# STEVEN
# SPIELBERG

## Father of the Man

# STEVEN SPIELBERG

## Father of the Man

### His Incredible Life, Tumultuous Times and Record-Breaking Movies

ANDREW YULE

LITTLE, BROWN AND COMPANY

A *Little, Brown* Book

First published in Great Britain in 1996
by Little, Brown and Company

Copyright © Andrew Yule 1996

The moral right of the author has been asserted.

A CIP catalogue record for this book
is available from the British Library.

ISBN 0 316 91363 4

Set in Plantin Light by M Rules
Printed and bound in Great Britain by
Clays Ltd, St Ives plc

Little, Brown and Company (UK)
Brettenham House
Lancaster Place
London WC2E 7EN

'My heart leaps up when I behold
   A rainbow in the sky;
So was it when my life began;
So is it now I am a man;
So be it when I shall grow old,
   Or let me die!
The child is father of the man;
And I could wish my days to be
Bound each to each by natural piety.'

*William Wordsworth*

'The childhood shows the man
As morning shows the day.'

*John Milton*

'I use my childhood in all my pictures, and all the time. I go back there to find ideas and stories. My childhood was the most fruitful part of my entire life. All those horrible, traumatic years I spent as a kid became what I do for a living today, or what I draw from creatively today.'

*Steven Spielberg*

# Acknowledgements

In as much as I have been gathering up Hollywood snapshots of Steven Spielberg in interviews conducted over several years, this book has been almost a decade in the making.

Over lunch with Quincy Jones at his Bel Air villa, he talked warmly of his relationship with Spielberg, how *The Color Purple* was brought to his attention, his dedication to bringing the book to the screen. (Spielberg took Directors' Guild minimum for the movie, then ploughed most of it back when it ran over budget.) I interviewed another admirer, Neil Canton, at Spielberg's Amblin Entertainment headquarters on Universal's backlot, where we talked of the making of the various *Back to the Futures* in which Canton had been involved as executive producer. Back in Bel Air, Peter Bogdanovich gave me his account of the dramatic cast change on the first in the series that saw Eric Stoltz abruptly replaced by Michael J. Fox.

In London Terry Gilliam talked of his unsuccessful attempt to have Spielberg intervene with his 'elder brother', Universal's Sid Sheinberg, to have *Brazil* released in the States. Also in London, I sat with the no-nonsense David Tomblin, Spielberg's first assistant director on several movies, from *Raiders of the Lost Ark* to *Empire of the Sun*. Conceding that Spielberg was indeed a formidable taskmaster, Tomblin added that he drove himself harder than anyone.

Between London, New York and Los Angeles, I covered many other filmmakers where the conversation touched on Spielberg. Last, but far from least, I met with Denis Hoffman, the producer who backed Spielberg when he was a complete unknown in the film industry.

The one oddity I came across, something I hadn't encountered in writing any previous book, was a reluctance on the part of many other interviewees to speak other than under a promise of anonymity. The common explanation I was given: 'Even though I'll probably say at least fifty per cent good about the guy, and that's all you quote, I might get the blame for any unattributed quote you use.' Bearing that in mind, I decided – once the information thus gained was double-checked – not to use any names where mixed messages were conveyed. Their timidity, I should explain, was not confined to underlings scared they might never work again. Far from it. Following Spielberg's refusal to cooperate, one Academy Award winner – having already agreed to talk and having provided his home phone number – failed to return calls.

Staff at the Museum of Modern Art Film Studies Section in New York City were enormously helpful in sifting through the dozens of articles written about Spielberg and his movies over more than twenty-five years, unearthing features in *Rolling Stone* (by Chris Hodenfield, Randall Sullivan, Lynn Hirschberg and Michael Sragow), Los Angeles *Times* (by Joyce Haber), New York *Times* (by Bernard Weinraub), *Interview* (by Bianca Jagger and Andy Warhol, Susan Pile and Tere Tereba), New York *Post* (by Jerry Talmer), New York *Daily News* (by Dave Kehr), New York *Observer*, *Cinema Papers*, *Forbes* (by Randall Lane and Robert La Franco), Los Angeles *Reader* (by Michael Kaplan), *Vanity Fair* (by Edward Klein, Kim Masters and Peter Boyers), *City of San Francisco*, *Village View*, *Village Voice* (by Tom Allen) *Variety*, *Time* (by Jordan Bonfante, Adam Cohen and Jeffrey Resner, and David S. Jackson), *Newsweek* (by Michael Meyer and Charles Fleming), *Soho Weekly News*, *Cinema Reader*, *Take One*, *Penthouse* (US and UK Editions), *New Yorker* (by Stephen Schiff), *Hollywood Reporter*, *Millimeter* (by Donald Chase), *TV Guide* (by Richard Turner), *Premiere*, *Prevue* and Boston *Globe* (by Jay Carr). Books consulted in the process included: *You'll Never Eat Lunch In This Town Again* by Julia Phillips, *Special Effects* by Ron LaBrecque, *Outrageous Conduct* by Stephen Farber and Marc Green, *Skywalking* by Dale Pollock, *Wired* by Bob Woodward, *Master of the Game* by Connie Bruck and *The Devil's Candy* by Julie Salamon. Also studied were TV interviews given by Spielberg's mother Leah Adler to David Hartman on *Good Morning America*, by composer/conductor John Williams to Hugh Downs on *20/20*, by Spielberg to Steve Fox on *20/20*, and by Spielberg to Dick Cavett on *DC*.

To all of the above, the named and the anonymous, my grateful thanks.

# Contents

# 1

## Basket Case

*'Walt Disney was my parental conscience, and my step-
parent was the TV set.'*

*'The first scary thing I learned to do as a child was to turn
off the light.'*

<small>STEVEN SPIELBERG</small>

*It grew overnight into a palpable thing, a live entity with darkly mock-
ing features that fed on his deep-seated feelings of inadequacy. It grew
and grew until he was unable to see over, under or past it, until its poi-
sonous shadow threatened to obliterate the rest of his life, stretching
beyond any known horizon into a remote, inaccessible, uncertain future.
The grey light of dawn, when at last it came, only served to confirm that
today was the day – the day he'd been dreading for weeks, the day when
he, Steven Spielberg, together with the rest of his elementary class of
fifty pupils, was due to run a mile to gain a grade.*

*The awful reality outdid even his worst imaginings. The remainder of
the class had crossed the finishing line, leaving just two trailing behind.
One – a skinny, spindly legged boy, tall for his age, large head precari-
ously balanced on a pipe-stem neck – was a hundred yards short; the
other, forty yards further behind, was a mentally retarded youth, his
chubby features red and running with sweat, his legs wobbling and chaf-
ing as they rubbed together.*

*Suddenly the entire class was rooting for the straggler, shouting,
'C'mon, c'mon, beat Spielberg! You can do it! Beat the wimp! You can do
it! Run, run!!'*

*Although the encouragement had a galvanising effect on the disad-
vantaged kid, it was never going to be enough to save him from coming
in last – short of a miracle, that is. And this had never been intended as
a miracle mile. As Spielberg looked behind, he found himself rationalis-
ing that he might as well be hanged for a sheep as a lamb. That, and a few
other considerations. 'Okay, how am I going to make it look real?' was the*

1

*thought that ran through his mind. 'How can I take a tumble and make it look real?'*

*A few seconds later he took his dive, stepping on his toe and tripping over, head-first, on to the red clay of the track. The tumultuous cheer and loud whistling that greeted his fall was immediately followed by renewed exhortation: 'C'mon, John, run, run! Beat the wimp! Beat Spielberg!!'*

*Bleeding from a scraped nose, Spielberg made a convincing show of struggling to his feet as his competitor thundered up behind him. The remaining problem lay in making it look as if he were still running to win, but not quite making it. An affected limp helped enormously. Now they were neck to ungainly neck, now Spielberg was slipping half a pace behind, now a whole stride, now the kid was a chest ahead, now an arm's length as they reached and passed the finishing line.*

*Spielberg watched as his classmates hoisted the kid shoulder-high and carried him all the way back to the showers in a triumphant victory procession. For fully five minutes he stood alone on the track, his chest heaving, hot tears of both shame and exultation coursing down his face. In his entire young life he never felt better and he had never felt worse.*

Obsessed with electronics since his boyhood, Arnold Spielberg had spent most of World War II as a radio operator in a B25, part of a bombing squadron nicknamed the 'Burma Bridgebusters'. Leah Posner was an aspiring concert pianist before marrying Arnold and settling into domesticity in the Avondale suburb of Cincinnati, Ohio, where her husband secured employment, after a resumed stint as student at the University of Cincinnati, at the giant General Electric plant that dominated the area. Their only son, Steven Allan Spielberg, weighing in at 6 lbs, 10 ozs, was carried to full term and born on December 18, 1946, at 6.16 pm, in the city's Jewish Hospital. The couple were later to be blessed with three more children, the sisters Anne, Sue and Nancy. The boy's earliest memory, dating back to when he was just six months old, is of being wheeled in a pram down the dark aisles of a synagogue, being peered at by a series of heavily bearded individuals silhouetted against a sudden, silent explosion of velvety red light, and being handed biscuits by the group of black-clad Hasidic elders.

In 1949, following a move to Haddonfield, New Jersey, the burly, bespectacled breadwinner of the family continued to pursue his career as a pioneer computer engineer and burgeoning workaholic. Time was still found, after his kids had clambered into bed alongside him every Sunday morning, to read out loud from the Comic Section of the local newspaper. It was during a visit to Philadelphia in 1953 that Arnold took his son to see his first movie, Cecil B. DeMille's *The Greatest Show on Earth*. 'It's going to be bigger than

2

you,' he explained in advance, 'but that's all right. The people in it are going to be up on a screen and they can't get out at you.'

Spielberg recalls a mixed experience. Despite what his father had told him, he had still expected to see a *real* circus, where he could *smell* the animals and *taste* the sawdust. What was this business with a *flat screen*? Eventually his imagination took over, but it took a while, long after the lights had dimmed. (Another unexpected development; they were going to watch a circus *in the dark*?) His reaction to the slightest threat of violence or scary moments was either to clutch his father's coat sleeve, or bury his face in his hands.

That first encounter was followed over the next few years by carefully selected visits to movies his parents considered suitably non-threatening and non-scary. Limited in the main to Disney fare, his favourites were the little cartoons that supported the main features. They too had their share of violence, but it was 'okay' violence where, squashed flat one moment, the indestructible characters could spring back to life the next. Full-length features were a different matter. After witnessing the wicked queen turn into a hideous old crone and a skeleton crumble into dust in *Snow White and the Seven Dwarfs*, the eight-year-old burst into tears and began shaking. For three nights afterwards he had to crawl into bed with his parents. Watching *Bambi* proved a no less traumatic experience, 'because the fire killed the family'. At *Fantasia* the 'Night on a Bare Mountain' sequence found him cowering under his seat. Surely Disney was supposed to delight and enthral – not terrify?

At this early stage young Spielberg was a walking basket case of neurosis, from which a lifetime of phobias would linger – a dread of bugs, a fear of flying, a terror of elevators, a distrust of rollercoasters, even a hatred of furniture with feet, which he constantly anticipates moving across the room. And it seemed that the more his parents tried to protect him from the relatively mild media violence of the day, to the extent of draping a blanket over their television set, the less they succeeded. With *The Mickey Mouse Club* and Mickey Rooney in *The Atomic Club* representing the limit on authorised viewing, Spielberg had his answer. When his parents were out, he'd wait until the babysitter had fallen asleep, then creep downstairs and watch TV with the sound turned low. Later, when he himself was old enough to qualify as the babysitter, he grossed out on every illicit delight the tube had to offer, daring his sisters to snitch on him. And he was wise to his father's device of leaving a hair across the 'On' switch of their 19″ RCA. He carefully memorised its position and replaced it after each mammoth session of *Dragnet*, *Soupy Sales*, and *The Honeymooners*. The natural limit to this overdosing by the self-confessed 'TV junkie' was a 10.30 pm curfew imposed on programming by the local television authority.

Even without the fuel supplied by Disney and television, Spielberg's imagination ran riot. It took just a backyard tree appearing to move in the wind with its long twiggy fingers to scare the impressionable boy. The creaking door of a closet produced a sense of dread at what might be about to emerge from its dark interior. The slightest suggestion of a groaning bedspring bespoke a monster lurking below, waiting to spring into life. A crack in the wall? Weird creatures dwelt there. His sister's clown doll? An evil grin betrayed its true nature. The flip side to Spielberg's 'terror' was that it came, more often than not, with a delicious *frisson* attached, the 'scared to look, hiding your eyes, but unable to resist peeking' syndrome. Put simply, he *enjoyed* being scared.

The move to Scottsdale, a suburb of Phoenix, Arizona, where his father continued at General Electric in computer development, was made in 1954. His surprised parents found their son, notwithstanding the prospect of leaving behind the upsetting tree and creepy cupboards, reluctant to move. His mother bribed him with the prospect of a pony of his own – a promise she signally failed to keep, as her son teasingly reminds her to this day. Diminutive, elfinfaced Leah, with concerns of her own, had checked out the town's credentials in advance. An encyclopedia she consulted alarmingly described Arizona, with its warm, dry climate, as a barren wasteland. Only after the move – when Scottsdale, a burgeoning cow town unaware of the revolution about to take place in its midst, turned out to be a pleasant surprise – was the publication date of the reference book checked out. It was 1920.

Try as he might to fit in at school, Spielberg failed. A painfully slow reader, he broke into a flop sweat at the thought of having to stand up in class and read aloud. With neither the aptitude nor physique for games, he was dubbed 'the retard' by his new schoolmates, and laughed to scorn when he vomited outside, accompanied by several others – all of them girls – after being asked to dissect a frog in biology class. The only time he remotely felt at one with the music of the spheres was when, following music lessons from his mother, he learned to play clarinet and marched in the school orchestra from the fourth grade on. Rodeo parades were a problem; concentrating on his keys and trying to keep in step, he trod on more 'horse pie' than anybody he knew. He was the last kid in class to don a Davy Crockett outfit of coonskin hat and chaps, and carry the essential powder horn and flintlock rifle. He suffered for the omission, the rest of the class coming after him with the butt-end of their rifles and chasing him home.

Being the only Jewish kid in his school class deepened the acute

4

sense of 'separateness' he felt. It was something he had always been aware of, a basic, elemental factor that made him 'different' from the rest of the mainly Gentile community. The discovery that their ranch-style house was the only one in Scottsdale not lit up at Christmas added to the embarrassment of belonging to an Orthodox Jewish family. The outward perception of his parents' worshipping, their synagogue visits on Friday nights and on High Holy Days, all added to his feelings of isolation. More than anything else in the world, he longed to assimilate, be just like 'everybody else', be *accepted*. Although he was never *ashamed* to be Jewish, it created unease on several occasions. The lowest of the low points came when a gang of his schoolmates gathered outside his home and chorused, 'The Spielbergs are dirty Jews! The Spielbergs are dirty Jews!'

Fievel, his maternal grandfather – Arnold's father had passed on before his children were born, leaving a widow, Rebecca, who chose to remain in Cincinnati – always wore a trailing black coat, black hat and long white beard which made him embarrassed to ask his few friends over at night.

More often than not grandpapa would be in a corner *davening*, either that or emerging from the attic where he kept his stock of sundry haberdashery items, the belts, tie-clips and cuff links he hawked. How to explain the praying old man and his buckles and braces to his WASP pals, even if they were just a collection of scrawny necked wimps like himself, trying to make it through the school year without getting their faces pushed into the drinking fountain? Worst of all was when his grandpapa would call him in at meal times while he was playing in the backyard with his friends. He would pretend not to hear when the old man, using his Hebrew name, would cry, 'Shmuel! Shmuel! Come on, now! It's dinner, Shmuel!' (Fievel's wife Jennie had died soon after the move to Arizona. Born in 1881 and college-educated, she had been a formidable presence in Cincinnati, well known both for her public speaking and radio broadcasts. Her last pronouncement on her grandson to Leah was uncannily perspicacious: 'Mark my words, dolly, that boy is going to make a name for himself in the world.')

A regular sprinkling of anti-Semitic remarks at school led to a futile attempt to reshape what Spielberg perceived as his 'big schnozz'. A large piece of duct tape was employed, one end curved round the tip of his nose, the other high on his forehead, designed to turn the offending object skywards and limit any further growth. His self-consciousness eased only when his face 'grew into it' with the passing of the years.

Not that the Spielberg household was *entirely* kosher – not with

Leah's love of lobster. While his mom was surreptitiously cooking up a pair of prize specimens one day, her son licking his lips at her elbow, a knock came on the door. Peeking out the curtains, Leah could have wished the earth would swallow her up. 'Quick, Steven,' she cried, 'get these lobsters out of here while I let Rabbi Kravitz in!' The crustaceans spent the next hour under the bed in the master bedroom. Spielberg and his mother laughed until they cried after the rabbi left, before getting down to the serious business of the feast. Eventually, bowing to the inevitable, his parents gradually eased off from their observant Orthodoxy.

As a youngster Spielberg was vaguely aware of something elders discussed called 'the Holocaust', otherwise known as 'the Great Murder'. He knew it was something bad that had happened in the past, something 'those murdering sons of bitches' had carried out, even that relatives of his parents in Poland and the Ukraine had been victims. An encounter with the living survivors of the death-camp victims his mother was tutoring in English, went straight over his head. Only one aspect of the meeting remained vivid in his mind: one of the group performed a magic trick with his concentration camp tattoo, the '6' twisted around to make a '9'. As the years passed and the full horror was slowly spelled out, his parents explained, 'We're telling you this so you can tell your children one day.' It wasn't that Spielberg was unimpressed – far from it – but he chose not to pursue any further study beyond the oral history Arnold and Leah provided. To a kid growing up the world was full of present-day distractions and problems.

All that other stuff was in the past, so why bother?

# 2

## In Focus, In Frame

*'My father had that WWII ethic. He brought home the
bacon, my mom cooked it, we ate it.'*

STEVEN SPIELBERG

*'We never said no. We never had a* chance *to say no.
Steven didn't understand the word. We all worked for him.'*

LEAH ADLER

In the evenings it was either grandpapa Fievel holding forth about
the old days, or his dad and a half-dozen colleagues discussing the
latest developments in technology over a twelve-pack. During the
day it was his mother and her friends drinking coffee and gossiping,
or tinkling their way through chamber pieces. All seemed to combine in a conspiracy to rob young Spielberg of the privacy he
sought at home in Scottsdale. Energy-draining claustrophobia
threatened to close in even as he crammed towels under his bedroom door to smother the cacophony. The only other refuge in the
daytime was the family den, which meant straining to hear Pinky
Lee on TV while awaiting the Good Humor Man's chimes, the
high point of the day.

His real childhood domain was his bedroom, the one inviolate
kingdom over which he ruled supreme. His parents indulged a
fondness for pet birds by gifting him a pair of parakeets. Spielberg
gradually got them used to being out of their cage and trained them
to live on the curtain rod, adding to his collection until he had eight
of the creatures up there, thoroughly starching the curtains. His
mother ventured into her son's kingdom as seldom as she had to,
faithfully collecting his dirty laundry, crunching her way across the
birdseed-covered floor, hating the free-flying birds and the mess
they made. Her son doted on them, and that was enough for Leah.

Spielberg's memories of Scottsdale are of a place where excitement was nowhere to be found, where it had to be self-created.

Enter the master of mischief. Plastering peanut butter on a neighbour's window seemed like a great idea at the time, not so great when he was given the task of cleaning if off. He'd terrorise his sisters by day, locking them in closets, continuing the campaign after they'd fallen asleep by sneaking into their rooms with a flashlight under his chin, shaking them awake and yelling, 'I'M THE MOOOOON!!'

For months he petrified Anne, Sue and Nancy with a story that he had a World War II pilot rotting away in his bedroom closet. Daring them to face this horror – an invitation they accepted only with fearful trepidation – he waited until dark, opened wide the closet door, and shone a flashlight on a plastic skull wearing suitably placed goggles and a helmet. The sisters were still screaming hours later.

Sue remembers the 'creative torture' they all endured. 'One time he came into my bedroom with his face covered in toilet paper like a mummy. He peeled off the paper layer by layer and threw it at us! He was a delight, but a terror. And we kept coming back for more.'

Nancy recalls all the sisters playing with their dolls while their brother sat singing to himself as if he were on the radio. Suddenly he interrupted the broadcast 'to bring an important message'. He announced that a tornado was coming, and he would save his sisters by flipping them over his shoulder to safety. But if they dared to look at him, they would turn to stone.

'His badness was so original that there weren't even books to tell you what to do,' says Leah. 'One time he cut the head off one of Nancy's dolls and served it to her on a platter, surrounded by lettuce and tomato. Steve was *not* a cuddly child!'

Leah's Father's Day gift to her husband of an 8mm Kodak movie camera caused considerable excitement in the Spielberg household, with a whole series of silent home colour movies being turned out that revealed – among playful, coyly posing sisters; smiling, sunbathing blonde mom complete with fetching can-can; dark, broody, confident dad – a decidedly puzzled Steven looking, with his enormous forehead, squinty, close-set eyes and triangular visage, like something that had tumbled from another planet. The camera soon fell into his hands after his constant criticism of his father's lack of technique, for it seemed that Arnold raised being out of focus or frame to the level of an art form. 'If you know so much,' he retorted to his son, 'why don't *you* try?'

Young Spielberg's initial 'try' produced *The Great Train Crash*. Once the film was processed, even Arnold gasped at the lifelike collision created. *And* it was in focus, *and* it was in frame – his son's model trains looked just like multi-ton locomotives. If only a realistic soundtrack could be added, the illusion would be complete.

Spielberg's earlier answer to the impossibility of wading through a copy of Nathaniel Hawthorne's *The Scarlet Letter* had been to draw matchstick men on the corner of every page and flick through them, producing a tiny animated cartoon. Terrific though it was, the pleasure had remained confined to him alone. It wasn't good enough. He wanted to share the experience, transmit the kick. His alternative to serious reading had been comic books like *Classics Illustrated*, where the pictures largely told the story. He had been able to understand the stories perfectly long before he was able to understand the words. Through them he had been transported into other worlds, even beneath the ocean in Jules Verne's *20,000 Leagues Under the Sea*, where he could shut his eyes and *be* Captain Nemo. Now, thanks to the miracle of the camera he had inherited, he could tell his *own* stories in *moving* pictures – and unlike matchstick men they could be shared with an audience. He felt a great release.

That the Spielbergs were avid backpackers led to a whole series of Great Outdoor mini-epics shot in the Rocky Mountains – 'Father Chopping Wood', 'Mother Digging Latrine', and young Spielberg's first 'horror' film, 'Young Sister Removing Fishhook From Right Eye'. Now it was his father who turned critic. 'Why'd you show this?' he'd ask. 'Why didn't you show that instead?'

Whenever he wanted to avoid confronting the real world, Spielberg took to sticking a camera to his face, pointing and shooting. It almost always worked. And apart from anything else, his escapades made him the centre of attention. They were the perfect way to compete with his sisters for his parents' attention: 'Hey, I'm here too! Look what I can do!' He wanted approval, and the camera gave it to him. The 'applause junkie' had emerged.

Without stopping to figure out the whys and wherefores, Spielberg was following in a family tradition in these early leanings. Fievel, an immigrant from Russia, together with several other relatives, had initially entered vaudeville in the New Country as well as maintaining their Yiddish theatre roots; an uncle was a Yiddish Shakespearean actor. Leah could see the direction in which her son was heading, although so far there was no discussion with her husband about what it might lead to. There was neither need nor possibility. As far as Arnold was concerned his son was following him into computer engineering and that was that.

From the age of ten Steven took over the family home, turning it into a miniature studio as more and more equipment was acquired. Soon the house was filled with dollies, floodlights and heavy electric cables. 'Mom, we're filming tomorrow,' he'd announce. 'Okay, tomorrow we're filming,' Leah would reply. Cue 'The Terror of the Burning Doll's House' aka 'Castles of Fire'. Leah remembers her son 'ruling his three younger sisters. And me too, actually. Our living room was where Steven did his filming. We never said no. We never had a *chance* to say no. Steven didn't understand the word. We all worked for him.'

Anne recalls a weekly routine: 'Every Saturday morning my parents would escape from the four of us. The minute they were out of the house I would run to my room and block the door. Steven would push it all the way, then punch me out. Sue and Nancy would get it next if they had done some misdeed. Then, when he was through doling out punishment, we would all get down to making his movies.'

Bullied at school, Spielberg had become 'the little bully' at home. And his mischief-making gained cinematic dimensions. At a showing of *The Lost World* at Phoenix's 1200-seat cinema, a movie palace with not one but two balconies, he waited in the 'gods', together with a few pals, for the most terrifying moment in the picture. Right on cue, accompanying the process with vomiting sounds, they emptied a mixture of white bread, milk, parmesan cheese, creamed corn and peas over the unfortunate patrons below them. Then they ran for their lives down the fire escape.

The head of the house came home one day with something he declared was nothing less than 'the future', in the shape of a tiny transistor. Arnold watched as his son took it from him, looked at it uncomprehendingly – was it candy, bubble gum, seawater taffy, what, *what*? – and promptly swallowed it. Arnold laughed, but only briefly. Then the smile changed to a glower. A science-fiction fan who sensed the rapid dawning of science-fact, he regarded the future as something not to be trifled with. At the same time, regardless of the different career paths he had in mind, Arnold aided and abetted his son in the hobby that would soon take over his life.

'It was chaotic and creative at our house,' he says of those days. 'I'd help Steven construct sets for his 8mm movies, with toy trucks and papier-mache mountains. At night I'd tell the kids different tales about characters like Joanie Frothy Flakes and Lenny Ludhead. I see pieces of me in Steven. I see the storyteller.' Apart from that, Arnold made another singular contribution to his son's upbringing. In the Russian army his own father had been a sharpshooter, a skill he had handed down to his son. Now Arnold in turn passed it on to Steven.

Sue acknowledges her dad's influence. 'Steven's love and mastery of technique definitely came from our father. Mom was artistic and whimsical. She led the way for Steven to be as creative as he wanted to be. We were bohemians growing up in suburbia. And everything was centred on Steven.'

Even when the young moviemaker wasn't showing off his own output, extra money was earned during summer vacation by renting out catalogue classics like *Davy Crockett* and charging twenty-five cents a ticket, unspooling them through his dad's Bell and Howell projector in the family living room, with his mother and sisters selling soda and popcorn during intermission. To raise more money for equipment Spielberg initiated a tree-debugging service during school breaks. The charge was seventy-five cents a tree, and at twenty to twenty-five trees a day he could come out on a good week with $75.

One day, after he'd decided to take over the family kitchen to capture on film cherries exploding from a pressure cooker, Leah dutifully headed for the supermarket and stocked up with umpteen cans of the heavily syruped fruit. Her son was content only when the contents of each can had been captured spurting over the kitchen walls, burgundy-hued goo trickling down the brand-new hand-rubbed ash cabinets. In all the years that followed in Scottsdale, Leah's morning routine, after getting up, brushing her teeth and percolating the coffee, was to pick up a sponge and make another attempt to remove the juice stains.

Distinctly *avant-garde* tendencies were discerned when she asked her son to photograph the family in their convertible. What Spielberg chose to focus on instead were the hubcaps. As Leah puts it: 'I should have known that meant something!'

The emergent director's first home movie with 'actors' – a few fellow scouts got up as cowpokes, playing out a stagecoach robbery he called *The Last Shootout* – lasted three and a half minutes, was brought in on a budget of $10, and earned its youthful filmmaker an Eagle Scout photography badge. Adept as he was at issuing orders to his family, he found there was an even greater kick to be had from bossing outsiders around. Next up was a fifteen-minute war picture *Escape to Nowhere* that called for realistic special effects if it was to have any chance of winning the amateur moviemaking prize he had in mind. His answer was to dig two holes in the ground, place a balancing board loaded with flour between them, then cover the whole thing with a bush. When his schoolboy 'Nazis' ran over them, the flour produced a perfect geyser. It was enough to win him the first prize of $50.

Within a year he had graduated to a forty-minute war movie, *Battle Squad*, starring, in a cunning move born of desperation, the hulking jock who tormented him most at Phoenix Arcadia High. 'He was my nemesis,' Spielberg recalls. 'I *dreamed* about him. So I said to him, "I'm making this movie about fighting the Nazis and I want you to play this war hero." At first he laughed in my face, but later he said yes. He was this big fourteen-year-old who looked like John Wayne. I made him this squadron leader in the film, with helmet, fatigues and backpack.'The casting was inspired, as from that moment on the jock became his director's faithful protector and best friend. It was a heady power high and a taste of the control in which he would revel in the years ahead. 'I knew what I wanted back then,' Spielberg recalls, 'and it wasn't what my dad wanted. I wanted *Hollywood*.'

Back in the real world, Spielberg and his sisters were brought face to face with the fact that their parents' marriage was falling apart. Constant rowing between them had become more and more open, less and less avoidable as the years passed. 'I don't think they were aware,' Spielberg has said, 'of how acutely aware we were of their unhappiness – not violence, just a pervading unhappiness you could cut with a fork or a spoon at dinner every night. For years I thought the word "divorce" was the ugliest in the English language. Sound travelled from bedroom to bedroom, and the word came seeping through the heating ducts. My sisters and I would stay up all night, listening to our parents argue, hiding from that word. And when it travelled into our room, absolute abject panic set in. My sisters would burst into tears, and we would all hold one another.'

Spielberg saw his mother as 'just like a little girl who never grew out of her pinafore . . . like a big kid', with so much energy and encouragement to offer that she made everything fun. He sees his father as neither hero nor villain, simply acknowledging that his parents were two entirely different, utterly mismatched people. 'I went to my dad with things,' he recalls, 'but he was always analytical. I was more passionate in my approach to any question, and we always clashed. I was yearning for *drama*.'

An early introduction to his goal of filmmaking in Hollywood came courtesy of Universal Studio's guided tour. Originated by the company's founder 'Uncle' Carl Laemmle in the 1920s, the tours had just been reinstated following two years of extensive updating; Spielberg bought his ticket during a summer vacation in Canoga Park spent with cousins.

Hiding behind soundstages after the tour bus had departed, the seventeen-year-old wandered the studio for several hours. This was his home, he decided, this was where he belonged. Some crazy kind of osmosis would take care of the details. As luck would have it, director John Ford was in a rare expansive mood when he found himself confronted with the intruder. While showing off his collection of Western prints to the choked-up, profusely sweating youngster – who could scarcely believe his luck – the crusty veteran had two pearls of wisdom to impart. 'When you understand what makes a great Western painting, you'll be a great Western director' came first. Next: 'Never spend your own money to make a movie.' His final words: 'Now get the hell out of here.'

Before he did, Spielberg also met Chuck Silvers, a senior editor on the lot, who listened sympathetically to his tales of amateur moviemaking. A pass was handed out for the next day so Spielberg could return without having to pay, and so he could bring along a few of his 8mm shorts. After viewing his work and offering a few words of encouragement, Silvers explained that he didn't have the authority to write any more passes. He wished him good luck, and told him to stick with his moviemaking. That was enough for Spielberg.

Next day, and for the rest of the Summer, wearing a suit and swinging a briefcase that contained a sandwich and a few candy bars, he breezily walked past the guard and gave a friendly wave. The hope was that he would pass muster for 'some mogul's kid'. It worked. Disappointingly, it was the only thing that did. Despite virtually squatting in offices on the lot, no one among the writers, editors and dubbers to whom he spoke showed any interest in what he had to offer. Their indifference sent Spielberg back to Phoenix more determined than ever to produce something that would change their minds.

Borrowing $400 from his father, he produced and directed a 140-minute science-fiction movie, *Firelight*, a tale of hostile UFOs. Employing mainly student actors from Arizona State University, it had aliens harassing the Earth's scientists, running circles round the National Guard, and stealing an entire city to reassemble it on their own planet. It was great fun to shoot at weekends, with Spielberg using all his powers of persuasion to have the local airport shut down a runway for one scene, a hospital to throw open its emergency room for another. Sister Nancy found herself enrolled in the venture, playing a kid reaching up in her backyard toward the mysterious light in the sky. 'Steve had me looking directly at the sun,' she recalls. '"*Quit squinting!*" he'd yell. "*And don't blink!*"'

Although it was shot silent, Spielberg had a sound strip applied to *Firelight*. There was a sense of considerable pride when his father hired the local cinema (World Premiere! March 24, 8 pm!) and the movie was shown for one heady night only in Scottsdale. It recovered its cost and came out, on a box-office gross of $500, with a clear $100 profit. Spielberg regards it as a tragedy of sorts that most of the film was promptly lost the day after the premiere in the family's move to Saratoga, a suburb of San Jose. So he should, for what remains contains lighting effects of space ships hovering and swooping that would not have looked out of place in many a Monogram or Ed Wood epic, even a Roger Corman programmer (scratch that; Spielberg's effects were too good, *and* in colour).

The family's relocation to Northern California came courtesy of a job offer from IBM that Arnold was unable to refuse. Spielberg's resultant transfer to Los Gatos High School brought no respite from the verbal anti-Semitism he'd been forced to endure in Scottsdale. Classmates would cough the word 'Jew' into their hands as they passed by. This even turned physical in the last semester of his senior year when a fist in the mouth during a touch football game, and being tripped and stepped on during a scrimmage, escalated the abuse beyond the jeers and laughter of the past. Pennies were thrown at him in the study hall, there was the constant threat of being beaten up. Although the school was only walking distance from home, the situation soon reached the point where, for his own safety, he had to be picked up by his parents. This was his most humiliating experience to date, and one that has stayed with him. 'It was my six months of personal horror,' Spielberg recently declared. 'And to this day I haven't gotten over it, nor have I forgiven any of them.'

Neither their idyllic surroundings of beautiful rolling hills and lush vineyards, nor the prospect of a move into a house his father had designed, was enough in the final analysis to paper over the cracks in Arnold and Leah's marriage. Arnold had dabbled for several years in the stock market. Several investments turning sour served further to exacerbate already-existing tensions. Despite having waited six years for the final split to come, Arnold's departure – just two days after the family's new home was completed – was no less devastating for Spielberg and his sisters. Suddenly he had to make an unwanted transition from irresponsibility to man of the house. No longer could he simply be the teaser, the tormentor of the family, killing off his sisters on a regular basis with his little 8mm epics, nagging his mother to afford him more leeway in his moviemaking forays. His family had to be protected, and the duty was his. Overnight, he had to grow up and face the adult world. A distinct feeling of resentment set in.

Spielberg's recollections of his childhood do not add up to an idyllic picture, and certainly, by his account, there were more than a few tortured moments. He has perhaps coloured his memories more than he realizes. Friendless, abused, a laughing stock . . . ?

14

According to his sister Anne: 'He had more friends than he remembers having. I don't think he realised the crushes that some girls had on him. Some of my friends had *major* crushes. If you looked at a picture of him then, you'd say, "Yes, there's a nerd. There's the crewcut, the flat-top, the ears, the skinny body." But he really had an incredible personality. He could make people *do* things. He made everything he was going to do sound like you wished you were part of it.'

Spielberg's first choice after graduating from Los Gatos High would have been UCLA and their tantalising film school programmes. That was ruled out because of his C-average grades. His second choice of USC, which also featured film tuition, turned out to be over-subscribed. That left California State College in Long Beach, where he chose to major in English. At least there, he reasoned, he'd be *physically* close to Hollywood.

Two years after his first visit, ducking out of college for three days every week, Spielberg was back at Universal, sneaking in once more to watch filmmakers at work, hoping to persuade some of them to take another look at his work. He found himself ejected from an editing room by Mervyn LeRoy and from several sets, among them Alfred Hitchcock's *Torn Curtain*, where he caught a glimpse of the dictatorial master at work. Then a curious Charlton Heston wondered who the pesky kid was being repeatedly escorted from the set of *The War Lord*. Even so, briefly watching Franklin Schaffner and Hitch at work on their movies, he learned something of great importance: that unless one knows what's in a director's mind and how he's going to cut his material, there's little or nothing to be gained by hanging around on a set. He would learn more by studying the dubbing and editing processes.

Although this time he had something more than shorts to show, it still wasn't enough, even for the supporters he found. They were embarrassed when he asked them to remove their pictures from the wall so he could project his 8mm efforts. 'If you make your films in 16mm, even better 35mm, *then* they'll get properly seen,' he was told.

Working in the college commissary to raise the necessary finance, Spielberg took them at their word. 16mm film was bought, a camera was rented. Whatever it took . . .

Spielberg has good reason, apart from the movie itself, to remember a screening of Stanley Kubrick's *Dr Strangelove . . . Or How I Learned to Stop Worrying and Love the Bomb*. As he waited in line outside the movie house in San Jose, his sister Anne ran up to him with a letter. 'Look,' she cried, 'it's from Selective Services.'

15

Opening it, he could feel his heart pound. There it was: 'Report for your physical.' The two hours watching Kubrick's satirical masterpiece, nobody's idea of a recruiting poster, were spent with mixed emotions.

Over a period of a year, in between successfully avoiding the draft, Spielberg made a short feature entitled *Amblin'*. The movie was produced under the auspices of a young man in his twenties named Denis Hoffman, who ran a company called Cinefx he'd set up with two partners to provide titles and opticals effects for movies. The budding entrepreneur also managed a pop group named October Country and had hopes of breaking into movie production. Having undertaken several commissions from Universal, Hoffman was alerted by a friend at the studio's post-production department, Julie Raymond, that there was this kid who'd been hanging out there, looking over shoulders, watching and learning, who wanted to direct movies. Why didn't they get together, chew over the possibilities, maybe join forces?

When Hoffman met Spielberg for the first time over lunch early in 1968, he was immediately impressed by the youngster's unbounded enthusiasm. He struck him as someone who was extremely focussed and aggressive. So aggressive, in fact, that he had already fallen out with an earlier partner in the actor Tony Bill, a huge rift having developed that neither care to discuss to this day.

Spielberg told Hoffman how desperate he was to direct a project that would bring him to the attention of a major studio, something that at the very least would set his foot on the bottom rung of the ladder. He outlined his family situation to Hoffman: Left on her own, with three daughters to support, there was no way his mother could contribute financially. And his father, disappointed over his refusal to consider a career in computers, had refused to help. At Cinefx Hoffman had what he lacked – access to finance, equipment, a sound stage, and the professional know-how to put a project together.

In Hoffman's recollection, Spielberg was prepared to sign a contract of any kind, whatever in the world it took, if Hoffman would only back him. In practical terms, he offered to pay Hoffman ten per cent of his earnings over the next three years in exchange for backing. Instead, Hoffman came up there and then with what he considered a more equitable and less onerous formula, one that also reflected the faith he had in his young partner-to-be: in exchange for production facilities and financing for that vital initial project, Spielberg would undertake to direct a feature of Hoffman's choosing within ten years, for a fee of $25,000, plus five per cent of

16

the profits. It truly was cast-your-bread-on-the-waters time, for if Spielberg proved a bust, the contract would be worthless. It amounted to an article of faith.

The initial story outlines Spielberg turned in for their first collaboration were considered by Hoffman naive and unrealistic. (At this point all Hoffman had seen of Spielberg's most recent work was footage of bicycle racers he had begun shooting, then abandoned.) He decided to lay down a few guidelines that would oil the wheels and enable the still-green Spielberg to function. First off, Hoffman decreed there should be no dialogue. That would eliminate any sound problems on location, as well as arduous and time-consuming (ie, expensive) post-synching. Instead, extensive use would be made of music utilising October Country. Cinefx's optical effects would add the final polish. 'Let's make it as clean and creative as possible, with minimum distractions for you as first-time director' said Hoffman.

Spielberg eagerly accepted all of his producer's suggestions and finally came up with the concept of a boy and girl who meet in the Mojave Desert and hitchhike their way to the Pacific Ocean. The title, *Amblin'*, was 'a collaborative decision' between the two. With a budget set at between $8,000–$9,000, *Amblin'* was filmed in August 1968, mainly in Pear Blossom, California, with Hoffman driving the 140-mile round trip daily to process what had been shot, then conducting production meetings at night. Back at Cinefx, with the production already heavily into overages, filming continued for several days on Hoffman's indoor stage facility. The final budget ballooned to close on $20,000, and Hoffman would later throw another $5,000 into the pot to promote the movie. In all, ten people contributed their time and expertise to the production, under Hoffman's weather eye, with composer Michael Lloyd writing original songs for October Country, as well as an evocative background music score. That the budget had been more than doubled was accepted philosophically as the price of backing an inexperienced first-timer; to Hoffman it was the results that counted in the end. And they were looking good.

From the time of that first meeting their relationship had grown, with Spielberg often camping out overnight and spending time with Hoffman, his wife and kids at their home in Outpost Drive, near Mulholland in the Hollywood Hills. Money required for meals? Sure. A loan of Hoffman's buggy to get around? No problem either. The oral agreement dating from their first lunch together was formalised on September 28. With friendship and trust on both sides, there had been no hurry to make it legal.

A couple of months later *Amblin'* was ready for unveiling. Since

17

the negative was held at the Technicolor lab within Universal Studios, the twenty-four-minute movie was handily situated for a providential borrowing.

Universal's president in charge of TV was thirty-two-year-old Sidney Jay Sheinberg, and after a feature screening one night, Chuck Silvers prevailed on him to watch 'this young guy's short film'. Sheinberg agreed and was suitably impressed. He liked the way Spielberg had selected the performers and developed their relationship, he admired what he saw as the maturity and warmth in the movie. Taking in the close-to-mirror image of himself that Spielberg presented in the hastily arranged follow-up meeting was something else again. Sheinberg recalls a 'nerd-like, scrawny creature' appearing: 'The surprising thing was that he looked just like me.'

'You should be a director,' he informed Spielberg.

'I think so too,' came the rapid agreement, 'but I'm still at college. I haven't graduated yet.'

'Do you wanna graduate college or do you wanna be a film director?'

A TV contract at Universal or back to college? Oh, *real* tough. Spielberg quit college so fast – to hell with graduation – he didn't even stop to clean out his locker. His seven-year deal was drawn up and signed a week after the offer was made.

Sheinberg's on-the-record recollection of another conversation with Spielberg is puzzling: 'The big thing with Steven was he wanted me to promise him that he would direct something before he was twenty-one-years old. I told him that I would cause that to happen.'

Puzzling? Only in so far as Spielberg didn't join Universal until he was on the verge of his twenty-*second* birthday in December, 1968. What was going on? If Sheinberg's recollection is correct, Spielberg had understated his age by one year. Why had he bothered?

MCA founder Jules Caesar Stein had begun his working life as an eye doctor, booking bands on the side back in the thirties to stretch his income. The rapid stranglehold MCA had gained – first over musicians, then over acting talent following a move to Hollywood – had earned MCA the title of 'the Star-Spangled Octopus' and brought accusations of Mafia involvement that continued to swirl around the company for years.

Under the guidance of Stein and his deputy, Lew R. Wasserman, Universal had enjoyed an unrivalled series of hits in the first half of the sixties that seemed fully to justify the decision to abandon their agency, bowing to a government decree that prohibited the running of an agency *and* studio at the same time. It was a move that Stein in particular had made with great reluctance.

MCA-Universal's line-up of hits had included remakes of *Imitation of Life* and *Back Street*; Doris Day's sparkling run of 'cash comedies', *Pillow Talk*, *Lover Come Back*, *That Touch of Mink*, *The Thrill of It All* and *Send Me No Flowers*; Stanley Kubrick's *Spartacus*; Hitchcock's *The Birds*; Robert Mulligan's *To Kill A Mockingbird*; Stanley Donen's *Charade*; Andrew McLaglen's *Shenandoah*; Ralph Nelson's *Father Goose*, and George Roy Hill's *Thoroughly Modern Millie*.

To Spielberg, and to most of the outside world in the latter half of the sixties, Universal and its parent company looked the very picture of a well-run business enterprise, its movie studio flush with big stars and major projects, its factory-style TV division humming away. The appearance was deceptive. Universal was a studio in crisis, reeling like almost every other major from a decade of falling cinema audiences and three years of ill-advised movies, their earlier record-breaking run of hits now a fading memory.

Eyeing a $100-million-debt mountain, unprecedented in MCA's history, Jules Stein was not a happy man. Ancient loyalties were being strained to breaking point. It was ironic that at the very moment Sid Sheinberg was taking young Spielberg under his wing, Stein was resolving to fire Wasserman, his deputy of over thirty years. Everyone at the studio felt the cold breath of Stein's anger and frustration. Blood-letting was on the cards.

And sooner, rather than later.

# 3

## Sid Sheinberg's Apprentice

*'I think all children experience filmmaking. When their
parents buy them a birthday present of little characters,
soldiers, little men – when I was a kid, it was cowboys –
and the kid lies down on the shag rug on his stomach,
holds the little figure up right by his eyes so it's very
realistic, and gets an angle on that shoulder, puts the other
shoulder at arm's length in the other hand, and goes,* bang,
bang, bang, bang! *– that's the beginning of filmmaking.
We all start out as filmmakers. And I guess I never grew
out of it.'*

STEVEN SPIELBERG

*'You know, you live life and you give birth, and then one of
your children turns out to be Steven Spielberg ... People
ask me if I knew Steven was a genius. I didn't know* what
*Steven was!'*

LEAH ADLER

Spielberg's first assignment at Universal was the middle segment of
a three-part television pilot, *Night Gallery*. Its author and originator,
Rod Serling, was a talented pioneer of live-TV dramas, including
*Requiem for a Heavyweight* and *Patterns*. With sponsors wary of
backing what they regarded as similarly 'heavy' fare, irrespective of
their worth, Serling had turned in frustration to *Twilight Zone* as a
means of expressing social comment disguised as easily digestible
twenty-two-minute dollops of science fiction. With the cancellation
of the series, Serling now saw *Night Gallery* as his ticket back to TV
after a five-year hiatus. He presented himself to Spielberg as 'a
great, energetic, slaphappy guy' who gave him 'a fantastic pep talk'
predicting that the entire movie industry was about to change
because of young people being given breaks. It was music to

Spielberg's ears. More pertinently, the nervy Serling emphasised that not one single word of his script must be altered!

Spielberg was understandably nervous. Not only was *Eyes*, his *Night Gallery* episode, the first professional work he had ever shot, but the star was the formidable – in prospect at least – Joan Crawford. The sixty-three-year-old star, a decade after her come-back in *Whatever Happened to Baby Jane?*, had accepted with some trepidation the role of a blind, manipulative millionairess prepared to do whatever was necessary to regain her sight for twenty-four hours. The story's kicker: it coincides with New York's famous power black-out. Their first introduction found Crawford the pro greeting Spielberg at her door already wearing a blindfold. Her terrified director watched as she lurched around her apartment. When he suggested going out to lunch, she took off the blindfold, looked at him in disbelief and said, 'I'm not going to be seen in public with you! People will think you're my child!'

Suddenly there he was, just six weeks after signing his contract with Universal, on an actual sound stage, surrounded by sixty crew members and one fretful superstar, all of them awaiting *his* directions. Serling's dialogue immediately presented a problem. There was a *tremendous* amount of it, and Crawford, while still a total trouper, had difficulty reciting it word for word. Cue cards and occasional soothing words from co-star Barry Sullivan saved the schedule from a worrying initial slippage.

Spielberg moved swiftly to squash rumours of Crawford's discontent with her role, with the dialogue, even, heaven forbid, with her inexperienced director. Crawford was 'terrific, totally professional', one reporter was informed. Then he gilded the lily somewhat: 'She relied on me to direct her more than I ever thought she would.'

Rod Serling's wife Carol recalls their relationship as somewhat less harmonious: 'Joan was *climbing the walls* while they were filming. She was calling Rod all the time.' When Spielberg invited the star out for dinner – this time she accepted – he was careful to ask a friend along to keep the conversation flowing. Movie buff that he was, Crawford still had him tongue-tied.

If Crawford had her concerns, Spielberg's producer, William Sackheim, had even more, to the disconcerting extent of reshooting sizeable chunks of his work to achieve what he considered 'normal-looking TV'. Unceremoniously dropped were the 'experimental' shots and long pans Spielberg had coaxed out of veteran cameraman Russell Metty. If Spielberg felt any sense of awe that he was dealing with another industry great, this time on the technical side – Orson Welles' *Touch of Evil* was among Metty's recent credits – he

21

tried hard not to show it. Only a restricted few, like a sympathetic Barry Sullivan, were aware of the insecurity that was gripping him.

Apart from the close friendship forged with Crawford's co-star, it was not a happy time. The word around Universal was that the *Good Ship Spielberg* had sunk on its maiden outing. A concerned Sid Sheinberg later confirmed rumours that 'the picture couldn't be put together'.

Spielberg was regarded as untouchable for a year, with no other producer at Universal-TV prepared to work with him. 'They thought Steven was *avant-garde*,' says Sheinberg. 'So many people take bows for his success now, but at the time they complained because he wanted to put the camera on the floor.'

'I was so traumatised,' Spielberg recalls. 'The pressure of that show was too much for me.' He acknowledges that he used a lot of 'fancy shots'. 'Some of the compositions were very nice, but I'd usually be shooting through somebody's armpit or angling past someone's nose.' Suffocating and panic-stricken in the enforced freedom, he was brought face to face with the painful truth that Universal's TV-factory was no place for experimentation. Yet he desperately needed to work. He canvassed producers at Universal, offering to do anything they cared to offer. There were no takers.

A side-trip to Columbia's Burbank Studio led to an introduction to Peter Guber, already known as 'the Electric Jew' because of his sudden, dazzling bursts of enthusiasm for whatever project took his fancy, followed, all too often, by an equally sudden power outage when he moved on to something else. Spielberg was grateful that Guber deigned to look at his modest product reel, since he was one of the few who bothered. Nothing came of it, but at least Guber allowed him to hang around the studio.

Lest anyone think Spielberg was living off the hog as a result of his Universal contract, think again. He started humble, just like his boss before him: Sheinberg had joined MCA's legal department in 1959, on the very bottom rung, at $125 a week. Spielberg's take-home pay was $100 a week, per his recollection (gross $275, according to Sheinberg) of which $130 a month was shelled out in rent for a modest apartment. And when Spielberg maintains that no one would hire him, there were in fact temptations. Like fast bucks from producers of hard porn triple-XXX movies, their offers made over lunches where he was invariably left to pick up the bill. The tabs he had to accept, the offers he managed to resist. He would be a serious filmmaker or nothing.

During the dry spell from shooting, Spielberg flailed about in every direction, frantically trying to get a leg up from episodic TV to his real goal of features. He kept his ear to the ground both on his own and through his agent, the smooth, jocular Mike Medavoy, he talked himself up, he polished his resumé, he fought off frequent panic attacks. He met a young filmmaker named George Lucas at a UCLA student film festival and was impressed with his prizewinning *THX1138-4EB*. They hung out, together with Lucas's classmates Hal Barwood and Matthew Robbins and their mentor John Milius. Spielberg collaborated with Barwood and Robbins on a script for *Ace Eli and Rodgers of the Skies*, an adventure epic set in the early days of aviation. When the movie division of Universal passed on the project, Medavoy decided to cast the net a little wider.

Producers Richard Zanuck and David Brown were based at Twentieth Century-Fox when they received the submission for *Ace Eli*. Son of the famous Darryl F., the wiry, compact Zanuck was determined to demonstrate that his father's showmanship had been inherited, while *Cosmopolitan* editor and author of *Sex and the Single Girl* Helen Gurley Brown had already provided her husband, the tall, urbane Brown, with the basis of his first success. Although the team liked the script for *Ace Eli*, and went on to buy it, they balked at hiring a raw newcomer like Spielberg to direct. John Erman was chosen instead. It was another bitter disappointment, although for the Zanuck/Brown team *Ace Eli* would prove an ill-fated production. After a long period on the shelf, the movie was sneaked out to a few theatres, ambushed as 'tepid' and 'muddled' by critics, and body-swerved by the ticket-buying public.

Spielberg was going nowhere fast. Meanwhile, over the months of inactivity, mingling with casual acquaintances at other studios and shooting the bull with fellow strugglers, casual remarks alerted him to the parlous state of Universal. After three years of lousy movies, Lew Wasserman's venerable neck was on the line? It seemed barely possible.

For Jules Stein and his wife Doris, 'the hosts with the most', the glow of a hit movie lent sparkle to their upper-crust gatherings. A succession of embarrassing flops, although not on the same scale as his old gangland associations, had the reverse effect. Stein enjoyed both the social and political benefits of his philanthropic and charitable pursuits; the Jules Stein Eye Institute at UCLA had been completed in 1966 at a cost of $6 million, after a fund-raising campaign run by the couple, who personally contributed $2.5 million. Stein was less enthusiastic about the loss of privacy that MCA's entry into the world of movies had brought; Universal's hits and misses were subject to intense public and industry scrutiny. And he loathed being associated with the low-grade movies Wasserman seemed intent on churning out with grim regularity. The Sorcerer had turned socialite, and his Apprentice wasn't living up to his aspirations.

With a three-day grand-slam party organised for the Spring of 1969 to celebrate the opening of the twenty-storey, 500-room Sheraton inside Universal City, the Steins looked with mortification at the 'Big Movie' Wasserman had lined up to climax the event. The word was already out in the Hollywood community that *Sweet Charity*, the expensive Bob Fosse musical version of Fellini's *Nights of Cabiria*, was a stone-cold disaster. And as if to add insult to injury, the movie was about a goddam *prostitute*. What would all his high-toned friends think? The more Stein thought about it, the more he regarded Wasserman's latest offering as the final straw.

Stein summoned vice-presidents Taft Schreiber, Berle Adams, and several other executives to a meeting from which Wasserman was notable by his absence. 'We don't have a good picture,' Stein spelled out. 'Lew's never made a good picture. *Why can't we get rid of Lew?*'

# 4

## Surviving the Bloodbath

*'Directing is eighty per cent communicating and twenty per cent know-how. If you can communicate to the people who know how to edit, know how to light, and know how to act – if you can communicate what you want so that what they're doing is giving you your vision, that's my definition of a good director.'*

*'Directing is very hard. It's very, very hard.'*

STEVEN SPIELBERG

Word of his imminent execution reached Lew Wasserman at his Beverly Hills home, where he lay confined with a mild blood disorder. The news sent him reeling, and it was only with the help of his wife that he was finally able to calm down. After talking it through with Edie, a masterplan was cooked up. Part One: they would leak a story that he was hospitalised with a heart attack, virtually at death's door. That would hamstring Stein for the moment, at least until his precious party. Part Two would be reserved for the party itself.

Hollywood scribe James Bacon was Wasserman's mouthpiece of choice for the *coup de grâce*. During the Sheraton's launch, Bacon revealed that Stein, 'a mere band booker' until he met Wasserman, intended cold-bloodedly to dismiss the man who had helped build his fortune at MCA.

Dreadfully embarrassed, Stein proceeded with the board meeting he'd planned. Instead of *firing* Wasserman however, he *extended* his contract. There were conditions attached, like the appointment of a fresh executive to take charge of theatrical movies, but this would take another two years to achieve. Although Wasserman had survived the palace coup intact, blood-letting was still on the agenda in the night of the long knives that followed his triumphant return. Berle Adams, who had accepted the position of acting presidency during Wasserman's absence, was first to feel the cutting edge of his expertly thrust blade, with a clutch of VPs following close behind. 'If Wasserman wants to tell it,' said Adams two decades later, 'he can tell it his way. I won't tell it my way, because nobody would believe it. He's too big a man in the business and I wouldn't *dare* tell my side of the story.'

When *Night Gallery* was finally transmitted a year after completion, on November 8, 1969, the patched-up 'Eyes' proved the stand-out episode, easily eclipsing the two other segments from directors Boris Sagal, a TV regular, and veteran Barry Shear. Although Spielberg's name was up there as director, those in the know were aware of the re-shoots. Heels well cooled following his involuntary exile, Spielberg was offered more work only as a direct result of Sid Sheinberg's intervention.

'His career stalled on a number of occasions,' Sheinberg confirms, 'and I had to restart it. I've been involved in starting, or restarting the careers of a significant number of directors, but it was different with Steven. Because it wasn't just getting that *first* job. It was having to get *a number of jobs.* To the point where more than one person wondered, "What the hell is it with Sheinberg? Why am I being leaned on so much to use this kid?"'

The result of Sheinberg's first arm-twisting (and, let it be said, no one in the business does it with either greater expertise or more obvious enjoyment) was an episode of *Marcus Welby, M.D.* entitled 'The Daredevil Gesture'. This time Spielberg agreed to shoot in typical TV style, instead of the experimental 'hole in the ground' approach that had alienated so many in his professional debut. 'I got a lot of that out of my system and became less preoccupied with mechanics,' he later admitted, before claiming, 'I began to search instead for the *literary* quality in scripts.' A pep talk from Sheinberg probably had a lot more to do with it.

During 1970 Spielberg had another bruising experience with the assembly-line system of episodic-TV. NBC had picked up its option on *Night Gallery* for a series, and Spielberg was assigned to shoot the first half of a two-part episode entitled 'Make Me Laugh'. A few days before shooting wrapped a decision was made to replace one of the actors. Instead of being retained to direct the scenes with his replacement, a new director, Jeannot Szwarc, was ushered in. All in all, *Night Gallery* had not proved a happy association.

Now, however, it was onward, if not necessarily upward. If you believe Hollywood lore, this is how it came to pass: one day Sheinberg came across two clearly disconsolate producers, George

Eckstein and Richard Irving. 'What the hell's wrong?' he asked. 'We've got to get a director,' one of them allegedly replied. 'We've got this very special *Name of the Game* episode to shoot. And no director.'

'I've got just the guy for you,' said Sheinberg. 'Use Steven.'

Meaningful glances were exchanged. 'Is this right for him?'

'What are you talking about? He's terrific.'

'Do you think he can do it?'

Sheinberg claims the conversation terminated when he switched into his semi-selling, semi-ordering mode. Not only was the job Spielberg's – Gene Barry gets hit on the head, passes out, wakes up in the twenty-first century, and you have a ninety-minute *Name of the Game* episode entitled 'LA-2017' – but his introductions to Messrs Eckstein and Irving were to prove fateful, both to Spielberg's career and also in his personal life.

Meanwhile, he was farmed out to direct two episodes of *The Psychiatrist*: 'The Private World of Martin Dillon' and 'Par for the Course'. From there it was on to the 1971 premiere episode of *Colombo*, 'Murder by the Book', on once more to an episode of *Owen Marshall*, 'Eulogy for a Wide Receiver', that same year. Treading water it may have been, but Spielberg was also learning his craft.

During a visit to New York in 1971 Spielberg was introduced by a mutual friend to another young director, Brian De Palma. Although the two of them could hardly have been more different in looks and personality, they hit it off immediately. Maybe it was the contrast between them that helped cement their relationship. Physically De Palma towered over Spielberg's medium height. Spielberg mixed an innate shyness with a spark of determination that carried him through most situations; De Palma was darkly intense, formidable even. Spielberg was California laid-back, De Palma New York-wired.

Certainly there was no sense of competition between them, for it was clear that De Palma was coming from a different, darker corner. Unlike Spielberg, he had bypassed TV work and gone straight into movies after graduating from Sarah Lawrence College and teaching a film class there. *The Wedding Party*, featuring young hopefuls Robert De Niro and Jill Clayburgh, had been shot in 1963/4 and edited as more money dribbled in. It had finally seen the light of day in 1969, by which time De Palma had pressed ahead with *Greetings*, an anarchic lesson in the fine art of draft-dodging that may or may not have proved of more than passing interest to Spielberg. *Hi, Mom* had kept De Palma off the streets until the call had come from Warner Bros with an offer to direct *Get To Know Your Rabbit*, a comedy to star Tommy Smothers of the Smothers Brothers team. Grateful as he was for the opportunity, De Palma faced the prospect of working in the Hollywood dream machine with considerable trepidation, having heard numerous tales of bright New York hopefuls returning disillusioned, bloody *and* bowed, from the West Coast.

Sure enough, when Smothers took against De Palma at an early stage, Warner Bros did not hesitate to support its star. The result was the blinding humiliation of being unceremoniously dropped from his first studio picture. With commiserations exchanged as Spielberg listed his own setbacks, the two men promised to keep in touch.

Spielberg never stopped looking for that special subject that would catapult him into features. Along the way, several critics began to take note of his work, remarking on his occasional quick cuts away from the action, or his restricting the pivotal part of a scene to the corner of the frame, making it look like something glimpsed from the corner of an eye. He was beginning to discover the difference between technique for its own sake and technique in the service of dramatic effect, the happy medium between showing off and applying his craft. Working in TV also taught Spielberg to think on his feet, although there were few compensating illusions that he was working in an art form. It was a job, pretty much like any other, a learning experience in a sweat shop.

For a while Spielberg was unsure if he wanted to continue. There was little stimulation, and none of the gratification that even his home movies had provided. He could feel his enthusiasm being slowly smothered. He *had* to make the break into movies, not only to get back the passion for filmmaking, but for the sheer sense of fun and exhilaration as well.

The crucial break came when Spielberg's secretary slipped him a copy of the script for a TV movie by *Twilight Zone* writer Richard Matheson. *Duel* was a psychological thriller based on a harrowing real-life experience Matheson had endured after falling foul of a psychopathic truck driver on the open road. With Spielberg's imagination immediately captured, the next stop was producer George Eckstein's office. Impressed with the young man's bubbling enthusiasm, and with decent memories of their earlier collaboration on *Name of the Game*, Eckstein and Sheinberg sought the green light from their customer, the ultimate end-user, a young man very much on the move – Barry Diller, at thirty-three in charge of ABC-TV's *Movie of the Week* slot. Diller watched one of Spielberg's episodes of

*The Psychiatrist* and thought, 'What good work . . . This guy is going to be out of television so fast.' His observation was based on the fact that the TV episode played like 'a director's film', and his belief that TV was not a director's medium.

Spielberg was given a budget of $300,000 to make *Duel* and a shooting schedule of ten days; in the event three extra days were required to bring the seventy-two minute feature home. When considering the lead actor, Spielberg remembered Dennis Weaver's nervous twitch in Orson Welles' *Touch of Evil*; it was enough. For his Everyman he wanted that touch of vulnerability. Weaver laughs today when he recalls being asked if he minded working with Spielberg, considering his then-spotty track record: 'I must be the last actor on a Spielberg picture who was asked to give director approval!'

No one, least of all Spielberg, knew that *Duel* would provide his ticket to the big screen.

# 5

# Little Screen . . .

*'My mom and dad put their faith in Judaism and Roosevelt.'*

STEVEN SPIELBERG

*'When Steven was little, he would insist that I lift the top of the baby grand so he could see the strings when I played. Then he would fall to the floor, screaming in fear.'*

LEAH ADLER

'When Sid Sheinberg smiles at you,' said one colleague, 'it's the smile of a shark before he takes your arm off.' Before too many years had passed, many other shark comparisons would be made, not least because of a movie his protégé Spielberg turned out. Apart from the formidable Sheinberg, two other young Turks had been recruited by MCA back in 1959.

Frank Price broke into the company when he sold his first script to Universal-TV. The young man's weekend 'open plaid shirt and good ol' boy' act was only let down by fairly frequent bursts of pomposity. That didn't impede his rapid ascent, thanks to success with shows like *Ironside*, *The Virginian* and *It Takes A Thief*. By the early seventies he was one of the top executives in the company.

Ned Tanen began in MCA's mailroom and within a few years was given $750,000 to start up MCA Records. Operating on high-voltage charm and a short fuse, his crackling energy quickly enabled him to make his mark as an undoubted comer.

With promotions in the air after his skin-of-the-teeth survival, Lew Wasserman carefully weighed up his team's relative strengths and weaknesses. Jules Stein was still very much around, and since he was monitoring his every move, they had to be skilfully made.

*Duel* became one of the highest rated features in the *Movie of the Week* series when it was shown in November 1971. It copped

Emmy nominations for best cinematography and best sound editing, winning the latter. In an unprecedented move Universal decided to buy the movie back from ABC, have Spielberg shoot new footage to increase the length – also increasing the eventual budget to $450,000 – and release it theatrically outside the US. The end-result in 1973 was a worldwide gross of $9 million, 'breaking box-office records in London, Paris, Tokyo, Amsterdam and Rio de Janeiro', according to an overheated Universal press release. It served as an accurate forecast of things to come.

There was a 'Grand Prix' from the International Fantasy Film Festival in Avoriaz, France in February 1973, and a special jury award for 'Best First Film' at the Italian Taormina Festival a few months later. Spielberg accepted the honour in person during a tour sponsored by Cinema International Corporation, Universal's European distribution arm. It was on a side-trip to Rome that the opportunity arose to meet Federico Fellini.

For Spielberg, nervous, shy, hesitant, at the very beginning of his career, lunch with the great man was like stepping into another world. Here he was, thousands of miles away geographically, and about a million light years artistically, from Universal's TV factory. When the gates of Cinecitta opened, he could sense history pouring out. Rossellini, De Sica, Visconti, all of them had worked here, transmuting words and feelings into unforgettable images that transcended national barriers. Although it was true that their art-house movies were watched by Spielberg more from duty than for pleasure, the bragging rights among his contemporaries back home would be incredible. He'd actually broken bread with Fellini?!

The maestro was in good form that day, beaming benignly, every inch the great man welcoming a neophyte to his table. After lunch Spielberg summoned up the courage to ask if he might take a photograph. Fellini agreed, then was somewhat amused to see his young guest produce a small, cheap camera. If one picture can take the place of a thousand words, Spielberg seemed intent on achieving several thousand, or at least plenty of directorial coverage. After snapping away a half-dozen times, Fellini smilingly signalled that enough was enough. Back at Universal, Spielberg wrote a note of thanks, adding that he had pinned one of Fellini's photos in his office for good luck. Maybe for inspiration. At least partly for show.

Spielberg also met up with a fellow-American director in Rome. After enormous success with *The Last Picture Show*, *What's Up, Doc?* and *Paper Moon*, Peter Bogdanovich was filming his adaptation of the Henry James classic *Daisy Miller* in the city as a vehicle for his inamorata and star, ex-cover girl Cybill Shepherd. He'd been shooting on authentic locations at the Pincio and the Coliseum,

31

and was relaxing with Shepherd at the Rome Hilton when Spielberg dropped by.

Bogdanovich was someone whose company Spielberg enjoyed. Although he was flip, brattish, and downright cocky about the constant presence of the peaches-and-cream Cybill, he still gave an impression of vulnerability, of someone who didn't – yet, at least – believe all his publicity handouts. Bogdanovich introduced Spielberg to his assistant, a tall, athletic young man named Frank Marshall. The name and the face stuck for future reference.

Prizes and lunches with movie greats apart, Spielberg had been gratified by a glowing review for *Duel* from the veteran English critic Dilys Powell, who singled it out for praise at the Cannes Film Festival and had spread the word among her fellow-scribes. Spielberg had also been thrilled to discover a whole different atmosphere among European writers, reporters and journalists, a feeling that they genuinely loved movies, and were far more ready than their US brethren to embrace, idealise and lionise filmmakers.

In the frantic meantime Spielberg had shot a second TV movie, *Something Evil*, and a ninety-minute pilot, *Savage*. Although Robert Clouse had written his demonic possession script two years before *The Exorcist*, Spielberg heard about the William Peter Blatty novel in the middle of shooting *Something Evil*. The similarities were unmistakable. Johnnie Whitaker, the 'sweet kid' from *Family Affair*, was cast against type, with Sandy Dennis and Darren McGavin as the harassed parents confronted with a malevolent presence.

*Savage* reunited Spielberg with *The Psychiatrist*'s writer/producer duo of William Levinson and Richard Link. They had created the pilot as a hopeful launch vehicle for the husband-and-wife team of Martin Landau and Barbara Bain, late of *Mission: Impossible*. Spielberg would have preferred to skip this retrograde step, and bitterly resented an assignment that represented, according to him, 'the last time I was ordered to do anything'. (Per Sid Sheinberg, one more order would follow. A significant one.) *Duel*, unfortunately, had yet to take off. And whether as *Savage*, *The Savage Report* or *Watch Dog* – the plethora of alternative titles giving just a hint of the doubts and consternation involved – the idea of the proposed Levinson/Link series died with its pilot.

Before the *Duel* assignment had fallen into his lap, Spielberg had worked for nine months with Joseph Walsh, a young writer he'd befriended. A seriously compulsive gambler, Walsh had a script he simply had to get out of his system, one that would attempt, through the adventures of two hardcore enthusiasts, to explain the mentality of those who lived to gamble. Spielberg's role in the relationship was not so much to help him write, more to react to Walsh's latest outpourings, as well as to give *Slide* a semblance of form. 'I don't know if Steven ever told me what to do – ever,' Walsh recalls, 'but when he didn't giggle like a little boy eating a cookie, saying, "This is great!" I knew something was wrong. I always took that as a gauge, and somehow I looked deeper into the scene.'

When Universal chose to pass, a deal was struck with the James Aubrey regime at MGM. Amazingly, it seemed that not only was the studio high on the project, but they accepted the package put up by Walsh's agent, the popular lad-about-town Guy McElwaine (who would take over Spielberg's affairs as well when Mike Medavoy left agenting behind). It looked all set: Walsh would produce *Slide* with Spielberg directing. It was too good to last.

One month away from the commencement of principal photography, a new regime took over at MGM and took a hard look at *Slide*. Well, all right, they decided, the project should go ahead – with just a couple of minor changes. First, there should be a Mafia 'sting' element added to make it more of a thriller. Second, it should be filmed at the Las Vegas club, Circus Circus, that MGM owned. Third, Dean Martin should head the cast. Fourth, the script had to be trimmed to a *precise* number of pages. Fifth, Walsh was out as producer.

Contractually, Walsh had the power of walking away and taking his baby with him. Disappointing Spielberg in the process – he was sympathetic to Walsh's plight, but hell, this was a theatrical movie he might be about to lose – Walsh walked. Under Spielberg's direction, he walked all the way over to the Zanuck/Brown team. This time it was Spielberg, without warning, who decided to drop the project and do some walking of his own.

Walsh's introduction to Hollywood had been salutary: presented with MGM's impossible conditions from what had seemed a done deal, then abruptly deserted by Spielberg, the friend who'd helped develop *Slide*. Shattered, he looked around for another home for his project. And found one when Guy McElwaine introduced him, through producer George Litto, to director Robert Altman. That McElwaine also knew Columbia's new head man, the immaculately buffed David Begelman, did no harm at all. That Begelman was himself a compulsive gambler and all-too-perfectly understood the motivations of the movie's characters did no further harm. That it was a small-budget roll-of-the-dice clinched the deal. Before Walsh knew it, *Slide* became *California Split*, a Columbia Picture starring Elliott Gould and George Segal, directed by Altman.

While the Writers' Guild Award Walsh accepted for his work on *California Split* boosted its box-office score not one whit, there was

33

almost universal praise for the movie Spielberg had chosen to put behind him. Walsh recalls meeting with his ex-partner soon after the opening and his description of it as 'truly exceptional'.

'I really saw how grudgingly he wanted to get that out,' says Walsh. 'Remember, this was going to be *Spielberg*'s picture, *the* picture.' Even while praising the movie, Spielberg was definitely feeling his oats and unable to resist adding that had *he* directed *California Split*, 'it would have made twenty-five, maybe fifty million dollars'.

Walsh understood what Spielberg was saying and readily acknowledges what his totally different approach might have achieved: 'Steven would have built that last scene, that gambling scene, into one gigantic orgasm, climaxing the last forty pages of the script until you were on the edge of your seats. He's a master at building it up, Steven is, whereas Altman comes from a whole different world, more of a European style. Steven could have manipulated that film into $50 million at the box-office, but he didn't know if he could have made a *better* film.'

Spielberg finally described *California Split* as 'much better than I thought it was'. To arrive at that conclusion, though, he'd had to see it 'over and over again'.

Back at Universal, Lew Wasserman had been forced to conclude that hurling projects willy-nilly against the wall and seeing which ones stuck, was no way to run a studio. Nor were so-called value-for-money double-bills, not with endless hours of pap available on TV for free. The answer that was forced on him, with the cash drain reaching ever more alarming proportions, was to greenlight just eleven movies for 1970. His new 'less is more' policy worked immediately. *Airport*, producer Ross Hunter's version of the Arthur Haley best-seller, was the biggest hit in Universal's history. For the moment, Wasserman's trademark horn-rim glasses were immune from further attack.

With the 1971 crop, it was back to square one. Now the obscure object of Wasserman's desire was emulation of Columbia's free-wheeling *Easy Rider*. Some of the movies that resulted were good, notably Monte Hellman's *Two Lane Blacktop*, but none turned a profit. The best his 'mainstream' could manage was a middling *Andromeda Strain*. Only continuing revenues from *Airport* enabled MCA to post a reasonable return for the year.

It was Ned Tanen, his 'happening' guy, whom Wasserman chose to guide him through the maze of *Easy Rider* wannabes. The dapper young man's success in completing the programme – including Dennis Hopper's *The Last Movie* after a year in production – led to his appointment as movie production chief in 1972. After years of

Wasserman's try-everything approach, all eyes were fixed on Tanen.

Decent returns from Martin Ritt's *Pete 'N' Tillie*, Hitchcock's *Frenzy* and John Sturges's *Joe Kidd* helped persuade Jules Stein that it was safe to shuffle off to the sidelines. In 1973 he appointed himself Chairman Emeritus and handed over chairmanship of the company to Wasserman, the man he'd sought to fire only four momentous years earlier. With Frank Price taking over as president of Universal-TV, Sheinberg moved up to Wasserman's overall second-in-command. This had to be good news for Spielberg.

If 'The Legend of Lew' had taken a battering in the troubled latter half of the sixties, the era was well behind him with his ascent to chairmanship not only of MCA, but of the Motion Pictures and Television Producers Association. One of his first successes with the group came when he settled a Writers' Guild strike that had halted TV production for four months. One writer told the *Wall Street Journal*, 'He'll take your hair, your arms, your legs and even your fingernails in a deal. But he won't lie to you. He'll *tell* you he's doing it.'

Rumours of continued Mafia involvement in the running of MCA, meanwhile, refused to go away, fuel for the flames provided by Wasserman's close relationship with mob lawyer Sidney R. Korshak. A strike averted? Or called off? No problem, if Korshak's number was on your Rolodex. As Robert Evans put it, 'Let's just say that a nod from Korshak and the Teamsters change management. A nod from Korshak, and Santa Anita closes. A nod from Korshak, and Las Vegas shuts down. A nod from Korshak, and the Dodgers can suddenly play night baseball.'

And with a nod from 'the Godfather of Hollywood', as Wasserman rapidly became known, who knows what could happen? How about the go-ahead for a new director's first theatrical feature?

Finally committed to making his first *intentional* big-screen debut, *White Lightning*, a thriller starring Burt Reynolds, Spielberg spent three months caught up in preparation for the movie, scouting locations and casting. Until, one day, he sat down and thought it through.

This was his first *real* movie. Was it up to scratch? Or was it nothing more than a glorified, by-the-numbers B-film? After much heartsearching, and much to the studio's astonishment, he turned the picture down. It was a move that could have jeopardised his entire future. 'I didn't want to start my career as a hard-hat journeyman director,' he rationalised. 'I wanted to do something a little more personal.'

While working with Joseph Walsh, he'd encouraged his friends

Barwood and Robbins to concentrate on a project they called *The Sugarland Express*. Pitched to Universal, it had been met with their monotonously regular lack of enthusiasm. There had to be a way . . .

Soon after the débâcle of *Ace Eli*, the Zanuck/Brown team had moved their shingle from Pico Boulevard and Fox to Warners' Burbank Studios. Eighteen months later, in a providential move for Spielberg, they relocated again, this time to neighbouring Universal. Their brief as independent producers tied to the studio was simple. Turn out mainstream blockbusters. As they were preparing to move, a meeting was set up with Spielberg's agent Mike Medavoy. 'You know and like Steven,' the team was reminded. 'Well, he's got a project at Universal, *The Sugarland Express*, but he can't get it off the ground. What he really needs is a heavyweight production team who can launch it.'

Zanuck and Brown read the script and were impressed, yet hesitated about pitching it to the same studio heads who had already turned it down. Their end-run was achieved by including it among a whole batch of other projects. Wasserman was diplomacy itself. 'We think Steve has a great future,' he told the team, 'but I have to tell you we have no faith in this project.' The truth, it emerged, was that Wasserman found little fault with the script beyond the fact it had missed its anarchy-flavoured sell-by date. He was still reluctant to turn his brand-new production team down, and on a relatively low-budget item. 'Make the film, fellows,' he said at last, 'but you may not be playing to full theatres.'

It was a prophetic statement.

# 6

# ... Big Screen

*'Sugarland Express did get good reviews, but I would
have given away all those reviews for a bigger audience.
The movie just broke even; it didn't make any money.'*

STEVEN SPIELBERG

*'He was my first, so I didn't know that everybody didn't
have kids like him. I just hung on for dear life.'*

LEAH ADLER

*It seemed almost too good to be true, yet there it was. Deep in the heart
of Jefferson, Texas, a dark, brooding Victorian edifice loomed into view. All
it lacked were the scudding clouds, jagged lightning and appliquéd gar-
goyles Roger Corman would have ordered up for his Edgar Allan Poe
adaptations. And, incredibly – yes, it turned out to be a hotel.*

*As Spielberg, his production manager Elliot Schick, and Diane
Bucker, head of the Texas Film Commission, exchanged glances of relief,
their only concern was whether or not there would be room at the inn. It
was, after all, ten o'clock at night, the end of another exhausting session
scouting locations for* The Sugarland Express. *Diane's blue four-door
Mercedes Benz, next door to brand-new and her pride and joy, had
clocked up hundreds of miles that day alone, and another long day lay
ahead. The thought of a comfortable bed for the night, many miles before
they had expected to find a hostelry to rest their weary bones, was irresistible.*

*The threesome quickly established that the hotel was empty of guests.
Two elderly ladies took them through the formalities of registration in the
vast reception area, then showed them to their equally capacious rooms,
complete with canopy beds and velvet wall-coverings that seemed to
speak of an age long since past. Spielberg was given the Jefferson Room,
where a sombre oil painting of Thomas Jefferson held court on the far
wall. His two companions had the Washington and Lincoln chambers.*

*Although the last thing on Spielberg's mind was to dwell on dead* presidents, indeed on anything to do either with the supernatural – all he wanted was a good night's sleep – he was unable to shake off the strangest feeling that someone, or something, was looking over his right shoulder. The sensation was so definite that he turned quickly a couple of times to check. There was nothing there, but each time he felt as if the thing, the spectre, whatever it was, had switched sides and was standing behind his left shoulder. He was being silly, he told himself. He was tired, it had been a long day – no, there it was again, the feeling was stronger than ever—!

Scared as he was, he told himself that he had to be practical. His travel bag lay at the foot of the great bed, and opening it up, he felt inside and extracted the still camera he had packed for recce shots. Attaching the flash, he began to scan the room, methodically covering every corner. As he moved around he noted with alarm an acute change of temperature from one area to the next, just a footfall apart. There was a definite cold spot in the centre of the room, with neither vent, pipe nor crack to offer any explanation. Suddenly there came a tap-tap-tap on the door. It was Diane. 'This place is real spooky,' she declared, shivering involuntarily. 'I mean – Steven, I can't explain it, but there's something going on here. Something – weird.'

'Not only is there something going on,' Spielberg replied, 'but feel this, Diane. I'm standing in a cold spot.' He stepped aside for Diane. Shivering even more, she said, 'Hey, not just cold, Steven, but ice-cold!'

'Let's get Elliott,' Spielberg replied. 'We're leaving.' Diane offered no argument and went to summon Elliott, who, already half asleep on top of his bed, proved somewhat harder to convince.

Spielberg blithely informed the two old ladies that they had decided to press ahead to a Holiday Inn sixty miles farther on, on the pretext that it would bring them closer to the locations they wanted to scout the following day.

On the stroke of midnight the threesome loaded their belongings back into the Mercedes and settled down for the journey. Diane turned the key in her infallible Mercedes, confidently anticipating the low purr with which she had become reassuringly familiar. Instead, the ignition went 'click-click-click'. What fresh hell was this? She tried again. The result was the same. The Merc was dead as a doornail, as a second 'click-click-click' confirmed. 'This isn't happening,' Spielberg declared, 'this is a joke.' After a moment of hollow laughter Diane made a third attempt. 'Click-click-click-click.'

Turning to look at Spielberg she indignantly spluttered, 'This simply can't be. I just got this car, it's less than a year old, this has never happened before.'

Clearly missing his bed, Elliott had his own solution. 'Let's go back to the hotel,' he suggested. 'I mean, this is ridiculous, I don't believe in ghosts.

The only reason I agreed to leave in the first place is because you wanted to leave and you're the director.'

That was Spielberg's cue: Yes, by God, he was *the director!!* 'We are leaving and I am going to get this car fixed,' he declared. Marching back into the hotel, he explained the situation and requested help in finding a mechanic. Yanked from his bed, the local repairman scratched his head as he beheld Diane's car. Although he had no idea where to start, there was one fix-all that would serve to get the party on the road. Unfamiliar as they were with the procedure, the threesome looked on in some wonderment as the worthy opened the hood and hot-wired the gleaming Mercedes. The party reached the Holiday Inn without further incident and gratefully booked in. Next day, after Diane had hot-wired her auto like a true professional, the threesome did the rounds of one-horse towns. Each time they stopped for a recce, the local townsfolk would gather round to take in the sleek blue steel of the Mercedes.

Only when they had to leave and open the bonnet, following the hot-wire procedure once again, was one old boy heard to mutter, 'You know, my Buick – I don't know, I just get in, turn the key and the damn thing starts. How much did you pay for that thing?'

It would be a wonderful wrap if the photographs Spielberg took in 'the Jefferson Room' had revealed a floating sea of ectoplasmic goo. Regrettably, there was just a series of faithfully recorded, decidedly drab old furniture.

Even as he was making his pessimistic forecast on the prospects for *The Sugarland Express*, Lew Wasserman felt secure in the knowledge that the Zanuck/Brown team had the makings of a real winner in another item on their slate, the Paul Newman/Robert Redford feature, *The Sting*. About another item they were involved in, a snake-filled B-movie thriller called *S-S-S-S-S-S!*, he rightly felt less sanguine.

*The Sugarland Express* was based on a real-life incident in 1969 that had riveted the attention of the media, in which a mother, herself newly released from prison, sprang her husband from a remand centre and set off to 'rescue' her baby son from a foster home in Sugarland, Texas. Goldie Hawn was cast as Lou Jean Poplin, the barely articulate – and renamed – lead character, William Atherton as her husband Clovis. Although Spielberg stopped short of awarding himself third writing credit with Barwood and Robbins, he split story credit with Robbins. Unless the pair had more influence over 1969's headlines than might reasonably be supposed, it's hard to figure how they justified the latter claim. Or does the explanation lie within the well-worn catch-all, '*Based on* a true story'?

With almost all of *Sugarland* shot on location, the logistics – not to mention the 'haunted hotel' Spielberg and his companions encountered along the way – proved formidable. Traffic had to be blocked off along considerable expanses of highway, with a convoy of forty-five police cars chasing the couple; the number of vehicles had been reduced by Spielberg from the real-life total of ninety-odd on the basis that the truth was just too incredible to be portrayed realistically. Apart, that is, from budgetary considerations.

Watching their young director in action impressed Richard Zanuck from day one. Prior to shooting the producer's attitude had been, 'Well, let's take it easy. Let's get the kid acclimatised to this big-time stuff.' Instead, Zanuck was bowled over by what he saw: 'The first day he was about ready to get this first shot, and it was the most elaborate fucking thing I've ever seen in my life. I mean *tricky* – all-in-one shots, the camera stopping and going, people going in and out. But he had such confidence in the way he was handling it. Here he was, a young little punk kid, with a lot of seasoned crew around, a major actress on hand, and instead of starting with something easy, he'd picked a very complicated thing that required all kinds of intricate timing. And it worked incredibly well – and not only from a technical standpoint, the *performances* were very good. I knew right there and then, without any doubt, that this guy probably knew more at that age about the mechanics of working out a shot than anybody alive at that time, no matter how many pictures they'd made. He took to it like he was *born* with a knowledge of cinema. And he never ceased to amaze me from that day on.'

It was MCA vice-president Jennings Lang – a man who'd nurtured Sid Sheinberg in the same way Sheinberg was now watching over Spielberg – who introduced Spielberg to John Williams. The maestro, a future Boston Pops Orchestra resident conductor, was already a veteran at Universal-TV renowned for his composing skills, as well as his ability to work to a deadline on an enormous variety of subjects. Spielberg had found the man who would supply his movie music for the next two decades and beyond. In turn, Spielberg introduced Williams to George Lucas. The result would be another lasting partnership, beginning with the soundtrack for *Star Wars* that helped elevate that movie to epic level.

Even the buzz that flew around Hollywood on Ned Tanen's first slate underestimated the goodies in store. Although he'd had no faith personally in George Lucas's *American Graffiti* – after an early preview he pronounced the movie 'unreleasable' and told his girlfriend he'd felt sick watching it – the movie proved a smash. On a minuscule budget of $775,000, *Graffiti* grossed an astounding $115 million at the US box-office. Even this was outdone, though hardly in costs to profitability terms, by Zanuck/Brown's *The Sting*, its $156 million gross another all-time high for the studio. While scarcely on a level with the leaders, Norman Jewison's freeform adaptation of *Jesus Christ Superstar*, Fred Zinnemann's crisply efficient *Day of the Jackal* and Clint Eastwood's ultra-violent *High Plains Drifter*, all provided juicy returns.

One way or another, although he had yet to score big himself, Spielberg was enjoying success by association. Certainly, his friend Lucas had streaked ahead of him. But here he was, allied with the top production team at Universal on *The Sugarland Express*. Couldn't be bad.

Zanuck and Brown previewed *The Sugarland Express* at the Cannes Film Festival in 1974 in an attempt to kick-start favourable word-of-mouth. Instead, the response was decidedly tentative, apart from an encouraging award for best script. Back home the production team realised they were in deep trouble when the entire resources of their office, working with Universal's marketing mavens, failed to come up with a convincing ad campaign for the movie, a single idea that would express in visual terms what *Sugarland* was about. They acknowledge that Universal experimented endlessly, taking whole cities and creating new approaches to the media blitz. Per David Brown, the commercial canker at the movie's heart lay in the two petty criminals with whom audiences were expected to empathise. Quite simply, they declined the invitation en masse.

Spielberg's initial reaction was to deny that the movie had failed at all, both to himself and to the outside world – and if it had, it was sure as hell nothing to do with him. This much you have to hand him: if his explanation for *Sugarland*'s flop was circuitous, it was also highly ingenious. 'For one thing,' a journalist was informed, 'we've pulled the picture, so we don't consider that it's failed in its opening. We're going to re-release the picture, because I think that the main failing of *Sugarland Express* was the fact that two other films came out at the same time that were thematically similar, *Badlands* and *Thieves Like Us*. And that the audience was wrapping all three films into one bundle. And I really think, in talking to other people, that they got the reviews – the good reviews of Terry Mallick's *Badlands*, which were really a turn-off because the theme of Terry's picture is a real downer – they mixed up my reviews with his and his with mine. I just didn't think that the general public were aware at the time that they were essentially different movies.'

Enough? Nope. 'The other big feeling was the release time. Nothing really made it that Spring, especially when six hits had come out from September to January – *Serpico, The Exorcist, The Sting, Papillon* – and my God, there were so many pictures making it, *American Graffiti* too, so many pictures making a lot of money, that just when we came out all those pictures had left their exclusive or flagship runs and that really spoiled it for the moviegoer, who today is so selective about what they go to see.'

There was yet more. 'And a third factor I feel was the advertising and publicity. In Universal's attempt to sell the picture I think they did a milksop job. They just dropped it on the country with no preparation, and a trailer I didn't like at all.'

Pausing only to take a quick breath, he summed up his reaction as 'more anger than disappointment' before producing yet another rationale: 'People saw it was Goldie Hawn's film . . . they thought it was "small".' Then there was the title: 'Most people thought it was a kids' film.'

Left with little alternative in the final analysis, Spielberg conceded that *Sugarland* was 'a sad film, a bitter-sweet film' – hardly blockbuster material, no matter how skilfully realised, misunderstood or misrepresented.

When it was suggested that *Sugarland* came off as a companion piece to Billy Wilder's *Ace in the Hole*, Spielberg acknowledged that it was no coincidence. I wanted to go further,' he claimed, 'in that these media events not only changed the shape of public opinion, but they also changed the people inside the car, and I thought that was important. Because the media could go right to the source, it affected the people concerned emotionally. More importantly, it affected the whole natural course of the event.' (If Spielberg's words were true back then, look around now – when not just thousands, but *millions* of viewers across the US, and *worldwide*, watched – live on TV – a flotilla of LAPD vehicles pursue O.J. Simpson and A.C. Cowlings along the Los Angeles freeway in a 'media event' that, while dwarfing the *Sugarland* spectacle in terms of coverage and viewership, was still presaged by Lou Jean and Clovis Poplin's odyssey.)

Despite the undoubted prescience behind Spielberg's pronouncement, as well as the uncompromising idealism he affected, he had astonishingly attempted to tamper with the tragic real-life outcome that had one of the participants shot to death. *Ace in the Hole* was all down to Billy Wilder. Can anyone imagine Wilder *volunteering* to change his downbeat ending to make a few extra bucks at the box-office? That was exactly what Spielberg did during production of *Sugarland*. He was the quintessential young-man-in-a-hurry, desperate for a hit, and if he'd been allowed his head, everything would have come up roses for Lou Jean and Clovis. It really would have been 'Story by Steven Spielberg'!

What ensued was a reverse case of the usual director/producer conflict, with Zanuck and Brown insistent on preserving the artistic integrity of the project. They rejected Spielberg's proposed happy ending as a compromise too far. Spielberg found himself ordered to make the movie they had all been so enthusiastic about in the first place.

The 'applause junkie' side of Spielberg, preserved intact from his boyhood, had been held in check. For the moment.

Spielberg was acutely aware of all the other emerging directors at the time, knew most of them personally, and constantly gauged his performance and status against theirs. Senior citizen Francis Coppola, with whom he shared an agent in Mike Medavoy, was ahead of all of them thanks to a jump start from Roger Corman. *Dementia 13* had been successfully parlayed into a run at Warners, *You're A Big Boy Now* leading to *Finian's Rainbow* and *The Rain People*. Along the way, pausing to turn out an award-winning script for *Patton*, Coppola had taken intern George Lucas under his wing, championing his *THX 1138* in 1970 along the way to his own big-time directorial breakthrough with *The Godfather* two years later at Paramount. Now, as well as juggling *Godfather II* and *The Conversation*, and dreaming of *Apocalypse Now* for the future, he'd produced Lucas's breakthrough, *American Graffiti*.

Spielberg's friend Brian De Palma had left his troubles at Warners behind him and had just unleashed his independently produced shocker *Sisters* (aka *Blood Sisters*) on an unsuspecting public. Now he was at work on a follow-up, *Phantom of the Paradise*.

Martin Scorsese was another NYU alumnus whose work as an editor at Warners had led to a directing shot from the ubiquitous Corman with *Boxcar Bertha*, then a move back to Warners for the groundbreaking *Mean Streets*. Now, in something of a departure, he was working at Burbank on *Alice Doesn't Live Here Anymore*.

Peter Bogdanovich, his host in Rome, was back from Italy, deep in the editing process with *Daisy Miller*, and planning the 'ultimate musical' to showcase his beloved Cybill, *At Long Last Love*.

And there was no shortage of comers. Jonathan Demme, two decades before *Silence of the Lambs* and *Philadelphia*, was about to start his first movie, *Caged Heat*. Michael Cimino was making his debut directing Clint Eastwood and Jeff Bridges in *Thunderbolt and Lightfoot* for United Artists, the company he would eventually send into eclipse with *Heaven's Gate*. A wild card from Czechoslovakia, with a setback in Universal's *Taking Off* behind him, Milos Forman was about to be given a second Hollywood chance by producer

43

Michael Douglas with *One Flew Over the Cuckoo's Nest*.

As if that wasn't enough, a host of other young wannabes were waiting in the wings. Besides Milius, Barwood and Robbins there was Allan Arkush, another from NYU who would travel the no-pay/low-pay Corman route, as had Bogdanovich and Demme, Monte Hellman, Gary Kurtz, Walter Murch, Paul Bartel, Jack Nicholson, Tony Bill, Joe Dante and Jonathan Kaplan.

Spielberg had no intentions of getting caught in the same trap that had snared Bogdanovich – his oft-declared adulation of past cinematic heroes. 'I don't look back to the thirties, to William Wellman and Howard Hawks, for my ideas and inspiration,' he declared. Instead: 'I draw from my friends – Marty Scorsese, Brian De Palma and George Lucas.' Neither, for that matter, was he all that enamoured of the works of European directors, despite his side-trip to worship at the feet of Fellini. 'If I weren't in the business,' he confirmed, 'I would never choose to see films by Bergman, Fellini or Ingmar Bergman.' So much for inspiration!

It was an intensely competitive time, with commercial success and critical acclaim, as ever, the twin benchmarks. Garnering one was great, garnering both a dream. It was all a question of priorities, and Spielberg had no doubt about his. 'I'm not interested in making small critical successes that nobody goes to see,' he declared.

Despite its commercial failure, *Sugarland* collected some excellent reviews. *New Yorker*'s Pauline Kael described Spielberg's direction, according to the handout Universal immediately prepared, as 'One of the most phenomenal debuts in the history of movies'. (The full version of her review qualifies this just a tad; her remark was prefaced, 'In terms of the pleasure that technical assurance gives an audience, *Sugarland* is . . .') Although she also criticised the movie as shallow and impersonal, Kael's notice contained an uncannily accurate prediction: 'He could be that rarity among directors – a born entertainer.' Pleasing, on a somewhat lower scale, was a comparison she chose: '*The Sugarland Express* has life to it. Not the kind of life that informs a young film like Martin Scorsese's *Mean Streets* – probably the best American film of 1973 – but the vitality that a director with great instincts can bring to commercial entertainment.'

Bearing in mind Spielberg's expressed admiration for *Ace in the Hole*, another major consolation was the unqualified rave *Sugarland* elicited from Billy Wilder: 'The director of that movie is the greatest talent to come along in years.'

Wilder's assessment gets no argument from me. I thought the movie was outstanding, both on a logistical and personal level, displaying an amazing technical assurance for a first major feature, while never losing sight of the human angle. The performances Spielberg elicits from Goldie Hawn, William Atherton and Michael Parks are among the best they've given – in Hawn's case her finest-ever – and he gave John Ford veteran Ben Johnson yet another autumnal chance to display the gravitas displayed in Bogdanovich's *The Last Picture Show*.

Both Kael's and Wilder's notices were formidable additions to any young man's resumé. Which begged the question: where had Spielberg acquired the life experience to bring off his triumph? Two answers suggest themselves.

First: from his vast storehouse of decidedly bitter-sweet child-hood memories, culminating in his parents' wrenching separation and divorce that catapulted him, kicking and screaming, into adult-hood. There were many elements in *Sugarland* that can be traced directly back to Spielberg's own experiences, all the way to Atherton playfully shining the torchlight on his face ('I'M THE MOOOON!!'). And one can see how the tale must have appealed to him in the first place, with its parents, no matter how disadvantaged, prepared to go to any lengths to reclaim their child.

Second: from watching lots and lots of movies.

Back in 1968 Denis Hoffman had been forced to correct a mistaken impression over *Amblin'*. Because Chuck Silvers, in his enthusiasm to show the movie to Sid Sheinberg, had ordered a copy struck from the negative at the on-site Technicolor lab, at Universal's expense, the movie had become known in the press and at subsequent festival showings – even though they'd been organised and financed solely by Hoffman – as 'Universal's *Amblin*''. As in the headline: 'Universal Wins Atlanta Film Festival'.

'I was only trying to do you and Spielberg a favour,' an embarrassed Silvers explained. 'Don't make more of a fuss than you have to, otherwise it could get nasty for me around here.' While accepting this with good grace – Silvers was known to be a decent, easy-going fellow – Hoffman managed to negotiate a retraction from the studio that appeared in *Hollywood Reporter*.

In the next few years Hoffman watched Spielberg's career take off with considerable satisfaction, more convinced than ever, as the first man to put his money where his mouth was, that he had made a sound investment in his friend's talent and prospects for the future. While keeping in touch, there was no question of any imme-diate pressure being applied on Spielberg to fulfil the terms of their contract. There was plenty of time for that, and projects a-plenty that Hoffman began to sift through. So *The Sugarland*

*Express* hadn't taken off. So what? It was a creditable piece of work that bode well for the future, and Hoffman had until 1978 to come up with a script that would reunite him professionally with Spielberg. Their ten-year agreement had a ways to go. And a contract was a contract.

Wasn't it?

# 7

# 'No Final Script, No Final Cast, No Final Shark'

*'I really like my contemporaries and I can get more out of George Lucas, who's a good friend of mine, than I can by sitting in a screening room and screening eight Preston Sturges films. I mean, I really can. I watch hundreds of old movies, so don't get me wrong, but I haven't learned that much from them.'*

*'I wanted to do* Jaws *for hostile reasons. I read it and felt that I had been attacked. It terrified me, and I wanted to strike back.'*

STEVEN SPIELBERG

The box-office failure of *The Sugarland Express* was shared in 1974 by another Goldie Hawn vehicle from Universal, *The Girl From Petrovka.* Two others from the studio went belly-up in the same year: Don Siegel's *The Black Windmill* and Roland Kibbee's *The Midnight Man.* Billy Wilder's *The Front Page,* his first-ever movie for Universal, was an ode to Lew Wasserman, his ex-agent and one-time bridge partner, and although it featured his well-tried team of Lemmon and Matthau, it did no more than OK. There were only two winners – *Airport '75* and *Earthquake* – but they were enough to carry the day for Ned Tanen.

Plucked from TV and 'coerced' by Lew Wasserman into accepting the post of Universal president, Sid Sheinberg decided he'd better learn the movie business fast, for although Tanen was the titular head of the studio, both their necks would be on the line unless they kept the ball rolling. 'The first thing I did,' Sheinberg recalls, 'was get into a state of anxiety as to what this company had that we could release in the theatrical area. And one of the properties that was in the works was this silly story about a fish . . .'

Following completion of filming on *The Sugarland Express*, Spielberg had been offered a variety of projects by the Zanuck/Brown team. None of them had captured his imagination. One day he picked up the galley proofs of Peter Benchley's novel *Jaws*, which happened to be lying on David Brown's desk. 'What is this about?' he asked himself. 'A porno dentist?' He read it just to relax. Instead, the adrenaline started pumping. He loved the basic theme of the common man up against elemental forces, a hero straight out of the Akira Kurosawa movies he had forced himself along to see. Once, that is, he got over what he considered 'the dry-land shit'.

'Sorry, Steven,' he was told when he expressed interest, 'we already have a director attached.'

It soon transpired that, having outbid the considerable competition for Peter Benchley's book in galley form – ponying up $150,000 with escalation clauses to $250,000, plus a percentage of the profits – the Zanuck/Brown team had been brought face to face with the grim reality of transferring the story to the screen. They had absolutely no idea of how to make the movie. Even Dick Richards, their first directorial choice, had disconcerted them by referring to 'the whale', betraying a certain lack of the *je ne sais quoi* required for the undertaking. In the four frantic days after Richards left to make *Farewell, My Lovely* for Lew Grade, other, established directors were considered ahead of Spielberg.

When they finally did offer it to Spielberg, his response was disappointingly equivocal: 'I just don't know. After all, it's only a shark story.' Well, the team felt, at least he got the species right! A week later, the adrenalin by now having drained completely, he let them know it was definitely out of the question. What did he know from sharks? What did *they* know? What did *anybody* know? Instead of moving onward and upward in his career, he saw *Jaws* as a backward step. After that first read, Spielberg had commissioned sweatshirts overprinted with 'Jaws'. The purpose: To psych everyone up that he was the guy for the job. Now the ruse backfired on him. To his dismay he found the Zanuck/Brown team wearing theirs when he reported to turn the movie down. 'We shamed him,' they claim, 'into staying on the project.'

Sid Sheinberg, as usual, has his own version of events. 'I literally *forced* Steven to do it,' he says. 'It's the only time in our careers I really ordered him to do something. I think he was upset with me for a while. "Why are you making me do this B-movie?" he asked.' Sheinberg also claims he turned to his protégé with the suggested approach: 'Why don't we simply make it *Duel* with a shark?'

Next came the problem of coming up with a script outline they could all live with. Spielberg swiftly made it clear to his producers that he had no intention of approaching the book with the reverence Benchley felt it deserved. For a start, he saw the *Peyton Place*-type subplot as pure soap. Benchley was still given first crack at the script, mainly because a Writers' Guild strike was threatened which would leave him unaffected, since he was not yet a member.

Everyone concerned expressed disappointment in that first draft, which seemed simply to be all the dialogue in the book transcribed, with descriptive passages in between. It was read while Spielberg, Zanuck, Brown and Benchley were staying at the Hotel du Cap in the South of France during the 1974 Cannes Film Festival, preparing to unveil *The Sugarland Express*.

The movie team collaborated on basic character and story changes in Benchley's version until – pausing only to turn down a last-minute offer from Paul Newman to direct *Lucky Lady* – Spielberg felt he could definitely come on board as *Jaws*' committed director. Needless to say, Sheinberg's 'order' may have had something to do with his decision. Zanuck was not only relieved, but totally impressed with the *chutzpah* his young director had displayed. 'I marvelled at the kid. He had only one picture behind him and that had not been released yet,' he says. 'He shared an agent with Paul Newman, and there he was, telling him that he *might* do *Lucky Lady*, but not with Newman. He was twenty-four-years-old, and he turned down Newman like he swatted a fly!' (For the record, Spielberg was twenty-six.)

Benchley would produce a total of three drafts before throwing in the beach towel. After his best effort had been duly tweaked by Spielberg, Zanuck and Brown, it was passed to Howard (*The Great White Hope*) Sackler for a redraft that didn't work, to John Milius for Quint's grim USS *Indianapolis* speech, finally to Carl Gottlieb, a college buddy of Spielberg's. Gottlieb stripped the novel down until it was three protagonists versus the Great White, or as he puts it, Melville's *Moby Dick* meets Ibsen's *Enemy of the People*. He worked on location on what were regarded as the final drafts with Spielberg, although on-screen credit remains shared between Gottlieb and Benchley.

Spielberg and the movie's art director, Joseph Alves Jr, decided after viewing everything from *20,000 Leagues Under the Sea* to *Moby Dick* that studio tanks were out – real life, all-at-sea locations were essential. That left the problem of 'Where?' Alves's wintertime recce trip for suitable locations included a stop-off at the Hamptons, which he decided were just too high-falutin' for humble fictitious Amity; something less tony had to be found, the town had to look convincingly 'resort'. En route to Nantucket he took a ferry to

Martha's Vineyard. This was more like it, he decided, taking in the generous stretches of golden beaches and dunes, sunbleached docks and picturesque inlets. There were many other factors that weighed in the Vineyard's favour. The twelve-ton steel submersible platform planned to support their manufactured 'shark' necessitated twenty-five–thirty feet depth of water and a level, sandy base; both were available. A sheltered bay was required to permit 180-degree pans over uninterrupted horizon; this looked like a given. These facilities had to be within a forty-five-minute drive or sail of a hotel able to accommodate the needs of more than a hundred cast and crew. Yes, Martha's vineyard had it all! And it was so *quiet*!

Casting for what Spielberg saw as the story's three 'authority figures' was of crucial importance.

First there was Martin Brody, the town's police chief, the person responsible for ensuring beach safety, an ex-New York cop looking for asylum for himself and his family from the violence and evil of the city streets. When Zanuck suggested Charlton Heston, Spielberg recoiled in horror. It had nothing to do with his admiration for the actor. 'What?' he exclaimed. '*Moses?* You want *Moses*? Everybody'll know he'll win! We've got to have an actor everybody'll believe!' Roy Scheider, former Golden Gloves boxer, late of Joseph Papp's New York Shakespeare Festival and Lincoln Center repertory, fresh from an Oscar nomination for his role in *French Connection*, was an early choice they could all agree on, and was first to sign on the dotted line.

There was Matt Hooper, the egghead ichthyologist, the above-it-all shark expert. Spielberg's first choice, Jon Voight – tall, blond, physically right for Benchley's hero – was unavailable. Richard Dreyfuss, not tall, not blond, but hot from the unexpected hit, George Lucas's *American Graffiti*, and about to get hotter with the imminent opening of *The Apprenticeship of Duddy Kravitz*, turned him down at first after Spielberg ran through the scenario. 'I'd rather watch this movie than have to shoot it,' he declared. He remained adamant at the end of their second pitch. 'The shark'll be a turkey,' he predicted, shrugging nonchalantly at the frustrated expression on the faces of Spielberg and Gottlieb. Finally, with only days to go before shooting was due to start, and with Joel Grey now under consideration, Gottlieb hustled Dreyfuss down to Boston for a third meeting with Spielberg. 'I don't want to do it,' Dreyfuss still insisted, 'because as an actor it doesn't do anything for me.' This time Spielberg and Gottlieb eventually wore him down, despite a situation Dreyfuss succinctly summed up as having 'no final script, no final cast, no final shark'. What it did have was 30,000 feet of shark footage shot off the Australian coast by underwater photographers Ron and Valerie Taylor, renowned for their *Blue Water, White Death* documentary. What it now also had was Dreyfuss wearing his Boston hat, glasses and beard, the ensemble judged ideal by Spielberg, who told wardrobe to shop around for 'two more of whatever he's wearing'. The bottom line behind Dreyfuss's eventual signing? 'The people around me said a) You have no money, b) There's an actors' strike coming up and that means no other work, and c) You'd be an idiot not to do it!' ('Whatever you do, don't read the book,' Dreyfuss's agent had also pleaded. With good reason – 'Matt Hooper' was chomped to death in Benchley's tome.)

A substitute victim was found in the novel's bald bounty hunter Quint, with a World War II true horror story up his sleeve that owed nothing to the Benchley novel. Instead, it was perfectly suited to the mindset of John Milius, Spielberg's USC buddy. The producers' ideal choice to play Quint had been Sterling Hayden, a seasoned actor known for spending weeks at a time on board his own boat. When that failed to work out, Robert Shaw was approached. He signed after listening to advice from his wife, Mary Ure. She had, after all, previously persuaded him to accept the role of the villain opposite Connery's Bond in *From Russia With Love*. That had been very much against the serious actor's judgement – Dostoevsky it wasn't – but the gig had increased his profile and led to the kind of payday of which he could only have dreamt while treading the boards of London's West End, let alone touring repertory halls.

*Jaws* was a not dissimilar situation – Shaw described the book as 'a story written by committee, a pile of shit' – but Zanuck/Brown's crock of gold, already sampled with *The Sting*, proved too much to resist. At the same time, his open contempt for Benchley's opus made the decision to play Quint with hair, rather than the author's skinhead, an easy one. Shaw would set up home in Martha's Vineyard 'Bel Air', Edgartown, with Ure and an ever-changing selection of their brood of nine kids from their own and his wife's previous marriage to playwright Harold Pinter.

Controversy continues to this day over who is really responsible for the *Indianapolis* speech. Take your pick:

*Take One* Peter Benchley: 'I don't know, I didn't see it being filmed. Shaw claimed he wrote it himself. I have heard it was any number of people. John Milius was said to have written it.'

*Take Two* David Brown: 'John Milius claimed he wrote that

famous speech. That speech was written by Howard Sackler, Milius added something and then Robert Shaw added a great deal.'

*Take Three* Carl Gottlieb: 'Robert Shaw wrote his own long speech about the *Indianapolis*. I willingly concede that the *idea* of a scene in which men compare scars as a macho ritual may have originated with Milius; his personal obsession with 'manly' behaviour is well known. However, the *Indianapolis* speech was written by Shaw, who was a gifted writer as well as an actor. He collated the research, and examined all the drafts of the speech by different screenwriters.'

*Take Four* Steven Spielberg: 'John Milius sat down at a dining room table and pulled out a pad of yellow notepaper. He asked for the facts, and then he began to write in longhand. It took him seven minutes to write a seven-minute monologue. It was perfect. To be fair, I have to say that Robert Shaw did revise it a little, because we had to bring it down to four or five minutes.'

*Take Five* John Milius: 'Steven needed a scene to tell why Quint hated sharks and we just came up with most of it over the phone.'

The physical embodiment of the shark itself had presented the greatest casting challenge. Landlubbers Zanuck and Brown had their own dream solution: 'Oh, we'll get a trained one!!' Even Dreyfuss's faux-ichthyologist was able to scupper that idea.

Translating the terror of the deep into a mechanical creature that could stand scrutiny in the clear light of day was no mean task. It was accomplished by Robert Mattey, the man who built the mechanical squid for Disney's *20,000 Leagues Under the Sea*. It was still, in Spielberg's increasingly panic-stricken view, risky and 'about as easy to operate as a 747'. He realised that the movie could easily turn out to be the laugh riot of the year, with the creature coming out of the water tail first. Whatever happened, the fact that they were using a man-made shark had to be kept under wraps at all costs. 'There's only one shark in this movie,' Spielberg solemnly assured journalist David Helpern, 'and it's real.'

Mattey's prototype polyurethane creation, nicknamed 'Bruce' by Spielberg in a capricious moment after his attorney Bruce Ramer, barely made it out of the water at all on his first pre-production launching, all twenty-four feet and one and a half tons of him sinking to the bottom. The second attempt was even more spectacular. The hydraulics inside his gut exploded.

By the time Spielberg arrived at Martha's Vineyard with director of photography Bill Butler, it was late spring, several months after Alves's recce, and summer was stretching ahead. He, Alves and Butler looked with some disquiet at the myriad boats dotting the horizon as far as the eye could see. What the hell was this? What hadn't been taken into account was the 'regatta season', now in full swing, of which there had been no evidence during the December trip. That, together with the fact that just about every large yacht and sailboat on the eastern seaboard converged on Martha's Vineyard at some point during the summer. What a difference a season made!

As he was settling in, a distinctly rattled Spielberg chose to sound off to *Newsweek* about his 'distaste' for the novel he was about to bring to the screen. The magazine hit the stands the same day the New York *Times*' Gregg Kilday arrived to chronicle the start of filming. Benchley seethed on the record, describing Spielberg as a 'B-movie literate' and predicting that 'one day Spielberg will be known as the greatest second-unit director in America'. By the time the two had actually met and buried the hatchet, their blood feud was all over the media.

As shooting began, worry was expressed that 'Bruce' lacked the sheer frightening bulk required to jolt audiences out of their seats. One idea was to use a short actor for long shots to make the shark look bigger. Carl Rizzo, the 'short actor' hired, decided he was already short enough and refused to share the proposed briny bath. On the third day of shooting the shark sank at sea, sending shock waves of panic through the unit and all the way back to Universal Studios. The secret that they had been filming with a phoney shark was broken by the New York *Times* scribe, making liars of them all. Worse was to follow, with a Washington *Post* photographer sneaking into 'Bruce's' dry dock and splashing the resultant image all over the front page of his widely circulated newspaper. David Brown was disconsolate. Who the hell would want to see the movie now?

Within a week the unit was two days behind schedule. Two Arriflex cameras were lost at sea, there was a near-miss with a $50,000 Panaflex. Roy Scheider cut open a toe that became infected, halting production for three days. Carl Gottlieb fell overboard and was nearly decapitated by a propellor. Spielberg was saved from drowning by his wet suit, then almost crushed to death between two colliding vehicles.

Constant heavy tides, freakish currents and unpredictable wind patterns dogged the resort. Many days nothing was shot until 4 pm, with the light completely gone a couple of hours later. Then there were all these goddam boats constantly sailing into view—! Scheider summed up Spielberg's frustration: 'Here we have two guys out in a rickety boat, hunting a killer shark, supposedly miles from shore. What kind of movie is this going to be if there is a family of four only feet away having a picnic on a sailboat?'

Even when Spielberg tried a 5 am start, the boats were there ahead of him; either that or the water was too choppy, with five-foot waves washing over the boat. Taking the boat into the harbour for close-ups didn't work either; a nor'easter blew up that lasted for six days. Weather apart, operating with a mixed crew from Los Angeles and New York presented a problem on its own; observing the relative pecking order involved was like walking on eggshells.

By the time 'Bruce' was fully functional the movie was 100 days behind schedule and 100% over its original $2.3 million budget. Three final, road-tested 'Bruces' built by an increasingly disenchanted Universal, cost the studio $450,000.

'I was out of my mind with fear,' Spielberg admits, 'not of being replaced, even though people were trying to fire me, but of letting everybody down. I was twenty-six –' (Spielberg was twenty-seven, and due to turn twenty-eight on December 18, 1974) '– and even though I felt like a veteran by that time, nobody else felt that way about me. I looked seventeen, I had acne, and that doesn't help instill confidence in seasoned crews. It was a nightmare, going into the ocean was like working inside an earthquake. Tourists intentionally tripped over cables and threatened to sue. Ruth Gordon was around. Walter Cronkite showed up with his family – the father of my living room on my movie set!'

One consolation for Roy Scheider among the tourists was getting to meet one of his idols, playwright Thornton Wilder. Unlike many of the Vineyard crowd, the venerable Wilder had no ambitions to appear in a Hollywood movie. Otherwise, the resort was jam-packed with bankers, lawyers and Wall Street dealers, none on a stipend of much less than half a million a year, all perversely anxious to cut themselves a deal as an extra. What kind of money could they expect? $2.50 per hour was the somewhat deflating answer.

Less of a consolation for Scheider was the way he saw his character of Police Chief Brody being transformed from the original straightforward, macho concept. Although he realised how important it was that Brody not act too self-assured, that he shouldn't necessarily have all the answers, he initially felt Spielberg was nudging him too far in the direction of ineffectuality. Peering through the glasses he was asked to wear, following Spielberg's instructions and bumping into things and falling down, he was worried.

If Spielberg had at least been in possession of a final, *final* script with which he was content, it might have been some compensation. Unfortunately, there was no such thing, even after all the hands involved. His solution was to invite Carl Gottlieb and the lead players to his place for dinner. From two hours of pooling ideas on tape, he and Gottlieb were able to extract eight or ten lines that became part of the script to be shot twelve hours later.

David Brown's arrival as Spielberg's partner in misery signalled the imminent arrival of MCA brass. Brown was quickly made familiar with one source of the money drain – the infamous 'Bruce'. 'That shark was like owning a yacht,' he recalls. 'We had to dredge a place for it to rest, park it, place a guard around it, strike it, hide it from the public.' (But not, alas, from the prying eyes of the Washington *Post* and its readers.)

Universal troubleshooters showed up after several weeks, took one look at the conditions under which Spielberg was labouring, collectively turned green, and promptly returned to base. The word among those remaining: 'Uh, oh, the other shoe is about to drop . . .!' Following their trip, horror stories from the location continued to leak daily to the filmmaking community. The result: undisguised glee that the latest wunderkind looked set for a fall. Spielberg was brought face to face with a grim reality of Hollywood, that there were many people more interested in seeing him fail than succeed. He knew that *Jaws* could break him as well as make him, for expectations were sky-high among the millions who had bought Benchley's book.

For a while the studio considered pulling the plug. Instead, they finally decided that the point of no return had been reached. Whatever it cost, the movie had to be finished.

# 8

## 'I Shall *Not* Return!'

*'If I hadn't been a Scout I'd probably have ended up as an
axe murderer, or a butcher in a Jewish deli.'*

*'I'll read the critics, but only months and months later. I
even read the pans.'*

STEVEN SPIELBERG

Storyboarding carried out in the pre-production process – including 400 individual pen-and-ink drawings committed to paper by an art director for the last third of the movie alone – helped Spielberg retain a grip on his sanity during the gruelling *Jaws* shoot. It was a piece of homework that gave him the security to get up in the morning. He needed it, for there was little else; he was the lone holdout during the entire process, refusing to take a break on the mainland. And he claims largely to have eschewed consolations of the flesh as a diversion from his troubles: 'You have no time for yourself except to eat, shoot your movie, plan your shots for the next day, sleep and forget women. When I'm making a movie I become partially celibate. I get into the routine of fucking *my movie*. I become mad Dr Frankenstein, with test tubes and electrical sparks, creating a living organism from dead parts!'

Others, according to Spielberg, were less consumed with the act of celluloid creation: 'I'm just trying to be honest . . . the sexual urge isn't as strong when I'm making a movie as it might be for several film producers I know, who take the opportunity to sport-fuck seven days a week.' A few years later, asked in a *Penthouse* interview if there was a lot of 'sport-fucking' on location, he answered, 'Does a bear shit in the woods?'

His buddy Brian De Palma happened to visit just in time to accompany Spielberg to see the long-awaited rushes featuring the latest 'Bruce' in action. The feeling as they sat down to watch was, 'Hey, if the shark doesn't work, we might as well all go home.'

'Afterwards,' De Palma recalls, 'it was like a wake. Bruce's eyes crossed, his jaws wouldn't close right.' Richard Dreyfuss chipped in with his ten cents' worth: 'If any of us had any sense, we'd all bale out now.'

Spielberg thought it would be a great morale-booster, to him at least, if he were permitted to dip into Universal's vast library of classic movies and show them to his *compadres* in the evenings in the log cabin he rented in the woods. Yes, the studio would supply a projector and send a few movies, no problem. For the first time in many weeks Spielberg felt a genuine sense of anticipation as he opened the box containing the first epic Universal had selected. All he could do was stare disbelievingly at the title that presented itself. *Ma and Pa Kettle On the Farm*?! Was this a joke, or a subtle message from someone at the studio? Neither, it turned out. There was simply no answer to: 'Well, you did say you wanted something cheerful, didn't you?'

As shooting dragged on, Robert Shaw became increasingly restive. With good reason. If he worked for more than ninety days in the US, he would have to pay taxes to Uncle Sam. Past the point of no return, he accepted the inevitable. 'Universal,' he declared, 'might as well pay my salary now straight into the IRS.' And he had other concerns over the scene where he took over from Matt Hooper as 'Bruce's' toothsome snack. 'What worries me,' he told Spielberg, 'is who's going to keep those mechanical teeth from sinking in too deep?'

'I will,' Spielberg promised.

Nervously chewing licorice one day, Shaw accidentally yanked the cap from one of his front teeth. Quick as a flash, Spielberg resourcefully wrote it into the script – Quint gets a tooth knocked out when 'Bruce' first attacks the boat. Spielberg's 'method' of handling the vastly experienced Shaw was to give him plenty of leeway; if he wanted a scene done a certain way, he tried to make the actor come up with the idea himself.

Relief from some of the tension was provided by a running battle of wits and wiles between Shaw and Dreyfuss. 'At your age I wasn't even *in* a movie yet, let alone *starring* in one,' Shaw spelled out one day. Then came the kicker: 'But I *was* a star on the stage!'

Dreyfuss in turn stage-whispered to one of the crew: 'Tell him Albert Finney is a better actor than he is.'

Shaw overheard and retorted, 'But Finney is – a *boy*! It's like saying to you that Ben Gazzara is a better actor than you are!'

When talking to reporters, Shaw was fond of suggesting they repair by motorboat to Oak Bluffs, the better to partake of Boston House's estimable scallops for lunch. Quaffing a concoction of half-port, half-brandy, he delighted in holding forth. One day the subject was directors, very much from an *actor*'s point of view. 'It's the most overrated profession,' he declared. 'They're all overpraised. It all began with this auteur business, the idea that directors are the sole "creators" of films. That is a piece of shit. Most directors only get in between the writer and the actor, between the creative material and the artist, and they obstruct things. They are so very anxious to present *their* vision.' No doubt his present director was excluded from his comments; Shaw was merely alluding to the profession in general.

Despite all the travails during shooting, there was still a part of Spielberg that remained disengaged enough to see how *Jaws* might have turned out a very different movie. Richard Dreyfuss was kept awake one night, after the script conference was put to bed, by Spielberg's alternative concept. Coolly, calmly, analytically, Spielberg went through the entire movie, scene by scene, explaining how else he might have shot it, how it might have been a film that would have called his attention to his own directorial technique instead of 'Where's the shark gonna pop up next?!' It might have been *Jaws – The Art-House Edition*.

Dreyfuss's frustration with the slow pace of filming was never going to be suppressed. During production he described the movie as 'A waste of my time as an actor' and railed, 'This business is fifty years old and they still don't know how to do it!' Interviewed on TV on *The Mike Douglas Show* he went further, lashing out at what he described as 'incompetence' on the set. When Zanuck and Brown took grave offence at this, Dreyfuss was re-booked on the show, supposedly to 'retract'.

'I *never* retracted that statement,' he claims. 'What I did retract was a comment I made about the film's producers. Brown and Zanuck are terrific producers. I'd really meant to blame what I took to be mismanagement by the studio. They didn't know anything. And if they did, they didn't care.' As for Spielberg: 'My criticism had nothing to do with him. He saved that movie. I admire him and like Steven enormously. But I didn't like Universal much – or Martha's Vineyard!'

Twenty years later, through a rose-coloured mist, the mercurial Dreyfuss would recall the making of *Jaws* as 'one of the most extraordinary collaborative experiences of my life'. We also have to credit him with providing most of the few flashes of humour that relieved the tension.

When he wasn't in the middle of the ocean, or on TV airing or clarifying his grievances, Dreyfuss – feeling his oats following the praise for his performance in *Duddy Kravitz* – operated a full-scale, non-stop 'babe alert', yelling indecent proposals through a giant megaphone at any nubile young thing who entered his line of vision. Surprise, surprise, nine times out of ten it worked! *Duddy* came through, with Dreyfuss dating anyone who would have him. 'You know why I'm getting so many dates?' he elatedly asked Spielberg. 'Because I have a forty-foot face!'

During dinner at Edgartown's Seafood Shanty one night, after a particularly trying day, not even Dreyfuss was able to raise a smile. Roy Scheider, subject to all the same pressures, decided it was just too much – if he didn't let off steam, he would explode. Grabbing a bowl of fruit cocktail, he reached over the table and emptied the contents over Spielberg's head. Dreyfuss's instant response was to throw red wine in Scheider's face. Not to be outdone, Scheider stuck his fingers into a heap of pâté and smeared it on Spielberg's jacket. Dreyfuss's next weapon of choice was a huge plate of ravioli, which Scheider afterwards claimed he had been wanting to sample in any case. Spielberg led the free-for-all that followed – while the rest of the diners muttered to themselves epithets not dissimilar to 'Fucking Hollywood riff-raff!'

Upset though he had felt that his character had drifted from the original concept, Scheider had rolled with the punches and coped like a champion. Before the movie was released, however, he was upset again upon hearing that several later scenes – in which Brody had asserted himself, neatly balancing his earlier tentative behaviour – had ended up on the cutting room floor. At the same time, he claimed to understand why Spielberg had used the scissors, that it had helped build an image of a man with whom the audience could identify, an average sort of person in those extraordinary circumstances. He expressed one regret: 'I just had to realise that the work I do in the film is not the kind that's going to be noticed. It's not an eye-catching role.' Scheider was dead wrong. He could well have gone back to being a reliable supporting player after *French Connection*. Instead, *Jaws* made him a star. The ultimate accolade came from Dreyfuss, his fellow cast member: 'Roy gave the best performance in the film.'

Through it all, Scheider's admiration for his director was undiminished: 'If there's a hero out of this whole ordeal,' he declared, 'it's Steven Spielberg. It's amazing that he's only twenty-six –' (!) '– but he never once lost his cool. The worst thing that can happen on a movie is when the director loses his dream, that wonderful fantasy in his mind of what he wants the picture to be. Steven never lost that. He had to make compromises, but even when things got tense, Steven was a rock.'

The 'hero', for his part, swore it would be a case of 'never again': 'My next picture'll be made on dry land,' he vowed. 'There won't even be a bathroom scene.' Even as he waved Martha's Vineyard goodbye, with reshoots under his belt that had had to wait until the end of the regatta season, he made another vow: 'I shall *not* return!' Even then, there still lay ahead a month of filming on the Pacific in what would end up as a six-month shoot, the longest in Universal's history.

There was a kind of terrible beauty about the symmetry, for it followed the same period of pre-production, with six months of post-production stretching ahead. 'Terrible' rather than 'beauty' would have been the word that sprang to the minds of Universal's accountants. By the end of the day the budget had soared from $2.3 million to $8.5 million.

Editing on the movie's last third of its eighteen-month odyssey provided happier moments as the troubled production was pieced together. *Sugarland Express* ace Verna Fields had already proved a tower of strength on location, inserting the real-life underwater shark footage, shot by the Taylors, into Spielberg's material. Back home, Fields set about overcoming the problem of consecutive shots of sea and sky that almost never matched due to the constantly changing weather conditions. As a result, several shots in the final cut followed scenes filmed months earlier. Then there was the conundrum of deciding how high the gore level should be pitched, drawing the fine line between what an audience would take and what would turn them off. Spielberg had filmed a particularly grotesque scene that had the first shark victim vomiting blood as the shark chews her up and drags her through the water. That, he decided, would have to go. There was more work ahead for Fields that neither she nor Spielberg had anticipated . . .

For the musical score Spielberg was reunited with John Williams, the two spending sessions together listening to Vaughan Williams and Stravinsky. Williams was excited as he urged Spielberg to sit near him at the piano. 'Here's the theme for *Jaws*,' he declared, going on to pick out a series of chords, ominously repeating on the lower notes. Spielberg began to laugh. 'Oh, no,' said Williams. 'This is *serious*. I mean it. This is *Jaws*.'

Although it grew on Spielberg, the earth signally failed to move. He had had something more melodic in mind, the salt-encrusted romance of the sea, the glorious, unfathomable mysteries of the deep. That was for elsewhere, Williams maintained, for another scene, maybe for another movie. 'You don't have *The L-Shaped Room*,' Williams pointed out. 'Steven, you've made yourself a *popcorn* movie.'

60

Williams was surprised to find his director, a closet clarinettist, sneaking in to play third clarinet while the *Jaws* score was being recorded. It was a precursor of things to come. At a future Boston Pops Tchaikovsky concert, Spielberg unexpectedly showed up again. At least on this occasion there were no 'horse pies' to avoid.

An early screening of *Jaws* produced a *frisson* of disappointment at 'Bruce's' long-awaited leap from the depths. It wasn't sudden enough, it wasn't scary enough. After a bit more fiddling at the hands of Verna Fields, it was. Thereafter the movie's preview reaction, first in Dallas, Texas, then in Long Beach, California, went through the roof. Except for one more critical scene, to which the audience barely reacted. Spielberg was puzzled, for he had intended it to be a real shocker, one that would jolt the audience out of its seats. It was the episode where Dreyfuss swims down to the old wreck and a disembodied head suddenly floats through a hole in the hull. Why, why, *why* didn't it work? Fields had the answer: it had been shot from the wrong angle. If Spielberg wanted to achieve the audience-jolter he had intended in the first place, it was back to the ocean depths. His reaction: 'God, Verna. Anything but that!!' The 'ocean depths' were promptly relocated to Fields's back-garden swimming pool, where a reluctant Richard Dreyfuss and his scuba gear were reassembled and the scene reshot, complete with strips of foil floating on top of the pool to simulate light reflecting off the ocean surface.

During a series of later previews at the Cinerama Dome on Sunset Boulevard, Spielberg asked a friend to audiotape audience reaction. After listening to the tape, he needed to know more. 'How did it go?' Spielberg asked.

'Great!' came the reply. 'It's all there on the tape.'

'Yeah, but I'm a little upset,' said Spielberg. 'When Robert Shaw gets eaten by the shark, someone was *applauding*.'

'No, that was me,' the friend admitted.

'*It was you?* But weren't you sad that Robert gets eaten?'

'Yes, I was. But it was done so great!!'

Spielberg's sister Anne had her own reaction to an early screening. 'For years he just scared us,' she reported. 'Now he gets to scare the masses.'

Unlike on *The Sugarland Express*, Universal had no problem labouring over the movie's promotion. Not with *Jaws* consciousness at its height, the book having sold a mind-blowing seven and a half million paperbacks before the film's release. Zanuck and Brown had done an exemplary job in coaxing Bantam's Oscar Dystel, who had paid $575,000 for the paperback rights, to use the same logo they planned for their movie.

61

We'll give Dreyfuss the last word on the prediction stakes. Despite his earlier 'turkey' pronouncement, the actor had undergone a swift change of mind after catching a New York preview. 'I was closer than anyone else in my estimate of what the movie would make,' he claims. 'Steven thought it would make maybe $38 million. While I was making it, I couldn't tell. It seemed like a piece of junk to me. But after that preview I called Steven and said, 'It's incredible! It'll make $200 million!'

Nothing, indeed, could stop the *Jaws* juggernaut, least of all Penelope Gilliatt's negative-plus review in *New Yorker*. 'The shark is plastic,' she declared, 'and the film is punk.' Her view was hugely in the minority. Apart from being an incredibly intense thriller, the movie had all the scale and drama of a grand seafaring adventure, shot through with humour, occasionally of the gallows variety, and expertly combining primal fear of the unknown with the struggle of the little man to assert himself and prevail despite overwhelming odds. The majority voted with their feet, marching into cinemas across America in record numbers in the spring of 1975. The movie opened 'wide' – in mid-seventies terms, that is – at over 300 cinemas across the US.

At the same time, until the astonishing grosses of $7 million in three days were known, Spielberg claims that Universal treated *Jaws* no differently from any of the other dozen movies on their release schedule, that it was only *after* the incredible opening cash burst that they really got their act together and began beating the drum that Zanuck and Brown had been tirelessly hammering on their own for months. In fact, Universal had booked thirty-second spots on every prime-time TV show, on all three networks, on three consecutive nights *before the movie opened*. It was a record TV spend, and the movie was immediately spread to an additional 100 theatres after its smash opening. After seventeen days the gross had climbed to $37 million.

With its eventual $260 million take at the US box-office, *Jaws* became the first movie ever to smash through the exalted $100 million net barrier on initial US release (net being the amount returned to the studio from the box-office after theatres take their cut, typically averaging fifty per cent). It easily bested the previous record-holder, 1972's *The Godfather*; since then only *The Exorcist* and Zanuck/Brown's *The Sting* had come close.

Spielberg was about to get his first real lesson in Hollywood economics. Under the terms of their contract the Zanuck/Brown team was due a whopping forty-one per cent of the net, their director just 2.5 per cent on top of his $50,000 salary. Although Guy McElwaine renegotiated his deal just before the movie's opening, increasing his cut to five per cent, the yawning differential that remained was not lost on young Spielberg.

*Jaws* helped redefine 'blockbuster' status. It changed forever the concept of 'wide opening', for up until then a movie had typically run for several months on 'platform' release in selected cities before being generally released. It redefined marketing spend and strategy; unlike on the slow roll-out, a mass opening demanded an ever-increasing record number of prints to justify hugely expensive national advertising. (In truth, a clever huckster named Joe Levine had been there before them, parlaying a cheap Italian import, *Hercules Unchained,* into a smash years earlier with almost identical tactics; the one huge difference was Levine's plan to have the cash in the till before lousy word-of-mouth leaked out and the circus moved on.) With *Jaws* the word-of-mouth was great, providing the cherry on top of the cake. Multiple visits.

There was a downside, but that was in the future. The success of *Jaws* would start to redefine the type of movies that were made, and especially those with which Spielberg would be identified. This carried with it a considerable degree of irony, as David Brown points out: 'Steven once maintained to me that there were films and there were movies, and that he would like to do *films* – never knowing he would become the biggest *movie*-maker of all time.'

Meantime, Universal brass were cockahoop. Jules Stein had a new sign painted and displayed outside his home: 'Beware Guard Dog – and Sharks'. 'I want to be the first to predict that Steve will win the Best Director Oscar this year,' Sid Sheinberg whooped. That he didn't, and that he wasn't even nominated, proved a major disappointment to Spielberg, let alone his supporters.

The news that one of the nominated directors was his lunch host Federico Fellini, up for his work on *Amarcord*, produced what might be seen as a surprisingly ungenerous reaction from Spielberg. 'I can't believe it!' he reportedly shouted, stamping his foot. 'They went for an *Italian*! They went for *Fellini* instead of me!'

At least the movie itself was in the winner's circle, and to lose out to Milos Forman's *One Flew Over the Cuckoo's Nest* was no disgrace. Oscars for Best Original Score, Editing and Sound for *Jaws* provided additional salve.

The box-office success of *Jaws*, Fellini's airing of the unequal struggle of Art vs Commerce apart, spawned several cash-in attempts. Peter Guber, the Columbia comer who'd viewed Spielberg's product reel back in his salad days, led the charge. First, he paid a staggering $500,000 for the rights to Peter Benchley's follow-up opus, *The Deep*. Secondly, he cast Robert Shaw. Third, he added the one element *Jaws* had lacked – sex appeal, in the shape of

Jacqueline Bisset in a wet T-shirt. So all he had was a conger eel instead of a Great White? Advertising would sort that out. It did too, his mammoth campaign securing a very respectable $125 million at the US box-office.

Lower down the totem pole – his favourite position, from where he built his fortune – Roger Corman assigned Joe Dante to direct *Piranha*. So the pesky creatures were small already, but hey, small and *deadly*! Made for peanuts, the movie earned a small fortune round the world.

Already deep in pre-production on his next movie, meaningful personal relationships seemed to be off the agenda for Spielberg. 'I didn't stop to notice if women were interested in me,' he claims, 'or if there was a party I might have been invited to. I didn't take the time to revel in the glory of a successful or moneymaking film.' Despite his protests, he did take time to revel in the glory of numerous one-night stands.

It was true that, as yet, he neither dressed nor acted the part of the big-time director. Turning up with Brian De Palma to talk to Francis Coppola at his Zoetrope headquarters in San Francisco, they were taken for film students and almost thrown out the door.

Back at Universal, a distinct sense of *déja-vu* set in. As he had on Hitchcock's *Torn Curtain*, Spielberg – still showing traces of the reverential student – sneaked on the set of the master's *Family Plot*. He watched as Hitch, sat in his chair with his back to him, seemed to sense the presence of an outsider. An assistant director was quickly summoned and given his instructions. 'Sir,' the AD politely informed Spielberg, 'I'm sorry, but this is a closed set.' The director of filmdom's biggest-ever hit had been given his marching orders. Which he meekly, and regretfully, obeyed.

*Soon after the release of* Jaws, *Spielberg was walking on his own down New York's Fifth Avenue when he was stopped by a lady requesting his autograph. Despite his innate modesty, being recognised produced a definite tingle, although there were disquieting elements of the professional autograph-hunter in the speed with which she eagerly produced and proffered a pen and leather-bound book from her voluminous handbag. And could she and her family possibly* have *seen* Jaws *as often as she claimed? If so, he mused, it would certainly account for a large percentage of the movie's take . . .*

*As he made to sign, wondering which greeting to use, whether to put it before or after the signature – he was, after all, new to this game, and determined to carry it off with a flourish – she edged a little bit closer, poked an elbow in his ribs in what she clearly felt was a display of fellow-*

*feeling between two comrades-in-arms, in the process almost jolting the pen from Spielberg's already unsteady fingers, and said, with an air of someone generously allowing a partner into a sweet deal, 'You know, Mr Spielberg, I have this daughter who's a wonderful singer.'*

*Spielberg looked up, interrupted in mid-flourish. 'That's great,' he told her. 'You should get her into Juillard.'*

*The slight suggestion of a petulant frown. 'She's like Diana Ross and Barbra Streisand. She wouldn't be* right *for Juillard.'*

*Spielberg beamed at the lady just a shade nervously. 'Diana and Barbra? That's a pretty good combination!'*

*A final stroke of the pen, and he handed over the book and pen and made as if to break into a stride. Too late. The lady had already grabbed his sleeve and was hanging on as if her next poppyseed bagel depended on it. 'Wait here a second,' she commanded, and ran into an adjacent building. Spielberg was left standing on the sidewalk, grinning inanely at the passing parade – but only for the less than sixty seconds it took for proud mama to produce awesomely gifted prodigy. 'This is Steven Spielberg,' she announced as she emerged. 'He made Jaws! So sing for the man already!'*

*Halfway through an ear-splitting version of* My Way *that started at the top and was left with no place left to go Spielberg decided that enough was enough. If he hung around much longer, he'd be late for a pressing appointment with a cappuccino. Then there was the brain damage he might suffer if the performance was allowed to continue. 'Yes, that's very good,' he declared, taking advantage of the middle break he thought the youngster would never reach. 'Let her finish school.'*

*Again his sleeve was grabbed. 'Wait! I have another daughter who's a miraculous dancer. Stay right here!'*

*'But—'*

*'Don't move! I'll be right back.'*

*One minute later the second infant phenomenon was making like Isadora Duncan on the corner of 57th and Fifth. Worse yet, an intrigued crowd was gathering. 'She's great,' Spielberg spluttered. 'But I gotta go.'*

*'One more thing,' the woman trilled, 'since you're here already. You have to meet my boy Jerry. He's a comedian. Hold it right there. Talk to Ruthie and Susan while I'm gone.'*

*The jokes were funny – except that by this time Spielberg was too embarrassed to laugh; for some strange reason he found himself unable to force his upper lip above his teeth. The result: a kind of horrendous rictus grin. Finally, the lady asked, 'So can you use them in anything?'*

*Spielberg sensed that the ordeal was drawing to an end – she'd run out of progeny. 'Send their pictures and resumés to my office,' he said, his tone pleasant, helpful. The door hadn't been shut, it was a civilised end to the encounter.*

*The woman's tone was like ice. 'That's what they all say,' she snarled, lip curling.*

*Spielberg was stunned. 'Who all?' he managed.*

*'Everyone we do this to,' she replied, disconsolately herding her flock back inside.*

*Then, with a contemptuous toss of the curls, 'Why should* you *be any different?!'*

At the end of each of their meetings after the release of *The Sugarland Express*, Denis Hoffman left convinced that the reignition of his professional relationship with Spielberg was just a matter of time. Except – well, he couldn't help noticing that he was becoming increasingly difficult to reach.

After the enormous success of *Jaws*, there was a definite sense of their relationship becoming arm's length. Several scripts had already been offered to Spielberg, in Hoffman's account, all of which were turned down for one reason or another.

Item: Hoffman had been referred to ex-Beatle Ringo Starr through a customer in his optical business who counted Ringo as a client. With his solo music career stalled, it seemed that Ringo was anxious to cross over into movies. Aware of Hoffman's contract with Spielberg, Ringo and his people saw their project as a perfect collaboration to reunite the producer and his director. After Spielberg read the script Hoffman submitted, he declared himself 'not crazy' about it: 'But I sure do want to meet Ringo!' Ringo and his entourage turned up at Hoffman's house bang on time, then were kept waiting, with no Spielberg in sight. With time ticking away, Hoffman sensed that his guests were probably regarding the whole thing as some kind of bullshit scam. When Spielberg eventually turned up, an hour late, the project was briefly discussed, together with general movie business. Then Spielberg proceeded to lecture Ringo on how to reform his career. Finally – and clearly, in the wake of his sudden, overwhelming success at the box-office, utterly full of himself – Spielberg placed a call to John Milius. 'J-o-h-h-hn?' he drawled exaggeratedly. 'It's J-A-W-S here!! Haw, haw, haw!!' Which went down like a lead balloon.

Item: Hoffman worked with Sal Mineo to secure the movie rights to *Fortune and Men's Eyes*, a play in which the actor had starred. He spent a year working on the script and touring locations with Mineo, Don Johnson – who'd also appeared in the original play – and Johnson's PR man and friend of Mineo's, Elliott Mintz. Spielberg's reaction: Nope, he didn't care for the movie's theme of homosexuality in prison.

Item: After doing the titles and special effects for Cornel Wilde's

*Beach Red,* Hoffman forged a friendship with the veteran actor/director that lasted until his death twenty years later. Together they submitted a project for Spielberg's consideration that Wilde's company would co-produce. Another rejection.

At all these stages, Hoffman maintains that he never pushed: 'Yes, he was rejecting everything I brought, a half-dozen submissions in all, finished scripts, treatments, the works, but I still trusted Steven to carry out his end of the deal. And I was very much aware that the worst thing anyone could do to a creative person is push something down their throats they don't basically care for. It had to be something we *mutually* liked. And there's something else. Spielberg has a way of making you feel very comfortable, that everything is going to be OK, you come away from meetings with a sense of elation. I fell into that.'

At one meeting after *Jaws'* release, Hoffman recalls Spielberg explaining that he was committed to doing *Close Encounters of the Third Kind* for Columbia; after that was completed, he declared himself ready to make their long-planned movie together. The problem was that Spielberg then began distancing himself more and more. Their meetings got further apart, and Spielberg began taking weeks to return Hoffman's calls. For the first time since signing their agreement back in 1968, Hoffman began to feel real concern.

The guillotine was finally dropped later in 1975. After many attempts to reach him, Spielberg called Hoffman. 'My attorney tells me that the contract is not enforceable.'

Utterly horrified, Hoffman asked, 'Steven, what are you talking about? We have an agreement—'

'You'd best talk to my attorney.'

Hoffman declined to talk to Bruce Ramer personally, and instead sought out the services of showbusiness attorney Eric Weissman. He was someone who happened, purely by coincidence, also to represent the Zanuck/Brown team. After contacting Ramer, a former colleague of his, someone he had known personally for years, Weissman came back with the shocking 'revelation' that Spielberg had been under twenty-one when he had signed Hoffman's contract in 1968, and was therefore, under California law, a minor at the time. The contract was void.

A shattered Hoffman decided to seek verification of the underage claim from the source. He called Spielberg and put the question directly to him: 'How old were you when you signed our contract in 1968?' Per Hoffman, Spielberg replied that he was twenty years old at the time, that he was born on December 18, 1947. It looked like the end of the line.

Hoffman felt as if he'd been punched in the solar plexus even as

67

he listened to the settlement proposed. Apparently Spielberg still felt he had a moral obligation to Hoffman, his 'underage signing' notwithstanding. He wanted to settle 'this thing' amicably. The deal that was hammered out: In exchange for surrendering all rights under the contract, as well as the negative of *Amblin'* and rights to the use of the name, Hoffman would receive a one-off cash settlement of $30,000.

Faced with this 'best deal' offer, Hoffman accepted. If he, or his lawyer, had checked Spielberg's birth certificate, Hoffman – pretty reasonably – maintains that he would have never dreamt of signing away the rights to a Spielberg movie for the microscopic mess of potage $30,000 represented. Instead, he took the word of Spielberg and Ramer, as relayed by Weissman, and as personally spelled out by Spielberg. Not only that, but every reference Hoffman checked in the press, whether from Spielberg himself, or from Sid Sheinberg, or simply from the journalist filing the story, confirmed the underage claim. Surely Spielberg couldn't have been *systematically* misstating his age all these years?

Oddly enough, as the months passed and the wound healed, Hoffman resumed his relationship with Spielberg. Instead of the increasing chill he had experienced prior to the settlement, Hoffman found Spielberg, now the pressure was off, much more friendly. Hoffman was invited to Spielberg's homes, first in Laurel Canyon, then in Coldwater Canyon, and on studio tours.

Careerwise, Hoffman decided he had no alternative but to plough on. He was still busy on the optical side of the business, and a TV pilot was in the planning stage. True, the wagon he had so perspicaciously hitched his hopes to back in 1968, long before anyone else had been prepared to back Spielberg's potential with vital hard cash, had broken down. As he looked back on all those wasted years of project submissions, Hoffman might have been excused at least a modicum of bitterness. Instead, he decided to put the whole thing behind him and get on with the rest of his life.

# 9

# Weird Lights in Space

*'We all get cheated by the studios, and it's rarely worth the legal hassle to try to get even. I personally don't think I've been cheated that much. Big winners like Jaws usually allow the producers to be generous and honest. It's on the low-budget pictures that we, directors and stars with percentage contracts, really get taken. Here the studios have all kinds of ways to prove that they have actually made no profits, so why should we be cut in on anything?'*

STEVEN SPIELBERG

*'Steven always had a highly developed imagination.'*

LEAH ADLER

*Arnold Spielberg stayed up reading for three hours after Leah had gone to bed. He had decided against going to sleep and disturbing his wife with the alarm when the appointed hour came. He knew that young Steven, his fifth birthday still months away, would be dead to the world in his own room, having turned in without the slightest inkling of what his father had planned.*

*On the stroke of 3 am Arnold made his way to the kitchen and prepared coffee, drinking a cup and pouring the rest into a Thermos. Thus fortified, he crept silently upstairs to his son's bedroom, quietly opened the door and tiptoed inside, pausing for just a moment to take in the sight of the sleeping boy peacefully dreaming his dreams. It seemed a pity to disturb his slumbers, and yet . . .*

*Reaching down, he gently shook his son's shoulder. Young Spielberg rubbed his eyes as he sat up. 'Dad, what is it?' he asked.*

*'Don't ask questions,' his father replied. 'Quick, get up. We're going out for a drive.'*

*'Going out? For a drive? But Dad, it's still dark, what...?'*

*'Don't argue, son, get up, let's go.'*

*'Okay, Dad, I'll get dressed.'*

'Don't bother, there's no time. Here, drape a blanket over your pyjamas. And take another one with you.'

'Why, Dad? Isn't Mom coming?'

'No, she's not. And don't ask so many questions. C'mon, hurry.'

Although he had no lack of trust in his father, Spielberg was frightened. This was strange, unusual, downright weird. Yet there was something in Arnold's tone that precluded further questions. All the way downstairs, through the kitchen and into the garage, the boy experienced a sense of unreality, a strange thrill of the impending unknown. As his father drove off in his wartime surplus Jeep, waving his way through the deserted New Jersey streets, it occurred to him that this was the first journey he had ever undertaken where he was unaware of the destination in advance.

Arnold was silent almost throughout the half-hour drive, offering no explanation as he drove along the dark country roads. All he asked at one point was that his son unscrew the top off the Thermos and pour some coffee. 'We'll be there soon,' he grunted after quickly swallowing the liquid and handing back the lid.

At last Arnold began to slow down, squinting as he did at the road-signs as he drew into a parking space at the side of the road that was crammed with vehicles. To Steven's astonishment he could see dozens – maybe a couple of hundred people – all lying on blankets in the field beyond, all of them looking up at the night sky. 'Has it started?' he heard his father hiss. 'Not yet,' came the reply, 'but it's due any minute now.'

Arnold swiftly found an empty patch, spread his blanket and lay down, motioning his son to do the same.

They did not have long to wait. Within seconds the sky was alive with a riot of colour as the magnificent meteor shower the weather bureau had predicted the night before filled the night with bright yellow arrows of wonder. Steven felt his imagination soar. No longer was he earthbound, or particularly interested in what he guessed would be his father's inevitable technical explanation for the phenomenon, the American Science version. (Which came soon enough – 'These meteors are space debris attracted by the gravitational pull of . . .' TUNE-OUT TIME!) Instead, he felt transported by a sudden jolting insight into the incredible, limitless power and potential of the universe. When Arnold was able to tear his gaze for a second away from the breathtaking spectacle, he watched his son's awestruck reaction with pride and a quiet satisfaction. He could have announced the expedition in advance, and in so doing removed all of the magic element of surprise. Instead, as his son would relate many years later, 'Dad had surprised and frightened the hell out of me.'

That memorable night apart, Spielberg's sense of wonder was sparked on a much less worrying excursion, this one to the movies to see Walt Disney's Pinocchio. Here, the lyrics of Jiminy Cricket's 'When You Wish Upon A Star' left the same indelible impression.

*Little wonder, then, that a telescope and an intense interest in stargazing preceded the wonders of his dad's 8mm camera. The twin inspirations for Spielberg's early* Firelight, *with its 'weird lights in space', can safely be attributed to that night trip and to little Jiminy Cricket. So can* Watch The Skies – *or, as it became,* Close Encounters of the Third Kind.

While Spielberg had been nursing *Sugarland*'s interiors scenes at Universal, producers Michael and Julia Phillips were suffering post-birth trauma over director George Roy Hill's shoulder on *The Sting*. This was the other baby being sired by the busy Zanuck/Brown, for whom the Phillips team had already brought forth the dead-at-birth *Steelyard Blues* at Warners. In between comparing notes and sneaking peeks at each other's dailies, Spielberg and the boyish, always-preoccupied Michael Phillips had discovered a mutual fascination with Unidentified Flying Objects – UFOs. The free-wheeling Phillips duo held *Duel* in high esteem; would it be such a leap to joining forces to depict the marvels of an alien landing? The zeitgeist seemed right. Mystical, man. Awe-inspiring. Sense of *wonder*. Spielberg, already dubbed 'Speelnuts' by the bold Julia, experienced a distinct *frisson* – and not only at the subject itself. There was a sense of daring in the idea of Zanuck/Brown's young bucks striking out together. Like that trip with his father back in New Jersey, it was a journey with an unknown destination.

The deal between Spielberg and the Phillips duo to develop *Watch the Skies* was signed soon after *Sugarland*'s US premiere in the Autumn of 1974. With the success of *Jaws* but a distant hope and dream, Spielberg was still far from a sure-fire commercial bet. Which helps to explain Universal's *laissez-faire* attitude, first in waiving Spielberg's seven-year TV contract, then in watching as he flipped over to Columbia with Michael and Julia Phillips.

'Adventure thriller' was the partners' choice of description for their project, mainly to avoid confusion with *Star Wars*, the 'sci-fi epic' in which George Lucas was trying to scare up interest. (With both Spielberg and Lucas beating him to the outer-space punch, Francis Coppola decided to ditch the drama he'd been cooking up for NBC-TV. Developed with future best-selling author Carl Sagan, Coppola's tale had dealt with earth's first response to a visitation from friendly aliens . . .)

To ensure their bonding at the hip survived, the Phillips pair agreed to sign on the dotted line with Spielberg's newest agent. The glamorous lad-for-all-seasons, ICM's Guy McElwaine, was famous for the Saturday afternoon TV football fests at his Beverly Hills home where hot dogs, ketchup, beer and liquor were among the items of nourishment and stimulants for regulars Alan Ladd Jr, Joey Walsh, David Giler and Dan Melnick.

Julia Phillips pitched the package for what was to become *Close Encounters of the Third Kind* to David Begelman, along with Martin Scorsese's *Taxi Driver*. Although he may not have known it, Spielberg was already being cross-collateralised. 'If Marty's a bust, Steven will finish it,' she promised, although Begelman probably wasn't losing too much sleep over Scorsese's $1.3 million budget in any case. Then it was on to *Close Encounters*. 'I don't know what he means by it,' her laid-back approach ran, 'but Steven wants to make a movie about UFOs and Watergate. And I want to do it with him.'

That Columbia was edging back from bankruptcy and could barely finance a *barmitzvah* on its own short of a tax-shelter arrangement, let alone an actual *movie*, was deemed a zillion years from the point. This was Hollywood, where anything was possible. Or was it? Even the doughty Begelman, the ultimate gambler, had to wonder.

Spielberg's first skeleton script submission to Begelman depicted the frustrations of a US Air Force officer forced to cover up UFO sightings. At the urging of Michael and Julia Phillips this was handed over for reworking and extension to their *Taxi Driver* scribe, Paul Schrader. His first full-length script, *Kingdom Come*, at least had the virtue of establishing the central character of Roy Neary. Unfortunately, there was little else of immediate appeal. Julia Phillips advised Begelman not to read it, claiming that it would only turn him off the project. Worse, she maintained that Spielberg, who hated what he saw as Schrader's morosely Calvinistic reworking, would not be interested in directing it. $25,000 was shelled out on a second draft before the parcel was passed on yet again to *Sugarland*'s Hal Barwood and Matthew Robbins. Many others along the way produced ideas, Spielberg's set to the tinkling strains in the background of Mike Oldfield's 'Tubular Bells'. Schrader contributed the eventual title, which was promptly abbreviated to *CE3K* during production. (Encounters of the first kind: when some mysterious object is spotted in the sky. Second kind: when the object comes close enough to leave physical evidence. Third kind: when spacecraft are sighted and when the observer has an encounter with the occupants.)

Still in the Never-Never district of La-La Land, possibly as a result of all the fairy dust she was ingesting on a daily basis, the bouncy, *ne plus ultra* Julia, with Spielberg in close attendance, produced a first-budget estimate of $2.8 million for the movie. Never mind that their special effects guru Douglas Trumbull would ask $3 million on his own, nor that the pre-production overall figure would rise to $12.8 million, with a final cost north of $20 million. This was a *big* baby!

No matter how big, Trumbull was not about to be overawed. His track record included the special effects for Stanley Kubrick's *2001 – A Space Odyssey* and *The Andromeda Strain*. Then he had made his own directorial debut with the cult classic *Silent Running*, the movie whose robot gave George Lucas the idea for R2D2 in *Star Wars*. Invited to join forces with Lucas, Trumbull had declined, deciding he had plumbed that route thoroughly. Instead, effecting the descent of the astrodome-sized mothership for Spielberg captured his imagination. How to create what had to be a truly awesome sight? Would he rely on highly detailed miniatures, as he had in the past? Or could he work out a combination of neon, fibre optics and quartz halogen bulbs that would meld together to produce a truly majestic effect? Probably both, he decided, by the time his *Close Encounters* lab facility at Marino De Rey – complete with printing, developing and editing rooms, electronically operated control booths, a wood shop, metal shop, paint shop and miniature-set construction shop – was fully operational.

Taking a brief break from the task of winning Begelman over to *Close Encounters*, Spielberg and Phillips took off for New York and the opening of *Jaws*. They were like a couple of kids out on the town, riding around in cabs taking home movies of lines for the movie. Spielberg, like all of the *Jaws* team, had hoped for a hit – but this . . .! Nothing less than box-office history was being written.

A short taxi ride took the pair from their Sherry Netherland Hotel to Columbia's East Coast office at 711 Fifth Avenue, where they met studio president Alan Hirschfield and his financial adviser Herbert Allen. Sure, *Close Encounters* was going to be spectacular, both men were assured, worth every penny of whatever the final cost would be. The incredible opening of *Jaws* almost made the claim believable. Suddenly Begelman's hesitation in giving the green light was a thing of the past. The money? No problem now, thanks to the prospects of risk lay-off through investments by EMI and Time Inc., and to funds sourced from West Germany. Where there's a will there's a way, even in Columbia's near-terminal, clapped-out case.

All five writers responsible for *CE3K* script drafts were successfully persuaded to back off claiming credit after Julia Phillips prevailed on Spielberg's behalf. Through Writers' Guild arbitration he would have *sole* 'written and directed by Steven Spielberg' attribution at the beginning of the movie's titles, *as well as* 'A Steven Spielberg Film' credit over the end titles. Spielberg as auteur? Despite subsequent disclaimers of the theory as applied to movies – it's a *collaborative* effort, he has invariably maintained – the young man was beginning to swallow his own publicity. And develop a distinct streak of ruthlessness.

Writing credit has always been an important one for Spielberg, despite his enormous success as a director. So it's instructive to hear how he tiptoes through the tulips on the subject of relative 'authorship', secure in the knowledge that a title like 'A Steven Spielberg Film', which he fought for and won, will become the ultimate yardstick in the public's mind. 'I believe everything begins with the writer's concept,' he has said. 'For a movie even to be made, somebody has to be attracted enough to the writer's script to say, "I commit X number of dollars to this." The minute a director starts working on it, it becomes another individual's concept. He becomes the creative ramrod. I think there should be – if the movie succeeds – a kind of shared credit. If it's a big failure then it's the director's fault. And when a director writes his own script, as I did for *CE3K* – [!] – it's *still* a collaborative art.'

Collaborative believer or not, Spielberg erected a road-block for one ex-colleague who had diverted attention from him in the past. There was talk, swiftly quelched, of bringing in Verna Fields as an associate producer on *CE3K*. Maybe in another lifetime, Spielberg declared, but not this one, not after the bold Verna had grabbed so much credit for putting *Jaws* together, swinging on his coattails to an Academy Award, VP-ship of Universal, and a public statement from the studio that Fields would direct a movie if she ever found a project that appealed to her. (She never did.)

He argued that she had worked the same 'I saved it!' number on his pals George and Marsha Lucas with *American Graffiti*, that there was no way she was getting away with it a third time, especially on his shift. And look what happened to Richard Dreyfuss during *Jaws'* post-production, when Fields had added inserts of him in the water, filmed in her swimming pool – *pneumonia* already!!

Spielberg didn't know it then, but at a future Eastman-Kodak 'Filmmakers at Work' shindig held in Rochester, New York, Fields would use unedited footage from *Jaws*, snapping her fingers as the clip unspooled to illustrate all the points at which she'd inserted her all-important cuts. At the same time, she always adamantly denied 'saving' *Jaws*. All she ever wanted to illustrate was her undoubted *contribution* to the movie's success. Fields had crossed the line. Although a warm surface relationship was maintained, she would never work with Spielberg again, and to hell with her *Jaws* editing Oscar. The Curse of Spielberg did not, however, extend to the Son of Verna, Rick Fields. Although employing Rick gave him back-door access to the Verna magic, *CE3K* would also mark the beginning of a relationship with another editor that continues to the present day. Michael Kahn had a history stretching back to his start as a nineteen-year-old apprentice at Desilu working on *Hogan's Heroes*. The rough and tumble of television work would stand him in good stead on his many outings with Spielberg.

During early pre-production on *Close Encounters*, in the company of fellow-nerds Marty Scorsese and Brian De Palma, Spielberg regularly mingled at weekend soirées at the Phillipses' oceanfront hideaway. The company was stimulating, as was the coke, booze and sex for those whose tastes ran in such directions – like just about everybody, in one permutation or another. Spielberg was invariably the spectre at the feast, the loner, the one at the far end of the buffet table, nervously devouring one dip-laden cracker after another.

Julia Phillips became convinced that she could handle the assistant producer chore on her own after the Phillipses' marriage broke up in July 1976, six weeks after *CE3K* began shooting. The settlement: he was assigned day-to-day on *Taxi Driver*, she on the same basis to *CE3K*. And never the twain did meet.

The account of how Richard Dreyfuss landed the role of Roy Neary varies, depending on whether it's Spielberg or Dreyfuss doing the telling. 'I wrote *CE3K* for a forty-five-year-old,' says Spielberg, 'but Dreyfuss talked me into casting him. I didn't want Rick and Rick knows that. I wanted Jack Nicholson, but Rick had heard me talking about *CE3K* all through *Jaws* and said, "Cast me in it."'

Accurate? Not a word of it, according to Dreyfuss. First admitting that his mother used to say he didn't so much tell a story as spell out variations on a theme, he goes on to claim that Spielberg does exactly the same. 'Of course I knew about *CE3K* when we were doing *Jaws*,' he agrees. 'But since Neary was a much older character it never occurred to me that I might do it. Then, after we finished *Jaws*, Steven gave me his first draft of *CE3K* to read, just as a friend. I read it and loved it and went by his office and said, "This is the best idea for a movie I've ever read. I just wish I were ten years older." I didn't talk him into anything!' He smiles and adds, 'Oh, after putting my two cents in, I did sort of hang around his office a lot . . . I never thought of the role as a great acting opportunity, but I *was* desperate to be associated with that picture. I knew it could become something colossal.'

Desperate he may have been, but Spielberg and his associates were dismayed when the actor's agent, Meyer Mishkin, demanded $500,000 plus five gross points for his services. It was the same deal, Mishkin swore, that he'd wheedled out of producer Ray Stark for *Houdini*, a movie that must have slipped its ropes; it still hasn't been made. Sandwiching myth and reality, Mishkin was merely following a tried and true Hollywood recipe.

Since Michael and Julia Phillips had split 2:3 in Spielberg's favour on fees and points, and their two-year-old deal called for net profits, not gross, they decided to fight their corner. In the end Mishkin backed down, settling for net for his client. And a tad less than $500,000 in salary.

# 10

## Perfect Small Moments vs
## Barnum and Bailey

*'I don't think I'll ever top* Jaws *commercially.'*

STEVEN SPIELBERG, 1976

*'I love juxtaposing, you know, the cosmos with a real sort
of suburban reality. I love anything that is contrary to
what we're used to. And it's essential for a film like this to
base it here, on Earth. You really have to believe in Earth
before you can believe in flying saucers.'*

STEVEN SPIELBERG on *Close Encounters of the Third Kind*

The bulk of shooting on *Close Encounters*, Douglas Trumbull's miniatures apart, took place in four enormous disused dirigible hangars in Mobile, Alabama, and at Devil's Tower Mountain in Gillette, Wyoming. Secrecy was all at every stage of development and shooting up to the movie's release, since they had no wish to invite either a Roger Corman rip-off, or a TV *Movie of the Week* scooping their big-buck effort. Even Richard Dreyfuss was shown the door a couple of times after turning up without his ID badge. For the benefit of the press Spielberg guardedly described the movie as being about 'extraordinary encounters in middle-class suburbia'.

As if to counter the fact that he had no personal experience with UFOs, he claimed at one point that he had begun incorporating them in his dreams. 'They seemed as real as being awake,' he recalled, 'and they always involved the same thing – my bedroom window and something in the sky. The dreams weren't telling me anything, I didn't have the feeling they were coming from a force that was telling me how to write the script or giving me dialogue or scenes. But somehow they gave me a living experience of what it would be like to have a real UFO experience. They set a mood, a tone, if you will, for my film. Each dream, or encounter, was more vivid than the one before, and each was very seductive. I would wake up angry that what had happened was simply a dream, because it seemed so real, and when it stopped, I wanted to know so much more.'

Since sixty-five per cent of the movie took place at night, and since no film existed that was fast enough to photograph it naturally, Spielberg decided to synthesise. Each 'night effect' would become a 'special effect'. On how convincingly the scenes could then be married to Trumbull's own 'special effects' would rest the success or failure of the movie on a technical level. Spielberg's intention was that people would walk out of the movie with more questions on their mind than they had when they walked in. He wanted them to consider the possibility that we are not alone in the universe, that the stars were not some kind of nocturnal wallpaper to be viewed indifferently. His imagination had been fired with his father's night trip to the meteor shower. He wanted to present his audience with an equally awesome experience that would fire *their* imagination. Instead of 'Take me to your leader', his aliens and their human reception committee would communicate by using the musical twelve-tone scale, a constant natural law to which any intelligent life form could relate.

Spielberg agonised long and hard about the scene where the aliens emerge from the mother ship. Should they walk, fly, skip, jump, *what*? And how to achieve the most naturalistic effect? What everyone thought was the ideal solution fell decidedly short. The aliens, it was decided, would be played by children, some as young as six, recruited from Mobile dancing schools. Clad in leotards, with rubber masks and flippers covering their face and hands, the tykes would fly out of the craft, suspended on wires. That was the theory.

The practice, by the time the mother ship's doors opened, found most of the kids suffering from heat exhaustion and hanging, rather than flying, from their wires. Scratch that idea. Now only one 'alien' would lead the way out, and it would be a $90,000 puppet operated not by strings, but by sixty separate levers. Julia Phillips brought in Carlo Rambaldi to build the creature, presaging another little extra-terrestrial several years down the line. Behind this 'main man' the recruited kids would be wittering, twittering and shimmering, earthily sweating in their enormous bald caps and face masks, even as they were bathed in soft, ethereal light.

The same soaring-budget pressures that had almost blown *Jaws* out of the water were back in force on *CE3K*. What had changed

78

was Spielberg's previously accommodating attitude with his crew. On *Jaws* he had kept his cool while all around were losing theirs. On no fewer than five separate occasions on *CE3K*, after visibly simmering with anger at the constant delays, he blew a fuse and stormed off the set. 'Wow, one hit and he's D.W. Griffiths already,' one seasoned technician was heard to mutter. With Julia Phillips around to talk him back down, Spielberg cooled off and went back to work. 'I'm not the easiest person to work with in terms of my crew,' he admitted, clearly implying that this was nothing new. 'When I say I think something should take two hours, and they say four, and it takes six – yes, I get angry.'

The difference, many felt, was an arrogance mixed in with the anger that had not existed before. It was an arrogance that seeped all the way through to his office staff, where no matter what they achieved, it never seemed enough. As ex-secretary Kathy Switzer later put it: 'Steven could be very charming and captivating. But it was so easy to dissatisfy him, to disappoint him. You could perform miracles, and it was never enough. There was never a "Good job". Instead it was, "Couldn't you have gone one step further and had me made God!?"'

On other occasions the milk of human kindness flowed in sufficient quantities for Spielberg to cook up enough of his favourite *matzo brei* to treat the entire 150-man unit. (His mother's reaction to this particular piece of news: 'I never knew he could cook. From me he just learned how to eat.') Spielberg, once again the soul of modesty, claimed that preparing the dish was 'the only real thing I do all day'.

Dreyfuss caused palpitations following a local Mobile radio show in which he took part over the July 4 weekend. The first half of the programme went well enough. Diplomatically declining to describe what the movie was about, the actor parried with 'Talking about something like this destroys it. Can you imagine someone talking about the Mona Lisa and telling you, well, it's this woman, and she's got a funny smile on her face?' So far so good. Then, out of the blue, the politically minded, outspoken Dreyfuss launched into a broadside on the evils of the Ku Klux Klan. Death threats immediately inundated the station.

The actor was flown to safety for a couple of days, then spent the rest of the movie confined to quarters, two hefty bodyguards forever at his elbow. At least on this occasion, having learned his lesson on *Jaws*, Dreyfuss kept any criticism of the production team or studio to himself. On *CE3K* it was the process of making a special effects movie that chafed. 'I'm OK in it, I'm not good,' he declared, once shooting was over. 'The special effects are put in later, so I spent a lot of time doing this . . .' He mimed looking around, above and below, his expression changing from one of horror to awe to delight. 'You do it on rocks and in houses and in canyons and in valleys, and they pay you *enormous* amounts of money,' he amplified.

Observing Spielberg at work, Phillips began to realise that he operated at opposite ends of two extremes, either capturing 'small perfect moments' or going all out for 'Barnum and Bailey' effects. In between: zilch, his tantrums apart. She also became unnervingly aware of his manipulative side. During the shoot he'd made Gary Guffey, the movie's littlest hero, his best buddy – all in the interests of getting the best performance possible out of the kid. After failing to get the required emotional wallop from Guffey for one crucial scene, Spielberg took the boy aside and told him that the movie was finished, that he wasn't going to see either him or the rest of his friends any more. That piece of calculated, some would say callous intelligence, produced the tears Spielberg sought.

The unkindest cut of all, as far as Phillips was concerned, was being informed at the end of filming that she would 'revert to the standard position of producer'. As in: she would have nothing more to do with the project. As in: she was fired. An interview Francois Truffaut had given to the New York *Times*, in which he'd been highly critical of her performance, had helped not one whit. Come to that, it seemed that Truffaut had been unimpressed with most of what he saw on this, his first American movie. 'Shooting was very slow,' he declared, 'even for an American movie. On occasion we only did two shots a day. We were on call from eight in the morning even if we didn't shoot until five in the afternoon.' There was one compensation for Truffaut among all the delays. It gave him time to work on the script for his next movie, *The Man Who Loved Women.*

Phillips's head would be only the first to roll. Spielberg took time off during post-production to attend the wedding of David Begelman and his latest bride, Gladyce. By that time he had met all of the principals – Begelman, Stark, Columbia president Alan Hirschfield and financier Herbert Allen – soon to be locked in one of the sorriest power struggles in Hollywood history.

Begelman himself was next to feel the axe, after it was discovered he'd been working a scam at Columbia to pay down his gambling debts. The scandal began when actor Cliff Robertson had a memory lapse over receipt of a Columbia cheque for $10,000 in 1975. Nor, for that matter, could he recall having done any work for the studio during that period, yet there it was on his 'Statement of Miscellaneous Income' from the IRS in 1976. It turned out that the cheque had been made out to him, but cashed by Begelman. Other embezzlements and misappropriations hiked the traceable total to $75,000.

Alan Hirschfield closely followed Begelman out of Columbia's revolving doors after refusing to regard the embezzlements as the mere 'aberrations' Stark and Allen portrayed, and to agree to Begelman's reinstatement and rehabilitation.

Spielberg waxed philosophical as *CE3K*'s opening date approached, postponed from Columbia's ideal dream-date of Easter to December 1977. He remained relatively unaffected by the blood-letting all around him at Columbia. His main concern was the movie, as well as his place in the pecking order of Hollywood and the growing degree of power he was accumulating. 'I just had to reach this point in my career where I had enough autonomy to make this movie right,' he declared, 'as opposed to having to make it in twenty days for a million dollars. Maybe I'll look back and wish I had made it for that, but right now it couldn't have been made the way it's coming out had I not had the time and money.'

Still there was considerable nervousness as the opening date approached. Columbia's stock had climbed from a low of $8 in the Spring of 1977 to $17 in September, boosted solely by expectations for *CE3K*. It was one hell of a responsibility for any movie, and for any one director, to carry. The pressure on Spielberg as he sweated away with his editors was overwhelming. 'If the movie doesn't do business, Columbia's stock will definitely bomb,' warned Charles M. Lewis, veteran film analyst at Balfour Securities.

Although Spielberg had openly expressed many concerns about the fate of *CE3K*, it remains easy to underestimate the additional tremendous tension he bottled up inside. At least, he might well have consoled himself, that bothersome business with Denis Hoffman was out of the way, and settled well ahead of the deadline of 1978.

A couple of nights before *CE3K*'s opening, Spielberg got up from watching TV and walked outside into his garden. It was a glorious night, still and calm, the inky-black sky filled with needle-point stars. All of a sudden he was unable to hold himself in check a minute longer. Feeling that he was completely coming apart, he began crying like a baby. In a few minutes it was over, and he was back watching television, his mini-nervous breakdown over.

A sneak preview of *Close Encounters* was held under a cloak of intense security at the Medallion movie house in Dallas, Texas. The audience was selected and contacted by phone, asked if they would like to see a free, unspecified movie. To collect their tickets, they had to turn up at the Medallion Shopping Center, with ID in the form of a driving licence, complete with photo. Despite these and other precautions against unwanted guests, not least the presence of three armed guards at the entrance, *New York* critic William Flanagan bribed one of the ticket-holders and smuggled himself past security to take his place among the citizenry, pen at the ready. 'I can understand Columbia's anxiety about *CE3K*,' he wrote. 'In my humble opinion, the picture will be a colossal flop.'

D-i-s-a-s-t-e-r!

The critic could have been right. Based on audience reaction at the sneak, Spielberg set about making changes. As he later explained, 'I had the opportunity to see how the film played. Film is not necessarily a dry cement process. I had the luxury of retouching the painting.' Out went a rendition of 'When You Wish Upon A Star' over the closing credits. Out went fifteen minutes from the flabby central section.

The movie survived some truly lethal reviews. 'The dumbest story ever told,' Molly Haskell declared in *New York* magazine, adding that Spielberg's pseudo-religion was 'as phony as the pseudo-science on which it rests.' Per Rex Reed: 'This might be the most expensive gibberish ever put on a screen.' Over to Andrew Sarris at *Village Voice*, who chose to personalise the put-down: 'I have seen *Duel* and I have seen *Sugarland Express* and I have seen *Jaws* and I have seen *Close Encounters*, and after all this exposure to Spielberg's precocious "talent" I conclude that he would have made a competent second-unit director in the days when movies still contained drama and narrative and recognisably human feelings . . . *Close Encounters* is a gooey, melted marshmallow of a movie with nothing more at the core than more gooeyness masquerading as godliness.'

As usual the public made up its own mind, flocking to the movie in sufficient numbers to register a box-office score of $128 million in the US, $300 million worldwide. Columbia was saved, and Spielberg had a second huge hit.

*Close Encounters* provided Spielberg's second lesson in Hollywood economics. Although his cut of the profits had been increased from five per cent on *Jaws* to a whopping 17.5 per cent, he wound up with only $5 million from the movie's worldwide gross. How come? Because his 17.5 per cent, impressive as it sounded, was *net* – after the studio deducted overhead, interest and distribution fees. 'Gross points', on the other hand, would have given him a share of the revenues from the first dollar the studio earned. The only problem: no director had demanded and been given gross since Alfred Hitchcock, and that in a deal brokered by the formidable Lew

Wasserman. Although it was too late to change tactics for his next movie, *1941*, a future collaboration with George Lucas would land him on the right track.

Spielberg was nominated for 'Best Director' for *Close Encounters*. (This time his *movie* was overlooked, a reversal of the *Jaws* procedure. Confused?) Other nominations were for Cinematography, Art Direction, Sound, Editing, Visual Effects, Original Score, and to Melinda Dillon for Best Supporting Actress. Of them all, only cinematographer Vilmos Zsigmond made it to the podium.

Underscoring public gullibility, UFO sightings increased to three and four a day following the movie's release – almost all, as government officials were quick to point out, from individuals in remote country areas with nothing much else to do with their time.

Spielberg regards the 'Special Edition' of *CE3K* he re-edited and partly re-shot in 1978 as the movie that would have been released in the first place had he been granted two more months in the post-production process. To him the entire second act of the original film was always 'very unsatisfying', especially with regard to the pacing between the Dreyfuss and the Truffaut scenes. The changes for the new version involved radical editing of the second act, a much-heralded additional sequence where Dreyfuss enters the mother ship, a few extra shots at the beginning of the picture and a new sequence of the discovery of a 350-foot liner in the middle of the Gobi Desert. Douglas Trumbull tub-thumped how majestic the interior of the mother ship would be; instead, what we got looked like the foyer of New York's Ziegfeld movie house, where, appropriately enough, the movie received its Showcase Presentation.

The length of the 'Special Edition' was about the same as the original version, since Spielberg had excised the tiresome 'Gonna Build a Mountain (Of Mashed Potato)' sequence and considerably tightened up the still-rambling middle of the movie. The ending was stretched out by sliding in extra padding that added little, some felt nothing at all, in terms of impact.

There was no doubt, however, as to how Spielberg compared the 'finished' *CE3K* to his breakthrough hit. '*Jaws* is a movie I could have played on a toy xylophone,' was his surprising declaration, 'but *Close Encounters* made me stretch further, it required all eighty-eight keys. When you take a dip-stick and measure *Close Encounters* against *Jaws* from an artistic standpoint, *Jaws* is half a pint and for me *Close Encounters* is two quarts.'

For many, this author included, *Jaws*' salty, nourishing half-pint was worth many times *CE3K*'s lo-cal half-gallon.

★

Before he entered drugs and alcohol hell in the late seventies, Richard Dreyfuss was known for his drollery, sharp wit and pin-sharp observation. Now that he's been back with us for over a decade, clean and sober, his observations on Spielberg are no less relevant than they ever were before, not least because, old substance addictions apart, they have so much in common. 'If you ever need an insight into Steven,' says the survivor of *Jaws*, *Close Encounters* and, into the eighties, *Always*, '"When You Wish Upon A Star" is it. What comes out of Steven unconsciously is that he's a big kid who, at twelve years old, decided to make movies. And he's still twelve years old. He's focused every one of his powers and capabilities on making movies and blocked everything else in the world out of his personality.'

It was true that the social upheaval that had shaken America in the sixties and seventies had completely passed Spielberg by. Ask him, however, about the upheaval at Universal, and he could provide a blow-by-blow account. Had he ever been drafted, he claims he would have gone to Vietnam with no regrets. Once there, he would have volunteered for special duty as a combat cameraman. Pfc Spielberg would have been the one setting up a 400-foot dolly shot tracking dense jungle foliage, recording the lurking terror behind every leaf and branch. Dissatisfied with the effect, he would have been the first serviceman in history to have insisted on shipping a Chapman crane out. 'I never believed in anything before I believed in movies,' he declared as the seventies drew to a close, 'and it's only now that I'm realising there's an entire backlog, an interesting and embarrassing gap for me to begin filling in.'

The problem was: How?

Spielberg had two answers.

The first: by 'living around, growing up'.

The second? By 'making more movies'.

Say what you like about David Begelman – and plenty has been said, before and after his death in 1995, about the man's exploits, his self-admitted weaknesses, his many undoubted qualities, his *chutzpah* – but his belief in Spielberg, in Michael and Julia Phillips, and in *Close Encounters* even as the budget soared into the stratosphere, saved Columbia Pictures. It was the one throw of the dice he must have relished to his dying day, one successful spin of fortune's wheel that nobody could take away from him, not even the self-inflicted gunshot that ended his life . . .

'I met a real heartbreaker last night,' Spielberg winsomely informed Julia Phillips the morning after a 1976 screening of Brian De

Palma's *Carrie*. Heartbreaker or no, and Spielberg's description turned out to be not far from the mark, blue-eyed brunette Amy Irving was certainly a beauty. Spielberg, instantly smitten, grabbed George Lucas's arm before the screening. Their conversation went something like this: 'George, that girl over there, who is she? Do you know?'

'Sure I do. That's Amy Irving. She's in Brian's movie. You want an introduction?'

'You've met her already? How come?'

'Easy. She came along to audition for Princess Leia in *Star Wars*. I turned her down.'

'Oh, *great!*'

'It gets better. She met Brian at the same audition, and that landed her the role in *Carrie*. Her mom's in the movie too, Priscilla Pointer. And hey, didn't you once work with her uncle?'

'Her uncle? Not that I'm aware of. Her *uncle?*'

'Come on, Steven. Wasn't he your co-producer on the Gene Barry *Name of the Game* episode you directed?'

Suddenly it clicked. One of the producers had been George Eckstein, who'd gone on to hire him for *Duel*. Then there was his partner, Richard *Irving*. Sid Sheinberg's introduction to the team had already paid off handsomely in career terms. Now he not only had a connection with which to break the ice with Amy Irving, he was about to be introduced to her mother, at least on film. Although his friend's movie had two other attractive young actresses cast in prominent roles – Nancy Allen as the 'bad girl', and Betty Buckley as the 'nice schoolteach' – Spielberg had eyes for no one but Irving as the Gothic yarn unfolded.

Amy Irving was struggling to make her way in Hollywood. Her role in *Carrie*, a low-budget entry that would prove a surprise hit, would go some way to establish her, as did *The Fury*, her follow-up for De Palma. Meantime, she was resentful of the fact that her breakthrough, and those of so many other young actors, had little or nothing to do with talent or training, simply that their 'look', their 'type', filled demands of the moment. It was not the firmest foundation, she considered, on which to build a career. Her youth had been spent first in San Francisco, where her father, Jules Irving, ran the Actor's Workshop, then in New York following his appointment as director of the Lincoln Center Repertory Theater. Although her grandfather was a Russian Jewish immigrant – she had that in common with Spielberg, on the paternal side of the family – Irving had been reared as a Christian Scientist, with neither religious customs nor traditions of any denomination observed by her family. Having a mother who was also in the business, she'd been raised to believe in artistic values. It was about the work, stupid, not the money. The result: disillusionment had set in with exposure to the real world.

De Palma's obliging introduction went even better than Spielberg had hoped. He summoned up the courage to ask the enchanting creature out, she accepted, and one date led to another. Double-dating with his pal De Palma was long since nothing new, and the practice between Spielberg and Irving and De Palma and Nancy Allen soon became common, as did the sight of De Palma toting a videocamera around to record their outings.

After being quoted in the columns of *Penthouse* that in high school and college 'bright women' had intimidated him, 'but not any more', Spielberg had landed himself with the acid test in the brighter-than-bright, sharp-as-a-tack Irving. 'It's nice to have a friend who's also a confessor, your lover, a second voice in your head,' he had rhapsodised to the magazine. 'To me a sensuous woman is one who, first of all, has a knowledge of herself. She isn't a drifter. She is goal-oriented. She has a sense of humour about herself and enough energy to light her life on fire and keep it burning until she has what she wants. And still not be satisfied.' Although he had described Irving to a 't', it begged the question: would such a paragon of ambition, humour and passion ever subordinate herself to the point of virtual disappearance? One thing the free-spirited Irving certainly was *not* was the archetypal homemaker of Spielberg's dreams.

At first Irving seemed fine as far as Julia Phillips could tell. Until she felt the daggers slipping between her ribs every morning after she, not Irving, had accompanied Spielberg to the various showings and awards ceremonies for *Taxi Driver*. Although it was strictly business with Phillips, in the service of tub-thumping *Close Encounters* – one furtive, exploratory, ill-judged French kiss with Spielberg apart, when the earth stubbornly declined to move – Irving clearly felt that her territorial rights were being infringed.

Phillips sees Spielberg's taste in women as on a par with hers in men. As in: not so hot, borderline disastrous. She had regarded his reported flings with Sarah Miles and Victoria Principal as bad enough, let alone the bimbo he'd been bopping pre-Irving, whom he'd had the nerve to 'test' for the key role of Jillian in *CE3K* that eventually went to Melinda Dillon.

Even Spielberg had had the grace to admit, after hitting with *Jaws*, he'd gone 'a little bit crazy' with the suddenly available opposite sex, trying to make up for lost time when they'd been annoyingly *un*available. Even then he would still claim he was too busy with moviemaking 'to become a real hedonist'. Which isn't to say he didn't try real hard.

Irving's reaction to a screening of *Close Encounters* was to weep copiously, and not just at the movie's climactic scenes. It was more than that, friends were solemnly informed. She had glimpsed nothing less than 'the beauty of Steve Spielberg's soul'.

After that it didn't take much coaxing to have Irving move in to Spielberg's modest Laurel Canyon 'bachelor funky' pad, where the furnishings were all but hidden under piles of scripts, where framed movie posters plastered the walls, and where his rapidly growing collection of original movie soundtrack albums were stacked high.

The idyll was short. In record time, according to Phillips, Spielberg had second thoughts and stutteringly begged her to coax Irving back out. Phillips' reply amounted to: 'You've made your bed, honey, now lie in it.' Which he did. And did. And d-did. To the extent of the couple weathering their initial storms and following De Palma and Allen in becoming engaged.

Many still felt their relationship was the opposite of what Spielberg craved and needed. After the disharmony with which he had grown up, with all the simmering tension between Leah and Arnold that constantly threatened to boil over, and finally did, the last thing he wanted was a programme re-run. Yet, all too often, that's exactly what he got.

Both were able to convince themselves, for a while at least, that their engagement would somehow take the sting out of the fierce competitiveness that grew up between them, that the more they were joined as a couple, each could share in the other's triumphs.

It was an interesting theory.

Many, many moons after their experience together on *CE3K* – during which time nary a word between them was exchanged – Julia Phillips braced herself for a visit with Spielberg on the set of *Poltergeist*. She was astonished when he asked for a puff of her joint. What had happened to 'Speelnuts', the 'straightnik'? She was almost relieved when he damn near choked. Perhaps in an attempt to write '*finis*' to the *CE3K* saga, he told her, 'I'm sorry I wasn't a good friend.'

'Oh, that's OK . . . nobody was,' she mumbled in reply. After the killer-diller, venom-laden speech she had rehearsed over the years, ready to trot out on just such an otherwise moist-eyed, touchy-feely occasion, she knew that her response was, to put it mildly, somewhat less than adequate. But what the hell, it would have to do until the Great Leveller came along . . .

It took several years before Paul Schrader was prepared to give his side of the story on *CE3K*'s script credit – and confirm that he had withdrawn from arbitration 'at Steven's request'. Unsurprisingly it was something he had come to regret, since he'd been given profit points in the movie tied to credit. If he'd chosen to fight the issue, he'd probably have been a couple of million dollars richer today. 'That's the way it happens,' was his philosophical last word.

# 11

## 'Are They Laughing?'

*'There are two great rewards that I heap upon myself
when I'm directing. The first is when I get the idea months
before I start shooting and I jump up and down and I
drink my Dr Pepper and I go out and celebrate. And the
second nicest moment is when I'm in the editing room and
I cut that concept together and it works; the best-laid plans
actually paid off. In between, the making of the movie is
just pure warm shit.'*

*'If a film works it's usually because of the characters and
not the special effects. Empathy with the people is
important because you sure can't empathise with a shark
or ninety police cars or a space ship.'*

STEVEN SPIELBERG

*With his wide-ranging absorption of cinema lore, Spielberg was more
aware than most of Universal's history, both ancient and modern, and as
he made his way to Malibu he found his mind wandering back. Back to
the* old *stuff, way back, long before even Jules Stein and Lew Wasserman
had roamed Lankershim Boulevard, let alone Sid Sheinberg, Ned Tanen
and Frank Price. All the way back to 'Uncle' Carl Laemmle, the little
Bavarian immigrant who founded the company in 1912. Spielberg had
a very special reason to refresh his memory.*

*Laemmle had sailed from Bremerhaven as a thirteen year old to join
his brother Joseph in Chicago. Ten years had been spent holding down a
series of ill-paid jobs as he struggled to master English. Joining the
Continental Clothing Company in Oshkosh, Nebraska, he had worked
his way up from bookkeeper to manager. During a visit to Chicago in
1905 he noticed a line of people outside a converted store. They were
waiting to see a moving picture show. Deciding on a mad gamble,
Laemmle located premises in the city and opened his own 'nickelodeon'.*

*By 1908 he was operating a small chain of the establishments, many*

89

*of them mere ex-parlours, and had begun thinking of making his own movies. The Universal Film Company was founded in 1912, the name deriving from the 'Universal Pipe Fittings' emblazoned on a van outside the new enterprise's first board meeting. Within a year the company was enjoying its first hit with a sensation-packed white slave traffic exploitationer,* Traffic In Souls. *Laemmle had advertised the movie as 'A $200,000 spectacle in 700 scenes with 800 players'. Nothing much in Hollywood changes, Spielberg may have ruefully reflected – the hits still have their budgets exaggerated, the flops have theirs minimised.* Traffic in Souls *had been produced for $57,000 and turned a profit of $450,000.*

*While looking for a permanent plot on which he could build – as would many screenwriters over the years – word reached Laemmle of a 200-acre parcel of land in the San Fernando Valley, north of the Hollywood Hills, ten miles from the city of Los Angeles. The site was purchased for $150,000, and 'Universal City' was open for business by March 1914 both as a studio, and as a thrill-tour for the public. (Fifty years almost to the day before Lew Wasserman would reopen the tour after remodelling.) 'See how we blow up bridges, burn down houses, wreck automobiles!' Laemmle's pitch ran. The 25 cents admission included a boxed lunch.*

*Although Laemmle employed some of the finest talent in the world at one point or another – Irving Thalberg, before he was snatched away to MGM, Erich Von Stroheim, Lon Chaney – he soon became notorious for his use of relatives. In 1929 he appointed his son, Carl Jr, to run the studio. He made directors of brothers and cousins like Ernst and Edward. On one movie,* The Notorious Gentleman, *the billing read:*

*Carl Laemmle Presents*
*A Carl Laemmle Jr Production*
*Produced by Carl Laemmle Jr*
*Directed by Edward Laemmle*

*As the eminent wit Ogden Nash put it, 'Uncle Carl Laemmle has a very large faemmle.'*

*One faemmle tie that had worked out extremely well involved Laemmle's nephew, a young man who got his start in the twenties on two-reeler westerns, romances and comedies, from* Stolen Ranch *and* The Love Trap *to* Hell's Heroes. *Like so many others, he moved away from Universal to achieve his greatest successes. The movies that made his reputation?* Dodsworth, Wuthering Heights, The Little Foxes, The Best Years Of Our Lives – *and they were just for starters. His name was William Wyler.*

*Spielberg had heard that Wyler lived in a beachhouse at Malibu, and on the offchance of meeting and talking with him, he decided to check out the address he'd been given. As he approached the house, he suddenly felt ridiculous. Wyler might be away, he might be unwell. He might also have no idea, or couldn't care less, who this presumptious young pup was. Why hadn't he tried to make an appointment first? Spielberg's mouth was dry as he nervously knocked on the door.*

*Wyler himself opened up, recognised Spielberg immediately, gave a broad smile and said, 'Come on in. Let's talk movies.'*

*Which they did. For several hours. Spielberg sat there enrapt as Wyler spoke. He had so many questions he wanted to ask this legendary figure, and wished – how he wished – he'd brought a microphone along to record some of the reminiscing. He did learn one thing that was particularly encouraging – that he should never be ashamed of making hit movies. Wyler, it seemed, would have been unhappy even with the best of his movies had they failed to make money. And he would trade all of the French 'New Wave's' efforts for the type of popular hits he'd helped Sam Goldwyn turn out.*

*Wyler had served his apprenticeship under Uncle Carl and his regime almost forty years before Sid Sheinberg had given another young man his big chance, on the selfsame soundstages. It would be going way too far to say that a baton was being passed. There was, however – at the very least – a distinct sense of continuity, the scribbling of a small footnote in history, the closing of a circle. Hey, maybe there* was *something in the gospel of respect to an earlier generation that the likes of Bogdanovich preached. Remembering his earlier, brash young man's pronouncement on the subject, Spielberg decided that his conversion was something to keep under his hat.*

Spielberg first met twenty-four-year-old Robert Zemeckis in 1975, along with his writing partner Bob Gale, on the Universal lot during a film class visit. This was on the very eve of *Jaws*-mania – in fact, Zemeckis was the friend who taped the audience response at the Cinerama Dome and clapped heartily as Robert Shaw disappeared into 'Bruce's' gaping jaws. Spielberg was struck with the fourteen-minute award-winning student film they proudly unveiled, *A Field of Honor*, complete with filched *Great Escape* soundtrack. He promised to keep in touch.

Back at USC Zemeckis and Gale produced a script they originally called *Hollywood '41*, which became, in various versions, *The Great Los Angeles Air Raid* and *The Rising Sun* before its eventual emergence as *1941*. John Milius, their USC professor, encouraged his protégés to develop their idea, regarding it as an ideal directorial vehicle for himself. The team had travelled a similar route before, when Milius had shown interest in two of their previous scripts.

*1941* was based on a little-known incident Zemeckis and Gale had unearthed in newspaper files detailing Japan's so-called 'attack' on California under the banner headline, 'Battle Enemy Air Raiders Over Los Angeles'.

It was true that a stray submarine had fired a few shots at an oil refinery north of Santa Barbara, missing the target, landing in a wooded area, and causing all of $200 worth of damage. If it could happen in Santa Barbara, though, could San Pedro, Long Beach, Santa Monica, even sacred Malibu be far behind? The seas had to be watched for subs, the skies for planes. The real scare had come at 3.12 am the morning after the sub attack, when an 'aircraft' flying over Los Angeles – actually it was a weather balloon – was taken by panic-stricken observers for the second wave of the assault on Fortress America. For two solid hours the night had been lit up by a combination of anti-aircraft fire, and the klieg lights that had hitherto been reserved for movie premieres.

To keep the wolf from the door while MGM was looking at the project, Zemeckis and Gale undertook several television assignments before landing an option deal at Warners for another invasion-based idea they had dreamt up, the effect on four New Jersey kids of the Beatles, *I Wanna Hold Your Hand*. Six months were spent developing and reworking their script, which Zemeckis was hoping to direct, accompanied by threats that they might be fired from their own project. When Warners dropped their option altogether, Zemeckis and Gale's young production team of Tamara Asseyev and Alex Rose contacted Spielberg and succeeded in transferring the project across Burbank.

Universal studio head Ned Tanen was offered a cast-iron deal. In exchange for Universal buying the script and financing the $2.6 million feature, Spielberg would act as executive producer on *I Wanna Hold Your Hand*. If his faith in Zemeckis as director of the movie proved unjustified, and Tanen would be the sole arbiter, based on the dailies, then Spielberg would take over. Tanen, no mean judge of talent himself, read the script, and within twenty-four hours of Spielberg's offer, gave the go-ahead. The dailies must have been more impressive than the insipid finished product, for halfway through the shoot, Zemeckis was handed a three-picture contract at Universal.

In the meantime, John Milius had given up on *1941* and gone surfing with *Big Wednesday* instead. At that point the project was offered on a plate to Spielberg, with the proviso that it be channeled through Milius's A-Team Productions (his chosen combat designation courtesy of the Green Berets). Still in pre-production with *CE3K*, Spielberg 'didn't even think', by his own account, but

92

grabbed it. Robert Zemeckis – regarded by Julia Phillips as nothing more than 'an incredible pest' on the set of *CE3K*, where he had no apparent function she could discern, other than as a buddy of 'Speelnuts' and eagerly looking on and asking dumb and dumber questions – had spent eight weeks with his writing partner Bob Gale on *CE3K*'s Mobile location, screening old war movies and working on *1941*'s script in the evenings.

Milius took *1941* to Universal after being told by Spielberg that he didn't want to work at MGM. Initially sceptical that Spielberg was really attached, Universal turned it down. Off Milius went to Columbia. When they acquired the property and Spielberg was confirmed, Universal – realising that oops, we boobed – suggested to Columbia that they get together to share the risk.

Twin logic was at work, for although both studios were keen to snare 'the new Spielberg', *1941* was an expensive son-of-a-gun, even at its original $21.5 million budget. Sure, *Jaws* had been successful, and *CE3K* was looking great, but could Spielberg be trusted to stay within budget? And hey, this was a *comedy*. If Spielberg foundered in the notoriously difficult genre, he wouldn't be the first. Yep, joint venture definitely seemed the smart option. Universal would handle US distribution, Columbia would take over foreign.

Spielberg had been a huge fan of NBC's weekly *Saturday Night Live* ever since the first show and its hilarious *Jaws*-inspired 'Victims of Sharkbite' sketch. On a visit to New York he made a point of meeting with the cast at One Fifth Avenue, an art deco bar and restaurant they used for after-show partying. 'I'm thinking of making a World War II comedy,' he told John Belushi. 'There's a terrific role of a Japanese sub commander. If I ever make the movie, you're it.'

From then on the two men kept in touch. The comedian's subsequent film debut in John Landis's *Animal House* made a fortune for everyone, although Belushi was paid just $35,000 at the time; only years later, anxious to sign him up again, did Universal agree to a retro-bonus of $250,000. Despite his manager, Bernie Brillstein, pronouncing *1941*'s script 'not very funny', and pointedly reminding his client that Spielberg was no comedy director, Belushi was high on the project. And he was a huge fan of *CE3K*. 'How can I turn Spielberg down?!' Brillstein was asked. Eyeing the fee of $350,000, Brillstein dropped his objections. Suddenly – yes, he could see that his client had a definite point . . .! Meantime, Belushi's role was no longer the Japanese sub commander, he was Wild Bill Kelso, demon P-40 bomber pilot. Dressing up a friend of his, Belushi invited Spielberg to meet 'Sergeant Tree, tank commander'. Oh, you want your *Saturday Night Live* sidekick in as well? No problem. Dan Aykroyd had landed his first movie.

Although Spielberg's claim that he was 'dragged hopelessly through the streets' by the movie's 'crazo script' may sound a little out of character, maybe he really did feel, for the first time, part of the zeitgeist of the decade, the square accepted into the hippy, happy world of the *SNL* team and their high jinks, the doofus embraced by the in-crowd, hot-stepping out in a brand-new direction.

His avowed intent was not only to tap into the *SNL* comedy vein, but to re-create the madcap humour of the Ben Turpin, Harold Lloyd and Charlie Chaplin silents he had enjoyed on late-night television in his youth, to make a 'celebration of sight gags'. Another model was the anarchic *Hellzapoppin'*, which he claimed to have watched 'hundreds of times'. Since Turpin, Lloyd and Chaplin, not to mention Olson and Johnson, were unavailable, Spielberg called on Chuck Jones, semi-retired doyen of Warners' cartoon department, to advise on slapstick timing.

It was also time for Spielberg to drop at least one longtime collaborator. As he would later explain, 'The only person I've had a perfect association with is John Williams. John notwithstanding, I find it healthy to change. After doing three pictures with Joe Alves – *Sugarland*, *Jaws*, *Close Encounters* – I found that we could no longer work together. I was beginning to look around for new talent. New, young, untried people.'

John Williams the only person he's had a 'perfect' relationship with? Per one leading Hollywood writer: 'That tells you a whole lot more about Spielberg than it does about the people who helped him through the early part of his career, who covered his ass, who covered up the flubs. Then found themselves up to their asses in ice and snow doing time in Outer Mongolia. You want to know the main reason he refused to do a sequel to *Jaws*? He'd have been forced to work with the same crew again, and he knew they hated his guts.'

Four blocks of Hollywood Boulevard, built entirely to scale on the Burbank Studio lot as the standing set for *1941*, were a wonder to behold. Here was the Ambassador Hotel in all its ornate, gilded glory. Walk a block and you stood in front of Grauman's Chinese Theatre, complete with its forecourt of cement imprints and signatures of the stars. Meantime, hundreds of sketches were being prepared that would be transformed into intricate miniature planes, submarines, automobiles and buildings by a forty-man team. In a reversal of the usual procedure they were filmed, carefully pre-lit, well in advance of the live action sequences to which they would be added.

Spielberg allowed himself no let-up during the first few, relatively carefree weeks on *1941*. Based in a sickly green one-storey ex-storage building on the Burbank lot, he was like a general marshalling his troops during the week, laughing along with the outrageous antics of Belushi and Aykroyd, at weekends retreating into the intimacy of the cutting room to work on the 'Special Edition' of *CE3K*. Then the problems began.

Leaving the camera running to catch the odd, brilliant glimpse of Belushi at his best, lines discarded, improvising like crazy, became routine. That in itself was no hardship, except in the cutting room, where the best ad-libs often came at the end of an otherwise blown take. Although Spielberg had been aware of Belushi's drug use, it had never crossed his mind, untutored as he was on such matters, that it would create a problem on the movie. When Belushi began turning up late, Spielberg tried to hide his annoyance. Not wishing to ruin the delicate relationship he had with the comedian – what do you do when the laughter dies in the middle of filming a comedy? – his initial mini-reprimands were couched as light-heartedly as he could make them. When they failed to work, he called on Aykroyd to have a serious talk with his friend.

It hardly helped. On December 5 Belushi turned up ninety minutes late. Shambling past Spielberg after practically falling out of the limo that had brought him, he barely made it to his trailer. Suddenly the dam burst. This was the second time in two days the comedian had kept the entire unit waiting. Spielberg was having enough problems making the comedy work without hanging round a set that had cost a fortune to build, with upwards of 150 people unable to work because of the absence of one guy and his over-indulgence.

The crew tensed as they watched Spielberg fling his script down and follow Belushi into the trailer, banging the door shut behind him with enough force to knock it off its hinges. 'You can't do this to me!' they heard him scream through the walls. 'You can do this to anyone else, but not to me. You're getting more money than Dreyfuss got on *Close Encounters*! For $350,000 you're going to show up!'

The incident passed, and for a while Belushi achieved some semblance of punctuality, usually when his dealer was due with a connection. The drug supplier had reason to be grateful to the comedian. The set of *1941* was a veritable wonderland of contacts. By one estimate close on two dozen users were enjoying music while they worked. 'What's Spielberg's bag?' the candyman, eager for the big score, asked a technician one day. 'Working,' came the reply, 'and hey, don't even fucking *dream* about it. You'll blow it for all of us.'

Belushi's discipline soon slipped again. Waiting in his trailer between takes, he began shifting cocaine in ever-increasing quantities, eagerly joined by his fellow-actor, Treat Williams. Cast as the hot-to-trot Sitarski, Williams remained completely in character during wild nights out with his new best friend.

There were a few personal pleasures among what Spielberg would come to describe as the 'utter horror' of *1941*. Like a new home in Coldwater Canyon, bought and paid for with $49,500 of the money from *Jaws*. Like the Porsche that replaced the bullet-ridden Merc 280 jalopy he'd bought for $400 off *Sugarland Express*. Like the herbal tea his new housekeeper Berthe provided at strategic intervals. Like the valuable antique billiard table he acquired. Like the over-the-borderline-hideous, back-lit, stained-glass panel of 'Bruce the Shark', a gift from a grateful Sid Sheinberg, that greeted visitors as they stepped inside the front door. Like the sight of olive-tanned Amy Irving parked among the Navajo rugs in his capacious den. Like the company he kept with Irving's pals Rob Reiner, Penny Marshall, Tim Matheson and Lisa Eichhorn. Like the sushi he enjoyed, perhaps to soak in the appropriate atmosphere, at the Imperial Gardens, a Japanese restaurant based on premises previously occupied by director Preston Sturges's eatery. Like hanging out with his own pals and 'leader of the bratpack' John Milius, accompanying him on skeet shoots, hoping to soak up a smidgin of his ersatz machismo. 'He's our scoutmaster,' Spielberg gushed to one scribe. 'He's the one who will tell you to go on a trip and only take enough food, enough water, for one day, and make you stay out longer than that. He's the one who says, "Be a man. I don't want to see any tears." He's a terrific raconteur, a wonderful storyteller. John has more life than all the rest of us put together.'

Milius was the first to agree, and to extend the metaphor into filmmaking. 'If you want to see the difference between generations,' he suggested, 'look at the difference between any of our movies and *Black Sunday* and *Marathon Man*, really foul movies by the Bel Air circuit. It's *easy* to be cynical. It's *hard* to be corny. Guys like George Lucas and Steven and me make our own stuff and we have producers who run the organisation for us.

Milius's 'bratpack' at that time, aside from his producing partner 'Buzz' Feitshans and nerds-of-honour Spielberg, Lucas and Brian De Palma, was rounded out by fretful, mumbling Paul Schrader, and the writing teams of Willard Huyck/Gloria Katz,

Barwood/Robbins and Zemeckis/Gale, with Francis Ford Coppola installed as honorary elder statesman when he deigned to visit.

Rather than frequent fashionable watering holes like Ma Maison, the pack was more often to be found in Denny's, off the Golden State Freeway in the San Fernando Valley. Either that or wolfing down cheeseburgers, french fries and malts at the 24-hour Bob's Big Boy in West Los Angeles. Wives were encouraged along as well as girlfriends, with Marsha Lucas and Celia Milius more often than not in attendance along with Amy Irving and Nancy Allen. The swapping of ideas that took place at these get-togethers carried echoes of kids bargaining with baseball cards. Points in each of their movies were traded-off, Milius landing one per cent of both *Star Wars* and *Close Encounters*, with Spielberg and Lucas on a similar percentage of *Big Wednesday*. Milius's seven minutes of work on the *Indianapolis* speech in *Jaws*? 'I never received a dime for it,' he says, 'and if Steven ever gave me a dime I would feel insulted.'

His pals apart, *1941* gave Spielberg the opportunity to meet and work with someone he and Milius, and millions more besides, considered 'the greatest samurai of them all' – Toshiro Mifune. Cast as the commander of the Japanese sub that Spielberg had first thought of for Belushi, Mifune walked into their first meeting wearing a business suit, jet-black hair thinning, still handsome, smiling, able to talk very little English. After formal exchanges of handshakes and gifts, Mifune got down to business through his interpreter: 'Now here's where the submarine is wrong . . .!'

As the shoot dragged on, correcting details of Japanese submarines proved the least of Spielberg's problems. One stunt after another nudged the budget farther and farther north. Emergency meetings were held, explanations demanded, rushes examined for crumbs of comfort. Belushi behaved; Belushi stopped behaving. The point of no return had long since been reached, with the final bill advancing on $25 million. It was a case of finish the damn thing PDQ.

Since her feature role debut as Roy Scheider's wife in *Jaws*, Lorraine Gary had been cast in Universal's *Carwash*, then Roger Corman's low-budget *I Never Promised You a Rose Garden*. A year later, in 1978's non-Spielberg follow-up, *Jaws II*, her payday had raised eyebrows, not to say questions from disgruntled MCA shareholders. *A quarter of a million dollar*s!? When Universal's Sid Sheinberg was asked if she was worth it, 'Yes, she is,' he snapped back.

The reason for his new-found sensitivity? Lorraine Gary was

Mrs Sid Sheinberg. 'I'll sue them if they accuse me of any impropriety,' her husband barked. In case there were any lingering doubts, 'I'm litigious!' he amplified.

It turned out that Gary's 'basic pay' for *Jaws II* had been $100,000. Still hefty by late-seventies standards for a non-name, the sum had been for a twelve-week contract, after which she was to be paid $10,000 a week. When the schedule ballooned to six months, overtime had kicked in, to the tune of a further $142,349. 'I got an extraordinary amount of money,' Gary acknowledged, 'and it will never happen again in my lifetime. But I *could* have negotiated for a piece of the picture . . .!'

Bronx-born Lorraine Gottfried had met her future husband when they were fellow students at New York University. Since their marriage she had appeared in scores of TV movies, the vast bulk of them for Universal. So how had she landed the role in *Jaws*? Per Gary, it had come about in the gym both she and Spielberg attended: 'We were working out one day when he told me he had seen me in a *Kojak* episode and that I'd be just right for the role of Ellen Brody.' Gary was less thrilled when she discovered that her character had so few lines to speak. But it was a feature movie, as opposed to TV. And to her credit, she gave a fine, convincing performance, making the most of her every scene.

Cast next in Spielberg's *1941*, Gary chose to agonise publicly on the pros and cons of high-placed connections, describing marriage to Sheinberg as a distinct career handicap. 'Some directors were afraid to hire me in case we had a disagreement on the set,' she explained. 'And I think there are other times that people wouldn't use me because they didn't like Sid.' Whatever the reason, after *Just You and Me, Kid*, also in '79, Gary had to wait another eight years for her next movie starring role, her last to date. The movie? *Jaws III – The Revenge*. For Universal.

Despite Spielberg's misgivings about the movie's reception, he was determined to have *1941* presented as 'A Steven Spielberg Film'. Anything less, after *CE3K*, would be seen as a come-down. Even the threat of a challenge from the Writers' Guild of America failed to deter him, although he'd stopped short, for once, of claiming any writing credit. His half-joking, half-in-earnest prediction that he would 'spend the rest of my life disowning this movie', would turn out to be wholly prophetic.

A sneak preview held in the same Medallion Theater in Dallas where *CE3K* had made its bow, confirmed his fears. He was met by one worried-looking studio 'suit' as he emerged halfway through the screening with a worried, 'Are they laughing?' Mostly, Spielberg had to report, they were not.

A planned November 8 opening was postponed, mainly at the behest of Spielberg and Sid Sheinberg, and re-scheduled for December 14. Spielberg was apoplectic when he heard that fifteen MCA executives who had attended the sneak had badmouthed the movie. 'Who needs *them*?' he raged. 'The preview was for *me*, to analyse and correct my mistakes, as I always do. But they brought in a computer-selected audience with a lot of staid older people, rather than the young *Saturday Night Live* audience this film is aimed at. Why didn't these MCA guys just stay home and watch *Laverne and Shirley*?'

Spielberg was disconsolate after the screening. Normally around to provide at least a modicum of comfort and support, Amy Irving was off in Texas shooting *Honeysuckle Rose* with country singer Willie Nelson. And busily denying rumours of a romance with her grizzled co-star. Spielberg was not amused.

'I don't know how this movie will come out,' he told one scribe. 'And yes, I'm scared. I'm like the Cowardly Lion, and two smashes back to back have not strengthened my belief in my ability to deliver. I can't correct the overall conceptual disasters about *1941*, but I can get little pieces here and there that I think will help speed the piece up.'

Spielberg was crushingly aware that if he absolutely failed he would be at the mercy of what comics called 'the death silence', when, instead of the expected laugh, a yawning black hole opens up. 'A comedy is an elusive, chameleon-like beast,' he agonised, 'and it's really an area of film that I'm not going to make a habit of. It's too fucking tough, panhandling for your supper.'

If this confessional sounds ultra-frank for a moviemaker coming off a production that ended up costing $27 million, you have to credit Spielberg not only with honesty but with perspicacity. If neither diplomacy or tact. Or was it all part of a disowning process? 'It wasn't a film from my heart,' he protested. 'It wasn't a movie that I constructed, dreamed about for ten years, although I have shed blood on it as if it were my own. Rather than a bastard adoption, I like to think of it as a project I was forced to take because of my own state of mind. For the most part, it's a picture made by people who aren't dealing with a full deck. That is why, I think, it was important for me to get it out of my system.' On, let it be said, Columbia and Universal's joint tab.

The reviews of *1941* were truly dire. 'A comedy almost devoid of humour, one of the most crashingly inept comedies of the past decade,' said Bruce Williamson in *Playboy*. *Newsweek* called it 'Spielberg's misguided missile', adding, 'Only the jokes die.' In the New York *Daily News* Rex Reed described it as 'A stupid farce based on a stupid idea.' In the New York *Times* Vincent Canby concurred: 'It is simply not funny.' To Stephen Farber in *New York* the movie was 'the most appalling piece of juvenilia yet foisted on the public'. Per Gary Arnold in the Washington *Post*, it was 'a hectic, smug, self-destructive farce, an appalling waste of filmmaking and performing resources . . . pointless, hateful, an artistic disgrace'. Over to Neal Gabler in Soho's *Weekly News*: 'What *1941* proves finally is that the Japanese didn't have to worry about destroying Hollywood. All they had to do was to wait years and let Steven Spielberg do it for them.'

Although unsurprised, Spielberg was devastated by the critical savaging. Were they reacting to the budget excess, rather than the movie itself? Or was this the long-expected backlash after the twin successes of *Jaws* and *Close Encounters*? Spielberg's feeling was that, even if *1941* had been a hit, critics would have been waiting for him to fail with his *next* project after that: 'After a certain amount of success critics are always ready to pounce if you fall off that pedestal they imagine you've built for yourself. *1941* is not a bad picture, but it isn't a great one. Still, it doesn't deserve the amount of flak it's gotten.' A pause, a grin, then a disarming concession among all the bullshit: 'By the same token, it did deserve a ruler across the knuckles.'

In no time flat the movie became joined at the hip in cinematic lore with another feature that had rocketed out of control, John Landis's *The Blues Brothers*. Spielberg found the juxtaposition unflattering. Much as he admired Landis as a director, he sensed a ploy. 'Landis loves to chase away the slight grey cloud of *The Blues Brothers* from over his head by bringing up *1941*,' he declared. 'While the rest of the world has forgotten *1941* and the fact that it made $50 million in worldwide film rentals, John hasn't. He mentions *1941* in the same breath as *The Blues Brothers* as if we should be ashamed of them.'

Finally, though, Spielberg swallowed the medicine: 'Until *1941* I thought I was immune to failure. But I couldn't come down from the power high of making big films on a large canvas. I threw everything in, and it killed the soup. *1941* was my encounter with economic reality . . . !'

Spielberg was shattered by the drug death of John Belushi. To him the man had been the exact opposite of his movie image, a sensitive individual looking for love and approval, at his most outrageous when he was most insecure. The panic that resulted had found creative expression in his amazing gift for comedy, albeit, more often than not, of the slobbery, gross-out variety. Belushi, 'the messy side of all of us', had grabbed social responsibility by the scruff of the neck and subverted it to his own form of public expression, doing things everyone thought of doing, but which society preached were unacceptable. No matter whether he was playing *Animal House*'s fraternity brother Bluto, 'Wild Bill Kelso', or Jake, the Blues Brother, he was always 'the guy that we secretly want to be, that unkempt side that exists in us all'.

Despite their rocky passage on *1941*, there was talk of the two getting together again on *Continental Divide*, an original script by Lawrence Kasdan that Spielberg urged Universal to buy. The male lead was a city tabloid columnist who travels to meet and get the scoop on a bird-loving country recluse. It was a mismatch comedy-of-opposites that carried echoes of the heyday of Spencer Tracy and Katharine Hepburn.

The only problem: Spielberg was unsure of how to proceed, and in what capacity. Maybe a script polish would tip the scales, together with Belushi's input. Or what if he brought in Messrs Barwood and Robbins to produce and direct under his wing? With that in mind, Spielberg summoned his long-time friends and collaborators to Coldwater Canyon. The idea: Belushi would meet with them and the whole thing would proceed from there. Or not, as the case might be.

It was very much a case of 'not'. Belushi turned up late, obviously the worse for wear, poured drinks all round, glared balefully at Barwood and Robbins, demanded a list of their credits, poured more drinks, and hovered menacingly over Robbins before being spirited away by his escort. Sickened, Spielberg passed on the idea of having anything to do with Belushi on *Continental Divide*. Barwood and Robbins, thoroughly intimidated by the comedian's off-putting wildman performance, seconded the motion. They all remained keen on the movie itself, though, and reluctant to let it go.

Other actors were discussed as possibilities for the role. Richard Dreyfuss was one, although he had problems of his own at the time, then there was talk of Peter Falk, George Segal, maybe even Dustin Hoffman. A combination of Jill Clayburgh and Robert De Niro was on the cards, then Clayburgh and Al Pacino – *very* briefly – before someone whispered scrap that, no, no, no, they've got too much history together. How about Streisand and Redford, together for the first time since *The Way We Were*. Sure, except that would require an exchange of genders: Streisand the tabloid terror, Redford the ornithologist. Naw, it wouldn't work anyway, the malls would be expecting *The Way We Were II*.

101

By the end of it all the fairly slight *Continental Divide* was buckling under the weight of all the casting discussions. 'OK, enough!' Barwood and Robbins jointly declared. There were, after all, other fish to fry. Their lives didn't have to revolve around the craziness of casting *Continental* Goddam *Divide*.

It was time for Belushi and Bernie Brillstein to pull a power play of their own. Sure, it would have been great to get Spielberg, Universal was informed – not that he'd done much with John in *1941* – but there were plenty of other directors in town who would kill for the chance to take over *Continental Divide*. Directors, moreover, who were a damn sight more comfortable with comedy than Spielberg. And dig this, if John doesn't get the role, Universal can kiss goodbye for ever to the comedian.

It boiled down to *Jaws* and *Close Encounters* in one corner; *Animal House* in the other. Universal listened. And hired Michael Apted to direct *Continental Divide*, Blair Brown to co-star with Belushi. Spielberg? He was paid $100,000 to back off.

That Belushi bent every known rule on screen enabled many to identify with him. Maybe it was the delusion that he could continue the antics in real life that helped destroy him. 'Overall, I could have been more involved in John's life,' Spielberg admitted. 'He reached out. But I felt that he would *consume* me. I am a control freak and want to deal on *my* terms, *my* hours. His life-style was so opposite of mine. I liked him, and there is a tear in my throat about John. Always will be.'

As if to confound any cynics who mistakenly saw her pairing-up with Spielberg as any kind of a career move, Amy Irving chose to go her own way. Soon after her return from Texas and *Honeysuckle Rose*, there was a temporary change of mind. Yes, her fiancé was informed, she would play opposite Harrison Ford in *Raiders of the Lost Ark*. The notion lasted until the middle of a three-week trip to Japan the couple undertook in January 1980. They left amidst talk of marriage, with Irving predicting she'd be pregnant by April. Instead, she broke off their engagement after a stand-up fight in the land of cherry blossom and returned home alone.

According to a diplomatic close friend, 'There was an awakening of sorts and they realised they weren't meant for each other.' *Raiders of the Lost Ark*? Forget it. Now Irving vowed that her career would remain hers alone. Her life too, at least as far as Spielberg was concerned.

Even Spielberg's pals who liked Irving felt a deep sense of relief even as they mimed sympathetic epithets. Since they had never seen the relationship as anything less than turbulent, her exit had to be good news, if not in the short term, then certainly for Spielberg's long-term peace of mind. He needed someone to fall in with his every whim, someone he could bend to his will and be his fun companion, someone who would subjugate her career for the greater good. His, of course.

Irving was never going to fill that bill.

# 12

# Castles in the Sand

*'With every film I find out a little more about myself.'*

STEVEN SPIELBERG

*'A director can't just say he's going to make the best film possible. He's got to work for a price.'*

GEORGE LUCAS

*After the many months spent planning and shooting* Close Encounters of the Third Kind *Spielberg was weary. Inspired but tired, and desperately in need of a break. George Lucas's suggestion of a vacation in Hawaii came out of the blue. Sitting on a beach, watching the waves and soaking in the rays provided living proof that a time and a place for everything exists, even in Spielberg's hectic schedule. After his smash hit with* American Graffiti *– all but disowned by the muckety-mucks at Universal before its release – Lucas was facing another depressing situation with the sci-fi follow-up he had unexpectedly chosen,* Star Wars. *Oh sure, Twentieth Century-Fox and Alan Ladd Jr were making bravely enthusiastic noises, yet the silence from the normally frenetic Hollywood buzz-industry was deafening. And a mere middling success was so much less than what Lucas had set out to achieve. Now even that seemed beyond his grasp. Good friends who had seen the movie were down on it. 'Oh, jeez, it's too bad, George, I really feel sorry for you. Better luck next time' had been a typical reaction. Spielberg had sat and listened to the trailer being booed at a screening of Fellini's* Amarcord, *and although this was hardly Lucas's intended audience, it had made him cringe in his seat. All in all, Lucas simply didn't want to be around when* Star Wars *opened. Hawaii seemed like a good place to be instead, especially if his pal Spielberg were there to hold his hand, congratulate – or, much more likely, to commiserate.*

*During a rambling conversation on what paths their careers might have followed if they'd chosen differently, Spielberg recalled at one time volunteering to join the James Bond franchise after* The Sugarland

Express. *When the chuckles died down, Lucas leaned forward conspiratorially. 'I've got something up my sleeve even better than James Bond. Have you ever herd of the Lost Ark of the Covenant?'*

*Spielberg, his mind still back in Burbank cutting* CE3K, *sipped his Dr Pepper contemplatively before replying, 'Noah's Ark?'*

*'No, no, no, no, not Noah's Ark,' Lucas spluttered. 'The Ark of the Covenant contains the Ten Commandments that were brought down from Mount Herob by Moses.'*

*'Oh.'*

*Lucas's idea, it swiftly transpired, was based on earlier conversations with director Philip Kaufman. It involved a 1936 movie-serial type archaeologist-cum-adventurer in a hunt for the Ark, racing against time to prevent Adolf Hitler – whom Kaufman was aware had been highly superstitious and into astrology – from getting there first, enabling him to gain the upper hand in his quest for world domination. Lucas's inspiration was in the* Adventure Theater *television shows of his youth, and reaching further back, those thirties serials.*

*Spielberg's mind spun back to his boyhood in Phoenix and the revival movie house that showed the old weekly cliffhangers. The memories came flooding back – cartoons first, then two feature films, a serial sandwiched between, masterworks like* Tailspin Tommy, Lash LaRue, The Masked Marvel, Commander Cody, Flash Gordon *and* Spy Smasher. *Boy, they were great . . . weren't they?*

*The day after their beach-side conversation, which climaxed with Lucas constructing an enormous sandcastle, an extraordinary phenomenon took place all across America. It was the day* Star Wars *opened. Lines had formed hours before the first show. Lucas was telephoned the grosses while having dinner with Spielberg. He actually* smiled *for the first time since his arrival in Hawaii.*

Indiana Jones *and* Raiders of the Lost Ark *would have to wait their turn as Lucas turned his attention to an immediate* Star Wars *sequel, while Spielberg began work on* 1941.

Depressed after the high-budget failure of *1941*, as well as the disappointing outcome of *I Wanna Hold Your Hand*, the initial Zemeckis/Gale collaboration he'd backed, Spielberg took a call from Paddy Chayevsky. It seemed that he had just had director Arthur Penn fired from *Altered States* and was seeking someone to take over the troubled production. Much as Spielberg admired Chayevsky's work – he'd been a big fan from *Marty* through to *Network* and *The Hospital* – he declined after lunching with the writer. Perhaps the movie's theme of spiritual, mental and physical deprivation reminded him too much of the entire *1941* process he'd just undergone. More likely, he wasn't ready to tackle such a controversial subject.

Instead, Spielberg finally got together in 1980 with George Lucas to develop the character of archaeologist-cum-adventurer Indiana Jones in *Raiders of the Lost Ark*. Their first organised meeting to kick the subject around took place in Lucas's cramped little office across Lankershim Boulevard from Universal. Spielberg's first reaction to the lead character's name was, '*Indiana*? George, that's the name of your *dog*!!' Later, to get them in the mood, Spielberg had Universal delve into their archives and dig up *Don Winslow of the Navy*.

As he and Lucas watched all fifteen episodes, hoping to rekindle that first fine careless rapture, they found themselves bored stupid instead, all their roseate memories rapidly fading. Weren't they great? Uh . . . not really, they had to admit, in the final analysis. The acting was *so* wooden. The plots were *so* ridiculous. The scripts were a *joke*.

Although he had already agreed to go ahead, the question uppermost in Spielberg's mind as he left Universal's screening room was, 'How can I get out of this?' Even Lucas had to concede, 'These things sure don't hold up twenty-five years later.' Anything remotely like a reproduction of what they had just endured was quickly ruled out of the question. Instead, they would create an original movie, albeit with a tip of the fedora to Don, Tommy, Cody, Flash and all the rest of the cardboard heroes they had cheered on so uncritically as kids.

Having already met Lawrence Kasdan through *Continental Divide*, Spielberg talked him up as a possibility for *Raiders* and arranged an introduction to Lucas. When a chord was struck between the two, Lucas laid down the precise formula for the writer: sixty two-page scenes, six dramatic situations for the hero.

For Lucas the character and situations had to be played dead straight, emulating his *Star Wars* formula, without mocking the genre in any way. Knowing winks were out. Spielberg saw 'Indy' (Kasdan's irreverent abbreviation) as the dishevelled Bogart character in *Treasure of the Sierra Madre*, while Lucas had a vision of a suave sophisticate in between archaeological digs. And he had one important stipulation. His morals had to be several notches above those of Han Solo in *Star Wars*.

Five consecutive nine-hour days were spent as Lucas, Spielberg and Kasdan, locked in together, paced the floor and acted out their ideas for plot and situations. Whoever shouted loudest held the floor as all their pent-up, wet movie dreams coalesced. Finally Philip Kaufman, Lucas's original story partner, was called in for 'additional embellishments'.

Securing their first choice of Tom Selleck for the lead lay in the hands of CBS-TV, since they had Universal's pilot for *Magnum P.I.* in the can, and held the option on future episodes. Selleck's availability for CBS's projected series suddenly became a top priority. On its own Universal would probably have played ball with Spielberg and Lucas. The network, hearing of the big-time interest being expressed in Selleck, dug their heels in and nixed Selleck's big-screen chance.

After a multitude of other hopefuls had been looked at, Harrison Ford's 'grizzled irrepressibility' made him a natural choice for Spielberg. This meant Lucas swallowing some of his straight-arrow preconceptions. (Ford's acerbic initial reaction to the buttoned-up Lucas and his first goody-goody concept: 'George, the man's a *grave robber!*')

The main reason Ford had been so low on the list of potential 'Indys' had nothing to do with Spielberg, everything to do with Lucas's desire not to hire *any* of his *Star Wars* stalwarts, in case, his reasoning ran, the audience got confused. It was the same odd attitude he had adopted after *American Graffiti*, while casting *Star Wars*. Having heard that Lucas wanted a completely fresh batch of faces for his 'science-fiction movie', Ford hadn't even bothered putting himself forward. Instead, feeling that his career had stalled, he'd put his acting career on hold after Francis Coppola's *The Conversation*. He'd turned to carpentry, first to fix up his falling-down family home in the Hollywood Hills, then to undertaking outside work to justify the high cost of the tool kit he'd acquired.

Working away at a portico entrance in Coppola's Zoetrope Studios one day, he'd watched as George Lucas and Richard Dreyfuss strolled into the office. Hey, wait a minute, Dreyfuss had been in *Graffiti* too, what was going on? Lucas said hello, and would he like to read opposite all the actors he was testing for roles in *Star Wars*, purely to help him out? So convincing was his Han Solo opposite all the would-be Luke Skywalkers and Princess Leias who turned up – Amy Irving among them – that Lucas cast him, much to Ford's surprise. Since *Star Wars*, Ford had struggled to establish himself outside that series. None of *Heroes, Force Ten from Navarone, Hanover Street* or *The 'Frisco Kid* had achieved that goal. *Raiders of the Lost Ark* would change all that, and provide Ford, as well as Spielberg and Lucas, with a brand-new franchise.

If there was one thing more important to Lucas than *Raiders of the Lost Ark* – The Movie, it was *Raiders of the Lost Ark* – The Deal. His one-man-against-the-Hollywood-system was about to reach its double-barrelled apotheosis as he met with Spielberg to hammer out their joint demands. 'We're supposed to be creative people,' was his rationale to his somewhat disbelieving partner, 'so come on, let's make a *creative deal*. Let's go for a deal *that will make history*.' (Lucas, a few years later, on the subject of the LA establishment: 'Hollywood doesn't care about films. They live to make deals.' Stifle that laughter.)

Lucas's terms were enough to make any studio head blanch, let alone Spielberg. And that's exactly what they did. Despite the lure of a movie from the men who had jointly brought forth *American Graffiti, Jaws, Star Wars, Close Encounters of the Third Kind* and *The Empire Strikes Back*, their proposal was turned down by every studio in town. Bar one.

Here's why: to get the movie, the backing studio had to put up the entire negative cost of $20 million. There would be no distribution fee for the studio (generally around thirty-five per cent, taken off the gross rentals) and no interest charge (normally twenty per cent) levied on the $20 million put up. After the negative cost was recouped by the studio, there would be a 60/40 split between Lucas and the studio up to $50 million in rentals, a 50/50 split up to $100 million, a 40/60 split thereafter.

How about Spielberg? He would be well taken care of too, though not quite on the same scale as Lucas. After recoupment, but before any division of the gross rentals between Lucas and the studio, Spielberg would collect ten per cent up to a take of $40 million; for anything over $40 million, again before any division, this would be increased to fifteen per cent. These were the terms Lucas handed to his lawyer, Thomas Pollock, with instructions that they were not negotiable. With Lucas alone, it might have flown. With free-spending Spielberg along, it crash-landed. Even at Universal.

Only one studio head, Paramount's Michael Eisner, was even prepared to talk. Gangly Eisner and the diminutive, bespectacled deputy he referred to as his 'golden retriever', Jeffrey Katzenberg, were high on *Raiders*, and determined to land the project. Lurking in the background through all the negotiations was their boss Barry Diller, late of ABC and *Movie of the Week*, champion of Spielberg's *Duel*. Left to himself on this occasion, he too would have passed. But his boys were so keen . . .

Knowing that his was the only game in town, Eisner squeezed a distribution fee, an overhead percentage *and* a partial recoupment of their marketing costs for Paramount. Okay, it was way below what the studio normally expected, but it was better than Lucas's punitive first demand. And the split changed on a sliding scale. Now, if *Raiders* took $40 million, Lucas would collect $11.2 million (the sum including his $4 million producer's fee). Spielberg would get $3.5 million (including his $1.5 million director's fee).

108

At gross rentals of $100 million Lucas would get $36 million; Spielberg $12.5 million; the studio, with earlier profits eaten up by cost of prints and their share marketing, would get $26 million. While it was true that only three movies up until then had exceeded $100 million in gross rentals (over $200 million at the box-office) it was also incontrovertibly true that all three had emanated from either Spielberg or Lucas.

Catching the distinct scent of the sweetest aroma of all to a studio, the possibility of a dripping roast in the succulent shape of a franchise, the canny Eisner secured rights, not merely options, to sequels. Eisner was also well aware of the second fortune Lucas had made on *Star Wars* – The Merchandise. Maybe Indiana Jones didn't offer quite the same opportunity, maybe he did. Who knew? Whatever, Paramount would have a share of that bounty too. The studio had turned away *Star Wars* and was not about to make a similar mistake.

There was only one tiny but significant catch with Eisner's counter-deal. If the budget of $20 million was exceeded, there was a stiff penalty clause – any excess would be made up by Spielberg and Lucas personally. Fond as Lucas was of his partner, this spooked him. After all, no budget of Spielberg's since *The Sugarland Express* had been regarded as sacred, and that, he knew, was why their original terms had been turned down by Universal, Columbia and Twentieth Century-Fox – fear of the big-spending half of the partnership. And Lucas still bore the scars from his experience on *The Empire Strikes Back*, where director Irvin Kershner, over budget and out of time, had pushed him to the edge of personal bankruptcy. He vowed there would be no repeat of that scenario.

Frank Marshall, who had come to Spielberg as a refugee from Peter Bogdanovich's camp when that director's star began to wane, found himself signed to act as line producer on *Raiders of the Lost Ark*. An ex-political science major at UCLA and the son of Jack Marshall, the film scorer, jazz arranger and record producer, Marshall had first met Bogdanovich in 1967 at a birthday party held at director John Ford's house for his daughter. Bogdanovich was present because of a documentary he was making on Ford, Marshall courtesy of the fact that his father had scored two of Ford's pictures.

Bogdanovich and his wife, the effervescent Polly Platt, had taken Marshall under their wing, starting as gofer on *Targets*, progressing by stages through *The Last Picture Show*, *What's Up Doc?* and *Paper Moon*. He'd stayed on after their marriage had broken up, working with Bogdanovich and his new lady Cybill Shepherd on *Daisy Miller* (meeting Spielberg for the first time in Rome in the process)

109

and *At long Last Love*, sticking with the director when Shepherd was forbidden by David Begelman to appear in *Nickelodeon* after the failure of their last two collaborations. By this time political science had long since been regarded as something to fall back on for Marshall, if the worst came to the worst.

Through the Bogdanovich/Platt connection he was drafted in to line produce Orson Welles's on-again, off-again *The Other Side of the Wind*, followed by Scorsese's documentary on The Band, *The Last Waltz*. With Bogdanovich's activities temporarily on hold, he teamed up with director Walter Hill to associate-produce *The Driver*, then to executive-produce *The Warriors*. Line, associate, executive? In Marshall's case it was all part of the learning process leading to his ultimate goal of directing, an ambition Spielberg would help him achieve in the fullness of time. Meantime, having the strapping, handsome Marshall around at his beck and call gave Spielberg the same high he'd experienced after recruiting the school jock for his home movie.

Another trusted lieutenant of Spielberg's was Kathleen Kennedy. Raised in Northern California, Kennedy had graduated from San Diego State University in 1975 with a degree in telecommunications and film, her early nursing ambitions pragmatically forgotten. At NBC affiliate KCST-TV, Kennedy served her apprenticeship as camera operator, video editor, floor director and news commentator before emerging with her own talk show, *You're On*.

While *1941* was in production, Kennedy was alerted by her roommate, Mary Ellen Trainor, that Spielberg was looking for secretarial help. It wasn't so much the job, but what it might lead to, that spurred her to seek the position. Her humble first credit was as 'production assistant' on *1941*. 'I wanted to know everything,' says Kennedy about her 'apprenticeship' with Spielberg. 'If Steven took a meeting, I went into the meeting. I didn't wait to be asked. I figured the worst that could happen was I'd be thrown out. I felt comfortable voicing my opinion. When you're Steven Spielberg, you need to have someone around who can do that.'

Although many considered her constant dancing attendance on her boss as just a tad excessive, Kennedy's approach paid off. One day Spielberg asked that she 'pay attention to what goes on with *Raiders*'. The reason? 'Because you're going to produce my next film.'

Kennedy's Irish heritage is apt to sneak through the charm from time to time. She can be abrasive, usually when she feels she is being shortchanged in terms of either time, money or effort. Back then her concern was to cocoon Spielberg from everyday concerns that might distract him. 'Our titles don't mean anything,' she would claim of her relationship with Spielberg and Marshall. 'We like to think of ourselves as one little family. We do everything together.'

Kennedy has been more forthcoming than most in offering insight into the way Spielberg interacts with his associates and acquaintances. 'Steven has trouble with a level of intimacy,' she once claimed. 'He gets close to people to a point, and then it begins to break down, because I don't think he is always comfortable communicating his feelings. His inability to trust very many people creates a certain amount of personal loneliness for him. But I also think it comes from just wanting to be by himself and be close to some creative, inanimate world he can live within, rather than deal with the real world and real people. I've sometimes witnessed him doing this thing: I see him withdrawing, and he's going into a place where he's more comfortable. He goes to that place, and it is completely devoid of other people and other pressures. It's almost Zen-like. And he comes out with extraordinary things. He goes there just like a monk. And he doesn't even know what it is.'

The chemistry between Kennedy and Marshall was good from the start, leading to much more than their merely working together. As their romance developed, they decided to keep it a secret from Spielberg. Just as surely as he might well approve, they reasoned, he might also turn around and disapprove. If that happened, where would that leave their careers? Their concern was not as far-fetched as it might sound. Spielberg had been known to cut associates dead if they displeased him, or showed any initiative of their own – like going out and casting their lot elsewhere. When one aide told Spielberg's mother that she had tendered her resignation, Leah had only one question as she smilingly searched the girl's features: 'And have you ceased to exist yet?'

Finally, it got to the point where the lovebirds felt they had to tell Spielberg. Imagine their relief when he beamed his approval. There were other relationships that interwove in the couple's lives. Marshall's best friend was Spielberg's protégé Robert Zemeckis, who was soon to marry Kennedy's ex-roommate, Mary Ellen Trainor. Along the way, it did no harm to the prospects of all concerned that Marshall's former college roommate was Michael Ovitz, boss of Hollywood's most powerful agency, CAA.

With his engagement to Amy Irving broken off soon after the opening of *1941*, both events tended to be lumped together in Spielberg's mind. 'It's almost a good thing that everything happened at once and I got it over with,' friends were told. Those who knew him best sensed that the end of the affair had left him with the worst emotional scars since the break-up of his parents, as well as

111

being wary and suspicious of all women. Spielberg was glad to leave all comfortable trappings and familiar settings behind and lose himself in *Raiders*. 'It's not a bad time for me to be out of the country,' he acknowledged. 'A change of scene seems in order.' The movie was a providential, tailor-made escape.

Lucas had drawn up a tight schedule of eighty-five days with four locations set – in Tunisia, Hawaii, the northern French coastal city of La Rochelle and at Britain's Elstree Studios. Grabbing the bit between his teeth, determined to put the past behind him and show his friend he could do it when he tried, and aided by the incredibly elaborate storyboards he'd prepared, Spielberg took great delight in not only sticking to the schedule, but shaving days off as he went along. He acknowledges that he never worked so hard in his life. Contrarily, many of the compromises he came up with worked to a scene's advantage, the alternative, speedier arrangement often proving 'fresher and better for the movie'.

Starting with what he called a 'David Lean epic on paper', Spielberg ruthlessly cut out seventy per cent of all the shots, paring right down to the bones of the story. All of the 'wonderful moments and shadows and dolly shots and coverage' were feasted on and dwelt over before, like 'some kind of psychotic slasher', he ripped the bulk of them out, ending up with no more than ten set-ups a day to shoot with interior lighting, and a maximum of twenty shots a day that depended on exterior sunlight. As he describes it: 'I orgasmed in the first two months of my preparation, then I essentially tore it up and just told the story.' Within each shot, however, he compensated by packing in as much action, style and humour as the scene could hold. He saw it as the kind of picture old Hollywood journeymen like Sam Wood, Victor Fleming, John Farrow or Michael Curtiz would have turned out, made to order, no fancy frills, yet with every button punched.

Whenever Spielberg looked as if he was going off at a tangent, Lucas put his foot down. In one scene Spielberg wanted to give the head German, Toht (Ronald Lacey), a wooden arm, into which he attaches a banana clip and fires through one of his fingers. When his sleeve falls away, a gun is revealed where his right arm used to be; he's lost it, per Spielberg, in 'some kind of weird, Hitlerian experiment'. That would put their show into a different category, Lucas protested, something between *Star Wars* and James Bond, not to mention horror movies. The gunfight remained, the gimmick was dropped.

Lucas kept up the pressure for a utilitarian approach, eschewing the technological angles Spielberg kept coming up with. One scene Spielberg envisioned – which would certainly have been stunning –

was the discovery by the hero of a secret hangar chock-full of fighter planes, clearly a half-century ahead of anything known in the thirties, developed by a Von Braun-type genius, their gleaming sides emblazoned with swastikas and iron crosses. 'No', Lucas again decreed. Yes, audiences would gasp, he agreed, then go next door, take in the new Bond movie, and gasp just as much. 'You're right,' Spielberg conceded.

Lucas's theory throughout was to go for a kind of retro-technology, the antithesis of what Spielberg often came up with. 'We must have an old "Flying Wing" and a truck chase in the film,' he urged. Lucas's 'Flying Wing' never actually flew, although it was apparently aerodynamic, but it certainly taxied and turned on its axis convincingly, as well as contributing dramatically to a spectacular chase. Spielberg's favourite scene was where Marion (Karen Allen, replacing Debra Winger, his first choice after Irving) tries to get Rene Belloq (Paul Freeman) soused and is drunk under the table herself. 'I'm from the Al Pacino school of acting,' Allen, direct from her stint with the actor in *Cruising*, had tongue-in-cheek informed Spielberg at the outset. 'You're going to get introduced to the Sam Peckinpah school of action,' he had countered.

Sure enough, Allen next found herself involved with 7,500 reptiles assembled for the snake pit encounter. Spielberg almost blew all the shooting days he'd saved until a handler was found to deal with the squirming mass. Although Spielberg himself had no fear of the creatures – bugs were a different matter entirely – he saw that many of the crew did, high rubber boots and reinforced canvas trousers and jackets notwithstanding. Oddly enough, Karen Allen seemed relatively unaffected. Too much so, Spielberg considered. Her screams of terror signally failed to convince. Maybe if . . .

The sadist in Spielberg was about to come out to play. Dropping a few live snakes on the unsuspecting actress's head did the trick. *Now* her screams of terror were for real! Oh, there was no need to worry, not with plenty of anti-snakebite serum imported from India, together with a doctor standing by. Until, that is, someone checked and found the serum had passed its sell-by date.

To keep things moving, and lighten just a little the considerable load Spielberg was carrying, the second unit shot much of the truck chase, while Frank Marshall found himself entrusted with footage of the monkey running away, crouching in baskets, vaulting over Arabs.

The economical Lucas went on to take his emulation of old serials literally, making shameless use of footage from other movies, like a shot of a DC3 flying in over the Himalayas that was lifted from Columbia's *Lost Horizon* remake, and a 1930s' street scene from

113

Universal's *The Hindenberg*. A planned 200-acre site of the archaeological dig at Tunisia, Lucas's old stamping ground from *Star Wars*, was reduced to seventy acres, saving $750,000 in extras, cranes, period vehicles and sets.

In describing Spielberg as a master filmmaker, George Lucas singles out in particular, 'master of invention, master of necessity'. He has in mind the *Raiders'* scene showing a North African tribesman menacing Indy, elaborately flashing his sword as a prelude to a savage fight with the hero. Harrison Ford was in the fourth week of a truly diabolical case of the runs as he awaited instructions from Spielberg as to how he should react. Spielberg wanted the whole nine yards, a full-scale battle to the death that would be one of the highlights of the picture.

'Steven, how long is this going to take?' Ford asked.

'The rest of the day,' Spielberg replied.

'I'm too sick. I can't go on disappearing to the bathroom every five minutes like this. Let's get it over in an hour so I can get back to my hotel.'

'The only way I can shoot this scene in an hour is if Indie just takes out his gun and shoots the guy.'

'Fine. Let's just shoot the fucker.'

Even as Spielberg shook his head, he was taking in the laughter from the crew. Hey, maybe that *was* the answer . . . The 'master of necessity' went ahead and filmed what became a favourite audience scene.

Never seen outside without sunglasses to protect him from the glare of the sun, Spielberg took to wearing them indoors on many occasions as well. An affectation? No. He found he was becoming increasingly sensitive to any bright light.

Back in Hollywood the prophets of doom were hard at work, predicting that Spielberg would never finish the picture, let alone on time. Lucas would take over, push Spielberg aside, grab the reins. Little did they know that Spielberg had secretly shaved twelve days off the schedule.

Editor Michael Kahn found that he had George Lucas to contend with as well as Spielberg. 'When you work with the Spielbergs and the Lucases, anything goes,' he maintains. 'Anything that works, that is. If I say to Steven, "I can't do it", he's got to have every confidence in me to know that if *I* can't do it, *nobody* can do it. Because, should George or Steven go in and make it work where you can't, you've lost all credibility. They won't trust you again.'

Kahn says that the key to working with Spielberg comes down to the word 'feeling', that the most valid thing he can say to his director

114

is 'It doesn't *feel* right': 'When Steven sees a scene, he knows right away how he feels about it. And when he says to me, "I don't know if it feels right", we discuss it, I sense his input, and we communicate on that level.'

In finishing *Raiders* within the $20 million laid down, the considerable downside of Eisner's terms had been avoided. The extraordinary upside would be the largest profit margin in Hollywood history for Lucas and Spielberg when the movie was released.

With *Raiders* about to open, Spielberg appeared relatively detached from the excitement and hoopla. 'Too much time seemed to elapse between when I agreed to do it and when I actually started,' he explained. 'I wanted to move on to smaller, more personal projects. It's no reflection on the quality of the work; that's just where I was in my career and in my life. Now that I'm through, I'm glad I did it. *Raiders* was a film to clean out my system, blow the saliva out of my mouthpiece.' As he had on *Jaws*, he pointed out that he could have made *Raiders – The Art-House Edition*. 'I could have done it as a neo-Brechtian *film noir*, with multiple shadows out of Carol Reed or Orson Welles, like *The Third Man* and *Touch of Evil*. But then I realised that what could be a turn-on for me could wreck a gravy-train movie. Why *impose* production values, visual noise? I just worked to tell the story. But I was *happy* making this movie, largely because of George Lucas and Harrison Ford. Both were full-time collaborators.'

Lucas had his answer to several critical charges of 'juvenilia' in *Raiders*. 'Spielberg and I both see movies through youngsters' eyes,' he claimed. 'I don't make intelligent movies.' For someone who had started off his career with the introverted *THX 1138*, it was quite a turnaround. Although that movie had directly expressed Lucas's true feelings about the world, he realised that it had failed to find an audience because people already *know* how grim life can be, they don't need to shell out hard-earned dollars to be reminded. Art, he declared, was for others: 'Francis Coppola likes to think of film as art. I don't take it that seriously. Art is for someone to figure out a hundred years from now.' Lucas had learned the same lesson Spielberg had absorbed after *Sugarland*'s flop.

Critics also expressed concern at *Raiders*' non-stop parade of asps and cobras, red-hot pokers and melting skulls, with sixty deaths graphically portrayed by gun, poison, propellor blade, knife and act of God. Questions were raised about the PG certificate cavalierly handed out, many arguing that had *Raiders* been an independent film or foreign import, rather than a major studio release, the ratings board would not have been nearly as accommodating.

115

'There's some strong stuff in it,' Lucas acknowledged. 'I feel some responsibility to the kids who'll see it because my name is on it, and Harrison's and Steven's. But I never wanted to be like Disney, and I don't want to let myself get painted into a corner.' He agreed that the concepts in *Raiders* were 'extremely violent', but defended them on the basis that 'the treatment was not repulsive'.

So who was to blame for pushing the mayhem envelope? According to Lucas: 'Steven got carried away in a couple of places, but we cut back on the blood.'

Spielberg had a different story to tell. 'Even though George is a benign, magnanimous individual, he likes movies with excitement, and that often calls for close calls, constant jeopardy. George could definitely "out-violence" me. My violence is more psychological. To me, the moments that are exciting are the ones that occur just before the trigger is pulled. The threat is more horrific than the shot. In *Duel*, what's scary is this big truck bearing down on Dennis Weaver's Valiant. The only blood you see is when Weaver bites his lip. *Raiders* is more in George's vein. It's the only film of mine in which *scores* of people are violently eliminated. But George's violence is kids' violence, it's intentionally scary-funny. And the villains in *Raiders* are *arch*-villains.'

Far from being turned off, the public embraced *Raiders*, making it the top US grosser of 1981 with $242 million at the box-office. Inevitably, the demand for a sequel became overwhelming. Not least from the delighted Paramount Pictures team of Diller, Eisner and Katzenberg.

Spielberg was puzzled. Although he'd hailed European critics back when they were praising *Duel*, *The Sugarland Express*, and to a lesser extent *Jaws*, they'd been disappointingly harsh, in relative terms, on every movie he'd made since. Oh, the tabloids were still on his side – with the exception of *1941*, which nobody had liked – but it hurt that the paens of praise were no longer automatic from the highbrow press. Some were even, God forbid, writing him off as someone who had peaked early. Back in the US, an article in *Time* magazine also incensed him. It wasn't that Richard Schickel was critical of *Raiders of the Lost Ark*, simply that he was high on praise for what he described as 'a producer's film'. Spielberg felt that his contribution had been unfairly downgraded. And went to surprising lengths to attack the writer.

A 'source close to Spielberg', widely considered the ever-voluble Kathleen Kennedy, was quoted as saying, 'The piece over-emphasised George's contribution to what was a close collaboration with Steven. He has a right to be upset that *Time* had Schickel do this story.' Meaning someone other than Schickel should have been assigned? Emphatically, according to the Spielberg camp, for hadn't Schickel made a documentary for Lucas in 1980, and therefore become unfairly biased in favour of his ex-employer? The message from Spielberg, the alleged youthful innocent, was clear: Don't throw sand in my face, and don't step on my blue suede shoes!

Schickel was at a loss to understand Spielberg's huff, pointing out that he had made eighteen TV documentaries without once feeling beholden to whoever had last paid his salary. And that had remained the case with Lucas.

The whole storm in a tea-cup quickly blew over, but not before industry fingers were wagged at Spielberg: 'Petty, petty!'

# 13

## Snake-Oil Salesman

*'There are only two things that I am a bully about – where
to put the camera and where to make the splice. Otherwise,
I think I'm very loose as a director and open to anybody's
ideas. I think I'm able to digest everything everybody else
thinks, and then come up with my own choices.'*

*'I really have no formula or method. When I'm caught
with my pants down, and I wish I had a formula, that's
when I have the most fun – in the editing room. Directing
is not my happiest time.'*

STEVEN SPIELBERG

*That Spielberg's maternal grandmother had been in failing health for
some time took little away from the shock of the 2 am news relayed from
the convalescent home in Phoenix to her daughter in Los Angeles: 'Your
mother has passed away.'*

*An even greater shock followed three hours later in a second phone
call.*

*Inexplicably, incredibly, Leah's dead mother was on the line – and
there was fear as well as pleading in her voice. 'Help me,' she moaned, her
voice echoing as from a great distance mere geographic miles could not
explain. 'He's coming to get me! He'll be here at any minute! I'm terrified!!'*

*Leah, her eyes swollen from hours of barely controlled weeping, stared
at the phone as her mind attempted to grapple with what she was hearing. Her mother was calling from beyond the grave?! She jerked her
head from side to side as bafflement was added to terrible grief. It
couldn't be! Her mind must be playing tricks. It was beyond reason, it
was – her rational mind struggled to keep its hold – a sick prankster
playing a joke.*

*'Please don't scare me like that,' she cried. And hung up.*

*Later that morning, out of the blue, a long-lost relative presented*

*himself at Leah's front door. It took several minutes and considerable*
*prompting before she recognised the resemblance from old photographs. It*
*was her uncle, her mother's brother. He'd been completely out of touch for*
*decades since running away from home as a boy to join the circus. Leah's*
*blood ran cold even as she ushered him into the house. All her life her*
*mother had been deathly afraid of her brother, opening up only on rare*
*occasions to recall how he would terrorise her as a child. Now some*
*preternatural instinct had drawn him back on this very morning . . .*

*Her mother's words echoed once more down the measureless canyons*
*of space and time: 'Help me! He's coming to get me! He'll be here at any*
*minute! I'm* terrified!!'

The origin of *Poltergeist* lay in Spielberg's desire to make a 'real
scary ghost story'. He saw movies with Victorian Gothic settings like
*The Uninvited, The Haunting* and *The Innocents*, well crafted though
they were, as 'the antithesis of what was scary'. Instead, he would set
his tale in a typical 800-home tract in the Southwest among everyday, nine-to-five accountants, grocers and teachers, people plugged
into and comfortable in the mainstream of life, the flip side of which
made them least able to deal with a supernatural invasion of their
cosy front parlours.

Apart from the 'haunted hotel' incident while on location for
*Sugarland Express*, and the spectral, inexplicable phone call from
beyond the grave to his mother, Spielberg did not have to look far
beyond his own imagination and childhood fears for inspiration –
the closet and the endless chasm that lay beyond, the monster that
had lain beneath his bed, silently waiting to devour him in its gaping maw the minute he fell asleep, the sinister clown doll that came
to life in the gap between eye-blinks, the phantom tree whose roots
reached to the very depths of hell . . .

Spielberg would be reunited on *Poltergeist* with studio head
David Begelman, 'made whole' again, temporarily, as studio head at
MGM/UA after the well-publicised Columbia scandal and the
community service he'd bluffed his way out of.

On the lookout for a beatific four-year-old for the juvenile lead of
'Little Carol Anne', Spielberg came across blonde Heather
O'Rourke lunching one day in MGM's commissary. His version of
the meeting: 'Who's the proud mother or agent of this child?' he
asked. Two hands immediately shot up, one belonging to the
mother, the other to the agent. Spielberg's memory was only partly
faulty. O'Rourke's mother Katherine was indeed on hand, but not
with her agent. With Heather's older sister Tammy instead. Maybe
that doesn't make for a slick enough story for his discovery of the
'They're heeere!' girl.

Spielberg chose twenty-year-old Dominique Dunne, daughter of novelist Dominick Dunne and Joan Didion, niece of author/screen-writer John Gregory Dunne, to play O'Rourke's older sister. Accidentally or on purpose, or a bit of both, in Oliver Robins he picked a younger model of himself to play the male juvenile lead.

When he refers to having 'written' the script for *Poltergeist* in five days, while still in post-production on *Raiders of the Lost Ark*, he concedes that he really means 'rewritten', since the project was commissioned by him as an original screenplay by Michael Grais and Mark Victor.

Here's how it pans out, per Spielberg: 'I actually wrote *Poltergeist*, but co-authored an earlier draft with Michael Grais and Mark Victor. I hired them to realise my original idea, but we were all involved in concert to dream up that first draft, and we all happily share credit.'

He amplified further to *Interview* magazine: 'When I wrote *Poltergeist*, when I *rewrote Poltergeist,* I had my whole office live in my house for five days. I wrote the film in five days, twenty pages a day. And I couldn't write alone, I knew I couldn't do it unless I had somebody to bullshit with and to tell funny stories with and to read the pages back. I really enjoy writing ten pages and saying, 'Everybody listen to this,' and I would read ten pages and they would ooh and ah and say, "That's scary." Or Frank Marshall would say, "No, that can be scarier," or, "That's not good enough," or Kathy Kennedy might say, "Why don't you do this?" I needed the presence, I needed all my little *Poltergeist* friends to be around me when I was writing.'

Spielberg's 'screenwriting' so far, apart from the story credit on *The Sugarland Express*, had amounted to sole writing credit on *CE3K*, leaving at least three others out in the cold. Now, on *Poltergeist* it was 'Screenplay by Steven Spielberg, Michael Grais, Mark Victor. From a story by Steven Spielberg'.

Curiously, it was the last time Spielberg would claim screenwriting credit on any picture. Why? Possibly because of the outcome of yet another battle waged on *Poltergeist*.

Since he was in simultaneous pre-production with *E.T.*, Spielberg hired Tobe Hooper to direct *Poltergeist*. He had first met Hooper in 1978 as an admirer of *The Texas Chainsaw Massacre*, the horror-fest the director had turned out on a $300,000 shoestring budget in six weeks. Meeting again in 1980, they'd discussed 'doing something' together.

*Poltergeist* was ready to roll in May 1981. This time, Hooper would be working with a budget thirty times greater than on

*Massacre,* with a reserve for special effects alone of $1.8 million for George Lucas's Industrial Light and Magic.

Producer Frank Marshall permitted himself a smile at the finished script he was handed, which seemed to him to be full of what he termed '$250,000 sentences' like 'All of a sudden the house explodes!' It was also riddled with grisly special effects, such as a parapsychologist having the skin of his face peel off in bloody lumps. Watching the dailies of that scene, Spielberg joked, 'I feel cheap!' Hooper's reaction, coming from the director of *Massacre,* was surprising. Maybe it had something to do with the enormous Italian lunch he had just consumed. He threw up.

Spielberg was very much around all through shooting – ostensibly as a humble line producer – but almost immediately, as Hooper, Marshall and the entire cast and crew were to discover, a lot more besides. Spielberg admits that the resulting 'situation' was 'frustrating for Tobe Hooper and frustrating for the actors, who were pretty torn by my presence and his every day on the set'. Still he denied that Hooper was merely hired as a 'decoy director' to circumvent union rules that would have frowned on Spielberg directing *Poltergeist* and preparing to shoot *E.T.* at virtually the same time. With rumours of dissent leaking daily from the set, a great deal of reading between the lines was required to get a sense of the day-to-day tensions that flared up.

'I don't know if it's better just to let speculation reign,' Spielberg declared once the movie was in the can. 'I think the film stands on its own as a really good movie without the controversy about who contributed what. It wasn't as smooth a sail as I would have liked originally, but what movie really is? All I'll say about my involvement as the line producer with Frank Marshall is that I designed the film; from the storyboards to post-production it's an overall design. I'm saying that I was the David O. Selznick of this movie. I won't go further out on a limb. I'll just say that I functioned in a very strong way. But if I had my choice to make another movie this way again, *forget it!*'

If he'd left it at that, it might have been possible to kill any future controversy. Instead, he chose to reopen the subject in a *Time* magazine article at the end of May 1982, just six weeks before *Poltergeist* was set to explode body parts at a cinema near you. Although Spielberg conceded that what he now termed 'my taking over' had less to do with 'Tobe's capabilities' than the fact he was 'bullish about my ideas', he'd have been far better keeping his mouth firmly shut.

MGM sold *Poltergeist* like the medicine man's snake-oil it was.

Trailers featured parapsychologists William Rol and Charles Tart, together with occult journalist D. Scott Rogo, solemnly pontificating on all manifestations supernatural. The studio's press kit contained an eleven-page document quoting leading quacks on the 'reality' of poltergeists, adding a list of 'notable' hauntings dating from AD 30 through 1968. The kit went on to claim that the cast and crew of the movie had undergone 'strange experiences' in their own lives, with testimonials from Jobeth Williams, Dominique Dunne, Beatrice Straight (a ghost had taken up residence in her Connecticut country house) – and Hooper (those following his dad's death, he claimed, had kick-started the movie in the first place).

Parapsychologist Thelma Moss, the real-life California-based 'ghostbuster' portrayed in the movie by Beatrice Straight, adamantly refused to buy MGM's snake-oil, no matter how cunningly packaged. It was one thing to make an out-and-out supernatural shocker, but to make spurious, po-faced claims for its authenticity, that was unacceptable. 'I'm not saying the things that take place in the movie couldn't happen,' she conceded, '*only that they haven't been recorded yet in history!* I just want to advise moviegoers now. Holes in closets don't lead to limbo; whirlpools don't steal children; trees don't swallow humans. For the most part, when I am called in professionally to observe a haunted house or one filled with ghosts, it's not the house that's crazy, it's the *people, they're* the freaks. I often advise psychoanalysis.'

*Poltergeist* was released one week before *E.T.* in July 1982, in what looked like an unstoppable Spielberg bonanza. *E.T.* certainly proved a bonanza on its own, but despite the healthy returns *Poltergeist* also enjoyed, Spielberg's collaboration with Tobe Hooper would provide the first of two bookends that would forever shadow and taint *E.T.*'s amazing success story.

The controversy over who did what on the *Poltergeist* set refused to go away. Following numerous complaints, Directors' Guild arbitrator Edward Mosk, on Hooper's behalf, sought restitution for Spielberg's remarks that he 'helped Hooper direct the film'. Also under fire was MGM for giving Spielberg a bigger credit on 2,000 *Poltergeist* trailers than Hooper ('A Steven Spielberg Production' in type *double* the size of 'A Tobe Hooper Film').

'To the extent that the trailer denigrates the role of the director,' the DGA's complaint ran, 'the director is damaged.' MGM was fined $15,000, payable to Hooper, and ordered to strike new trailers immediately in the New York and Los Angeles areas, with fresh prints all round for future engagements. Another, even more humiliating, part of the settlement required Spielberg to take out trade paper ads praising Hooper's direction. The result was a series of full-page announcements in the form of a letter from Spielberg to Hooper:

'Dear Tobe,
'Regrettably some of the press has misunderstood the rather unique, creative relationship which you and I shared throughout the making of *Poltergeist*.

I enjoyed your openness in allowing me, as a producer and a writer, a wide berth of creative involvement, just as I know you were happy with the freedom you had to direct *Poltergeist* so wonderfully.

Through the screenplay you accepted a vision of this very intense movie from the start, and as the director, you delivered the goods. You performed responsibly and professionally throughout, and I want to wish you great success on your next project.

Let's hope that *Poltergeist* brings as much pleasure to the general public as we experienced in our mutual effort.
Sincerely,
Steven Spielberg.'

That was fine, as far as it went. Until Kathleen Kennedy blew the gaffe on the whole crock of bullshit with her own, off-the-cuff explanation in a taped interview. Starting off by describing Hooper's contribution as 'minimal', she added, 'Tobe is a terrific low-budget, small-film kind of director, but he's not a Steven, and I think he got in over his head. He needs time to work, that's his basic style, but with the cost of movies today you don't have time to pat people on the back and say everything's going to be okay – all you have time for is to get the movie finished. At $50,000 a day you can't sit around and talk about it. And that's basically what happened.'

Columnist Rex Reed offered his own take on the ruckus: 'Every time Spielberg claims credit for himself in the plethora of publicity designed to inflate his ego beyond anything Orson Welles ever dreamed of, it hurts Hooper's chances of future employment. Through all this, Spielberg maintains the cagey demeanour of all genius kids who suddenly find themselves with $100 million in negotiable assets – never denying that Hooper directed *Poltergeist*, yet always giving the impression to interviewers that he did all the work himself, relegating Hooper to the position of vessel, observer and glorified errand boy.'

That, he might have added, went double for Kennedy's contribution. The perfect footnote to the whole brouhaha was Hooper's eventual claim that even the *original* idea for *Poltergeist* had been his, offered to Spielberg on a plate, and inspired by strange occurrences he had experienced – glasses breaking, knickknacks shattering, empty rocking chairs rocking – following his father's death.

Spielberg's *last* word arrived years later: 'Turmoil is essentially created by wanting to do it your way and having to go through procedures . . . That is why I will *never again* not direct a film I write.'

To put it more succinctly, *Poltergeist* and the acute embarrassment Spielberg suffered over those well-circulated trade ads – even though the dispute on this occasion was over who *directed* what, rather than *wrote* what – seemed to spell '*finis*' to his screenwriting forays, whether or not he was the director.

Apart from 'Story Credit', Spielberg the writer disappeared into a retirement that continues to this day.

Spielberg's visitor early in 1982 could scarcely believe his ears. Was his host actually going to pay for lunch? *An industry first?* Had he heard right as Spielberg stopped by Verna Field's table and asked, 'Verna, you got ten dollars?'

'Sure, Steven,' she replied, reaching into her purse and handing over the bill. After lunch the visitor watched with bated breath as the bill was placed on the table between them. Disconcertingly, Spielberg showed no sign of picking it up. After a while his guest picked it up, looked at it, put it back down. Eventually Spielberg too picked it up, still in mid-conversation. *And put it back down!*

Sighing, the visitor picked up the bill, paid, said his goodbyes and left. Wondering only what Spielberg had in mind for the ten bucks still in his pocket.

# 14

## The Alien Gardener

*'Any time I'm into a project, I immediately focus on the
antithesis of what I'm working on. So my reaction [to
Raiders of the Lost Ark] was to think of a very touching
and tender relationship between an extraterrestrial and an
eleven-year-old child who takes him in.'*

*'I hate crybabies, spoiled-brat actors who lock themselves
in their dressing rooms and won't come out and talk until
the director apologises. God knows, that's happened every
day in Hollywood. I'd rather hire a good actor and work
his tail off to be better than some pain-in-the-neck
superstar.'*

STEVEN SPIELBERG

*Spielberg had been absent from the set for only two days during the
entire* Poltergeist *shoot. Yes, it was back to Hawaii with his pal George
Lucas the day before the opening of* Raiders of the Lost Ark. *It had
worked with* Star Wars – *so maybe lightning would strike twice, especially with a little help from the construction of a second sandcastle.*

*Spielberg had stood at the back of the theatre during the first half of*
Raiders' *sneak preview, a complete nervous wreck. One minute it seemed
to be working just fine, the next minute he was not so sure. With previous movies there had been occasions when he was able to sit among the
audience and gauge their reaction, sense the waves of approval, enjoy
their enjoyment. Not with* Raiders. *This time, all he got was a flop
sweat.*

*Taking his cue from John Williams, he knew full well that* Raiders
*was pure popcorn. It was easy to digest, it didn't fill you up, it melted in
the mouth, and you could chow down on it endlessly. It was also, like*
Raiders, *enormously profitable. Its box-office bonanza was gratifying;
even more so were the 'Best Picture' and 'Best Director' Oscar nominations. This time Spielberg knew better than to get his hopes up. Rightly*

125

*so – for* Raiders *lost out to the Hugh Hudson-directed* Chariots of Fire *and to director Warren Beatty for* Reds. *If Spielberg was sore, he was not the only one. Hudson had a definite beef.* Chariots *was 'Best Picture', yet Warren Beatty was 'Best Director'? It seemed that Spielberg was not the only one suffering from Hollywood politics.*

In 1979 Spielberg had concocted a story he called *Night Skies* before turning it over to writer John Sayles for development. Ron Cobb, art director on John Carpenter's *Dark Star* and George Lucas's *Star Wars*, was set to direct for Spielberg, with extra-terrestrial creatures designed by Rick Baker. Despite Sayles valiantly reducing eleven proposed aliens down to five, Frank Price at Columbia (moved over from Universal-TV) decided to pass. The studio's research department claimed that the movie's appeal would be limited to children, and Price had another 'We are not alone-er' in the works with John Carpenter's *Starman*. Price still held on to the rights, for there was the small matter of development costs to be recovered before the project could be placed elsewhere. Spielberg and Baker then had a falling-out over costs, while Spielberg and Sayles differed on concept.

Spielberg had never been completely sold on Sayles's depiction of Scar, the alien leader, as a hostile force. Something cuter and cuddlier was more in line with his thinking. What if the 'little alien' got left behind and was stranded on Earth, alone and scared?

Years later the story came back to him during the Tunisia location of *Raiders of the Lost Ark*, first on a fairly uncomfortable car ride from Netta to Souse, then while scouring the desert for scorpions; Yes, what if—!

Hectic time though it was, surrounded by cast and crew of hundreds, measuring his daily progress against the tightly pre-set schedule, shaving a day here, a day there, Spielberg still found moments when he experienced the pangs of personal loneliness and isolation. The story of the displaced, lonely extra-terrestrial, never far from his mind, began to loom ever larger.

What he needed was someone to run it by. Harrison Ford was out of it, stricken with those infamous runs. 'What about Melissa?' Kathleen Kennedy suggested. Melissa Mathison, co-writer of *The Black Stallion* and *The Escape Artist*, was on hand as Ford's girl-friend while working on material of her own. She would prove an inspired choice, providing exactly the sympathetic ear required.

'It was like, when you were a kid and had grown out of dolls or teddy bears or Winnie the Pooh, you just wanted a little voice in your mind to talk to,' Spielberg explained. Then he began describing an imaginary creature, not too far removed from the friendly

126

aliens who stepped out of the mother ship for thirty seconds in *Close Encounters*. Mathison's reaction to his notion of young children offering succour and shelter to the creature from outer space was immediate and highly gratifying. She wept and agreed to drop the project she was on in order to write the script for what became *E.T. – The Extra-Terrestrial*.

After pitching ideas and character relationships back and forth during the remaining weeks of the shoot, Mathison – armed with a tape recorder – visited Spielberg during *Raiders'* editing process. Together they plotted *E.T.* out, scene by scene. Single mother. Dad run off to Mexico. Lonely, introverted son. Sassy sister. Friend from outer space. Her finished script was delivered ten weeks after the unit's return from location. Unsurprisingly after the enchanting first half of *Black Stallion*, she turned out to have exactly the innocent childlike vision Spielberg sought, best summed up by the reason she gave for concealing E.T. in a forest: 'A forest is *magical*. There are *elves* in forests.'

Whimsy such as this apart, Spielberg realised that in *E.T.* he was reacting to the most traumatic event ever in his life. No, not Amy Irving's departure.

The day his father walked out of the family home for ever.

With Kathleen Carey, a talent scout for Warners Music, Spielberg enjoyed his first meaningful relationship since Amy Irving. Following the break-up he had embarked on a whole series of affairs with nineteen and twenty-year-olds. ('They were all nice girls, but I was playing big brother', he maintains.) After moving up the age scale and dating twenty-four-year-old Valerie Bertinelli, veteran of the CBS soap, *One Day at a Time*, he'd been introduced to pretty, blonde Carey, a thirty-three-year-old divorcee. A major romance soon developed, one that both parties hoped would lead to something permanent.

Spielberg saw hope in a reversal of the usual situation in his relationships with women. 'Amy and I must have been together about a year and a half before we got to be friends,' he spelled out, 'but Kathleen and I were friends *before* we were lovers. That makes a real difference.'

Although she spent considerable time with him in Coldwater Canyon, and they shared most weekends at the Malibu beachhouse he'd acquired, Carey continued to keep a place of her own in Los Angeles. To draw her even closer, Spielberg persuaded her to leave Warners and join MCA's Backstreet Records label.

'We've just been so busy on our careers that we haven't dealt with each other on a marital basis,' he parried questions. 'But now we're thinking about it. Kathleen has taught me there's a life after movies.'

'Steven inspires me in my career,' Carey reciprocated, 'and I help him to be a more rounded person. He was always so busy working before he never had time for a real relationship. He needs friends, not people telling him how wonderful he is.'

Although Carey was certainly a refreshing change – she described 'his idea of exercise' as 'sitting on the beach eating Häagen-Dazs ice cream while I run a mile' – maybe she wasn't 'show-bizzy' enough to last. Maybe the still-insecure Spielberg *needed* those constant reminders of how 'wonderful' he was.

Rumours of a fling with Debra Winger around this time tended to dilute the lovey-dovey factor between him and Carey. Winger even agreed to play a tiny role in *E.T.* Look carefully, and you might recognise the feisty, unbilled actress, heavily disguised as the hatchet victim in the movie's Halloween sequence. Not only that, she was one of the 'voices' of E.T. According to Spielberg, this was the 'electronically distorted voice of an eighty-two-year-old woman in Sausalito'. What he neglected to mention was that Winger's voice was in the mix too. 'I recorded all E.T.'s lines,' she confirmed. 'I said "Elliooottt" and "E.T. phone home" and "Ouucchh!" I worked one day on the film.'

Spielberg's relationship with Winger had got off to a stormy start. He had originally wanted her for the role that went to Karen Allen in *Raiders of the Lost Ark* and was infuriated when she turned it down as offering 'no stretch'. 'He didn't speak to me for six months,' said Winger, 'but we got to be good friends.'

Sid Sheinberg's recollection of *E.T.*'s genesis begins with a dishevelled, bejeaned Spielberg arriving in his office. 'I want to talk to you about something,' he was informed. 'There's this script that's been in development at Columbia, but they don't really want to make it. Why don't you take it home and see if you like it? Maybe you can get it, and I'll make it for you.'

Sheinberg liked what he saw, an approach to Columbia's ex-Universal-TV chief Frank Price was made, terms were negotiated. *E.T.* was moved over to Universal, there was elation all round. After stopping off at Columbia and Paramount, Spielberg the wanderer had returned. The trade announcement went out immediately: 'We at MCA-Universal are thrilled and flattered that Steve has chosen to renew his relationship with us, and that we will have the opportunity to further benefit from his unique talents. We consider Steve part of our family and hope that he will always look to Universal as his home.'

The death of MCA founder Jules Stein in the Spring of 1981 came as a profound shock. Eighty-five years old or not, many had been convinced that old Stein would outlive them all. He had been one of the most remarkable and controversial figures of the twentieth century in 'show business' – a term he came to detest. He wanted to be remembered as 'Dr Stein', the appellation to which he reverted in the seventies as he withdrew from the monolith he'd created, anxious to escape the hurdy-gurdy image of the 'ex-band booker'.

Stein took many of MCA's secrets to the grave with him, details of deals, payoffs and associations that may never be unravelled, vendettas neither forgotten nor forgiven, real and imagined slights for which retribution had long since been extracted. And 'the biggest, toughest Jew' he'd ever found, who turned out on at least one crucial occasion to be even tougher and smarter than he'd have liked, was left to carry on the tradition from the confines of the Black Tower's ultimate power centre. The King was dead! Long live the new King – Lew Wasserman!

Sorrow was mingled with a more immediate regret. Even as his pallbearers – Jimmy Stewart, Cary Grant and Ronald Reagan among them – were carrying his coffin aloft, a staggering thirty-seven per cent was being wiped off MCA's value. With something badly needed to redress the balance, Wasserman and Sheinberg took an anxious look at their upcoming slate.

Naturally a Spielberg project could never be overlooked, but if only he were at work on some kind of potential blockbuster, instead of the merely profitable little picture they expected *E.T.* to be.

Spielberg saw his extra-terrestrial creation as nothing less than the interstellar ambassador of peace and good humour, and declared himself happy to be back working in a space-related subject, like 'a big kid adjusting to Christmas in summer'. As for the lead human character, the boy Elliott, he saw him as the archetypal Beatles' 'Nowhere Man', drawn from Spielberg's own painful childhood memories. Looking back, he could see that he'd been forced into making movies to become quasi-popular, to find 'a reason for living after school hours' while most of his peers were out playing sports or starting tentative experiments with girls.

Nine-year-old Henry Thomas, Sissy Spacek's 'older son' in *Raggedy Man*, was asked to test for the role of Elliott after film editor Ed Warschilka Jr sent over a reel from the movie. Kathleen Kennedy wanted to hire him on the spot. 'It sounds corny,' she admits, 'but you do know when a special kid comes into the room.' After a fairly pedestrian reading of a prepared text, it was an improvised, videotaped session with casting director Mike Fenton that sold Spielberg. Thomas started talking about how E.T. was his friend, and why should anybody have the right to take him away and hurt him? Tears were streaming down his face as he spoke, and in no time at all both adults followed suit. Spielberg still saw the boy as an adult actor rather than the kid his resumé claimed, an extremely controlled, methodical performer capable of offering 'a bread crumb at a time' rather than the over-the-top 150 per cent many child actors believe they're expected to deliver. There was no question of dithering. 'Okay, kid, you've got the job,' he immediately declared.

Seven-year-old Drew Barrymore's test was something else again, for she was nothing if not wildly inventive. Originally one of the 100 kids interviewed for *Poltergeist* before being bounced in favour of Heather O'Rourke, Drew arrived for her *E.T.* test claiming to be the lead singer in a local punk band. Already impressed with her performance in Ken Russell's *Altered States*, Spielberg felt secure in the knowledge he'd found Gertie, Elliott's mischievous, uninhibited younger sister. It was perfect casting for the precocious youngster, as he later confirmed: 'You don't restrain Drew. You give her a wide field.'

Fifteen-year-old Robert McNaughton, with a track record of television and stage work, was hired to play Elliott's older brother. 'What do you like to do in your spare time?' Spielberg asked at the interview. 'Ride my bike,' McNaughton replied. Well, there *was* a lot of that scheduled . . . !

Impressed by Peter Coyote's performance in Walter Hill's *Southern Comfort*, the actor had been one of many tested by Spielberg and Lucas after losing out to Tom Selleck for Indiana Jones. The many facets Coyote was capable of portraying convinced Spielberg he would be ideal for the initially sinister leader of the scientific community in *E.T.* who turns out to be an all-round good egg. Dee Wallace's calling card was her performance in Joe Dante's *The Howling*. Perfect for the role of the harassed single mother, Spielberg considered.

As for E.T. himself (herself/itself), he/she/it was a mixture of special effects, mechanics, electronics and actors, a mime and two midgets included. There were three different 'versions': one was a lightweight electro-mechanical device bolted to the floor, capable of thirty points of movement in the face and thirty more in the body. Another, more complicated body was auto-electronic for close-ups and sophisticated shots, with eighty-six separate points of movement, servo-boxes dangling from its carcass employing many more cables than the electro-mechanical model. The third was a suit, cableless and capable of only ten points of movement, custom-designed and padded to be worn by little people hired for E.T.'s walking scenes, which in the end occupied just fifteen per cent of screen time. 'We wanted E.T. to look as ugly as possible,' Melissa Mathison explained, 'so that you *eventually* learned to love him.'

*E.T.* was tightly budgeted at $9.5 million, with Spielberg personally responsible for cost overruns. With this in mind, he chose to shoot studio scenes at Culver City's Laird International Studios, ducking Universal's loaded overhead. The special effects bill came to $800,000, with George Lucas's Industrial Light and Magic once again doing the honours. Filmed under the title *A Boy's Life* so as not to give the game away entirely, the movie afforded Spielberg an opportunity to repay a long-standing debt in exemplary style. That he did is to his credit, although the truth behind the apparently spontaneous gesture is somewhat more prosaic. While Allen Daviau had been his cameraman on *Amblin'*, and his assignment on *E.T.* brought him his first feature after two short subjects and several commercials, Daviau had to line up with every other applicant for the job, hustled along endlessly by his agent, and forced to submit test footage to prove he had the chops for the job. Those under the impression that the 'old pals act' had been invoked, or that Spielberg was acting out of an old loyalty, are sorely mistaken.

On the set one day Spielberg had to yell at Drew Barrymore to get what he wanted, and only then did he discover that John Drew and Ildiko Jaid Barrymore's daughter (and the legendary John Barrymore's granddaughter) had gamely turned up with a temperature of 101 degrees. He hugged her for fully ten minutes and sent her home. 'Most directors just say, "Sit here and turn camera left",' Drew later admiringly declared. 'Steven *shows* people.' Never having really got to know her own father, a wandering soul dubbed 'the battling Barrymore' by the press – her parents had separated before she was born— Drew immediately fixed on Spielberg as the ultimate father figure.

Henry Thomas found it 'pretty hard to relate to a machine with twelve guys working it'. On Spielberg: 'It was basically a business-like relationship. He was the director. My role was to listen to him.' A pause, then: 'He'll listen to you, though. That's why he's a good director.'

Making *E.T.* and having 'supervised' *Poltergeist* provided Spielberg with a contrasting summer and autumn. It was a time, surrounded by kids, that brought out the 'frustrated father' in him, made him yearn as never before for a brood of his own. Kathleen Kennedy was informed that the summer would tell him once and for all if he was suited for parenthood. Reliving all his childhood insecurity as the movie progressed left Spielberg physically and emotionally drained. 'It was tortuous,' he would later recall. 'My pubic hairs turned gray!'

The veil of secrecy surrounding *A Boy's Life*, which extended not only to the phoney title, but also to each member of the cast being forced to sign a contract agreeing not to talk to the press, was well maintained right up to the very first preview. Even the poster artists were kept in the dark, with the now-famous Michelangelo-inspired finger-touching between Elliott and E.T. the only permitted initial artwork, and carried out based solely on Spielberg's descriptions, with all film clips withheld. 'Is this what you want?' Spielberg was asked as the umpteenth sketch was submitted. 'No,' he replied, mentally tut-tutting. 'The fingers should be longer, and the skin should be a different colour . . .'

It was back to the drawing board yet again to get *precisely* the correct image.

Sometimes it pays to pass comment on someone else's work, sometimes even the best-intentioned remarks can be either misunderstood, misconstrued or downright twisted. And not only by outsiders, but often for the party they were meant to compliment. Such was the apparent case following Barbra Streisand's decision to unveil a rough cut of her magnum opus, *Yentl*, for Spielberg's perusal. Apart from anything else, he was keen to see how Amy Irving had performed under the diva's direction. 'Don't change a frame!' La Streisand was informed after the screening.

That would have been fine on its own. Except that somehow the press got a hold of it and implied that Streisand had gone to Spielberg looking for advice, that he had 'helped her out'.

'Do you know how *repulsive* that is to me?' Streisand ranted. 'I *hate* it. It's like they're already taking my film away from me.'

Paranoia in paradise? Par for the course.

132

# 15

# The Bliss-Out

*'I didn't care for Indiana Jones and I hated 1941. When I told him he said, "Don't talk to me, Dad!"'*

ARNOLD SPIELBERG

*'My wish list' (after parents' divorce) 'included having a friend who could be both the brother I never had and the father I didn't feel I had any more. And that's how* E.T. *was born.'*

STEVEN SPIELBERG

Sid Sheinberg called Lew Wasserman and his wife to fly to Honolulu to catch the first public preview of *E.T.* Then he panicked. If it were a disaster, the doughty Wasserman would be distinctly unamused. Incredible relief was felt as the movie unspooled. 'That first screening,' said Sheinberg after the event, 'I don't think there's ever been an experience like it – and I surely will never have another one like it in films. It truly was like a religious experience. It must be a little bit like the way people feel when they think they've seen God.' The normally brusque, hard-to-move Sheinberg sobbed along with Spielberg when it was over.

One of the reasons Sheinberg claims he was so moved by the ending of *E.T.* was the similarity he saw to his relationship with Spielberg, the protégé who had come so far: 'It's in the nature of his life and his career that sometimes he goes away. And that's very sad . . .'

Another telling indication of the success *E.T.* would go on to enjoy was its unprecedented reception at the Cannes Film Festival, where it was the closing black-tie gala presentation. Spielberg, Frank Marshall and Kathleen Kennedy stood there, stunned and temporarily speechless, as the notoriously difficult-to-please audience rose to its feet and gave an extended standing ovation. Although it was shown out of competition, many felt it could easily have been

133

a contender for the 'Palme D'Or', the festival's main prize, had it been entered.

Apart from that, and a similar reception as the closing night gala presentation at the Edinburgh Film Festival in September, Europe had to wait until Christmas to see for themselves what all the fuss was about.

For the most part critics agreed with Sheinberg's assessment, with Kenneth Turan in *California* hailing the movie as 'A triumph almost beyond imagining', and Pauline Kael echoing the sentiment with her euphoric description of *E.T.* as 'a dream of a movie, a bliss-out'. On the other hand there were the hard-bitten, cynical bunch who do not mind so much being manipulated, but to hell with the strings blatantly showing. Like Britain's Kenneth Robinson. Maybe he went just a *little* too far in tagging *E.T.* 'the worst film I have ever seen', although he's entitled to his opinion. Certainly, as with *Close Encounters*, there was an incredibly ramshackle central section to contend with. There were also moments of great charm, notably when Elliott shows off his toys to the creature.

*Variety* was right on the money in describing *E.T.* as 'the best Disney movie Walt Disney never made,' although not, perhaps, in the complimentary way it was intended. Spielberg had calculatedly loaded up a live-action movie with shameless gobs of sentiment considered palatable in the past only when doled out in cartoon form. He had slavishly followed the Disney formula *to the frame*, in all its unabashed glory, right down to the creature 'dying' near the climax, only to be brought back at the last minute.

One of the most revealing Spielbergian stories has composer John Williams fretting out loud to his director that his over-ripe, if-you-have-tears-prepare-to-shed-them-now concerto played over the climactic *E.T.* scenes was, even for them, too highly calibrated, strung just a notch too high. Maybe they should modulate it just a little, ease it on down? 'It's *shameless*, Steven,' he declared, wringing his hands. 'Will we get away with it?'

Spielberg fixed his good friend and collaborator with an owlish, inscrutable stare. It was as if he had the wisdom of the ages to impart, the key to the universe, the perfect baton to conduct the music of the spheres. Which he incontestably has, in popular terms. 'John,' he intoned, 'movies *are* shameless.'

Although it was doubtless spoken in semi-jest, Spielberg had just offered up one of the main keys to his enormous success. Taste, skill, luck, judgement, all of these play a part. But none as much as that single realisation, and the common sense to keep it in the forefront of every moviemaking decision. If, that is, you want to sell loads of tickets, and manipulate the resultant audience until the pips squeak. Or maybe more than just squeak . . .

To the allegation that his approach to grown-up romance in movies lacks any perceptible degree of conviction, let alone eroticism, Spielberg would later answer, 'I think I have an *incredibly* erotic charge. It's one of my ambitions to make everyone in an 800-seat cinema *come* at the same time.' Could this be the wave of the future?

More seriously, Spielberg absolutely denies the charge of 'Master Manipulator' levelled at him. 'Unless you are a preposterous ass,' he claims, 'you never sit down and say, "This movie is going into the hearts of America." I've never felt that way about any of my films. I plan for failure and I'm surprised by the success. I don't think any of us can plan to make a movie that reaches out and makes $100 million. I'm not trying to burst any bubbles here. I'm just telling you the truth.'

And protesting too much?

Critic Dave Kehr, one of the leading lights on the New York *Daily News*, produced a compelling take on Spielberg's work in the wake of *E.T.*'s release. 'Spielberg's way to fight the movie-isation of television was the television-isation of movies,' he suggested, 'to take TV situations, TV emotions, and give them a larger, more mystic life on film. *E.T.* is hi-fi television, with superior depth and detailing, superior scale. The movie does have a beginning and an end, but in between only isolated jokes and autonomous episodes – the drunk scene, Halloween – in place of an evolving plot. Soggy structure is always a Spielberg problem, but that doesn't seem to bother audiences. The self-contained set-pieces are what hold both audience and Spielberg's interest and we enjoy them as we would a series of Saturday morning cartoons, in independent ten-minute chunks. Most of the middle scenes could be rearranged without damaging the film's tempo or effect.'

Spielberg offered his own take for all nay-sayers once *E.T.*'s grosses of close on $400 million in the US were added up. 'If I really wanted to take reviews seriously,' he declared, 'I'd show my films to all the critics in rough-cut, so at least if they wanted to take me over the coals they could then. If there was one good idea I could make the change, I'm very generous about that kind of thing. But we don't do that, so I just don't really bother myself with reviews, I read them sometimes a year later.'

Back in the mid-seventies producers Richard Zanuck and David Brown had scoffed at Spielberg's suggested licensing of Bruce the shark. Now that Lucas, first with *Star Wars*, then with Indiana Jones' fedoras, had proven the value of marketing tie-ins – as if, post-Disney, further proof were really needed – Spielberg experienced no such difficulty in selling the idea of loveable little *E.T.* Walking Toys, Action Toys, Cuddly Toys, Collectibles, Spaceships and 'Elliott' Bicycles, to name but a small selection. The resultant bonanza would go on to yield an estimated $1 billion in merchandise sales internationally, with a healthy percentage finding its way back to Spielberg's coffers.

Fully paid product placement, for years a Hollywood staple, reached a new peak of success with *E.T.*, with a delighted spokesman for Reese's Pieces claiming a sixty-five per cent increase in sales after being featured in the movie. A representative of M&Ms, who had been offered the slot and turned it down because of the prohibitive price demanded, categorically denied any corporate embarrassment.

A whole series of unfortunate off-notes were sounded above and well beyond the tumultuous success of *E.T.*

Spielberg's relationship with Drew Barrymore had been one of the highlights of the movie for both of them. And, unlike many others, it continued long after the movie was completed. He offered her career advice, advising her to stop making commercials if she wanted to be taken seriously as an actress. She listened. He spent three separate weekends coaching her for her courtroom scene in *Irreconcilable Differences*. She learned. She wrote a script – only eight pages long, but they were enormous pages, and written in her child-like scrawl. Spielberg read it and provided the title: *Terms of EnDrewment*. They planned a double date: he was to escort her to the premiere of *Indiana Jones and the Temple of Doom*, she would return the compliment, taking him along to the opening night of *Firestarter*. She loved it, despite the last-minute cancellation of both outings when she had to report to North Carolina to film *Cat's Eye*. 'She will be bigger than Tatum O'Neal and better than Meryl Streep,' Spielberg predicted.

Even as she described him as 'one of the few adult people that I respect,' she wistfully added, 'yet he will always look at me as a child.' Maybe not, for there was talk that Spielberg was so smitten that he intended to wait for her to grow up so they could marry. Many of Drew's Sundays were spent at Spielberg's Malibu home.

Although they remain friends to this day, it's on a different basis. The change began with Drew's first two incarcerations in a California rehab centre. Drug and alcohol abuse is common in Hollywood. Not so common at thirteen years of age. The 'child' had become a 'wild child'.

Spielberg still apparently saw Drew as the merely precocious kid he had first met. His Christmas gift to her as a fifteen-year-old? An arcade-sized Ms Pac-Man.

Thankfully, Drew found her way back from substance abuse, and today is one of the most sought-after young actresses in Hollywood.

Bruce McNaughton, young Robert's father, formally complained to the New York *Daily News* on behalf of his son, Henry Thomas and Drew Barrymore, about the lack of publicity accorded *E.T.*'s human co-stars. Not only that, there seemed to be no fan mail for them – surprising for a movie that was breaking records and had likeable kids in leading roles. When McNaughton's mother checked, she discovered that thousands of letters had been diverted by Universal straight to Spielberg's office for use by his 'E.T. Fan Club' – without bothering to inform either the young actors or their parents. Contacted at Amblin, Spielberg's spokeswoman Peggy Siegal huffily declared, 'If Bruce McNaughton doesn't like it, well, from now on he can take care of his son's mail himself . . .!'

Hollywood buzz had Spielberg and Dee Wallace falling out over her place in the credits, and his attempting to have her blackballed when she refused to yield. Wallace was already on record as being dismayed at how secretive Spielberg had been during production. And certainly one of her favourite scenes in the movie, in which E.T. had crept into her bedroom as she slept and placed an M&M on her pillow, had been cut. (Whether or not it was because M&M wouldn't cough up the necessary placement money, it still hurt.) 'It would be sad,' said Wallace to Stephen Farber and Marc Green, authors of *Outrageous Conduct*, 'if someone of so much creativity and power could be so small. It doesn't make sense to me, but then stranger things have happened in Hollywood.'

Whenever Hollywood produces a blockbuster, there is a history of those clambering to board the bandwagon in a variety of ways. Not least plagiarism suits. *E.T.* would prove no exception. A $750 million lawsuit was filed by Lisa Litchfield, a thirty-eight-year-old playwright, claiming that the idea for the movie was filched from her 1978 one-act play, *Lokey From Maldema*. 'It's the people you've never heard of who crawl out of the woodwork like cockroaches to sue you,' said Spielberg.

Although he is undoubtedly correct, the next individual to poke his head above the parapet was scarcely unknown, except perhaps to the wider commercial audience. It was none other than the legendary Indian director Satjayit Ray, who made the allegation that

*E.T.* contained striking similarities to *The Alien*, a script Ray had circulated around Hollywood in the late sixties. Ray's subject: a lone
alien befriends a ten-year-old boy during a trip to Earth to study
plant life. Sounds familiar? The basic theme apart, he claimed that
several incidents from his script had been lifted wholesale, like dead
plants coming back to life . . . !

The Los Angeles *Times* ran the story in March 1983, at the most
embarrassing moment possible for Spielberg, on the very eve of the
Oscars ceremony. A furious, and – as it turned out – decidedly
paranoid Universal alleged that Columbia was behind the story –
specifically Columbia's Frank Price, the man who had given *E.T.*
the heave-ho, and who had a vested interest in badmouthing the
main contender against *Gandhi*, Columbia's and Price's pride and
joy. And yes, there was an Indian connection other than Ray himself
and *Gandhi*, for *The Alien* claim had been first circulated by Aseem
Chamhra, a student at Columbia University, who had picked it up
from an article in a February edition of *India Today*. After making a
few calls to India to check the story's authenticity thoroughly, he
had repeatedly tried to contact both Spielberg and his attorney,
Bruce Ramer, for a comment. None of his calls had been returned,
and the story ran in his campus newspaper.

Completing the picture, another writer, Barry Price, claimed in
the columns of the Los Angeles *Times* that Spielberg got the idea for
*E.T.* from 'a concept' he had submitted to the Walt Disney
Company years earlier.

A frustrated Amblin source commented, 'Do you realise that
Spielberg has been accused of plagiarising on every film, even
*Sugarland Express* and *1941* – and these were flops?!'

In the event the copyright infringement suit filed by Lisa
Litchfield was thrown out, the judge in the case finding 'no substantial similarities' with Litchfield's 'Lokey'. And 12,000 miles
away, Satjayit Ray's lawyers persuaded their client from going ahead
with his suit, on the basis that Spielberg had made 'the necessary
changes so that there is no case, there is no legal action possible in
these circumstances'. Dismayed as he was, Ray accepted the decision, while stoutly maintaining that 'Neither *E.T.* nor *Close
Encounters of the Third Kind* would have been possible without my
script of *The Alien*, which is available throughout America in
mimeographed form.'

Barry Price's case? It never got the length of a courtroom.

For Spielberg the price of his unprecedented success to date had
been a complete shut-out from major Oscar honours. So how was
*E.T.* going to be any different, especially when it was in the ring

against Richard Attenborough's worthy, critically acclaimed, heavy-duty *Gandhi*? Answer: it wasn't, despite a prediction from screenwriter William Goldman, author of the famous 'Nobody knows anything' theory of Hollywood, here inadvertently offering convincing personal proof. 'This is the middle of '82,' he wrote, 'and next year's awards are nine months away. I don't care. There's no doubt in my mind that *E.T.* will win.' Oh, yeah? Awards for Best Sound, Visual Effects, Sound Editing and Original Score (John Williams, shamelessly aided and abetted by Spielberg) were some compensation. Oh, and a hug from a teary-eyed Dickie Attenborough. Looking on was a triumphant Frank Price, who had spent so much of Columbia's money promoting *Gandhi*'s 'World Event' opening and Oscar campaign that the studio actually lost money on the movie's US release.

Several real-life tragedies invaded Spielberg's life after the openings of *E.T.* and *Poltergeist*, some in their immediate wake, others stretching into the future.

Michael Patrick Bilon, 35" tall, 45-pounds, one of the 'little people' hired to play the extra-terrestrial in his various perambulations, had spent many hours working inside E.T.'s forty-pound suit in steam-bath conditions. At the age of thirty-five he died of complications arising from pneumonia six months after the movie's premiere. Twenty-two-year-old Tamara De Treaux, 35" tall, 40-pounds, another who suffered in the cause, had her own comment on conditions inside the E.T. suit: 'Did you ever wrap yourself up in Cellophane?'

Dominique Dunne, the young actress cast as Heather O'Rourke's older sister in *Poltergeist*, was attacked and strangled by her lover John Sweeney on October 30, 1982, just three months after the movie opened. She survived on life support until November 4. Her death sent shock waves through a Hollywood community well practised in the portrayal of violence on screen, yet still inclined to disbelief when it penetrates their own lens.

Following the altercation with Tobe Hooper and MGM, and the tragic death of Dunne, Spielberg decided to have nothing to do with the sequels MGM demanded. *Poltergeist II* went ahead without him, as did *Poltergeist III*, both of them featuring Heather O'Rourke, the five-year-old he had discovered in the MGM commissary and cast as 'Little Carol Ann'. By the time the second sequel was completed, there were rumours of unease among the cast and crew of the movie. Life, it seemed, had imitated art, and stories circulated that part of the movie had been filmed, as in the fictional original, on the site of an old Indian burial ground. Whatever the truth of that, young Heather's sudden hospitalisation took everyone by surprise. Suffering from what was described as an 'extremely unusual' congenital intestinal condition, she went into septic shock and died, aged twelve.

Then there was the terrible accident that had taken place on the set of *Twilight Zone – The Movie* only days after *E.T.*'s opening.

*The more Vic Morrow thought about the helicopter scene he was scheduled to film, the more apprehensive he became. Gradually it became an obsession with him – the 'copter would crash and he would be killed. He could see it, he could describe – in graphic, horrific detail – exactly how it would happen, he could taste it.*

*There were two clear-cut choices – either to give in to his fears and duck out of the project, or to go ahead and defy the premonition of disaster.*

*Weighing everything up, he chose to honour the commitment. At the same time he made an appointment with his attorney, and presented him with an extraordinary request. If an accident should happen, he was determined to ensure that his dependents wanted for nothing. Could an insurance policy covering him for $5 million in the event of his accidental death be obtained, the contract to run for the duration of filming that one scene?*

*The policy was secured, the scene – for a television movie – was shot without incident, the policy allowed to lapse.*

*A few years later, at the age of fifty-one, Morrow was offered a role that would mark his return to the big screen, and in a major Warner Bros movie being co-produced by Steven Spielberg. It was like a gift from the gods – his first starring role in over twenty years. And although it too involved filming a scene with a helicopter hovering above him, Morrow could ruefully reflect that he had travelled that route before. All the worry, all those sleepless nights, all those unnecessary insurance provisions, none of them had been necessary.*

*And they were all but forgotten as he readied himself for what would prove the last role of his life – in* Twilight Zone – The Movie.

# 16

# The Dark Side

*'Oh, but I do have a dark side. Everyone does. I really believe that the best movies, the best stories, take you to the darkest part of your own – or the leading character's – personality, and then you rescue him. There's a rescue mission involved in all the best movies. And that person is saved from his own undoing or from what other people are doing to him. You have to bring people down to the bottom before you can recover in the operatic third-act finale.'*

STEVEN SPIELBERG, 1985

*'Lover of children? Or user of children?'*

JULIA PHILLIPS on Spielberg

The idea of a movie version of the old black-and-white TV show *Twilight Zone* started with an approach from Warner Bros, who had acquired the rights from Rod Serling's widow, Carol. Before his death at age fifty in 1975, just a few years after meeting Spielberg on the set of *Night Gallery*, Serling had himself intended to make the leap to theatrical features with the big-screen *Twilight Zone*.

Carol Serling wanted any movie version to be faithful to the concept her husband had created, worrying that it might be distorted in the wrong hands. After Warners refused her request for artistic control, she worried even more. As soon as she heard Spielberg would be involved, she felt that she could relax. Those anxious phone calls from Joan Crawford were all in the past. One of the things that won her over was Spielberg's request, recognising the impracticality of stretching a single story out to feature length, that she help select four episodes for the movie.

Spielberg was elated, convinced he had found the perfect vehicle for a collaboration with another *wunderkind*. He had first met John Landis at Martha's Vineyard during the filming of *Jaws*, with Landis brought in briefly to contribute a few jokes to the script. Although

141

that hadn't worked out, the two men had since formed something of a mutual admiration society – this despite the comparisons between *1941* and *The Blues Brothers* that both resented.

Landis had been a high-school dropout at seventeen, seguing straight into the mailroom at Twentieth Century-Fox before spending time in Europe riding the coattails of Clint Eastwood's *Kelly's Heroes* as a gofer. After the next-to-zero budget *Schlock* and the equally oddball click of *Kentucky Fried Movie*, the enormously successful *National Lampoon's Animal House* had registered him as a major Hollywood player. The resultant cash gusher, together with the returns from *An American Werewolf in London*, enabled everyone to overlook the excesses involved in *The Blues Brothers*.

Landis had played the cameo of a motorcycle messenger for his new best friend in *1941*, his 'acting role' providing a glimmer of the movie's budget overages: one day's work for Landis's brief scene eventually stretched to four weeks. To repay the compliment, Landis awarded Spielberg a day's work on *Blues Brothers* that *remained* a day. He played a clerk, Landis having informed his wife, Deborah Nadelman, the movie's costume designer, that he wanted Spielberg dressed like a real nerd. Instead, he turned up looking fairly stylish. 'What is this?' Landis reprimanded his spouse. 'In *1941* Spielberg had me covered with dirt. Why should I let him look this good?'

'Hey,' his wife replied, 'remember I work with him too!'

After *Raiders of the Lost Ark* – on which Nadelman had indeed worked – failed to win 'Best Film' at the 1982 Oscars, Landis had provided comfort. 'Steve, you've got to stop winning Oscars for other people,' he joshed, referring to the technical awards his movies regularly received, dating back to *Jaws* and continuing through *Close Encounters*. Landis gave his own explanation for Spielberg's shut-out: 'You're too young and too successful.' Others, meanwhile, rendered their verdict on Landis: 'Too obnoxious and too cocky for his own good.'

Landis was enthusiastic about working with Spielberg on *Twilight Zone – The Movie*, as were Warners' Steve Ross, Robert Daly and Terry Semel at the double whammy of capturing both men. With whiz kids like these behind the movie, how could it go wrong? Surely they were guaranteed a franchise that would run for ever, just like on TV? A deal was worked out that Spielberg and Landis would co-produce, as well as direct one episode each, with two other directors brought in for the rest. To save money, mainly stiff studio overheads, the movie would be produced independently for Warners' release. If the two men wanted to work out of their offices at Universal, then that was up to them, they were calling the shots.

Joe Dante, hot from *Piranha* and *The Howling*, was preparing *Gremlins* for Spielberg when *Twilight Zone* came up. The episode he was allocated, 'It's A Good Life', had first been written for the 1961 season. It was a story Spielberg had considered for himself before passing in favour of 'The Monsters Are Due On Maple Street'.

George Miller's involvement came about simply because he happened to be on the Warner lot one day and bumped into Spielberg. With his friend and partner Byron Kennedy, Miller had produced *Mad Max* back in Australia for $350,000; it had gone on to gross $100 million worldwide. Their sequel, *The Road Warrior (Mad Max II)*, released by Warners, had consolidated Mel Gibson's stardom. Miller was on temporary furlough from *The Dismissal*, an Australian TV mini-series the team was producing. His choice of the *Twilight Zone* episodes on offer was a remake of 'Nightmare at 20,000 Feet' from '64, with John Lithgow replacing William Shatner, the original passenger terrified by a monster he sees perched on the wing of an airplane in mid-flight.

In a departure, the first episode, 'Back There', together with a brief prologue, would be directed by Landis from his original screenplay. The segment involved Vic Morrow's Bill, a present-day racist character, being transported back 'through space, time and mind' to World War II, where he falls foul of the Nazis, on to the American Deep South, where he becomes the centre of attention at a KKK lynching, finally to Vietnam, where he comes under attack from American GIs.

Shooting on 'Back There' began on 1 June, 1982 on Universal's back lot, and three weeks later was complete save for one crucial scene. This had Vic Morrow's 'Bill' rescuing two Asian children from a Vietnamese village under attack from the air. This was set for night-time location work at Indian Dunes Motorcycle Park, a 600-acre tract of privately owned land near the community of Saugus and Six Flags Magic Mountain Amusement Park in the Santa Clarita valley, twenty miles northeast of Universal Studios.

Landis ran into a brick wall when he met with casting agents Mike Fenton and Marci Liroff to discuss hiring the two kids needed for the scene. Apart from the illegality of working children outside of daytime hours, the action he described 'sounded kind of dangerous', Liroff declared. The scene was crucial, Landis protested, and had to do with 'softening the Vic Morrow character', giving someone who was otherwise an out-and-out racist 'a redeeming quality'. Liroff was adamant.

'The hell with you guys,' Landis fumed, per Liroff's later testimony. 'We don't need you. We'll get them off the street ourselves.'

143

Alarmed, Liroff called Spielberg's office and mentioned his colleague's threat to Frank Marshall, warning him that what Landis intended to do was against the law. According to Liroff: 'Marshall said he would take care of it.'

Kathleen Kennedy, it has been claimed, anonymously called state officials to confirm the rules regarding the hours of employment permissible for children. The information was then passed to Marshall, whose idea of 'taking care of it' seemed to extend to authorising George Folsey Jr, Landis's associate producer, to hire the two kids illegally.

Was Spielberg aware of what was going on? According to Folsey: 'We wouldn't have hired the kids on a Spielberg picture unless either Spielberg or his people knew it. I mean, that would have been a terrible thing to do, put them in that position. The fact that Frank agreed to do it made me feel that it was okay, that it was really his responsibility too.'

That the whole affair was conducted surreptitiously can be seen from the sum of money that changed hands in the unlawful hiring of seven-year-old My-Ca Le and six-year-old Renee Chen. The legal fee for hiring children legitimately through the Screen Actors' Guild was $90; instead the parents of the kids were offered $500 each for one night's work. Yes, they would be working without permits, Folsey explained, because of the night-time shoot, but other than that it was strictly routine. No mention was made either of explosives or the helicopters that would be flying overhead in the scene. 'Special effects' would be used, they were told, but nowhere near the children. Folsey requested $2,000 from Warner Bros, and despatched a Spielberg production worker physically to collect it.

James Henderling, an executive at Warner Bros, would later testify that he suspected children were being hired illegally. Bonnie Radford had phoned him from Spielberg's office to ask how to go about hiring kids without going through the Screen Actors' Guild. After informing her that a permit was required, she called later that day to say the children were not needed after all. The request for $2,000 followed hours later. Frank Marshall co-signed the cheque, which was cashed into twenty bills of $100 each.

On the afternoon of 22 July, another Warners exec, vp Edward Morey, noticed on his copy of the *Twilight Zone* script that two children were required. That was funny, he thought, since a quick inspection of the call sheets listed neither any kids, nor the teacher/welfare officer required by law to be on the set with them. Curious, Morey placed a call to Dan Allingham, Landis's production manager. Allingham pleaded ignorance, saying that it was being taken care of, but not by him. Asked to check it out and get back to Morey, he agreed.

Morey heard nothing further concerning the children until he was rudely awakened at 3 am the following morning.

Landis's script instructions for the final scene read: 'The helicopter makes another pass and then one of the huts EXPLODES in a spectacular fireball. Bill, holding a child in each arm, makes a Herculean effort and runs for the shallow river. With the huts burning behind him, Bill runs as best he can across the river.'

23 July, 1982, 2.20 am: the actual scene at Indian Dunes Motorcycle Park is like something dreamt up by Hieronymus Bosch. Frank Marshall watches it all from a safe distance as six cameras – sited on either side of the river, inside the helicopter, on top of the steep cliffs behind – start rolling.

In the air: an olive-green 'Huey' UH-1B fifty-two-foot long helicopter, descending to twenty-five feet above the Santa Clara River basin, is buffeted by a mortar bomb explosion.

On the south bank, where bamboo huts huddle at the foot of the cliffs: a huge fireball mushrooms into the sky, followed by more explosions – six in nine seconds – blasting debris and flames that engulf the 'copter.

In the shallow river bed: Vic Morrow, a child under each arm, runs from the wooden pier and begins to wade across.

On the north shore facing Morrow: arc lights perched on thirty-foot-high scaffolding are rocked, like the giant chopper, by the mortar blasts deflected from the cliffs.

Standing alongside the arc lights: John Landis is signalling the pilot to get down, and to the machine gunner inside the craft to start firing his dummy bullets. 'Lower! Lower! Lower! Fire! Fire! Fire!' he yells into his bullhorn.

As the force of the blasts hits the helicopter broadside, it tips towards the camera crane on the north shore, narrowly missing it as the pilot frantically begins straightening up. Twenty to thirty degrees into the turn that would have got him clear, another explosion catches the craft from below, enveloping it in impenetrable smoke and suffocating heat. Now it begins spinning out of control, a combination of debris and heat jamming the tail rotor, the helicopter's sole anti-torque device, without which the craft is nothing more than a 6,000-pound tin can attached to a forty-four-foot diameter chopper blade whirling at 1655 revolutions a minute.

Dealing with a quiet river is one thing, coping with water whipped into a frenzy by the lurching 'copter's downwash quite another. By the time Morrow is halfway across, the children have slipped from his chest to hip level. Renee Chen slides into the water altogether as he stumbles and drops to one knee.

The unthinkable is only seconds away as Morrow, with deafening explosions blasting the cliffs and night sky behind him, and still twenty feet from the north shore, struggles to get back on both feet. As he does the helicopter crashes into the river bed, its right skid crushing Renee Chen to death.

As it keels over, Morrow is decapitated first by the propeller's leading edge, My-Ca Lee's head is removed by the next revolution. Succeeding spins of the blade as it keeps on relentlessly whirling add the final merciless touches.

Morrow never gets to say the final lines Landis had written for his character after reaching the haven of the north shore: 'I'll keep you safe, kids. I swear to God.'

Several members of the *Twilight Zone* crew had become alarmed at Landis's hyper-hyper, gung-ho demeanour during a July 21 run-through. An electrician had voiced reservations about climbing the arc light scaffolding as it swayed in the wash from the chopper's blades. According to cameraman Stephen Lydecker, Landis's response had been, 'Is there somebody on this electrical crew who's not too chickenshit to do the job?'

When John Connor, a second camera operator, voiced his concern to special effects director Paul Stewart that one of the planned explosions might bounce off the solid background of the cliffs, directing the force of the blast across the set, an assistant testified that Landis responded, 'If you don't want to film it, you can go home. I'll shoot it myself.'

When Lydecker talked to his director on the same subject, the claimed answer stunned him, whether or not it was delivered tongue-in-cheek. 'Well, we may lose the helicopter,' Landis declared before turning his back and ambling off.

By 3.30 am on the morning of 22 July, with only the brief shot in the can where 'Bill' and the kids are introduced, Landis announced it was quitting time. The children would have to come back for the rescue scene that night. For this they would be paid another $500 each.

A final run-through of the helicopter's flight on the evening of 22 July, when there was no Morrow and no kids in the river below, graphically illustrated just how dangerous the 'real thing' was going to be. Explosions rocked the craft, blistering heat seared the pilot and passengers, the blast from a water mortar in the river splattered the chopper and reduced visibility to nil. Back on terra firma, and thoroughly shaken, both pilot Dorcey Wingo and the cameraman on board, Roger Smith, were assured that no explosions would come near the 'copter again. Less assuringly, Landis told them, grinning, that what they had experienced was but a 'warm-up' for what was coming; 'You ain't seen nothing yet!'

Walking the set moments later with special effects director Stewart, Landis urged him to add to his already heavy quota of mortar bombs rigged to go off. To shut him up, Stewart maintained he had only another couple left; in fact, he had thirty. Stewart still surprised an assistant when he asked him to place an extra loaded mortar under one of the bamboo huts, since earlier in the evening, fearful of the inevitable flying debris, he had claimed to have reached an agreement with Landis that no explosives be placed in any of the huts.

Perhaps Vic Morrow was forcibly reminded of his awful premonition as he psyched himself up for the movie's last scene. It clearly carried an element of risk, and he realised that this would be magnified if everyone concerned were not fully *compos mentis*. Unit hairdresser Virginia Kearns would testify that Morrow was 'very upset' about arrangements for the scene, and after watching the special effects crew rigging the village, and personally inspecting one of the explosive devices, he also chose to talk to Wingo and Landis. The pilot passed muster; Landis was a different matter. To Morrow the pupils of his eyes told him all he needed to know.

'They're pinpoints,' he told Kearns. 'That son-of-a-bitch is crazy.'

Panic, hysteria and disbelief swept through the unit as the waters of the Santa Clara ran red and the full horror of what had happened to Morrow and the children sank in. The occupants of the helicopter were rescued and shuttled away in the makeshift ambulance service that was organised, with Landis among those taken to hospital. Frank Marshall was gone by the time police arrived at 2.45 am, having disappeared almost immediately following the crash.

After being treated for minor bruising, John Landis, the 'yelling and screaming' observed by the *Twilight Zone* crew reduced to a monotone whine, called his attorney, Joel Behr. Realising the probability of charges being brought against his client, Behr alerted criminal defence attorney Harland Braun.

Next Landis made the hardest call of all – to his buddy Spielberg, the man many felt Landis had been attempting to emulate as he upped the ante repeatedly at Indian Dunes, aiming for something bigger, better, louder and more spectacular than even

'Steve' could have achieved, the ultimate 'bigger bang for the buck'. Spielberg's first question, according to Landis, was, 'Do you have a press agent?'

The news found Spielberg at the very pinnacle of his career to date, revelling in the notices and incredible business generated by *E.T.* after its smash opening barely two weeks earlier, any lingering chagrin over the mortifying Tobe Hooper climbdown relegated in the general euphoria to the farthest recesses of his mind. The death of anyone in the 'service' of a movie stunt was tragic enough – but two children as well as a much-respected actor? Spielberg's mind must have raced. Although not directly involved, the production was being made under his aegis, with Frank Marshall, his trusted lieutenant, actually on the scene. And there was no question that the kids had been hired illegally. Guilt by association was almost inevitable.

And how many would recall the scene Spielberg himself had shot to chilling effect in *Raiders of the Lost Ark*, with Indy's bald adversary carved up under the propeller of the 'Flying Wing'? There was only one thing to do, and it had to be done immediately.

From that moment on, Spielberg and his entire staff began to distance themselves from Landis. Even the remotest association with such a terrible incident would be damaging, the rationale ran. As one of Spielberg's employees put it, 'Suddenly it was as if Landis didn't exist.'

While promising full cooperation with any investigative agency, Warners also moved to distance itself, one executive referring to the matter as 'John Landis's problem'. Their 'cooperation' did not extend to turning over a still photographer's photos of the fatal crash; strangely, these had also ceased to exist.

Safety investigators seeking Frank Marshall for questioning discovered he had decamped to Idaho with Kathleen Kennedy. He would return to Los Angeles only briefly en route to scout locations abroad, together with Spielberg, for *Indiana Jones and the Temple of Doom*.

Out of the country definitely seemed like a good place to be.

# 17

## Actions Injurious

*'Steven could not walk into a room where that episode was
showing. He had a physical reaction to it. He couldn't
bring himself to watch it. It upset him that much.'*

MICHELLE ZEISEL, Production Secretary
on *Twilight Zone*

*'If Frank Marshall went out on a Spielberg movie and
hired kids illegally, who ended up being killed, and
Spielberg didn't know about it, he would can Marshall
immediately. It's clear that Marshall and Kennedy told
Spielberg.'*

HARLAND BRAUN, Defence Attorney

*Something about the storyboard he had created for* Twilight Zone's
*Vietnamese village scene made the artist hesitate. There was something
tantalisingly incomplete about it, and no matter how he juggled, added
and subtracted palm trees and foliage, re-drew the shadows to make
them more threatening, heightened the explosions to render them more
terrifying, the sketch failed to satisfy him.*

*After what seemed like a half-hour of pencil-chewing – wait a minute!
Of course! In a previous stint at Paramount, he recalled the helicopter
carcass the studio owned. Perfect! Wouldn't it be absolutely terrific if . . .
yep, that was it, just the right touch. Although he hadn't been asked to
portray a downed chopper, it was too good to miss. If the unit decided to
go for his idea, he could tell them exactly where to find the craft they
needed. They could hire it from Paramount for relative peanuts.*

*They didn't. But the sketch the artist submitted almost led investiga-
tors to believe the 'accident' had been calculatedly planned, storyboarded,
laid out in advance. It was as if Vic Morrow's original premonition of
doom, bizarre enough on its own and now all too real, had been twice
foretold.*

When Landis and Folsey attended the funeral of Vic Morrow on Sunday, July 25, neither Spielberg nor Marshall were anywhere to be seen. Fighting back his tears, Landis delivered a eulogy: 'Tragedy strikes in an instant, but film is immortal. Perhaps we can take some solace in the knowledge that through his work in stage, television and film, Vic lives for ever. Just before the last take, Vic took me aside to thank me for the opportunity to play this role.'

The statement was dismissed by Al Green, Morrow's lawyer, as disingenuous and 'as phony as a three-dollar bill'. Virginia Kearns, the unit hairdresser who had heard Morrow describe Landis as a crazy son-of-a-bitch only seconds before he allegedly thanked Landis, must have had her own thoughts.

Landis's unctuous comments sat uneasily with his angry, 'hurt and bewildered' disclaimer of the slightest shred of responsibility for the accident. 'What is shocking to me and my capacity for naivete,' he declared, 'is how ignorant people are. This issue has incredible potential to totally fuck the industry. The idea that the director is responsible for safety on the set is one of colossal ignorance. Staggering. *Breathtaking*.'

A week after the deaths, following an uneasy quiet, came the first government action. On July 30 Landis, Folsey, Dan Allingham, and Warner Bros as a corporation, were cited for violating state codes and fined civil penalties of $5,000 each 'for taking actions injurious to the health of a minor and for having children work after hours'.

A second investigation, carried out by the California Occupational Safety and Health Administration (Cal-OSHA) concluded that all four had violated dozens of state workplace regulations. They levied $62,375 in fines, of which Landis was to pay $30,955, Warners $3,645.

That left the National Transportation and Safety Board (NTSB), who found themselves forced to sue Landis in federal court to extract evidence. They concluded that the crash had been caused by 'the detonation of a debris-laden special effect explosion too near the low-flying helicopter'. Blame was laid on Landis and Dorcey Wingo, who had his pilot licence revoked by the Federal Aviation Administration.

In January 1983, the Directors' Guild of America produced a declaration that film directors must assume final responsibility for safety on the set. Landis's attorney, Harland Braun, managed a new spin on the subject. Why, Landis wasn't really the overall director of *Twilight Zone* at all. He was merely the 'artistic director'. Following a *Rolling Stone* article by Randall Sullivan that ridiculed the idea, sixteen fellow-'artistic directors' signed a letter of protest. It was a basic truth of filmmaking, they maintained, that all directors had to rely on their colleagues to carry out the actual *making* of a film; no director could prevent a camera operator from shooting a scene out of focus, or even be aware it was happening. A director couldn't sit on a camera crane without the crane operator's permission, nor could he prevent that equipment from toppling if it were incorrectly operated. *Someone else was at the controls.* It was up to directors to *design* films, but they must depend on the technological skills and professional responsibility of experts regarding logistics, mechanics and safety. So how could the author of the *Rolling Stone* piece possibly have maintained that Landis had to assume total moral and legal responsibility for the deaths?

The missive was signed by Michael Apted, Francis Coppola, Joe Dante, Jonathan Demme, Richard Donner, Jim Henson, Ron Howard, John Huston, Irwin Kershner, George Lucas, Sidney Lumet, Frank Oz, Mark Rydell, Don Siegel, Billy Wilder and Fred Zinnemann. *Not* by Steven Spielberg, who may have decided that in turning the auteur theory on its head, the signatories had neatly skewered themselves.

Author Sullivan was quick to suss out that the form letter, signed in Xerox-copy, had clearly been cobbled together by Harland Braun. In his reply he pointed out that he had neither written nor implied that Landis should bear 'total moral and legal responsibility'. What he found incredible, though, was his denial of any responsibility for the accident . . .

The buzz that began to spread like wildfire around the Hollywood community in the weeks and months following the accident carried ugly rumours of substance abuse at the *Twilight Zone* location. By October a wrongful death civil suit had been filed by Morrow's daughters, Carrie Morrow and Jennifer Jason Leigh. Among other things they charged that the defendants – listing everyone from Landis to Warner Bros to Frank Marshall to Spielberg among nineteen individuals or corporations – allowed 'consumption of drugs and/or alcohol by participants' during filming.

A fresh wave of rumours had Spielberg himself present at the crash scene, then spirited away immediately afterwards. Carl Pittman, a truck driver for the special effects crew, fanned the flames when he told investigators flat out that Spielberg had indeed been there when the helicopter crashed.

Spielberg's reply to the letter from the National Transportation and Safety Board seeking clarification, officially denied his presence:

'In response to your request,' it ran, 'I was never at the Indian Dunes location of *Twilight Zone* on the night of the accident or any other time. I declare under penalty of perjury that the foregoing is true and correct. Executed at Los Angeles, California, this first day of December 1982.'

In sworn testimony dated that same month, Pittman told National Transport Safety Board officials and Los Angeles County Sheriff's investigators, that Spielberg had indeed been there, that he had a disagreement with him at the accident scene. It had been over the use of a car which a crew member had requisitioned for emergency evacuation of those on the set in need of medical attention.

'I was trying to get the roads clear so we could get fire equipment in here,' his testimony began. 'So I put her (the mother of one of the child actors killed in the crash) in a car with her friend and the driver, with instructions to take her to a hospital, (to) get her the hell out of here. A few minutes later, when we had another car down there, the other child's father by that time was starting to have some problems too, and so was John Landis. So I got those people in (second car) and instructed the driver to take them to hospital.

'At that point Mr Spielberg requested a car, so I got him a car – he needed to go to the phone; and I was mad enough at him that I had to walk away from him.'

Asked why he was 'mad', Pittman replied, 'He was too cold about it.'

Mr Spielberg was on the set, then? 'Yes, he was. In fact, I didn't want him to have the car; I wanted to keep it there in case anyone else (needed the car) – at this point, no one knew how many people were injured.'

Warner Bros was first off the mark in nailing the story. The studio, its release ran, 'categorically denies that Steven Spielberg was on the set the night of the unfortunate accident, nor was he on the set of the Landis segment at any other time. Any statement to the contrary is simply not true.'

Landis was next in line: 'Spielberg had nothing to do with the production of this particular episode at all . . . I mean, it's true, he has nothing to do with this.' While describing his client's answers as 'frank', Joel Behr asked that the transcript not be made available to the press – though not, as he was at pains to point out, 'because there's anything about it that anyone should have to hide'.

The NTSB officials decided against pursuing Spielberg further after Carl Pittman retracted his story. He didn't know Spielberg, he now claimed. He must have had him mixed up with Frank Marshall.

Their sudden wrapping-up of the case surprised and dismayed many in the community, not least those in the District Attorney's office. With a grand jury hearing set for May 1983, the DA and his prosecution team needed all the data they could glean from the board's findings to back up the involuntary manslaughter indictments they intended to seek against Landis, Folsey, Allingham, Stewart and Wingo. Instead, what they got from Don Llorente, NTSB's chief investigator, was the reported finding of three empty cans of beer inside the helicopter.

Homicide detective Thomas Budds of LA County Sheriff's Department, after questioning a variety of witnesses – and gaining an impression from their hedged answers there was a distinct fear of being blackballed in the future if they said too much – chose to discount Pittman's initial story and accept Spielberg's denial. He regarded Spielberg as a reluctant witness whose knowledge of the illegitimate hiring was probably marginal at best, and not worth the trouble it would take to pursue in the criminal investigation into the deaths.

Frank Marshall? He was a different matter entirely. As far as Budds was concerned, he *must* have known about the hiring, he *had* been there on the tragic night, remaining briefly to help organise a makeshift ambulance run. Although there was no question of Marshall being prosecuted, Budds regarded Spielberg's deputy as an important eyewitness to events leading up to the fatal crash.

An interview with Marshall, considered a top priority, proved difficult to achieve – this despite Landis having appealed to Spielberg personally after the preliminary hearing, asking him to intercede with Marshall on his and Folsey's behalf to corroborate their statements about the joint decision to hire the children illegally. In the event, the DA's office decided to concentrate on the manslaughter aspect, to the exclusion of child labour law violations.

After several attempts to set up meetings came to nothing, Budds was surprised to be informed by Marshall's lawyer that his client did not intend to cooperate willingly. Budds particularly wanted him to clarify a response one witness, asked how he had positioned the helicopter for the final shot, provided: 'On the last rehearsal I'm not certain . . . Was that the one filmed by Frank Marshall?'

The result, early in 1983, was a subpoena issued by the District Attorney's office. Sheriff's deputies, frustrated in their attempts even to serve this successfully, started a surveillance operation on Marshall's home, only to learn that their quarry had once again departed for foreign shores – this time European, 'to work on a variety of Spielberg projects'.

★

153

Warner Bros considered shelving *Twilight Zone* altogether, until one of their lawyers pointed out that this might be seen as an admission of culpability. That did it. Instead, the scenes with the children were removed, and a new ending devised. Many were surprised that the makers failed to provide a 'dedication' to the movie's victims. 'I know this sounds ridiculous,' a Warners' spokesman began his 'explanation', 'but the studio thought that such an action would only remind the public about something everyone concerned with the film is hoping will be forgotten.'

Left to Spielberg, he would have walked away from *Twilight Zone*. Warners had other ideas, and they were persuasive. First, there was the matter of a contract to honour. Without Spielberg's name and contribution, they would be left with three-quarters of a movie. Secondly, to correct any suggestion that he was being pressured, he was asked to consider how it might look if he ducked out, the 'admission of culpability' angle they'd been forced to swallow.

Although Spielberg acquiesced, he was wary of going ahead with 'The Monsters Are Due On Maple Street', his original choice, involving as it did more night shooting with kids. He called in *Duel* scribe and *Twilight Zone* veteran Richard Matheson. Could he suggest a gentler, kinder, more innocuous episode? When Matheson drew his attention to one of the originals by George Clayton Johnson, 'Kick The Can', Spielberg eagerly made the switch to the tale of old folks rediscovering their lost youth. As if Matheson's sugary adaptation wasn't enough, he brought in Melissa Mathison to sweeten it further under her nom-de-plume, 'Josh Rogan'.

Spielberg, anxious to have done with it and leave for London to attend a Royal Command Performance of *E.T.*, completed 'Kick the Can' in just six days. The moral support kissy-kissy gathering on the final day included Drew Barrymore and Debra Winger, then it was off to be presented to Queen Elizabeth.

The reviews of *Twilight Zone* were mixed, weighted almost universally in favour of the episodes by Joe Dante and George Miller. To Richard Corliss in *Time* magazine, Landis's segment 'hardly looked worth shooting, let alone dying for'. Per David Ansen in *Newsweek*, 'its poor quality and moralizing tone make the tragedy doubly obscene'. With Spielberg's 'Kick the Can' dismissed as 'hard-sell whimsy', the movie was saved only by the genuinely scary Dante and Miller contributions. The combination of live action and animation was pressed into effective service in Dante's tale of a cartoon-obsessed boy terrorising his family, while Miller's edge-of-the-seat suspenser had a movie monster far scarier than Serling's original monochrome hobgoblin.

Almost a year to the day after the accident, another bizarre tragedy occurred thousands of miles away from Hollywood – in New South Wales, Australia. Director George Miller had first met his partner, mentor and best friend, Byron Kennedy, while working as a medical intern in 1970. One year later, Miller's medical career abandoned, the 'Kennedy Miller' production team already had a documentary under its belt in 'Violence in the Cinema, Part 1'. The success of *Mad Max*, further down the line, made the partners wealthy men.

On July 16, 1983, Kennedy, an expert airplane and helicopter pilot known for his meticulous attention to all aspects of air safety, took off on a test flight in a 'copter used on *The Road Warrior*. After the motor cut off over Lake Burragorang, south of Sydney, Kennedy's back was broken as he crashed into the freezing water. He survived only until the early hours of the following morning, tended by the shaken but uninjured passenger, a neighbour's fifteen-year-old son who had come along for the ride.

Shortly before indictments for the involuntary manslaughter of Vic Morrow, Renee Chen and My-Ca Le were granted in June 1983, Alpha Campbell, Landis's secretary on *Twilight Zone*, received an anonymous phone call, a male voice informing her that if she said anything unfavourable to Landis 'you are aware you could lose your job'.

Faced with civil suits for damages from the parents of the children, Warner Bros VP Stanley Belkin made the outrageous allegation that little Renee Chen, all of six years old, had 'knowingly assumed' risking her life.

Spielberg chose not to go quite that far, not to be *quite* that ridiculous. What he did instead, however, in choosing to lay responsibility on the parents of the dead children, was just as shocking. His attorney's filing ran, 'Spielberg is informed and believes and thereon alleges that at the time and place of the events complained of, plaintiffs were not exercising ordinary care, caution or prudence to prevent the injuries sustained . . . and that, therefore, the injuries alleged were proximately caused by the negligence or comparative negligence of the plaintiffs.'

Initially Warners offered just $46,176 to each family, acting on their lawyers' advice that workers' compensation benefits were the families' sole entitlements. In the end each of the parents' suits resulted in a pay-out of $2 million from a combination of Warner Bros and the defendants' insurance companies. The civil suit brought by the daughters of Vic Morrow was settled out of court on undisclosed terms.

Landis and his co-defendants were back in court in January

1984, for a preliminary hearing they had requested to determine whether or not an actual crime had been committed, and if so, whether or not they were culpable. The judge gave his verdict on April 23. The first two counts of 'child endangerment' were dismissed, the three remaining narrowed the focus to Landis, pilot Dorcey Wingo and special effects man Stewart. It had been Stewart's responsibility, the judge decreed, to set up and ultimately control all special effects, while Wingo had ample warning that the set was dangerous. As for Landis: While others could reasonably claim to have had neither custody nor control of the children, it would be difficult, if not impossible, for Landis to claim the same. In his quest for cinema verité he had gone beyond the realm of simple mechanical direction, and had set up the combination of circumstances which, in the final seconds of filming, had caused death and destruction. A trial date was set for September 1986. If convicted, Landis and his associates faced six years in prison.

In July 1982, to celebrate the twin releases of *Poltergeist* and *E.T.*, *Time* magazine's cover heralded 'Steven Spielberg, Magician of the Movies'. The following Spring, soon after *E.T.* had failed to capture any major category Oscars, Spielberg was disconsolate, desperately seeking closure, and gave his first and only public reference to the accident on the *Twilight Zone* set.

'This has been the most interesting year of my film career,' he declared. 'It has mixed the best, the success of *E.T.*, with the worst, the *Twilight Zone* tragedy. A mixture of ecstasy and grief. It's made me grow up a little more. The accident cast a pall on all 150 people who worked on the production. We are still just sick to the centre of our souls. I don't know anybody who it hasn't affected.'

He was not above criticism of gung-ho directors and producers who took unnecessary risks with lives: 'A movie is a fantasy – it's light and shadow flickering on a screen. No movie is worth dying for. I think people are standing up much more now than ever before to producers and directors who ask too much. If something isn't safe, it's the right and responsibility of every actor or crew member to shout, "Cut!"'

The implied criticism of Landis was not lost on observers. Spielberg's distancing was all but complete.

With the *Twilight Zone* trial only a few months away in the autumn of 1986, lead prosecutor Lea D'Agostino concluded that the DA's office would be under fire for not pursuing the presentation of Frank Marshall's subpoena. If one of Spielberg's officials were seen to be above the law, what kind of message was that sending out?

Acting on information from Spielberg's office that Marshall was in London working on a movie, Budds presented an affidavit to a federal magistrate requesting an international subpoena, on the basis that Marshall was a material witness in a criminal prosecution and was evading questioning. Service of the subpoena could not force Marshall back to the US, but would render him liable to seizure when he did return. Armed with the subpoena, Budds flew to London and utilised the facilities of Interpol and Scotland Yard to track Marshall down to the studio at which he was based and his digs at the St James Club.

Working between Scotland Yard and the FBI legal attaché at the US Embassy, the necessary paperwork was completed in a few days and a US Embassy official despatched to the St James Club to serve Marshall. The receptionist called Marshall's room and was informed that he was going out for lunch, but would be back in the afternoon.

An hour later Marshall checked out and was whisked away in a chauffeur-driven limousine. Scotland Yard was unable to turn up his name on any commercial flights out of the country. With Spielberg and director Richard Benjamin in Paris on a promotional trip for Amblin's *The Money Pit*, speculation was that he'd departed on board Amblin's corporate jet.

When D'Agostino and Chief Deputy DA Gilbert Garcetti suggested that Budds head to Paris, the weary Budds demurred, protesting that enough was enough; further pursuit would be futile. Once again Marshall had given everyone the slip.

As late as November 1986, Landis's attorney Harland Braun, acting on his own initiative, suggested to DA Ira Reiner and Gil Garcetti that they would be remiss if they did not consider that Spielberg, Marshall and Kennedy had also been criminally culpable in the illegal hiring of the children: Why were they being 'shielded'? He amplified his concern in a letter that questioned how Spielberg had been allowed to deflect the investigation away from himself by simply submitting a letter stating that he was not on the set the night of the accident. What other major witness, he asked, could avoid questioning by signing a piece of paper? 'Your office never asked Spielberg a single question about the accident or the hiring of the children,' Braun accused.

His action infuriated Landis, Folsey and Behr, since the last thing they wanted was Spielberg being dragged centre-stage. Frank Marshall, a relative bug in the heap, was one matter; Spielberg, king of the heap, quite another. They debated whether Braun should be fired, but decided against it. Instead, Braun found himself relegated to Folsey's defence; Landis replaced him with ex-Watergate prosecution heavyweight James F. Neal.

This was the final attempt to provoke questioning either Spielberg or any high-ranking member of his staff on the *Twilight Zone* case. Throughout the process, high-priced lawyers working for Spielberg and Warner Bros had managed to ensure that their clients never had to go through the inconvenience even of making a deposition. One unfortunate in Spielberg's office, foolish enough to answer one reporter's telephone call, was berated by Kathleen Kennedy for 'disloyalty' to her boss. As for the failure to serve Marshall a subpoena, Garcetti's only answer was, 'If someone really wants to avoid having a subpoena served, there's not a lot we can do about it.' Thomas Budds put it another way, 'It's smart to avoid a subpoena rather than lie under oath.'

As the date for the start of the *Twilight Zone* trial approached the portents did not look favourable for Landis and his co-defendants. James Camoile, the explosives expert who had actually detonated the fatal blast, had earlier been granted immunity for turning state's evidence. Jim Gavin, a veteran Hollywood 'director coordinator', while agreeing that ordinarily the onus for accidents on the set should not be on the director, damagingly declared that in his opinion Landis 'went for the lowest dollar', not only for a cost-cutting pilot, but that he had purposely chosen one who 'wouldn't talk back'. Originally called to the accident scene by the NTSB, Gavin had also found that the crucial radio link between Landis, Paul Stewart and Dorcey Winger was 'lousy'. The trial lasted from September 16, 1986 to May 19, 1987, with lead prosecutor Lea D'Agostino stating she had sealed testimony from thirteen witnesses who claimed that Landis acted in the reckless manner he did because he considered himself in direct competition with Steven Spielberg, and wanted to show that he could 'do bigger and better' than Spielberg. One witness alleged that Landis had screamed obscenities at Winger to get the pilot to follow his instructions. Although D'Agostino's witnesses were dismissed by the defence as low-level crew members, many felt that the onlookers had sussed out the game. Casting director Marci Liroff – who had departed the Fenton/Feinberg agency to go independent, and has never worked for Spielberg since – was among seventy prosecution witnesses called. All four of the dead childrens' parents testified that they would never have consented to their working had the scene been described to them in advance.

On the witness stand, Landis went to great pains to stress his close ties with Spielberg, referring to him throughout as 'Steve'. His lawyers went to equal pains to bring Frank Marshall's name into play, aware that he was unavailable either to deny or to contradict whatever they chose to say. Landis testified that Marshall had been fully aware that the children would be in the shot with explosions and a helicopter. And yes, he insisted, he had personally explained exactly the same thing to the children's parents. He flat out denied that Marci Liroff had ever told him the scene 'sounded kind of dangerous'. He also denied having said to cameraman Stephen Lydecker, 'We may lose the helicopter.'

His demeanour through much of the trial was in marked contrast to the smirking, hip-beyond-measure Landis everyone had known in the past. In his place, for the most part, was a regretful, quiet-spoken gentleman, soberly dressed in dark tweeds, who, when he wasn't giving his carefully controlled testimony, or holding his wife's hand as he listened to other witnesses, was dabbing his eyes with his handkerchief as emotion briefly overcame him.

After deliberating for nine days, D'Agostino was incredulous when the jury brought in a verdict of 'not guilty of involuntary manslaughter' and all five defendants were discharged. 'I believe the verdict was based not on the evidence presented, but, rather, on the power of Hollywood,' she declared. 'If I live to be a thousand, I will never accept that verdict.'

D'Agostino came in for criticism from some jury members for letting the case drag on too long. She in turn criticised the DA's decision to prosecute only on the manslaughter charges, stating that child labour violations should also have been addressed. On this point she was in accord with several jury members.

As one declared, 'Their asses could have been in jail, and should have been. But not for what they were accused of.'

Several filmmakers were courageous enough to give their own take on the subject, and not only on the verdict, but on the spread of responsibility. Regardless of his friendship with Spielberg, Brian De Palma spoke his mind to the authors of *Outrageous Conduct*. 'I don't think Landis was railroaded,' he declared. 'It's difficult to imagine putting all those elements in one place – helicopters, explosions, children, night shooting – and not treading a very thin line. Landis's actions were definitely excessive.'

Per director James L Brooks: 'If you hire children illegally, pay them under the table, then they get killed, that sounds like criminal negligence to me.'

'Look at Landis's other films and the stunts he's done,' producer Marty Bregman suggested to Farber and Green. 'They're very, very risky. Of course the studio shares responsibility for hiring him. And so does Steven Spielberg. He was the producer.'

Under his stage name of 'Dr Fantasy', Frank Marshall is an

accomplished amateur magician whose wrap party shows have become a staple of every movie he works on. Even his best party pieces, however, pale into insignificance beside the disappearing act he laid on the Los Angeles DA's office. Not until 1990 did he utter a word on the subject of *Twilight Zone*. On location at the time for *Arachnophobia*, a movie he was directing for Amblin, Marshall dismissed his non-availability as 'all hype. There's no truth to it at all,' blaming investigators for not reaching him at the outset. The tragedy had been 'terrible and horrible for everybody. But it was an accident. Which is eventually what the jury decided.'

Spielberg's speech on culpability and acceptance of responsibility might have run truer had he ensured that his staff, and Marshall in particular, made themselves available to investigators, rather than proceed to lead them a global dance at taxpayers' expense, in flagrant disregard of the legal process that affects ordinary mortals unprotected by powerful corporations and individuals. The disturbing conclusion drawn by many: If you're Spielberg, or you work for Spielberg, there's no question about it: you are above the law.

At the end of filming a puff for CNN on *The Color Purple*, interviewer Sandy Kenyon dared to ask a hitherto laid-back Spielberg for a comment on the *Twilight Zone* case. The result was a sudden change of demeanour. Waving his arms like a wild man, Spielberg screamed for the cameras to be turned off. The interview was over.

If Marshall went from strength to strength in the wake of *Twilight Zone* so did Kathleen Kennedy. During 1983 Spielberg asked her to run Amblin Entertainment. From 'Production Assistant' credit on *1941*, to 'Associate to Mr Spielberg' on *Raiders*, 'Co-Producer' with Spielberg on *E.T.*, through all the travails on *Twilight Zone* – it had been quite a ride for the energetic, resourceful Kennedy.

For John Landis, the picture was very different. The ride with Spielberg was over. His star has dimmed in recent years with a sting of box-office losers, although in the immediate wake of *Twilight Zone* he initially went from strength to strength, enough to join *Variety*'s 'Billion Dollar Directors' club in a 90s supplement studded with congratulations from every segment of the industry – that is, with the notable exception of Spielberg or anyone associated with Amblin. George Folsey Jr has remained loyal, as has Joel Behr. 'I lived the *Twilight Zone* tragedy with him long after the verdict', says Behr. 'I can say first-hand that it had a profound effect on him. He has a special place in his heart, not only for children, but also people advanced in years and wisdom.'

If that might be regarded as a piece of Grade-A bullshit, Landis himself had inadvertently provided his own best defence well in advance of filming *Twilight Zone*. It's something that neither he nor any of his associates bothered to bring up at any time during the trial – perhaps because what stuck in the craw of most people was his inability to accept even shared responsibility. Nevertheless, for what it's worth, here's what he vowed to one interviewer back in 1980: 'You'll never seen on any movie I make, "A Film by John Landis." That's *bullshit*. That kind of pretension offends me, on every film you see "Melvin Schwartz presents A Film by Sam Klein". I feel that everybody – the grip, the technicians, that make-up man – is responsible for a movie.'

As for the implication of drug use on the set, in particular the pin-point pupils that Vic Morrow had observed, that notion was refuted by Jamie Lee Curtis, one of the stars of Landis's *Trading Places*. 'He never uses drugs,' she maintained. 'He's the straightest man I ever met. He drinks *Tab*!'

Still the incident's stigma remains. In 1988 the Directors' Guild voted to reprimand Landis, his assistant director and Dan Allingham for conduct 'unprofessional, inconsistent with their responsibilities, and extremely prejudicial to the welfare of the DGA'.

The tragedy was also unkindly recalled by Eddie Murphy, the comedian who achieved movie stardom in Landis's *Trading Places*, *Beverly Hills Cop* and *Coming To America*. With a spokesman confirming 'personal problems' between Murphy and the director, stemming from 'racial slurs' allegedly made by Landis's wife, the comedian appeared on Arsenio Hall's talk show. He would never, he declared, work with Landis again. In fact, he added, Landis 'has a better chance of working again with Vic Morrow than with me'.

Being Hollywood, and with Murphy's stock in freefall, he and Landis did manage sufficiently to overcome their differences to make *Beverly Hills Cop III* together despite the declaration.

In a perfect world, rules and regulations governing the employment of children after hours would have been tightened following the *Twilight Zone* incident. Incredibly, California State labour laws governing the use of minors have actually been *relaxed* in recent years. Younger children can now work later hours, and even pre-school kids can work after midnight. How about safety on movie sets after the accident? Annual complaints of safety conditions have more than doubled.

Judge Gordon Ringer had it right back in 1984 when he observed: 'This isn't nickelodeon time anymore . . . I should have thought that after seventy-five years somebody might have thought it inappropriate to put Lillian Gish on an ice floe and send her into the middle of Niagara Falls to make a movie.'

When the California Occupational Safety and Health Administration (Cal-OSA) was disbanded in 1987 and taken over by a federal agency unfamiliar with movie-related investigation, their fines of $62,375 originally levied in 1982 against Warners, Landis and others, were reduced on appeal to $1,350 after the agency took over.

By this time Spielberg and Landis had but one thing in common. The returns from their five gross points in *Twilight Zone – The Movie*.

Between $800,000 and $1 million each.

# 18

## 'The Sequel's a Prequel'

*'We are the pigs, the ones who sniff out the truffles. You can
put us on a leash, keep us under control, but we are the
guys who dig out the gold. The men in the dark tower
cannot do that. They know as much about making movies
as a banker does. But the power lies with us – the ones who
actually know how to make movies.'*

GEORGE LUCAS

*'Lucas and Spielberg may be making themselves and their
backers very wealthy. At the same time they are doing their
medium a profound disservice.'*

DAVID SHIPMAN, *The Story of Cinema*

Another sad loss occurred only months after the fatal accident
involving Vic Morrow and the two children. Any resentment both
Spielberg and George Lucas had felt in the past was forgotten as
the two men paid touching tributes to Verna Fields following her
death from cancer in November 1982. Apart from any subsequent
squabbling over who did what and when, they both had good reason. Lucas had been introduced to his future wife Marsha in a
makeshift editing room over Fields' garage in 1966; Verna was in
charge of editing during the *American Graffiti* shoot, Marsha had
taken over in post-production; Verna had edited Spielberg's first
theatrical feature, *The Sugarland Express*, as well as *Jaws*. Spielberg
recalled the scene reshot in Fields' backyard pool that had produced one of the biggest shocks in the deep-sea saga.

The tussle over credit for the movie still refused to quit, revived
yet again in a New York *Times* article in 1995 asserting that *Jaws*
had been virtually 'saved' in the editing room. Writer Carl Gottlieb
took up the cudgel on Spielberg's behalf on this occasion, replying
that 'without denigrating Verna Fields' contribution . . . the film
didn't need saving'. He then shot his argument in the foot by adding

that 'every frame of film an editor cuts is conceived and shot else-where by others'. This conveniently overlooked Fields' solution to what could have been the floating head non-event, as well as the list of shots, supplied to Spielberg on a regular basis at Martha's Vineyard, required to make sense of the footage she already had.

Gottlieb, now vice-president of Writers' Guild of America West, finished with a Hollywood happy-ending flourish: '*Jaws* was the product of a fruitful and happy collaboration, and Steven Spielberg is the true auteur of that experience.'

Hold everything. AUTEUR?

In the first place, Spielberg was a gun-for-hire. By the end of the movie, he was an undoubted hero who'd hung in through hell and – mostly – high water. But an 'auteur' on *Jaws* in the original *Cahiers du Cinema* definition of the word – the sole, or even main begetter of the movie, from concept to conclusion? Consider. Discuss. Debate.

Then credit Peter Benchley in the first place for tapping into the public's primordial fear of sharks and dread of the deep. Credit Richard Zanuck and David Brown with a sensational job of pre-publicity, for recognising what they had and following through magnificently, dragging Universal, kicking and screaming, with them. Credit Carl Gottlieb and all concerned with reshaping Benchley's book for the screen. Credit Bill Butler for shooting the movie. Credit designer Joe Alves. Credit Bob Mattey for creating 'Bruce'. Credit Verna Fields for her masterful editing and swimming pool facilities. Credit John Williams for synthesising 'shark dread' in musical form; even if his main theme owed plenty to TV's *Twilight Zone* there was lots more that was terrifically down-to-the-sea-in-ships, the very essence of grand nautical adventure. Credit Lew Wasserman, Sid Sheinberg, Ned Tanen and Universal for not giv-ing up on their young protégé when seaweed smeared the lens. Give Sheinberg an extra credit for forcing Spielberg to undertake the assignment. And last but not least, credit Spielberg with amaz-ing stoicism during production and with tremendous directorial skill.

Man of the match? Definitely. But *auteur*? Give me a break.

Spielberg's effervescent mother hadn't allowed the grass to grow under her feet following the split from her first husband in 1965. Three years later she married Bernard Adler, effectively allowing her son to revert from his unwanted 'man of the house' appoint-ment to continue living, and reliving cinematically, his childhood.

The Adler's restaurant, 'The Milky Way', was established nine years later in LA's West Pico Boulevard. Like Leah herself, the establishment is bright and cheery, and like Bernie, it is highly organised and *strictly* kosher. (Bernie hails from Poland and is a member of the Lubavitcher sect, than whom few are stricter.) Blue denim tablecloths, whitewashed walls and large French windows give it the look of a Parisian bistro, although the menu and its assortment of ethnic delights – Adler's Caesar salad, pot stickers, chimichangas, salmon puffs, cheese blintzes and cabbage rolls – tells a slightly different, but no less delicious story. Fried smelts are also on offer. 'Some people don't like them,' says the irrepressible Leah with a shrug, 'but I keep them on the menu for my kid.'

Catering mostly but far from exclusively for local Orthodox Jews, 'The Milky Way' is her husband's brainchild, as she is the first to acknowledge: 'Bernie runs the restaurant. He's the brains. Me? I'm the mouth.'

When her son took off into the kitchen to make himself a kosher pizza, Leah was none too impressed with the results. 'He should stick to making movies,' she declared. '*That* he's good at.'

She was much more thrilled with a birthday present her son handed over – a $5,000 gift voucher from Tiffany's. After telling everyone about it, someone suggested she take a closer look. When she did, she discovered that it wasn't for $5,000 at all.

It was for $50,000.

Amy Irving unexpectedly turned up to greet Spielberg at the airport during an early recce trip he made to India scouting locations for *Indiana Jones and the Temple of Doom*. Fresh from location work on the made-for-TV *The Far Pavilions*, her olive skin glowing, she looked large as life and twice as alluring. The night before, in front of friends, she had said, 'I wish I'd have a visitor and I want it to be Steve.' Next morning news came through that, purely coincidentally, Spielberg was due to land later that day.

Rumours of a reconciliation flew, then fizzled as the 'two great friends' went their separate ways again. Irving knew better. Absence had definitely made her heart grow fonder.

With Sri Lanka standing in for India, shooting began in May 1983 on *Temple of Doom*. Macau was the next stop, standing in for 1935 Shanghai, then it was off to Britain's EMI-Elstree Studios. Shooting was interrupted halfway through, and a three-week hiatus declared, when a pre-existing back condition of Harrison Ford's was reactivated, requiring him to be flown to Los Angeles for surgery on his ruptured disc. For the man who had laughingly described Indiana Jones' 'most impossible stunt' as 'keeping that hat on all the time', it was a painful reminder of how exacting the role was. Even with a double on hand, Ford had chosen to do many of the stunts himself.

Newcomer Kate Capshaw, cast as Ford's love interest, Willie Scott, was a different kettle of fish altogether from Karen Allen's cool, collected toughie, Marion. Spielberg saw her as 'a natural comedienne, a cross between Lucille Ball and Ann Sothern'. Before too long, notwithstanding the renewed connection with Amy Irving, he saw her as a lot more.

Capshaw burst into tears when Spielberg asked her to embrace a fourteen-foot python. 'Don't make me do this, and I'll do anything else you want,' she pleaded. Little did she know that 'anything else' would include being covered with creepy-crawly insects, including one seven-inch specimen draped across her palm practically standing upright and saluting. 'It wasn't hard to play Willie Scott, who was always bitching about things,' says Capshaw, 'because it *was* hot, the bugs *were* biting, and there was an elephant that was a pain in the butt.'

Through it all the actress was great company, loads of fun, ready for a laugh. And ready even for the occasional tumble with her director while the rest of the unit discreetly looked the other way. What was this? Surely a new departure for the buttoned-up Spielberg?

Kate Capshaw is a package of contradictions. Look beyond the carelessly tossed hair that can be blonde or reddish-brunette depending on her mood. Forget the giggles. Forget the coquettish smile, the air of playful seductiveness, forget the fact that her ideal casting would be sat before a mirror singing 'I Enjoy Being a Girl' in a Westernised revival of *Flower Drum Song*. This is neither fashion's plaything nor ethereal sophisticate, and Capshaw has no aspirations in either direction. Instead, there's metal beneath the down-home surface. The steel-blue eyes are the giveaway . . .

The only daughter of a beautician and airline operations manager, Capshaw grew up in the St Louis suburb of Florissant. Bob, the man she married in her senior year, was her high school teacher. After gaining a Master's degree in education, two years of coaching children with learning disabilities followed. During long vacations she acted in summer stock, taking time off for the birth of a daughter, Jessica, in 1977.

Although the couple agreed to split while still in Missouri, Capshaw – with an eye on an acting career – managed to persuade her husband to make a decisive move with her in 1978: 'We knew we weren't going to be married for long, but we both made a pact that we would come to New York, try to start a new life, and help each other do just that. We agreed to split whenever we could financially, which was weird, but I couldn't have come to New York without him, and he couldn't have come without me.'

There had never been any infidelity in the relationship, simply a gradual drifting apart, and for a while Capshaw resorted to therapy to get her through the roughest patches of '*This* is my life?' When the split was finally made in 1982 after six years of marriage, it was, per Capshaw, 'amicable, then unamicable, then amicable'. Modelling had provided a living during that first year in New York, and given her time to crystallise ambitions either of movie or Broadway stardom. Oddly, she never saw herself as a professional *actress*, simply – A Star. TV commercials kept the wolf from the door for a while until she landed a role in a rock-bottom budget independent movie, *A Little Sex*. It did nothing for her career, flopping as soon as it appeared in '82. The next movie, although no more successful, provided another turning point. The director of *Windy City*, Armyan Bernstein, would be the next man in her life. 'It's very boring falling in love with the director,' Capshaw confided soon after their affair became known. 'There's no way I thought it would ever happen to me!'

She laughed as she described their first date. 'We were as nervous as two people could possibly be. The reason? We were nuts about each other, and we hadn't done anything about it. It was probably about sixty degrees in the restaurant – and we were burning up! We were peeling off our clothes!! When we left, I walked into a closet instead of out the door. I should have known then I was in big trouble!'

By the end of filming *Windy City*, Capshaw accepted the fact that Bernstein had become part of her life. There were several problems. First, he lived in Los Angeles. Second, as she explained: 'I hadn't lived with anyone since my husband, and I didn't know how I felt about living with someone and not being married. But it seemed like the right thing to do. Armyan had never lived with anybody either, much less a woman and her child.' How did young Jessica react? 'She watched the long phone calls. She sensed my love and homesickness for Armyan. And I let her know that she could and should have a lot of feelings about Armyan – from not wanting him around, to seeing that he was a pretty good guy.'

Love conquered all in the end, and in no time flat the Bernstein household was rounded out by Kate, Jessica and a housekeeper. 'Kate has to be affectionate at least once an hour,' the deeply contented Bernstein declared.

Spielberg's entry into the happy picture was only peripheral at first, and arrived courtesy of an early morning jog involving casting agent Mike Fenton and William Morris agent Peter Meyer.

'I'm looking for someone to play the feminine lead in Spielberg's *Raiders of the Lost Ark* sequel', Fenton huffed.

'You're not using Karen Allen again? She was a knockout in the first one,' Meyer puffed.

'I know,' Fenton replied. 'But we can't.'

'Why?'

'The sequel's a prequel.'

'Oh.' Meyer paused for all of four strides. 'In that case, I know someone who'd be ideal. You want knockout? I'll give you knockout. Name of Kate Capshaw.'

She was nervous as she made her way to Spielberg's office. This could be her big break, or it could be yet another in a series of let-downs. Disconcertingly, it was clear from the outset, even as she was greeted by Kathleen Kennedy, that they had been expecting someone else. A mix-up had occurred, and she wasn't the girl in the photograph they'd been looking at. Oh, Lord, she thought, here we go again – that oh-so-familiar too young, too old, too blonde, too brunette, too tall, too small routine. Instead, Spielberg – once he'd recovered from his initial double-take – rose to the occasion and handed her a one-page monologue to read. It had nothing to do with the *Temple of Doom* script, but was a little something he'd composed that allowed her to register the variety of emotions 'Willie Scott' was to smoulder through in the movie, all the way from 'Eek, a mouse' to 'You'll be back in five minutes'. Capshaw dutifully, and impressively, tip-toed through the emotions, giving the ever-so-slightly poleaxed Spielberg time to admire the merchandise on display. Whatever her attributes might be as an actress, Capshaw was one spectacularly beautiful woman.

For the next two weeks Spielberg called from time to time, on each occasion offering little flurries of encouragement. Yes, he was in New York interviewing other actresses, but she should not be discouraged, she should hang in, no decision had been made yet. That was the situation until one afternoon when he called again. Pandemonium was raging at the Bernsteins. A brand-new house-keeper had just arrived, Jessica was waiting to be picked up from school, wallpaper hangers were threatening strike action.

'Steven,' Capshaw spluttered, 'you've caught me at a bad time. I really can't talk right now.'

'But I'm calling from New York and I just wanted to let you know—'

'Steven, can you call me tomorrow? I can hardly hear you.'

'Kate, would you please s*it down*? I want you to play Willie Scott.'

'Steve, I do *not* have time to talk about— *Whaaaat?!*' Capshaw began to cry after putting the phone down, her mind a torrent of mixed emotions. She had just moved to Los Angeles to be with Bernstein. Now she was faced with a five-month location shoot starting in Sri Lanka, wherever the hell that might be. How about Jessica's schooling? And, to get back to basics, how about the role itself? Did she really want it, 'big chance' or not, Spielberg movie or not? After all, it was hardly the sort of role Meryl Streep would deign to play. *She* would, though—!

Bidding Bernstein a fond farewell, Capshaw flew to Sri Lanka with Jessica on the appointed day. Becoming romantically involved with Spielberg was the last thing on her mind. What was it she had said about falling in love with directors back in '82? *So* damn boring!

At the start of the eighties Spielberg had expressed to journalist Todd McCarthy his 'little Utopian dream' of forming a company which would operate like a 'children's crusade' of filmmakers. The only way to crash the portals would be never to have made a film before, whether you were eighty years old or twenty. In the years ahead Amblin, named after the Hoffman-financed featurette that had brought him to the attention of Sid Sheinberg, rarely lived up to the concept. Unless, that is, Spielberg's TV series *Amazing Stories* is taken into account. Here he did take the opportunity to fulfil his promise, with Bob Balaban, Donald Petrie, Lesli Linka Glatter, Mickey Moore, Phil Joanou and several others given chances on a scale they might not have enjoyed elsewhere.

MCA's 'thank-you' to Spielberg for *E.T.* was Amblin's $3.5 million corporate headquarters, established on the far corner of the Universal lot. With major design credit claimed by Spielberg himself, perhaps the real inspiration derives from fast-food chain Taco Bell, although everything was executed in the best possible Tex-Mex, Pueblo Indian style. The company logo, deservedly so since the image is responsible for the edifice, is the encircled silhouette of a boy riding a bicycle bearing E.T. in the basket. Spielberg's reaction to Universal's largesse: 'What can I say? This is the most amazing gift I've ever received.'

The remarkable thing about Universal's gesture was that it came with no strings attached, apart from a mutually agreed overhead charge that would be factored into Amblin's output. If Spielberg felt that a project was more suitable for Warner Bros, he was free to go there for distribution or co-production facilities. As he did. And to Paramount, of course, for further *Indiana Jones* adventures. 'I have no obligation to Universal, really,' Spielberg confirmed, 'unless you want to look at this wonderful building and apply the word "guilt"!'

Apart from Amblin's offices, where Indian rugs, exotic pot plants and ethnic pottery are scattered strategically throughout as if by some *feng-shui* expert, the low-slung, two-storey adobe-style building also comprises a video and pinball games room, kitchen, gym and screening theatre. An open gallery leads to a vegetable garden, fully stocked fish pond, coolly splashing fountains and a tree-shaded courtyard gently dominated by a pink marble bust of an Indian madonna and her children. To the casual visitor, of which I was one, there's a certain nagging degree of unreality hanging over the place.

Maybe it's the fact that everything is so carefully buffed, weathered, distressed, seasoned to perfection, neat and peachy-clean. Maybe it's the occasional sight of Spielberg first thing in the mornings. Conducting a production conference? Making casting choices? Discussing budgets? Maybe. But more often than not look for him in the kitchen, mixing up a mess of *matzo brei*. 'It's something I urge every young filmmaker to do,' he says. 'Gentile or Jew.'

# 19

# Home From Home

*'Steve Ross was very much what I wish my father was.'*

*'Producing came out of a feeling of impatience and ambition. Wanting to have more on my plate than I could possibly handle.'*

STEVEN SPIELBERG

Non-exclusive as his tie was to Universal, many were puzzled by Spielberg's favouring of Warner Bros as an alternative home for his projects. They wouldn't have been, had they known of his growing relationship with Warner Communications Inc. supremo Steve Ross.

'The day I first met him,' Spielberg recalled, 'he was on the phone, yelling at New York City. It had to be bigger, more ambitious, more colourful, *bigger*. I said to myself, "Well, that's a typical CEO. He builds empires." And then I realised he was talking about the 1981 annual brochure. He was like an art director. He had style, wit, pizzazz, he was creative. Being in his life was like being in a world that spun a lot faster than it is.'

Spielberg's introduction to Ross had taken place at WCI's sumptuous Villa Eden in Acapulco, during a weekend trip arranged by Terry Semel, one of Ross's deputies at the Warner studio. The exquisitely tailored, perfectly groomed Ross, his silver hair expertly parted to cover his growing baldness, was desperate to woo Spielberg away from Universal and land at least a portion of his future output for Warners. That the goal was attainable he had gathered from a briefly rumoured alliance between Spielberg and Disney that left the would-be participants remarkably tight-lipped, reluctant to deny outright that something might be in the air. Although it had indeed come to nothing – yes, *E.T.* really *might* have been a Disney movie – it encouraged Ross to imagine for the first time that a poaching raid on Spielberg might not totally be in vain.

He was smart enough not to take the overt route, at least not to the extent that Spielberg either noticed or seemed to mind. That follow-up would be left to Semel and Robert Daly, his foot-soldiers, once the softening-up process, with nary the slightest hint of favours being returned, was complete.

The Acapulco weekend package, which the likes of Barbra Streisand, producer David Puttnam and music maestro Quincy Jones also enjoyed, was just the beginning. The threesome might have given Spielberg a small clue as to what was going on, for everyone *except* him was tied in one way or another to Warners and, by definition, Steve Ross; Streisand through movies, although her record deal remained at CBS; Puttnam through a long-standing 'first-look' contract; Jones through his Warner-distributed Q-West label. In essence Villa Eden, situated near the resort town of Las Brisas, was a sumptuous rest 'n' relaxation spot for weary Warner troops.

Instead of the typical CEO Spielberg had imagined he was about to meet, the silver-haired and equally silver-tongued Ross exuded enough charisma to have made it as a movie star had that been his goal, rather than the funeral parlour to parking lot route he had travelled along the way to founding WCI. At Villa Eden Ross was a magnetic, solicitious host who took delight in anticipating and fulfilling his guests' slightest needs, so much so that few ventured outside its cultivated grounds. With swimming pool, tennis courts, a breathtaking view of Acapulco Bay, its own screening room and superb banqueting facilities, there was simply no need.

Despite warnings that Ross was only interested in him for one reason and one reason only, Spielberg was swept away by the man's forceful, yet easily charming personality. He claims he was 'cautious' for the first year with his new best friend, perhaps waiting for the sudden switch from socialising to the bottom line. It never came. At least, not from Ross. Why have dogs and bark at the same time? Over the years it was Semel and Daly who made the approaches, more often than not Semel, someone Spielberg had first met in the mid-seventies and regarded as a good friend. 'Steven was someone with no business history. He found Steve, who was much older, so fascinating,' is how Semel characterises the relationship. 'Steve was into things he knew only a little about – everything from art to fine wines to homes.'

Eventually, the softening-up process was complete, with Spielberg describing Ross as 'the single most generous person I've ever met in my life'. Differentiating between 'two kinds of generosity' as that of 'putting names on buildings' versus that 'which is selfless and done in complete anonymity', he maintained that Ross adhered to the latter. Never at any point did he seem to stop and ponder whose money was being splattered around: was it Ross's or was it Warners? Was it personal or was it business? Although his one per cent of WCI was worth millions, Ross remained an officer of the company responsible to his shareholders. Even so, he acted and spent as if WCI was his personal fiefdom.

Still Spielberg was seduced, seemingly under the impression, or content to believe, that Semel and Daly, in pointedly asking about his plans for new pictures, were acting independently of their boss. Or, hold on, maybe he wasn't as naive as they all thought. Even Sid Sheinberg, after all, was less than keen on some of the movies he pitched. What was so naive about having a second home for such projects, with the odd tidbit thrown in?

Ross went ballistic when he learned that Kathleen Carey, Spielberg's girlfriend, had been lured away from Warner Bros Music to MCA's Backstreet label. This was the exact *opposite*, he railed, of the traffic flow he had in mind. There had to be a way to redress the balance. He found one on discovering that Carey had become a 'special friend' to a disturbed nine-year-old orphan. Ross swung into action. Carey received a puzzled phone call from the orphanage: 'Why have seven colour TVs, seven VCRs, and eight hundred pounds of Christmas presents arrived here with your name on them?' Carey's first thought: 'Had Santa Steven been at work?' No, it turned out. Remembering that Kathleen had talked about the orphanage to Ross and his wife Courtenay, Spielberg had another thought: 'Was it Santa *Steve*?' After a brief denial, Ross chuckled. 'Look, don't look a gift horse in the mouth,' he suggested.

It didn't stop there. Far from it. During a visit to Ross's East Hampton pad, Spielberg was just a little taken aback, even in such autocratic company, to be told, 'I want you to live here. I want you to be my neighbour.'

'B-but people live in these houses,' he managed.

Ross's answer was to walk his friend a couple of doors down, ring the bell, and greet the old lady who answered with, 'Hi, how are you? This is my friend Steven Spielberg. I wanted you to know that you have a buyer – him – if ever you want to sell your house.'

A week later Ross began negotiations with the lady's broker, going on to have Warners purchase the property for later resale to Spielberg. It was several years before he moved in, after the property had been restructured by an architect introduced by Ross, and its interior decorated throughout by Ross's wife Courtenay. Bingo, Ross had the neighbour he wanted. And, more to the point, Spielberg weaving back and forth with his projects between Universal and Warner Bros.

★

173

If the controversy that had swirled for years around Steve Ross and his questionable business practices ever entered into Spielberg's considerations, no hint was given. The company's involvement in the Mafia-infested Westchester Premier Theater, in the unlikely setting of historic Tarrytown, had been well documented. Back in 1975, why had WCI invested in the Westchester in return for a sack of loose cash? And why had one of the original brokers, capable of damaging testimony against WCI, become a company employee, one prepared to take refuge behind the fifth amendment when the case came to trial, one whose legal costs of $100,000 were put up by his generous new employer?

At the end of the day, when the chips were down, Ross had moved swiftly to distance himself from Jay Emmett, his colleague and previous best friend, throwing him to the government wolves. Emmett had gone down along with WCI's assistant treasurer Solomon ('The company always had a need for cash') Weiss, who also doubled as Ross's personal accountant, and had handled the sack of greenbacks dumped on his desk in exchange for WCI investment in the Westchester. The partners in the venture? Heading the list, with a $1.4 million stake: the Colombo family's Richard 'Nerves' Fusco, the Gambino mob's Gregory De Palma, the Genoveses' Salvatore Cannatella.

To be sure, this was only part of the Steve Ross story, but how much farther back it reached was something that Spielberg, in the midst of being treated like royalty, chose not to delve into. Had he done so, he would have found that entering his father-in-law's funeral business had been only the first step on the ladder for Ross. That led to a tie-up with Kinney, combining funeral parlours with parking and car rental, all of them slush-fund friendly. Kinney's founder was bootlegger and bookie Emanuel 'Alabam' Kimmel, in association with Abner 'Longie' Zwillman, one of Godfather Meyer Lansky's sidemen. According to an FBI document in 1965, Kimmel was 'known to be a lifetime associate of several internationally known hoodlums'. Only with Kimmel's Kinney holding obscured behind a maze of dummy corporations had Ross been able to circumvent a Securities and Exchange Commission investigation and successfully take the merged companies public in March 1962. Seven years later Kinney National Services had taken over Warner Bros/Seven Arts to form Warner Communications Inc.

Almost from the very beginning of his career, Ross had been exposed to underworld figures, and had prospered mightily from the association. Kinney's slush fund, claimed to amount to $1 million a year, had been the 'green grease' that had oiled the company's wheels. $100,000 in a brown left on someone's desk to take care of a problem? No problem. As far as the FBI was concerned in their investigation of the Westchester Premier Theater scam, nothing had changed. Only Emmett and Weiss taking the fall had saved Ross, the 'real culprit' per government investigators. And even while the Westchester investigation was going on, Ross had been unable to stop striking other dubious deals, for which there was only one reasonable rationale.

In 1981 a New Jersey lawyer named Robert Petrallia was about to be indicted on charges of conspiracy and sixteen counts of mail fraud, following the collapse of his real estate tax shelter company with $38 million of shareholders' money. Just one month before his anticipated indictment, Ross had WCI buy eighty per cent of Leisure Development of America, a brand-new shell company Petrallia had formed, for $250,000, plus a commitment to spend $2.75 million. In addition, Petrallia and a whole bunch of 'associates' were handed 'signing bonuses' for applying their names on the dotted for WCI. Their stated intention: to start a chain of restaurants as a division of WCI, Warner Leisure.

There was one slight problem. The only experience either Petrallia or his associates had of restaurants was of being shown to their tables by a variety of maître-d's. One month after signing Petrallia pled guilty to a tax misdemeanour and was given a $1,000 fine, two years' probation, and ordered to serve 200 hours of community service.

The first any outside director heard of the 'Warner Leisure Follies' came in 1984, by which time the show was in its third great year. With $70 million of theirs and shareholders' money down the chute, the curtain finally, some would say mercifully, descended a year later.

The drive to capture Spielberg carried with it more than a hint of payback as far as Ross was concerned. Much as he admired Lew Wasserman's unassailable position in Hollywood, he was less than pleased with the icy tone Wasserman adopted in his rare references to WCI, and to Ross in particular. All right, maybe he *was* a Johnny-Come-Lately in Wasserman's definition of the term. If that was the case, he'd show Wasserman that even latecomers could steal a few pearls. Spielberg was missing his pet dogs? Easy. Ross despatched one of the Warner jets across the country to fly the little critters to East Hampton. To make Spielberg's mom feel right at home on her first Warner flight, Ross, aware of the restaurant in LA she and her husband ran, festooned the cabin's ceiling with 'Milky Way' candy wrappers. When Amy Irving eventually became Mrs Spielberg and they stayed in Paris at the Ritz as Ross's guests, they found their names embroidered on their bathrobes and embossed on the deluxe stationery. After spending a weekend as a guest at East Hampton, Spielberg, along with Michael Jackson, Quincy Jones and record mogul David Geffen, received a set of five hand-painted books as a memento of the occasion. Naturally, each was an original edition.

After all the wooing and wining, Spielberg's first trip into bed with Ross, *Twilight Zone – The Movie*, had proved an unmitigated disaster on every possible level. So had the second trip – for Ross, that is. Not for Spielberg. To be fair, there was good news and bad on the deal Ross struck with the object of his devotions to develop an *E.T.* video game. The good: an unbelievable $23 million *advance* against royalties for Spielberg. The bad: a colossal flop for Ross and Warners' Atari division that almost brought the company to its knees.

Despite research that showed less than a third of the economically necessary run of four million units was called for, Atari went ahead and manufactured and shipped the full four million. The result: 3.5 million unsold *E.T.* cartridges were returned. Many blamed the fiasco on the game's four-week development period against an industry norm of six months. Atari officials in turn blamed Spielberg, who had insisted when the deal was struck in July 1982, that the game had to be on the market before Christmas. Ross faced a storm of protest from fellow board members and shareholders that he had paid way too much to Spielberg in the first place. Like about $22 million too much.

Before Ross's largesse had manifested itself, Sid Sheinberg had planned to put the *E.T.* video game contract out to tender, to Coleco Industries amongst others, from whom he hoped to reap eventual royalties, based on a successful game being devised, of $15–20 million. Spielberg, meantime, had made it clear that he wanted Ross's Atari division to have the inside track. When the president of Atari's coin-operated games, Charles Paul, offered Sheinberg $1 million upfront and a seven per cent royalty figure, he was swiftly shown the door. Told back at base that a deal had already been worked out between Spielberg and Ross over the previous weekend at East Hampton, Paul was staggered. Why was Ross paying this enormous, unprecedented *advance*? How could he possibly justify $23 million? There had to be another reason. There was. Ross had just woven another strand of his silken web.

There was no saving the pathetic 'game' Atari engineers were forced to rush on to the market to meet Spielberg's timetable and with his contractual input. 'It wasn't a game at all,' said one Atari executive. 'It was a *thing* wobbling about on the screen.'

★

Another star revolving alongside Spielberg in Steve Ross's firmament was David Geffen, a young man even then flaunting the image of someone who could turn a profit on a dime. If Spielberg's arrival on the scene opened up all kinds of possibilities for Geffen, most would not be realised until more than a decade had passed. Meanwhile, the two mini-moguls found themselves competing for Ross's attention, although in Spielberg's case it was hardly necessary. He was the pristine, glittering prize; Geffen had been around a while and had a chequered, if spectacular history. 'We were sibling rivals,' Geffen confirms. 'I was jealous of Steven. But I respected him.'

Born in Brooklyn in 1943, Geffen had flunked high school and worked as an usher at CBS, then as a receptionist at a TV production company before landing in the mailroom of the William Morris Agency. There he swiftly rose to represent directors and screenwriters twice his age; a move to the Ashley-Famous Agency saw him concentrating on musicians' careers and provided his first introduction to Steve Ross when he gathered up Ashley-Famous, and Ted Ashley with it, for $13 million in 1967.

Convinced of Laura Nyro's talent as both singer and songwriter, Geffen abandoned his day job to manage her career. Soon he succeeded in signing her to a contract with CBS Records for a $4.5 million advance. Throughout the late sixties he added to his string of artists; when one act was turned down everywhere, he formed his own Asylum Records ('because it was all craziness'), a label that soon boasted Linda Ronstadt, Joni Mitchell and the Eagles. The sale of Asylum to Warners for $7 million in 1970 followed Ross's formation of WCI. Although more famous as a movie company, Warners' money, Ross had quickly discovered, came mainly from its record labels Atlantic, Elektra and Warner/Reprise; Asylum was a good fit. The sale made Geffen a millionaire at twenty-seven, the proud owner of a Rolls-Royce and several homes. 'He possessed an ego as large as all outdoors,' according to one of his colleagues at that time, 'and the energy of a hyperkinetic child on a sugar binge.'

With Asylum having absorbed Elektra, Geffen was bored and pining for a change by 1975. Ross's answer was to name him vice-chairman of Warner Bros Pictures under his old boss Ted Ashley. Instead of the creative buzz Geffen had expected, what he found instead, by his account, was a bureaucratic nightmare. After a year Ross fired him. Worse, under the terms of his $1 million-a-year contract, he couldn't work elsewhere. Worse yet, according to Geffen, a bladder tumour he had removed was found to be cancerous by no less an authority than the Cedars-Sinai Medical Center. The next four years were spent partying, getting laid, and preparing himself for the final curtain. Geffen shrugs off the alternative version some 'friends' circulated: 'If they think I had a nervous breakdown, I don't give a shit.'

When new tests revealed the cancer diagnosis had been in error, Geffen returned to the business he knew best and the welcoming arms of Ross. Geffen Records was co-financed by WCI on a 50/50 basis. Although the first two signings, Elton John and Donna Summer, struck out, the third – the result of a phone call out of the blue from Yoko Ono – scored a home run. In the year of John Lennon's assassination, Geffen's 'Double Fantasy' album from the ex-Beatle sold three million copies.

There remained the field of movies to conquer, and although boardroom wrangling had proved a bust, he was determined to prove himself on a project-by-project basis. For his first venture, again with backing and distribution promised by Ross, he chose a script by *Chinatown* writer Robert Towne, a lesbian coming-out-in-sports saga entitled *Personal Best*.

Steve Ross was nervous about allowing Towne, despite his writing credentials, to make his directorial debut with the movie, and a providential Writers' Guild strike during shooting gave him the perfect opportunity to close the movie down. Geffen was apoplectic. The man he'd looked to as a father figure had first fired him, then financed him, backed his movie, then walked away from it? Looking around for an alternative home, he settled on another William Morris alumnus with whom he was friendly – Barry Diller, late of ABC, now lording it over Michael Eisner and Jeff Katzenberg, his underlings at Paramount. Diller indicated that yes, he might adopt *Personal Best* when the strike ended. That sounded hopeful, except that later Diller would claim that the understanding struck entitled him first to see the existing footage before making a final decision. Geffen retorted that had never been the case.

Enter CAA's Michael Ovitz, muddying the water still further with a demand that, by the way, gentlemen, Towne's salary needed a considerable hike before he could possibly go forward. At this Diller dug his stilettos in even further. Unless he were allowed to view the rushes, the deal was *definitely* off. Geffen blinked. And Diller walked, leaving Geffen's neck on the line for millions spent.

The prospect of ever having a finished picture to sell became even more remote when Geffen himself pulled the plug on the re-started *Personal Best*, claiming that Towne was over budget and under schedule – and now, goddamit, he was spending his own money. Steve Ross relented finally and took the film back into the Warners' fold, but only after hijacking Towne's upcoming *Greystoke – Tarzan, Lord of the Apes* as compensation. When, after all these stops and starts and tribulations, *Personal Best* finally opened, it also closed in record time. It was not Geffen's finest moment. But he neither forgot nor would ever excuse Ovitz's opportunism in trying to score more for his client at his expense. It had been a Diller deal-killer, and one that could have seriously hobbled Geffen, millionaire or no. Thank God Steve Ross had come through in the end.

With Spielberg as the new object of Ross's affections, Geffen, sporting a carefully constructed preppy look and the close-cropped hair to go with it – a far cry from his 'Afro' of the seventies – looked around for a movie that would establish him as a contender, not an also-ran. For a while there was synergistic talk, heavily promoted from the sidelines by Ross, of Spielberg filming a version of Geffen's off-Broadway hit, *The Little Shop of Horrors*.

Instead, Geffen went ahead and filmed *Risky Business* without the benefit of Spielberg at the helm. Released in 1983, the movie established Tom Cruise as a star and Geffen as a movie player. Now Ross would see who the *real* star was!

Ross was deeply satisfied with the progress he'd made in recruiting Spielberg. So there had been that unexpected problem on *Twilight Zone*. Hey, the movie might still make some money, or at least break even. So the *E.T.* game had died the death. So what else was new? *Gremlins* was looking good. And look at Geffen go! Positively galvanised! *Risky Business*? *Big* business! If for nothing else, his courtship of Spielberg was paying off already, and in a way even he had not anticipated. Whatever, it was all grist to the Warners mill. And with any luck, there would be a lot more to come from the twin terrors.

# 20

# Third Time Lucky

*'After a movie I've had a family for perhaps as long as a year, usually about 100 people – cast and crew members. Then when it's over, they break up and go off and that's a really sad moment for me. Suddenly, there's nothing to do.'*

*'I remember being taken over to Terry Semel's house simply so Terry could sit me down and explain distribution, which I knew nothing about. Terry must have talked for four hours, and at the end of it I knew more about distribution and exhibition than I ever wanted to.'*

STEVEN SPIELBERG

Following the nightmare of *Twilight Zone – The Movie*, Warners unveiled Amblin's *Fandango*, a dour little item Spielberg had taken under his wing, the directorial feature debut of Kevin Reynolds. A couple of years earlier Reynolds had written a script, *Ten Soldiers*. MGM's adaptation, *Red Dawn*, directed by John Milius, had horrified and sickened him. The underlying message he had intended to deliver, that war destroyed people, had been distorted by Milius and the studio into a jingoistic, right-wing cartoon; instead of the Soviets being portrayed as real people, they had become caricatures in Milius's typical rootin'-tootin' gung-ho style. The only good thing the script brought him was an agent at William Morris, Mike Simpson.

When asked what else he could give Simpson to show around, Reynolds produced a twenty-two-minute short, *Proof*, that he had shot as a student at the University of Southern California. Nothing ventured, nothing gained, said Simpson, despatching a copy of *Proof* to Spielberg's office. Reynolds fully expected it to be returned unopened. Instead, he got a call from Spielberg inviting him to a meeting. He liked *Proof* and suggested it was worthy of being expanded into a full-length feature.

Reynolds had been eyeing the prospect of raising $1 million to make a feature independently. Instead, it was all systems go on what became *Fandango*, a $7 million Amblin-financed movie for Warners, with Frank Marshall and Kathleen Kennedy keeping an eye on day-to-day developments as executive producers. Steve Ross was jubilant. Universal's loss was his gain. For his part, the canny Sid Sheinberg probably suffered little loss of sleep.

Knowing he would be unable to consult with Spielberg during production of the movie – his benefactor was off to Sri Lanka to shoot *Temple of Doom* – Reynolds asked for a few words of wisdom to see him through. Spielberg gave him three: 'Just survive it.'

For his tale of five college roommates taking to the road for one last epic blow-out before turning into nine-to-fivers, Reynolds grabbed the opportunity to cast his buddy Kevin Costner, despondent after his role in *The Big Chill*, his major feature debut, had ended up adorning the cutting room floor.

Back from Sri Lanka, Spielberg was shown a late cut of the movie and emerged looking unhappy. In its final form, he made it clear, it was not the movie he thought Reynolds was going to make. Reynolds insisted that *Fandango* was what it was, exactly what he had always intended it to be. The two men agreed to disagree. *Fandango*, in Reynolds' cut, was handed over to Warners. Still listed as an Amblin production, the name of Steven Spielberg had nevertheless disappeared.

The movie's deserted three-week run at New York's Eastside Gemini Theater ended any notion of a wider release. When Reynolds philosophically declared, 'You pay a price for these things,' Steve Ross may have felt like seconding the sentiment. Reynolds accepts that the only reason the movie eventually got to play network television was the eventual popularity of Costner. As regards the 'conflict' with his original backer, there was certainly no lasting animosity. Spielberg called the director out of the blue one day and asked Reynolds if he'd be interested in directing an episode of *Amazing Stories*. The doughty Reynolds agreed, on condition he could rewrite 'You Gotta Believe Me'. Spielberg may have allowed himself a sigh of disbelief.

What *Fandango* undeniably achieved was the launching of the major-studio careers of both Kevins. If their well-publicised falling-out on both *Robin Hood – Prince of Thieves* and *Waterworld* continued the discord theme already established with Spielberg, well, there's something to be said for consistency.

No one will ever be able to take away from Steve Ross his reputation as one of the most skilful survivors in US business history. The collapse of Atari, already well signalled before the *E.T.* game delivered the *coup-de-grâce*, would have dragged many a company head down with it. Not Steve Ross. And even if it had, he'd have exited laughing.

Months before the collapse, faced with a mounting inventory consisting of millions of unsold cartridges, Ross had seen the writing on the wall. And declared publicly his intention to sell 360,000 shares of WCI stock 'for personal financial and tax planning reasons'. In case outsiders interpreted Ross's sale, his first since 1962, as in any way panic-inspired, WCI's subsequent announcement that it intended to buy in up to six million shares of its outstanding stock helped calm nerves and stop the stock slide. It was the signal for Ross to begin unloading. His price was considerably bolstered by WCI's proud, fearless six-million buy. Except that it never took place. The few shares of outstanding stock that were purchased amounted to just a fraction of that – just enough, hopefully, to convince any government snoop that WCI's *intentions* had been honourable.

Ross completed his unloading in the first half of November 1982, throwing an extra 120,000 shares into the pot on top of his originally announced figure. With the price boosted even further by his bullish announcements about 'Atari's continuing rapid growth', the top-up was simply irresistible.

Only weeks after Ross's $21 million cash-out, the Atari bubble burst, sending WCI's shares into freefall. With an investigation into the débâcle mounted by the Securities and Exchange Commission, and a simultaneous shareholders' litigation suit proceeding, Ross's back was to the wall. His solution was the same as in the Westchester Theater scandal – toss out a few minnows to deflect attention from himself. It worked again. Raps on the knuckle were imposed on a few lower-level WCI officers who had sold shares on the very eve of Atari's crash. Ross's earlier, massive stock sales, made even as he was doing everything in his power to tout Atari's continuing glowing prospects, were ignored.

'Steve must have had a hot line to God,' was Spielberg's admiring reflection on his friend's extraordinary luck. The comment was not, it should be said, about any one coup or Houdini-like escape. But it sure fits the Atari scam. About the thousands of investors suckered in the process? Such a hot line *they* should have had.

It would prove third time lucky for Spielberg's movie association with Ross. *Gremlins*' writer was Chris Columbus, a young dynamo who had grown up with movie director aspirations in the industrial town of Warren, Ohio. By the time he had graduated from film school, he had acquired the services of an agent and had two paid-for scripts under his belt, together with an assignment from CBS Theatrical for a script entitled *Summertime Blues*. In Columbus's second year out of college, after writing *Gremlins* on spec, his agent sent it along to Amblin. Spielberg liked the idea, but found the script 'just horrible'. Columbus stationed himself at Amblin during the eight subsequent drafts Spielberg demanded, running back and forth to Spielberg's office with each new batch of pages as if the script was a newspaper and Spielberg the city editor. Finally, it was in good enough shape for submission to a director. Who to choose?

Joe Dante was one surprised individual when he received the *Gremlins* script in the mail. Had it come to the wrong address? A graduate of the Roger Corman School of Hard Knocks, Dante had broken into directing, alongside his pal and fellow novice Allan Arkush, cutting theatrical trailers for Corman. Together they had gone on to co-direct *Hollywood Boulevard*, a $60,000 lampoon of their boss's pics. When Corman offered a choice of follow-up, the musically orientated Arkush chose *Rock and Roll High School*, co-written by Dante, while his partner chose *Death Race 2000*, starring David Carradine and newcomer Sylvester Stallone.

Next for Dante was John Sayles' first script, the unashamed *Jaws* rip-off for Corman, *Piranha*. Its success led to *The Howling*, which really put Dante on the map, albeit in low-budget terms.

The first meeting between Dante and Spielberg began with a nervous Dante 'apologising' for borrowing from *Jaws* in *Piranha*. Spielberg laughingly accepted. 'It was the *best* rip-off,' Dante was assured. (Worth remembering: the New York *Times'* Vincent Canby had originally posed the question: 'What is *Jaws* but a big-budget Roger Corman movie?' So maybe the favour had merely been returned.)

Dante didn't know at that point that an incensed Sid Sheinberg and Universal had been on the point of suing Corman's New World Pictures for the obvious similarities with *Jaws*. Spielberg, perhaps appreciating the 'homage', had pleaded with Sheinberg to drop the suit. If he hadn't prevailed, *Piranha*'s release could well have been blocked. 'I kind of owe my whole career to Steven,' Dante gratefully acknowledges. 'If my movie hadn't come out, I would never have directed another one.'

Dante was left entirely to his own devices during the shooting of his *Twilight Zone* episode, 'It's A Good Life', the story of a young-ster obsessed with TV cartoons who brings his favourite characters to life and terrorises his family. 'Because of the accident, nobody really wanted to be identified with *Twilight Zone*,' he explained, 'so I was working without anybody telling me what to do.'

When he then went on to shoot the anarchic *Gremlins*, he loaded the movie with in-joke references to Spielberg and his work. There was a cinema whose marquee advertised 'Watch the Skies' and 'A Boy's Life', the original titles of *CE3K* and *E.T.* There was a poster, designed in unmistakable 'Indiana Jones' style, plugging the appearance of a local DJ. One of the gremlins knocks an *E.T.* doll off the shelf in a toy shop. 'His imagination runs like a machine gun,' Dante said admiringly of his benefactor. 'Any two of his ideas would make a picture.'

So how much influence had Spielberg exercised on *Gremlins*? Had this been another Tobe Hooper/*Poltergeist* situation? Absolutely not, said Dante, pointing out that he had included all the Spielbergian references entirely on his own. 'He's so well known that I knew it'd be all right to do that,' he says. 'But listen, whatever may be wrong with this movie is mine, not his – he was still in Sri Lanka most of the time we were shooting.' Back from location on *Temple of Doom*, Dante even had Spielberg himself put in an appearance, gamely riding a scooter in one scene.

While proving a smash for Amblin and Warners with its bountiful US take of $148 million, *Gremlins* had more than one critic puzzled. One headlined his favourable notice 'More Spawn of Spielberg', while others labelled Dante 'Spielberg's Emissary to the Dark Side', someone who 'puts the id back in kid'. The perceptive Dave Kehr was back on the trail, expertly separating Spielberg's and Dante's separate 'authorial voices' on the movie. (Chris Columbus's contribution was left out of the loop, and rightly so, with Kehr obviously aware of the many drafts Spielberg demanded until the script had been tailored to his satisfaction.)

'Spielberg seems genuinely to have shared creative responsibility with Dante, yet their conjunction doesn't feel like a partnership; there are too many tensions in the end product, too many contradictions,' Kehr noted. He went on to delineate what he saw as the typical Spielberg scenario, the simple but ingenious formula – outside of the George Lucas-dominated 'Indiana Jones' chronicles – of 'a family melodrama invaded by the fantastic. In film after film a family that has somehow strayed from the Eisenhower-era model (generally it is the fault of the father) is regenerated through contact with a larger-than-life force. In some of the movies, the supernatural element is evil; in fighting it, the father rediscovers his lost masculinity and the family is saved – as in *Duel*, *Jaws*, *Poltergeist*. In others – *Close Encounters*, *E.T.* – the supernatural element is benign and loving; it introduces a new emotional centre to the imbalanced family.' The introduction of Dante, Kehr maintained, added an 'onslaught of disconnected images' to Spielberg's usual handiwork, producing 'a vivid illustration of that still mysterious something extra, something unique, that the act of filming imposes on a narration'. In other words, Dante had made his presence felt – and how!

The only aspect of Spielberg's contribution that I think Kehr underestimated was the replay of his childhood pranks that the movie surely represented. While Dante may have pushed the envelope further, *Gremlins* came over like the young Spielberg who'd locked his sisters in a cupboard, who'd served up the severed doll's head on a platter, who'd scared the life out of them after midnight with his combination of torchlight and 'I'M THE MOOOON!'

Which begs the question: apart from jacking up Amblin's strike rate, why had Spielberg chosen in the first place to hire an outside director for *Gremlins*? The answer he supplied rings absolutely true in the light of his travails with *E.T.*: 'I wanted to take a long vacation from anything with a wire trailing from its rear end that makes a creature smile when you pull it. Joe seemed perfect for the job.'

Perfect as he was, Dante sensed, and chose to articulate, the gap between the warmly appreciative front that Spielberg presents, and the cold, distancing reality that often takes its place. 'He's very available to being moved by what he sees creatively,' Dante notes, 'but not by the people around him. Put it on the screen and he can deal with it. He likes to have that piece of celluloid between you.'

With fifty toy companies licensed to produce *Gremlins* merchandise, all the way from cuddly hard and soft versions of Mogwai to pencil sets and jigsaw puzzles, Spielberg and his associates looked set for another profitable royalty run from a long-running franchise. The beleagured Steve Ross certainly needed it. The half-a-billion dollar loss WCI recorded for 1984, with the same prospect stretching ahead for the following year, would wipe out every cent the company had declared in profit since 1975.

In *Indiana Jones and the Temple of Doom* – to everyone's surprise – the supposedly sure-fire mixture of romance, adventure and thrills curdled. There were several reasons, apart from a sharp increase in the disturbingly overt racism inherent in the stereotypical villains.

First, there was an unusually heavy-handed script, courtesy of George Lucas's *American Graffiti* scribes, Willard Huyck and Gloria Katz, who would later bring the world, and the unfortunate Lucas, not only *Howard the Duck* but *Radioland Murders*. Most of what had been deftly achieved in the first movie had been coarsened in the multiplying, from the gore and noise level, right down to the characters' names; Lucas had been content to leave the rest alone after naming 'Indiana' after his pet dog. Now the heroine, 'Willie', was named after Spielberg's dog, and 'Short Round', the Asian kid, after Katz's pet pooch. Second, Spielberg was content to push the violence, mayhem and horror envelope even further than he had on *Raiders*. Strong stomachs were required even for an early banquet scene, with a pregnant snake being slit open and the revellers swallowing the wriggling offspring as the first course. Giant baked spiders followed, with a side-dish for 'Willie' of what looked like nourishing soup – except that it was replete with torn-out eyeballs. Dessert? Chilled monkey brains on the half-skull.

Censors zeroed in on one scene in particular, showing the still-beating heart of a sacrificial victim being pulled from his living body. (Oddly enough, the wound closes up and he continues to live long enough to be lowered on a mattress-like contraption, still screaming, into a pit of molten metal, above which he spontaneously combusts. Had the heart-plucking occurred to Spielberg later?) Cartoon-like though it was, the incident was severely trimmed for British release.

In *New York* magazine, David Denby provided a typical reaction, describing the movie as 'lurid and gloomy trash . . . heavy-spirited and grating'. On the other hand, the unpredictable, contrary Pauline Kael largely approved of *Temple of Doom* in *New Yorker*. She was also one of the few to single out Kate Capshaw's contribution for special praise: 'Instead of being a pallid little darling in distress, she's a broad in distress, and the situations gain from her noisy wholesomeness.' I agree with Kael, for right from her dynamite first sequence singing 'Anything Goes' in very passable Cantonese at the nostalgically named Obi Ben nightclub (in Shanghai?), to being dragged through the proverbial hedge backwards by her new partner, Capshaw, playing delightfully ditsy, was a joy. Described as 'enchanting' by one character in the movie, she girlishly accepts the compliment, the complete showgirl unable to resist a good review. 'Thank you very much,' she says. 'Thank you *very* much.'

The movie itself? No joy at all. Although it would be hard to top Spielberg for his handling of non-stop, hectic action sequences, screeching violence level or numbing intensity, on this occasion he went way over the top.

With widespread depiction of the movie as an ugly violation of trust, Spielberg moved quickly to distance himself, even to the extent of describing his involvement as 'only a hired hand'. Coming from someone with the power to make just about anything he chose, this was rich indeed. He added that he would not allow a ten-year-old to see the movie, that 'the responsibility to the children of this country is worth any loss at the box-office'.

There was even an element of equivocation and regret from

Spielberg that he had signed on in the first place: 'I got separation pangs. I knew that if I didn't direct *Temple*, someone else would. I got a little bit jealous, I got a little bit frustrated . . .' It seemed that the man who had refused to make a sequel to *Jaws*, who had decried all sequels as mere 'carny tricks', had sold out. For a very high price.

Notwithstanding the howls of protest concerning the excessive violence – which led directly to the creation in the States of a new motion picture rating code, PG-13 (Parental guidance suggested for children under thirteen) – audiences lapped the mixture up almost as eagerly as before. Although *Temple of Doom*'s $180 million at the US box-office was $60 million less than *Raiders*, it was hardly chopped liver. Unlike so many of the movie's cast.

Chris Columbus would write another three opuses for Spielberg before his twenty-eighth birthday, with *Home Alone* for Fox still in the future, as well as his own directorial hits, *Mrs Doubtfire* and *Nine Months*.

First he would provide Spielberg with the script for *Young Sherlock Holmes*, a decidedly less successful collaboration and one that would intensify the criticism of Spielberg that started with *Temple of Doom*. Were his people starting to work to a 'Spielberg formula', providing the master, way ahead of the future trend in rap, with 'sampling' from his own work?

When Spielberg had first read the script for *Young Sherlock*, it did strike him that the temple scene at the end was vaguely familiar. He still defended Columbus against any charge of cribbing: 'Chris wrote his temple sequence before *Temple of Doom* was released, and he hadn't read the script.' Well, yes – except that Columbus wrote *Young Sherlock* on assignment from Paramount, the studio simultaneously readying *Temple of Doom*'s release. That cross-pollination, whether intended or not, had certainly taken place, was later acknowledged by Spielberg himself when *Young Sherlock* was dubbed 'Indiana Holmes and the Temple of Goonies'. Director Barry Levinson also felt he'd been wrongfooted. 'It was a mistake on our part,' he said, 'because our movie came out the same year as *Temple of Doom* and we hadn't seen the Spielberg movie before it opened.'

'I should have been stronger as a producer,' was Spielberg's final comment on the subject.

Amy Irving's career strategy worked. After completing *Honeysuckle Rose* she took to the New York stage playing Constanza, Mozart's wife, in *Amadeus*. The notices were good. Then it was back to

Hollywood for Barbra Streisand's *Yentl*, which yielded her an Academy Award nomination for Best Supporting Actress.

Following their meeting in India, Irving re-entered Spielberg's life in earnest in 1984 when, despite all appearances to the contrary, he was at a personal low ebb. What should have been the overwhelming triumph of *E.T.* had been well and truly soured. First, by the Academy voters' latest shut-out; was there to be no end to their snubbing? Second, by the humble-pie three-course meal he'd been forced to swallow by the Directors' Guild, Tobe Hooper and MGM over *Poltergeist*. Third, by the *Twilight Zone* accident that haunted him still. Now, to cap it all, he was being pilloried for *Temple of Doom*'s sadistic excesses. And although still in occasional touch with Capshaw, she had gone back to Bernstein, her live-in lover in Sherman Oaks. Must have been something about that Valley air.

Soon it was confirmed that Spielberg and Irving's on-again, off-again affair was once more back on its precarious track. 'Now we're really in love,' she said. 'And here I am with the Prince of Hollywood. I guess that makes me the Princess.' When one reporter queried the absence of a ring, Irving defiantly replied, 'We're married in our hearts.'

Spielberg in turn declared, 'For the first time in my life I'm committed to another person.' Yep, this time it really looked like the couple had got their act together. And taken it on the road as well. Within a year he and Irving were married. With a child already on the way.

# 21

# Amazing Disgrace

*'If each studio would take $1 million profit per big movie
and invest it in film schools, we'd have the industry that
David O. Selznick and Irving Thalberg created. We must
become like Walter Huston in* Treasure of the Sierra
Madre. *We must put the mountain back.'*

STEVEN SPIELBERG, 1982

*'As much as I admired and loved* Citizen Kane, *I guess I
have a different outlook on life. I have more of a
bubblegum outlook than I think Welles did when he made*
Kane.*'*

STEVEN SPIELBERG, 1985

Speaking off the record, as almost all criticism of Spielberg is conducted, one prominent agent maintained back in the mid-eighties
that the director had developed into a rapacious dealmaker. 'No one
crafts better deals for himself than Spielberg,' he declared, 'often at
the expense of the talent he hires.' Spielberg hotly disputed the
charge, swearing that he never involves himself in negotiations, rely-
ing instead on his attorney and agent.

The barb 'at the expense of others' is impossible either to prove
or disprove. One could point to the list of talent who sign on with
the 'rapacious dealmaker' for picture after picture. One could also
list the talent unceremoniously dropped Joe Alves-style.

If not handling negotiations personally, as he claims, Spielberg's
handwriting is certainly apparent on every deal struck on his behalf.
According to his sister Anne (the only one of his sisters 'in the
business'; Sue and Nancy live entirely private lives, one working in
the jewellery business, one a housewife): 'He's a very tough bar-
gainer. He's a hard man to deal with . . . There are times when I'd be
tempted to take things other places, where I know I would get a better deal.' As she did with *Big*, the movie she co-wrote with Gary

189

Ross that starred her brother's neighbour, Tom Hanks. Produced outside of Spielberg's sphere of influence, at the only major studio where he has never hung his shingle, it landed Twentieth Century-Fox a major hit.

The bottom line with Spielberg's dealmaking is that he learned at the foot of master George Lucas, a man who makes Donald Trump's 'Art of the Deal' appear penny-ante. It was Lucas who was hellbent on achieving the 'deal of the century' with *Raiders of the Lost Ark*. If he didn't quite make it, he was beaten only by his efforts on the *Star Wars* trilogy. Then there was merchandising – again, Lucas was the mentor, having picked up the baton from Disney and run with it like a thing possessed. Even while he was embroiled in the first *Star Wars* saga, this is how he had it figured: since his movie was costing $10 million to make, and since it was basically Ol' Walt in space, he couldn't expect any more than the $16 million gross that had become par for the course with Disney at the time – in other words, a merely break-even movie. So how about licensing merchandise, like they did, to make up the shortfall?

It's true that for years Spielberg was known as being personally tight with a dollar. Lucas, on the other hand, has always been known to sprinkle his share of the treasure trove liberally round deserving cases, like making Alec Guinness a millionaire on the strength of his spit and a cough as Obi-wan Kenobe. There were few recorded instances, up to the mid-eighties at least, of similar Spielberg largesse, Leah's Tiffany token excepted. Credit Steve Ross with turning him around. 'I went from being a miser to a philanthropist because I knew him, because that's what he showed me to do,' says Spielberg. 'I was just never spending my money. I gave nothing to causes that were important to me. When I met Steve, I just observed the pleasure that he drew from his own private philosophy. It was a *total* pleasure, and it was private, anonymous giving. I have my name on a couple of buildings . . . but eighty per cent of what I do is anonymous.' (One of them is the Norman Rockwell Memorial at Stockridge, New England, where there's a 'Steven Spielberg-Warner Communications Inc. Gallery'. Tax deductible, natch.)

Which still leaves his reputation for being hell on wheels in cutting deals, squeezing the last drop of blood out of every contract, and for being a martinet to his film crews, demanding, impatient, dictatorial . . .

Some things never change. But they *can* escalate.

Spielberg's idea for Amblin's entry into TV was meant to re-create visually the 1920s' dime novels that contained up to twenty short stories and still fitted neatly into the pocket. More pragmatically, he intended to borrow from the format of the *Amazing Tales* series started in 1926 and owned by Universal Studios.

His cosy, not to say absurd notion of those supposedly innocent twenties and thirties, was of parents in bentwood rocking chairs reading to their gathered families, patting their heads to punctuate each homily while the fire reassuringly crackled in the hearth. His simplistic acknowledgement that TV had taken the place of family heads and their spoon-feeding was taken to its logical conclusion: *he* would take the place of the parent, *he* would be the TV surrogate dispensing a yarn each week to the huddled masses in easy-to-swallow twenty-two-minute bites. The hope was that his personally expressed need 'to be entertained faster and more economically' would be shared by the viewing public at large. On a more practical level, the series would provide a clearing house for ideas, mainly but not exclusively from Spielberg, of short subjects and stories unsuitable for the big screen because of their length.

Beginning with an introduction to NBC's chairman Grant Tinker that was arranged by *Family Ties* producer Gary David Goldberg, Spielberg negotiated a two-year deal with network president Brandon Tartikoff. It allowed for a budget of $800,000–$1 million per episode for the weekly series that was unprecedented in terms of both money and contract length. The calculation was that if the series was picked up beyond that time, Spielberg would come out with a profit around year five. If it didn't, he wouldn't make a cent. He also wouldn't *lose* a cent. At least, not unless he exceeded the average budget.

Spielberg's co-producer on the series, Joshua Brand, was in complete awe of his senior partner from the start. As a writer/producer Brand had worked with people who were good managers but not creative, as well as creative types unable to organise an orgy in a brothel. Spielberg, he quickly discovered, was able to don both mantles: 'He's got tremendous energy. He's kind of like an athlete who can run, hit and field for power – on the business level *and* on the creative level.'

Maybe the drawback for Brand, together with his other associates, was that Spielberg was *too* senior. He had long since arrived at the stage where his touch was regarded as golden, his every idea a gem, his every pronouncement holy writ. Only the likes of Marshall and Kennedy were in a position occasionally to temper justice with mercy, and even they had to tread carefully when the master was in full flight. Although Spielberg would hire both established as well as up-and-coming directors and writers for the series – including his sister, Anne – close on a round dozen of the tales, almost half the entire series, were 'based on stories by Steven Spielberg'. If *Amazing*

*Stories* represented a clearing of an elephants' burial ground of ideas, most of them, it swiftly transpired, would have been better left buried. But who at Amblin would dare to say him nay?

If they had, the burgeoning careers of several directors – Phil Joanou for one – might never have happened. Like Spielberg, Joanou had been fiddling with a movie camera almost as far back as he can remember, with twenty-two features of varying lengths under his belt by the time he graduated from the University of Southern California, where he spent three years studying film craft. His senior-year movie was *The Last Chance Dance*, which he looks back on as 'basically, an episode of "The Brady Bunch".' Maybe that factor alone unwittingly made it the perfect lure for Spielberg, who heard about it through the USC grapevine and watched it on the Warner Bros jet one October, courtesy of Steve Ross, en route from Los Angeles to New York. 'Can you meet with me next week when I get back? Is that convenient?' Joanou was asked.

'Any time in the rest of my life is convenient,' was Joanou's accommodating reply.

Halloween was the day set for his appointment at Amblin (worrying, but better than April Fool's, all things considered). The interview, during which Spielberg fired question after question in the friendliest fashion ('How did you film that high-school dance?' 'How about that crane shot?'), terminated in a clipped, anticlimactic, 'Thanks for coming', which left Joanou seriously thinking he had blown it.

Three days later his fears were laid to rest in a call from Deborah Jelin, Amblin's director of development. 'Are you familiar with *Amazing Stories*?' she asked.

'Of course,' Joanou replied.

'Well, Steven would like you to be the director of our Christmas episode.'

Eighteen months later, with the segment in the can, Joanou had a first-look deal and offices at Disney for his production company, Thunder Road. (Don't dress for Joanou's first Disney outing. Although his career has bubbled along elsewhere, nothing ever got made at the Mouse Factory.)

Newcomers like Joanou apart, Spielberg mustered an illustrious list of directors for *Amazing Stories*, that included Martin Scorsese, Clint Eastwood and Peter Hyams. Once the series was launched he had plans to go much further afield and work with Britain's ex-Monty Python team members, with Bernardo Bertolucci and Sergio Leone, with David Lean . . .

It was Lean who drew him up short, asking for six months to shoot his half-hour episode, with waiting time for weather on top.

Spielberg was incredulous. Until the magisterial Lean cracked a smile and said, 'Just joking, Steven.' Then proceeded to turn him down flat.

In the avalanche of publicity leading up to the first airing of *Amazing Stories*, Spielberg was asked to give a preview of what might be expected. The series, he replied, would be 'Avant garde . . . a couple are really wiggy. Some are quiet, others are action-packed. Some might even be considered art films. You've got to like Mulligan stew.' Imprecise? Maybe, but intriguingly so.

Spielberg himself directed the season premiere on September 28, 1985, 'Ghost Train'. Its budget had been blown in an excess of enthusiasm, with John Williams called in to score what Spielberg hoped would get the series off to a flying start. Confident that *Amazing Stories* would sweep all before it, NBC decided to go head-to-head against the reigning favourite on the 8 pm Sunday primetime slot, CBS's *Murder, She Wrote*. Maybe in a premonition of what was to come, maybe in a simple attack of pre-show nerves, Spielberg and NBC decided not to preview 'Ghost Train' or any other episode to critics. And last-minute reservations about his chosen showcase were expressed. 'When I go to the theatre,' he agonised, 'I sit in the fifth or sixth row, and I want the movie to overwhelm me. I want an environmental experience, one that I cannot get from watching television. The sad thing is, as good as our *Amazing Stories* look on film, they will lose about thirty–forty per cent of their poop by being on television.'

Even Spielberg's marked-down estimate of *Amazing Stories'* potential 'poop' turned out to be overstated, judging from the reaction to the initial 'Ghost Train' as well as subsequent outings. Tom Shales of the Washington *Post* summed up the general 'morning after' reaction: 'I hear America asking, 'What was so amazing about *that*?'

Richard Turner of *TV Guide* was puzzled. Well used as he was to the paranoia surrounding the output of certain entertainment luminaries, the secrecy surrounding Spielberg's *Amazing Stories* was re-writing the rule book. 'I can't talk about this,' one well-known, and clearly embarrassed actor had told him over the phone, pleadingly adding, 'You've got to understand.' What was going on? Surely a call to NBC would clear things up? 'Please!' the executive begged. 'I've got an 800-pound gorilla on my back!'

When more calls produced similarly panic-stricken deadends, the truth began to dawn on Turner. These people were *scared*. Not just scared, *terrified*. Spielberg's dreams were producing other men's nightmares?

Turner decided to dig a little deeper, ask a few more questions. How freakish and self-contained was the self-confessed 'control freak'? The launching of his TV series under the most highly controlled conditions possible – by satellite video – had certainly provided a clue. It was no coincidence, Turner discovered, that the publicity stories released about him were almost universally positive. Two separate sources testified that he was given to throwing out publicity pictures of himself where George Lucas was lurking in the background. When the Los Angeles *Times* had dared to portray *E.T.* with a coke spoon round his neck, an editor recalled the reaction from Amblin as 'instantaneous and a shriek', with an instant apology demanded – and granted.

An interview Turner set up with Spielberg was abruptly cancelled after the less-than-stellar debut of 'Ghost Train', the first so-called *Amazing Story*. It was rescheduled not once, but twice. On the appointed Sunday morning, Amy Irving rang from the Malibu beachhouse. Steven was sick and had to rest.

It took three months before he was available again. Three months while Turner absorbed further Spielbergiana. 'He grits his teeth in his sleep,' was the buzz regarding his Academy's Oscar denials. Fellow-campers at Amblin giggled about the fake-stone refrigerator and stalactites in the Jacuzzi room, where one pool was strictly for Spielberg's use alone. A neighbour at Malibu talked about the occasional visit from Spielberg and his consumption of 'about an eighth of a glass of wine'. According to one ex-associate, after confirming how 'extremely demanding' Spielberg waxes: 'His attitude is, this is the best job in Hollywood and you'd better appreciate it. People are scared of him and he assumes a huge place in people's minds. They see him as God.' And not a lovable God either, nor one who leads by the power of his personality, one who says 'hello' when you pass him in corridors: 'He doesn't observe the social graces except when he has to. He never asks anybody about their personal lives. His only subject of conversation is the movies.' Pissed off at one employee, he simply stopped talking to her until she quit. When his crew failed to deliver one effect he wanted in *E.T.* he told them, 'Well, you didn't get it. Think about that tonight.' According to one crew member: 'There was no "nice try" – nothing.'

What bothered Turner most of all during the three-month wait for an audience was the fact that ninety per cent of the people he contacted about Spielberg refused to talk to him at all. And those who did insisted on their anonymity. One even had an attorney present at the late-night rendezvous arranged. No one Turner spoke to for a moment denied Spielberg's virtuosity as a director. Their beef was with the 'vaguely unpleasant' aura that often accompanied his actions and the way he conducted himself personally, almost invariably in sharp contrast to the 'friendly elf' portrayed in publicity puffs.

Turner's close encounter with Spielberg finally took place at Amblin, with the tape recorders of both parties running. Once their small talk ('a little strange') was out of the way, together with a discussion on *Amazing Stories* – he wasn't alarmed about the ratings, although NBC was – Spielberg seemed uncomfortable when asked if he was difficult to work for. 'It's hard to say, I'm trying to think,' he began. 'I'm not a bully and I don't give orders, is what I won't do. I'm very collaborative, but what I try to do is inspire people who are collaborating that they've got to collaborate with me better than they have ever collaborated with anybody before. And so in that sense I'm demanding. I mean, I expect the best of anybody who works here.'

While noting the health-giving vegetables that had replaced the bowls of candies strewn around Amblin's offices, Turner also took in – amongst the many toys lying around – a rubber heart with an aorta that pulsed at the push of a button. 'Max loves it,' Spielberg offered. 'He calls it his *Temple of Doom* heart.' (Prompting Turner to think, 'Wait a minute. Max can't *call* it anything. He's *seven months* old.')

Turner left pondering how weird it was, that the only place where little babies talk, particularly referring to bits of their own father's cinematic history, was in the movies. Like them, Spielberg remained unreal.

After 'Ghost Train' it was downhill all the way. If plunging ratings weren't bad enough, the wave of hostile critical comment provided the *coup-de-grâce*. Describing the series as 'not so much monumentally dreadful as consistently disappointing', the New York *Times*' John O'Connor ridiculed Spielberg's much-publicised, rose-coloured 'family gathered round the head of the house' notion. 'What is the man talking about?' he asked. 'It's as if illiteracy and hardship, not to mention the Great Depression, never existed. It is noteworthy that more than one observer has commented on the decided scarcity of not only minority *issues* but minority *faces* in *Amazing Stories*. Obviously they might disrupt the lulling process . . . One looks at the consistent achievement of a series such as *American Playhouse* and can only shudder at the thought of how Mr. Spielberg might have interpreted James Baldwin's *Go Tell It on the Mountain*.' (When *Rolling Stone* queried the lack of 'minority faces', Spielberg replied that one had an all-black cast. It had just one black player.)

In the defence it mounted to the blandness of the first outings, NBC claimed that the early transmission time ruled out the 'more frightening' episodes in store, now apparently rescheduled for a later time. *Much* later, it turned out – in the vicinity of the grave-yard slot. After limping through the two seasons that Tartikoff had guaranteed, the series was unceremoniously cancelled. 'We started eleven new directors, eighteen new writers . . . *that* was amazing,' Spielberg-at-bay pointed out. 'When they cancelled the show, it was a shame for the whole industry.' Well, certainly for Amblin.

To borrow a title from Joe Queenan, several episodes of Spielberg's series could have been subtitled 'If You're Working for Me, Your Career Must be in Trouble'. Such was certainly the case with Scorsese's 'Mirror, Mirror'. Suffering from a severe case of mid-career crisis after the crashing flop of his brilliant but uncom-mercial *King of Comedy*, and the low-budget, unremarkable *After Hours*, Scorsese accepted the assignment as a 'filler' while a variety of studio committees stalled on his latest submissions.

Scorsese was allowed six days to shoot 'Mirror, Mirror'. It turned out to be a weak-as-water non-variation on 'The Man Who Haunted Himself' that Scorsese's *After Hours* writer Joseph Minion had half cooked up from a 'Story by Steven Spielberg'. Guest-starring Dick Cavett, it featured Sam Waterston as a horror-story writer and a young Tim Robbins as the black-clad Phantom who stares back at him from every reflecting surface. Take away stand-up domestic battles, Catholic guilt, subtext and Steadicam from Scorsese and what have you got? 'Mirror, Mirror' provided the shocking answer: just another Hollywood hack. 'The network neglected to tell anyone it was on,' Scorsese was unwise enough to complain. If they did, he should be grateful. Grateful also that Michael Eisner and Jeff Katzenberg at Disney handed him *The Color of Money* to end his spell in the wilderness.

With *Amazing Stories* being tabbed 'one of the biggest bombs ever produced for TV', Spielberg's golden touch had, it seemed, deserted him. His best decision, after packaging them for video release to squeeze out a few more dollars, would have been to for-get the whole thing. He couldn't, not while he saw a way to pluck triumph from the jaws of disaster.

On the face of it, 'Family Dog' looked promising. The only car-toon episode of *Amazing Stories*, the title character, designed by Tim Burton, amusingly manipulated his hapless human family. Animated by Brad Bird, and voiced by Bird and a stellar group that included Stan Freberg, Annie Potts and Mercedes McCambridge, it had enjoyed as decent a reception as any in the series. Although that isn't really saying a lot, it was apparently enough for Spielberg. Shouting, 'I smell *franchise!*' as if it were enough to *say* the magic word to have it materialise, 'Family Dog' was promptly burdened with the responsibility of justifying the entire sorry series.

It took until February 1991 before CBS belatedly but proudly announced that Spielberg's 'Family Dog' would soon be airing as a regular half-hour animated series. Puzzlingly, it took until November 1992 before ten episodes were turned over. Stories abounded that delivery had been hampered by indecision on the part of Spielberg and Tim Burton, by now an important player in his own right, with both men preoccupied on their movie projects. While that may have been part of the problem, Spielberg had been dissatisfied with the animation and had turned the project over to Canada's Nelvana Entertainment to be cleaned up. Three 'completed' episodes had to be totally revoiced. Even then, with $600,000 per episode laid out, CBS kept the series off the air for well over a year. By this time 'Family Dog' was being referred to as 'Spielberg's Albatross'. It was finally released only after a further $2 million had been laid out on the ten complete episodes, and *Jurassic Park* had made Spielberg's name irresistibly hot again. Judged elsewhere as 'Mean-spirited but not funny – a deadly combination if ever there was one', Ken Tucker summed up the general reaction in *Entertainment Weekly*: 'Beware of Dog.' And that's exactly what viewers did.

The prospect of any face-saving 'happy ending' to the entire bizarre *Amazing Stories* saga was gone.

Spielberg was not only aware at this stage of his limitations ('I can dump on me better than anybody else') but happy to elaborate on where he stood alongside other 'Movie Brats'.

'I don't paint in the strong browns and greens of Francis or in Marty's sombre greys and whites,' he conceded. 'Francis makes films about power and loyalty, Marty makes films about paranoia and rage. I use primary colours, pastel colours. When I see a movie like *Raging Bull*, I know I couldn't make it one-tenth as powerful or as quixotic as Marty was able to make it.'

Let alone *make* it, Spielberg was barely able even to *watch* much of *Raging Bull*. Its realism had him squirming with embarrassment. It made him feel like a voyeur, eavesdropping on individuals whose dignity and privacy he felt ought to be respected.

Jonathan Taplin, Scorsese's producer on *Mean Streets*, had his own take. As filmmakers he differentiates between Scorsese and the likes of Spielberg and Lucas: 'George and Steven came from a different point of view, a populist American point of view. They wanted to make movies that would move everybody. Marty? He just wanted to make movies that moved himself.'

As for his best friend, the increasingly idiosyncratic Brian De Palma, Spielberg saw him as trailing 'the scent of *film noir*' around with him, an unmistakable 'maverick, auteur, upstart European' – whether or not he actually hailed from Philadelphia. Whereas Spielberg never invited other filmmakers, not even De Palma, to watch his previews, he had nursed his buddy through every one of his. It hadn't been easy, for even the movies that turned out to be hits had endured early rocky passages, let alone De Palma's flops, however worthy. In *Blowout*, having Nancy Allen killed at the climax may have spelled the beginning of the end of their marriage, as well as helping to doom the movie at the box-office. Then Spielberg had held his friend's hand through the storm of protest that greeted the operatically orchestrated bloodbath of *Scarface*. Successful as the movie had proved in the end, with its remarkable afterlife on video, Spielberg dearly wanted to see De Palma enjoy the fruits of unqualified mainstream success. Instead, the cries of misogynism that greeted *Dressed to Kill* were repeated with *Body Double*. Spielberg and De Palma would have to wait another few years before *The Untouchables* touched all the bases, combining his darker sensibilities with commercialism.

If Spielberg saw the 'auteur' movies of Coppola, Scorsese, De Palma *et al.* as reflections of their own personalities, where did that leave him and his blancmange palette? Facing the facts, as he saw them at the time: 'I know I'm not a hard guy. I *know* that I have a dark side, but I don't have a *real* dark side.'

Nor did he share a real liking for either the American or European expression of man's dark side; they didn't 'reach' him. 'I've never been touched by *film noir* or trauma drama, psychodrama, anything having to do with the deep human condition,' he admitted.

Spielberg was in his late thirties when he made those statements. It would take another decade before he was mature enough to acknowledge and confront the dark side of his nature, to tackle a portrait of mankind at its most evil, perpetrating the single most heinous act of the twentieth century.

Meantime, he was about to grapple with his first 'adult movie' since *The Sugarland Express*, an adaptation of Alice Walker's Pulitzer Prize-winning *The Color Purple*. Cannily, he had no intention of throwing the baby out with the bathwater. If that was a complete financial wipe-out, the most likely scenario, he needed fall-backs at Amblin that would balance the books. Two names from the past, Robert Zemeckis and Bob Gale, would provide one such project, in spectacular fashion.

Meantime, there was an unexpected backlash from Pauline Kael, one of Spielberg's most enthusiastic early supporters. 'Why are movies so bad?' she asked. 'One hates to say it comes down to the success of Steven Spielberg, but . . . It's not so much what Spielberg has *done* as what he has *encouraged*. Everyone else has imitated his fantasies, and the result is an infantilisation of the culture. Spielberg, with his TV series, now rips off his own things. I can't think of any other director who's started paying homage to himself so early.'

If Spielberg had imagined that his initial involvement with Zemeckis and Gale would land him the successful producer's role Coppola enjoyed with *American Graffiti*, that never flew. Spielberg's guarantee to Ned Tanen was allowed quietly to lapse after *I Wanna Hold Your Hand*, while Zemeckis was granted the green light for a second feature, *Used Cars* – but at Columbia Pictures. Since not a single project with which they had been involved, certainly not *1941*, had been judged successful either on an artistic or commercial level, Spielberg might have been forgiven if he had dropped the team and moved on. To his credit he didn't.

Instead, the resistance came from Zemeckis, who didn't want his career 'permanently attached to Spielberg's'. He wanted to prove to himself, and to everyone else, that he could make a film without his friend's patronage. With Bob Gale he developed a screenplay in 1981, *Back to the Future*. Unfortunately, after peddling it all the way round Hollywood, only Columbia bothered to take up a tentative option. Even when Spielberg offered to intervene and place the project with Amblin, Zemeckis held out. 'Steven, if I were to do another movie with you, and it failed, my career would be over,' he explained. 'I would be perceived as a guy who could only get his movies made with Steven Spielberg.' Hot to trot as he was with *Back to the Future*, Spielberg was forced to agree. "Yeah, you're probably right,' he reluctantly conceded.

Having been impressed with *Used Cars*, Michael Douglas eventually came to the rescue, hiring Zemeckis to direct *Romancing The Stone* despite stiff opposition from Twentieth Century-Fox and their cries of 'He's got no track record.' Douglas's reply: 'Look at *Used Cars*. That's called *style*.'

With *Romancing The Stone* in the can and awaiting release, Zemeckis was hired by Spielberg's old team of Richard Zanuck and David Brown. No, not for *Back to the Future*. To direct *Cocoon*. Briefly, that is, for after taking one look at the first cut of *Stone*, Fox fired him. (Those Hollywood memories! Per Zanuck/Brown: 'We couldn't work out a deal with Robert.')

It was time to swallow his pride and crawl back to Spielberg with *Back to the Future* – before the future ran out, that is, and before Columbia renewed their option yet again.

'Talk about *Amazing Stories*,' Zemeckis enthused as he prepared to shoot *Back to the Future* for Amblin. 'Steven is one himself. I don't know how he could be having this baby and doing everything else he does.' (Actually, Amy Irving was having 'this baby', but we get the gist.)

'Everything else' would include the painful necessity of sitting down with Zemeckis to discuss the replacement of Eric Stoltz in January 1985, after six weeks of expensive shooting, half the entire budgeted schedule of *Back to the Future*. On the basis of Stoltz's performance in Peter Bogdanovich's *Mask*, Sid Sheinberg had recommended the young actor to Spielberg. The first Bogdanovich heard there was a problem was when Stoltz called to say, 'Peter, I just don't know how to work their way.'

Bogdanovich knew that Stoltz was an actor who was a little shy and who needed to be handled properly, and he was shocked and saddened when news filtered through that he had been fired. 'I phoned Spielberg,' Bogdanovich recalled, 'and he said, "It just didn't work out." It was a shame, a real setback for Eric, because of course everyone wondered what on earth was the matter with him. Basically, everybody else on *Back to the Future* was giving a TV kind of performance. Eric's deeper than that. He wanted to give more.' A Universal press release put it a little more harshly: 'His performance wasn't consistent with the original concept.' Although it was probably a good thing in terms of Stoltz's long-term career, it was a terrible slap in the face at the time. He was out, and *Family Ties*' Michael J. Fox was in.

The truth is that Fox had always been Zemeckis's and Spielberg's first choice for the role. When Spielberg had first approached *Family Ties* producer Gary David Goldberg about the young actor seguing over to Amblin, the answer was that Fox was unavailable. So as 'not to disappoint' the young actor, who had already made his movie debut in *Teen Wolf*, Goldberg didn't bother to tell him about the approach. The problem was that *Family Ties* still had two months of shooting left of its third-season run, and neither Spielberg nor Zemeckis was prepared to wait.

When both men eventually concluded that Stoltz 'didn't have the vulnerability and youthfulness for the part', Spielberg decided to try for his original choice again and sent a copy of *Back to the Future*'s script to Goldberg. And this time he called the actor directly. 'How would you like to do this movie?' he asked.

'Sure. When?'

'Monday.'

'I'll be there.' (While working the double shift necessary to accommodate both the movie and TV series, Fox asked the rhetorical question becoming more and more prevalent in Hollywood: 'How can you say "no" to Steven Spielberg?')

At last Spielberg's collaboration with Zemeckis was about to produce not only a hit movie, but a valuable franchise for Amblin's future. Moreover, the re-shooting of Stoltz's scenes would add only $3 million to the movie's planned $14 million budget. Following a preview of *Back to the Future* held at the Alfred Hitchcock Theater on the Universal lot, Sid Sheinberg announced, 'This is going to be the biggest movie of the year.' (He was right. *Back to the Future* went on to collect $208 million at the US box-office.) There was one other satisfaction involved, he gleefully noted, in the source of both *E.T.* and their latest hot property: 'It proves once again that you buy the best stuff at Columbia!'

If Francis Coppola had missed the boat with his friendly aliens saga back in the seventies, yielding to Lucas's *Star Wars* and Spielberg's *Close Encounters*, history was about to provide a weird repeat. His new movie for producer Ray Stark had the same time-travel theme as *Back to the Future*. At least this time his rival version actually made it to the screen, although TriStar yielded to the inevitable and decided to delay the release of *Peggy Sue Got Married* until *Back to the Future* had run its course.

When Zemeckis was asked later if he'd resented having to rely once more on Spielberg to get a project off the ground, he had his answer ready: 'Listen, Steven was the best executive producer a director could ask for. He cut the deal, worked very carefully on the ad campaign, marketing and release pattern. He looked at the first cut and made some great suggestions. What filmmaker wouldn't love to have Steven Spielberg look at the first cut and make suggestions? I'll tell you, most executive producers are ex-agents who ask you why a special effect that cost $1 million isn't in the final cut. Steven just says, "If it doesn't work, take it out." He didn't have much to do with the day-to-day work. He just told me he'd be there if I needed him. What could be better than that?'

# 22

## Rose-Coloured Purple?

*'Power should never be abused.'*

STEVEN SPIELBERG

*'He gets physically ill when a project is over. The people
involved become his family. He loves them and he hates for
it to be done and to leave everyone.'*

ANNE SPIELBERG

It was Warners' senior VP in charge of production Lucy Fisher, ex-
script reader in the mid-seventies at United Artists, ex-head of
production in the late seventies at Coppola's Zoetrope Studios,
who first handed Spielberg a copy of *The Color Purple*. 'Look, if you
like this,' she told him, 'understand that Quincy Jones is already on
board.'

Never a reader, Spielberg was encouraged by the fact that, whatever else its merits, *The Color Purple* was a slim volume. And once
he started, he was overwhelmed by the tale of two black sisters,
Celie and Nettie, and their enforced separation. 'I got angry, I
laughed, I cried,' he recalls. 'It was one of the best pieces of reading
I had picked up in years, a very strong emotional read.'

Also on board, it turned out, were two producers on the
Warners lot, Peter Guber and Jon Peters. Even before considering
a director for the movie, they had approached the legendary
music man Quincy Jones. 'They asked me about writing the
music, but I came back with a proposal of my own,' Jones recalled.
'Why didn't they let me have the whole project and allow me to
take it as far as I could? Okay, if I made a wrong turning, pull me
back. Otherwise, let me run with it. They agreed. My first question, once we got that out of the way, was "Who's going to
direct?" The reply was a couple of shrugs. Then I made the suggestion, "Maybe I can get Steven Spielberg." Needless to say,
they were all for the idea.'

Although the Guber/Peters team may have been sceptical, Jones was as good as his word. He and Spielberg, of course, had plenty of shared history. After meeting at Steve Ross's Acapulco hideaway they had talked about collaborating on a movie musical in the grand old style, to be shot on location in the streets of New York. That it hadn't happened was one of 'those scheduling things'. That was then, this was now.

'Luckily for me, "Q" came attached with *The Color Purple*,' Spielberg acknowledges. It also came attached with the rubber-stamped 'social conscience' Guber and Peters had been seeking from Jones' involvement in the first place. The power and profound sensibility Jones had brought to the music for the epoch-making *Roots* TV mini-series spoke for itself.

Another individual who claims responsibility for Spielberg taking on *The Color Purple* is Kathleen Kennedy. As far as Spielberg was concerned she murmured all the right things about his need for a departure in the type of material he chose, and the need to pick something that would demonstrate – for those who had forgotten about *Sugarland Express* – his versatility. Even allowing for an element of *Reader's Digest* paraphrasing, Spielberg's recollection of her pitch is something else again: 'You know it's a black story. But that shouldn't bother you, because you're Jewish and essentially you share similarities in your upbringing and heritage.'

Before a meeting with the authoress could be set up, Alice Walker had to be primed by Quincy Jones for the occasion. She had seen none of his movies – save, oddly enough, for an unspecified chunk of *Sugarland Express*, caught while surfing channels on her TV – and barely knew the name. 'I was sceptical,' she admits, 'because I didn't know his worth.' Except that, now she came to think of it, *Sugarland* had lingered in her mind long afterwards: 'The movie had a passionate intensity and sense of caring that I really appreci-ated.' Prior to Spielberg's arrival, she consulted with a group of friends, telling them that she was reluctant to give up her work, to 'sell out'. Their advice can be summed up as, 'Take the money, girl, and *run like hell*!'

The meeting got off to a shaky start, with Walker looking on in dismay as Jones and Spielberg arrived in a limousine so big it didn't fit into her driveway. The couple of hours that ensued tipped the scales for all parties, as one idea after another poured out, each party offering his or her own conception of how scenes should be staged. What was remarkable was how many times their views con-verged.

'Wouldn't it be great,' Spielberg suggested, 'if we had Shug

('Shug' Avery, the blues singer Celie idolises) singing beautifully in one room, and Squeak (the girlfriend of Celie's stepson) trying to imitate her in another room, right next door?' Even before Walker had time to say, 'What a lovely idea', another notion was being put forward.

'What impressed me at that meeting,' she recalls, 'was Steven's absolute grasp of the essentials of the book. Right away he saw everything visually. He knew the characters, knew the spirit.'

Spielberg came away equally impressed. 'I knew I was going to make this movie,' he recalls. 'I wanted the audience to feel every colour in Celie's rainbow, the rainbow she makes for herself and dives into headfirst.'

The fact that, rainbows apart, he was nervous about his ability to handle some of the book's explicitly sexual material, that the whole project would be a stretch, a challenge for him, served as the final spur: 'I love this *because* I'm scared to do it.'

The last point Spielberg and Jones mentioned at the meeting was that they wanted Walker to write the script herself. Although she had many misgivings – the 18-month round of endless inter-views that had accompanied the novel's success, and the award of the Pulitzer Prize, had left her exhausted – she agreed to give it a try.

'Most people just buy the book and shove the author under the rug,' Jones pointed out. 'That won't happen this time.' At every stage, he assured her, Walker would have the last word.

One of the things Walker mentioned during the meeting was that stand-up comic Whoopi Goldberg had contacted her about playing in the movie. She had already seen Goldberg perform as a stand-up comedian at the Valencia Rose, a small cabaret in San Francisco, and had been extremely impressed. Goldberg was contacted in New York and asked to come along to Amblin's mini-theatre. She was greeted by Spielberg, Jones, Lionel Ritchie and visiting 'King of Pop' Michael Jackson, and sailed through her audition. Spielberg started off the conversation afterwards with, '*God*, you're really talented. I'd love you to be in this movie.'

'I don't think so,' Goldberg replied, secretly hoping it wouldn't put Spielberg off. 'I couldn't take the responsibility,' she nervously rabbited on, 'I don't know the gears, I don't wanna mess up your movie.'

'Don't worry about that,' Spielberg replied with a reassuring smile, 'I'll look out for you.'

Goldberg had always imagined playing stalwart Sofia, but was coaxed into playing the lead role of Celie instead. All she could think about as she left for the plane that would take her back to New York was, 'The lead role in a Spielberg movie? In *The Color Purple*? Git *outta* here!!'

Black casting director Reuben Cannon was high on Tina Turner to play the role of 'Shug' Avery. (So was Goldberg. 'If I'm goin' to kiss a woman,' she declared, 'let it be Tina!') The comeback queen turned Cannon down, much to Alice Walker's relief – Ms Turner was not her ideal choice – stating that playing 'Shug' would have been just too close to home, a return to the South and the bad old days when she was growing up and on the road with Ike.

For a while Peter Guber let it be known that he wanted Diana Ross for 'Shug', which caused another Walker anxiety attack. Margaret Avery was cast instead. She had prayed, after falling in love with the book, that the role would fall to her. She already had a toe-hold in Spielberg's world, having played a small role in his telefilm *Something Evil* over a dozen years earlier. Danny Glover was cast as 'Mister', the harsh farmer to whom Celie is 'given', and who cruelly holds back a lifetime of correspondence between her and her sister Nettie.

Quincy Jones's contribution to the casting process was to recommend the hostess of a brand-new and controversial talk show being broadcast out of Chicago. As soon as he'd turned on the TV set in his hotel bedroom and caught *The Oprah Winfrey Show*, he knew he'd found the ideal Sofia.

After forwarding a single draft script, Alice Walker announced that she had given up ('I had no idea of just how tired I was'). What she did do was open Spielberg's eyes to a part of black history he'd known nothing about – the visible class distinction in the South during the twenties and thirties. Where he'd assumed that all blacks had lived in extreme poverty, scraping a living as sharecroppers (the movie and TV version of life back then) Walker set the historical record straight. Not only Spielberg, but most of her readers, she maintained, had confused her background with Celie's. The truth was that had Celie's father lived, Celie would have been a whole class above Walker's as a child.

*E.T.*'s Melissa Mathison was the first alternative writer to be considered. On this occasion the magic failed to materialise, the chemistry was deemed 'not right'. On the face of it thirty-one-year-old Dutch-born Menno Meyjes seemed an unlikely third choice to capture the flavour of life in a small Georgia town between 1906 and 1947. The author of several unproduced scripts and writer of *Lionheart*, a film about the Children's Crusade, Meyjes had already been considered by Spielberg for the *Raiders of the Lost Ark* sequel; *The Color Purple* would be his first major assignment.

Unlikely he may have been, but Meyjes was the first candidate to declare at the outset, after twice reading Walker's book, that he could see a way to dramatise the letters from Celie to her sister and to God. Voiceover, he declared, was the answer. Simple though it may seem, he was the first to come up with the idea.

After producing a first draft in three weeks, Meyjes met with Spielberg most mornings, occasionally on the set of Amblin's *Goonies* for what they came to call 'Bible Class'. Each clutched their copy of Walker's book and proceeded to underline passages and to discuss her intentions with each scene. 'Steve's very good at establishing an atmosphere of trust,' says Meyjes. 'I'd come back at the end of the day and show him my pages right off the typewriter.' Meyjes quickly discovered another encouraging Spielbergian trait: 'When you're working with Steve, he'll never see you at all unless he can give 100 per cent. If he can't, he'll tell you and make special time later.' After five months and five drafts, the job was done.

During rehearsals Whoopi Goldberg found it difficult to interact with fellow cast members Danny Glover and Oprah Winfrey. In Glover's case it was his professionalism that filled her with awe; with Winfrey it was her spontaneity. She felt in constant danger of falling between the cracks of the two extremes. 'You're gonna have to help me,' she told Spielberg, 'because I don't know what the hell I'm doing.' She reminded him of their first conversation after the audition at Amblin. Again there was that unflustered smile. 'You'll be fine,' he assured her.

The truth was that Spielberg too was 'winging it', having decided against storyboards. 'I wanted every day to be a new experience for me,' he explained. 'Usually I make my movies in my head, as you would design a house, and I come on to the set with the blueprint, and I build the house. And sometimes the best sequences – the best rooms in the house – are those that I do not have designs, or storyboards for, because of a crisis, someone got sick or we had to change plans. I've enjoyed the "winging it" parts of my movies more than the planned ones.'

Since the method involved constant script changes after viewing the dailies with Meyjes, it did little to help Goldberg's situation. Come to that, Oprah Winfrey was having problems of her own over her treatment from Spielberg. The reasons for his perceived 'coldness' towards her would only be revealed at the movie's premiere.

Before filming had begun in North Carolina in June 1985,

Denis C. Hoffman (*left*) and Steven
Spielberg at the Atlanta Film Festival,
1969 (*Denis C. Hoffman*)

Steven Spielberg, 1977
(*Aquarius Library*)

Spielberg and friend (*Aquarius Library*)

*E.T.*'s London premiére, with Drew Barrymore, Henry Thomas, John McNaughton, Spielberg and Princess Diana, 1983 (*Aquarius Library*)

Producers Frank Marshall and Steven Spielberg are seen on the set of MGM's *Poltergeist*, 1982 (*Aquarius Library*)

Spielberg on the set of *Indiana Jones and the Temple of Doom*, 1984
(*Aquarius Library*)

George Lucas (*right*) and Spielberg making their marks – in the
forecourt of Mann's Chinese Theatre, 1984 (*Corbis-Bettmann/UPI*)

Spielberg gives Whoopi Goldberg direction for a scene in *The Color Purple*, 1985

Ami Irving and husband Steven Spielberg at the Golden Globes, 1987 (*Aquarius Library*)

Spielberg, 1990
(*Corbis-Bettmann/UPI*)

Jon Peters (right)
and Peter Guber
(*London Features
International Ltd*)

Kathleen Kennedy
(*The Kobal Collection*)

Lew Wasserman
(*The Kobal Collection*)

Dustin Hoffman and Spielberg, 1991 (*All-Action Pictures*)

On the set of *Jurassic Park*
(*Aquarius Library*)

Spielberg, Mom and Kate
Capshaw at *Schindler's List*
post-Oscar celebration, 1994
(*Pictorial Press Ltd*)

Denis C. Hoffman today
(*Denis C. Hoffman*)

On the set of *Schindler's List* with Liam Neeson (*Aquarius Library*)

Jeffrey Katzenberg (*left*), Spielberg and David Geffen (*right*) pose for photographers after a press conference announcing the formation of DreamWorks, 12 October 1995 (*Corbis-Bettmann/UPI*)

Steven Spielberg after receiving an honorary Cesar award for his lifetime body of work, 25 February 1995 (*Corbis-Bettmann-AFP*)

Spielberg made one last stop. Director Richard Benjamin and stars Tom Hanks and Shelley Long were surprised and pleased that he took the trouble to drop in on the first day of shooting on *The Money Pit*. It was a project that had begun almost five years earlier as a script by David Giler, and had been nursed along ever since by Frank Marshall. A swift 'Hello, and all the best', and he was off.

Quincy Jones turned up in North Carolina 'just to watch', a procedure he observed every day of the shoot. At weekends he stood looking over Spielberg's shoulder as he edited the dailies. 'I need to feel what you're doing so I can feel the music better,' he explained. Although Spielberg normally prefers to edit alone, he made an exception in the case of Jones. Would he expect a reciprocation when the time came, while Jones composed the score? This was, after all, his first movie without John Williams. 'As much as he allows me to,' was Spielberg's modest response to the question.

Spielberg's deference to Jones was not extended to executive producers Peter Guber and Jon Peters. There could only be one master on a Spielberg movie. A clause in his contract prohibited their involvement at any stage of production. 'They owned the material,' Frank Marshall summarised, 'and they turned it over to us.' The first the duo saw of the movie was along with every other studio exec, at a Warners' screening.

The energetic Guber had moved on after his *Jaws*-inspired success with *The Deep* to produce *Thank God It's Friday*, then Alan Parker's *Midnight Express*, all the while trailing controversy in his wake. Producer Rob Cohen had already negotiated a deal for what became *Friday*, only to find it being torpedoed by Guber, who had a deal at Columbia, Donna Summer signed, and his own plans for a disco musical. On *Midnight Express* line producer David Puttnam sent a despairing telex to Guber from Malta that read, 'Every time I need any help, you vanish on me.'

In 1980, halfway through the production of a teenage-suicide saga, *Foxes*, Guber sold his Casablanca Filmworks to Philips/ Siemens, the Dutch electronics giant, and with their backing established Polygram Pictures with Jon Peters, a producer he'd met at Columbia on the set of *The Eyes of Laura Mars*. By this time every incredible chapter of the Jon Peters story had been observed with a mixture of envy, awe and disbelief by the normally blasé denizens of Hollywood.

Peters had spent his teenage years on the streets before establishing a highly successful hairdressing empire. In 1974 he was introduced to Barbra Streisand, who was searching for a short, modern cut for her role in *For Pete's Sake*. Doubling as her lover and producer, he steered Streisand through a remake of *A Star is Born* that defied critical scorn and his on-set tantrums to establish him as a Hollywood player. 'I bet my picture will outgross yours,' he boasted to Dino De Laurentiis, whose *King Kong* remake was also about to open. 'It's possible,' De Laurentiis conceded. 'My monkey doesn't sing.'

Successful as Guber and Peters had been apart, their touch deserted them during Polygram's three-year run, with the company admitting to a 'major loss', put at $80 million on their $100 million investment. A first-look deal at Warners signed in 1983 had brought Guber and Peters back with *The Color Purple*.

As anticipated, Spielberg's biggest problem with the material lay in its sexual frankness. It was not something he was used to grappling with, and there was one scene in the book he simply couldn't handle. His explanation: 'I didn't grow up that way.' The scene had 'Shug' Avery urging Celie to examine her vagina in a mirror. Many felt it was a key episode, in that it heralded Celie's 'coming out'. Spielberg concedes that 'Any woman director could have done that brilliantly, but I was afraid of it. I didn't know how to direct actors to do that.'

In the same way, Meyjes' dialogue failed to reflect the unadulterated frankness of the book, with its unashamed references to 'pussy' and 'titties'. Had these been retained, together with the vagina scene, no doubt it would have pushed the movie into another certification category, and severely limited audience size. Although at no point had Spielberg regarded *The Color Purple* as a potential blockbuster, there seemed little point in limiting its chances further. Spielberg's idea was to open the movie small, perhaps in thirty-five theatres across America, then let it build naturally, of its own momentum. Warners' marketing division saw matters quite differently. This was 'A Steven Spielberg Movie' after all, and to justify the kind of spend they had in mind, 150 theatres was the minimum required to soak up the juice. Spielberg reluctantly agreed to go along. The premiere on December 18, 1985, was perfectly timed to draw attention to the movie as an Oscar contender. And at last Oprah Winfrey was given the rationale behind her chilly treatment on the set. 'I realised how terrified you were, and that was working for you,' he informed her. 'That's why I never gave you any reassurance.' The talk-show queen *may* have bitten her tongue.

While the overall critical reaction was favourable – NBC's Gene

Shalit decreed that 'It should be against the law *not* to see *The Color Purple*' – those opposed were vociferous in their views. Julie Salamon of the *Wall Street Journal* was typical of the 'antes': 'He turned a wrenching, painful book into a feel-good movie.' Or, as Elvis Mitchell in LA *Weekly* put it, 'He turned the black experience into a themepark – Negroland.'

Had these people actually read Alice Walker's book? Spielberg's departures from the basic story were actually few and far between, and almost always in the cause of translating the story in filmic terms. Sad on the page, Nettie's departure is rendered heartbreaking in the movie. In the book the arrival of Nettie's first letter is virtually thrown away as Walker's otherwise impeccably assembled series of letters misjudges the proper dramatic sequence, whereas the movie *builds* to the revelation. Sofia's downfall and suffering in the movie is made graphically real to the point of being unendurable, and here Spielberg could be accused of exaggerating her situation to the point where her abrupt resurrection becomes unbelievable – a rerun of the Disney 'business' he pushed in *E.T.* But overall, he made a sincerely felt adaptation.

Predictably there was criticism that Spielberg had ducked the book's explicit sexuality and lesbian aspects. In fact, Celie's feelings for Shug were amply portrayed, with their tender kissing scene, Celie's first real awakening, leaving little to the imagination. And there was a world of heartbreak behind Celie's declaration to Shug: 'He blamed me for not being you.'

Most hurtful, from Spielberg's point of view, was the general backlash from the black community, bemoaning the fact that a 'honky white' had dared to take on a slice of black life. Whoopi Goldberg was ready with her reply. 'These people bitch and moan that you never see a black face in the movies, and as soon as there's a movie with a black face that is not singin' and dancin', they bitch and moan about it. These people are pissed off because Spielberg directed it, which to me is very ridiculous. It's like saying that if you're not a junkie, you can't tell anyone that heroin screws up your body. I say to people, cool the fuck out, and see for yourself what this man does with the movie.'

Spielberg's protégé Phil Joanou also rushed to defend his benefactor. 'Steven Spielberg is a great director,' he declared. 'I think he's been attacked unfairly . . . The fact is that now millions will see *The Color Purple* who probably would never have read the book. And no other director in the business could have gotten *The Color Purple* made into a movie.'

Joanou's estimation of readers versus moviegoers is on the money; less so his claim that no one else could have obtained a green light. The Guber/Peters team lucked on to Spielberg via Quincy Jones; the team would still have pursued the movie without him.

There was one other apparent result of Spielberg's perceived 'mishandling' of black history. Starting now, a young, untried but fiercely ambitious wannabe director vowed, he would raise himself to the point where he'd be able to put a more positive spin on the black experience. From the inside. His name was Spike Lee.

# 23

## Deep Purple

*'The great gamblers are dead, and I think that's the tragedy of Hollywood today. In the old days the Thalbergs and the Mayers came out of nickelodeon vaudeville, they came out of borscht-belt theatre, they came with a great deal of showmanship and* esprit-de-corps *to a little citrus grove in California. They were brave. They were gamblers. They were high rollers. There is a paranoia today. People are afraid. People in high positions are unable to say "OK" or "Not OK". They're afraid to take the big gamble. They're living for the odds-on favourite.'*

*'I'd like to be able to tell my child that it's all like it is in the movies. That we always slay our dragons, wake up from our nightmares, and that it's easy to tell the good guys from the bad guys.'*

STEVEN SPIELBERG

Under Lew Wasserman and Sid Sheinberg, Ned Tanen's slate of movies had made 'Little Universal', 'Uncle' Carl Laemmle's original creation, the undisputed top studio in Hollywood by the end of the seventies, with net profits from their 'Filmed Entertainment' division, a combination of TV and movies, totalling $685 million for the decade. Now, into the eighties, it looked like the studio might be propelled to even greater heights on the heels of *E.T.*

Spielberg's long-running feud with Frank Price – late of Universal-TV, late of Columbia Pictures and *Gandhi*, rejecter of *E.T.*, his all-round nemesis – was rekindled in 1983. In a hilariously telling example of Hollywood musical chairs, Price returned to Universal after Ned Tanen's departure for Paramount. His appointment as chairman of the newly created 'MCA Motion Picture Group' under Wasserman and Sheinberg was portrayed as a triumphal return in a *Variety* report headlined 'Expect Long-Ranging

Overall Reign'. Price's responsibilities were to include 'every aspect of motion picture production at MCA and Universal Motion Picture Groups including marketing, sales and distribution'.

*Every* aspect? Hollywood wise men stood by for inevitable ructions, for they were aware of the depth of feeling between Spielberg and Price, aware also of the *whole* story behind *E.T.*'s turnaround from Columbia to Universal . . .

When Price and Columbia had sold *E.T.* to Universal, the bill had included the $1 million in development costs already expended on the project – plus five per cent of *whatever the movie made*. Right there, as far as Spielberg was concerned, the very people who'd shown not a particle of faith in the project were reaping a bonanza. Not only that, but their bonanza was coming out of *his* hide! Now let's take a closer look at Price's decision to turn Spielberg and *E.T.* away in the first place . . .

Marvin Antonowsky, Price's original deputy at Columbia – shortly to rejoin his old boss at Universal – had indeed reported research studies back in '79 showing that only a bunch of kids would be standing in line for Spielberg's brainchild. Price was *still* willing to go ahead with the movie, *and* with *Starman*, in development at the same time – except that suddenly Spielberg's deal changed. According to Price, Spielberg arrived one day, flanked by his lawyers, with the revelation that he had a contractual obligation to Universal at least to allow the studio to *co*-produce *E.T.*

Remembering the nightmare of the last Columbia/Universal co-production, *1941*, Price balked at this. 'I was relatively pissed off,' he recalled to reporter Jack Mathews. 'I didn't want to go through the *1941* thing again. Nobody was in charge, it went incredibly over-budget. I said, "I am prepared to make *E.T.*, but I want it as a Columbia picture. I didn't want to split it with anybody."'

Spielberg was so angry at the perceived snub, not to mention the payday Price had negotiated in return for letting the movie go, that he vowed he would never work with him again. Now here Price was, just a few years down the line, snugly installed at Universal, and with Antonowsky in transit.

Spielberg swiftly let it be known that he would refuse to enter the same room as Price or his deputy. Then he decided, upon due reflection, that this wasn't formal enough. He demanded that an actual clause be inserted in his contract that he would never be required even to *talk* to Price. Two camps were established on the Universal lot. One reported to Price, one – Spielberg pretty much alone – dealt direct with Sid Sheinberg. The divided camp, while a source of great amusement to all who knew the background to the feud, would assume even greater significance to the outside world a couple of years down the line. In an irony impossible to invent, consider the competition Spielberg's Warner Bros release, *The Color Purple*, would be up against in the 1986 Oscars race. None other than Frank Price's Universal blockbuster, *Out of Africa*. And remember: Spielberg had already suffered at Price's hands in the Oscar stakes, when *E.T.* lost out to *Gandhi*.

Just to add an extra pinch of spice, there was a third Universal picture in the running for honours the same year that some regarded as Sheinberg's baby. It was not, oddly enough, a Spielberg movie, but Peter Bogdanovich's *Mask*, representing his return to a major studio after years in the independent wilderness.

The release of *Mask* in the Spring of 1985 sparked the first of two red-hot controversies that would swirl around Universal's Black Tower HQ as the year progressed.

Bogdanovich had handed over the movie, complete with Bruce Springsteen soundtrack, in the autumn of 1984. On returning from a European trip in December, he was stunned to discover that the studio had breached the 'final cut' clause in his contract. Gone was Bruce Springsteen from the soundtrack, together with several minutes of running time, including two key scenes. He decided on a showdown.

It wasn't an easy course for Bogdanovich to take. Since his last major studio release, *Nickelodeon* in 1977, things hadn't been easy for the director. Reunited with Roger Corman, he'd travelled to Singapore to shoot *Saint Jack*. One result was a fine, if uncommercial movie. Another was the break-up of his eight-year relationship with Cybill Shepherd. His romance with *Playboy* model Dorothy Stratten ended tragically when her estranged husband shot her to death before turning the gun on himself. The movie he'd made with Stratten, *They All Laughed*, had failed to gain a wide release and ended up bankrupting him. Then there were allegations of sexual misconduct with Dorothy's underage sister. All in all, Bogdanovich was in no shape to take on the might of MCA and Universal. Yet he felt he had no other choice. *Mask* was the life story of Rocky Dennis, a boy who'd been stricken with craniodiaphyseal dysplasia, a disfiguring congenital disease. With Rocky's mother Rusty closely involved, Bogdanovich regarded his accurate portrayal of her late son's story as a sacred trust.

Ironically, the movie opened to the best reviews Bogdanovich had seen for years. Brisk business, too. Four days after the opening, he called a press conference to announce an $11 million lawsuit against his producer Martin Starger and Universal. He listed the alterations the studio had made behind his back to his 'final cut', the change from Springsteen's music, which Rocky had loved, to Bob Seger's, which Rocky had never even heard. 'Universal will never pull this again on anyone when I get through with them,' he declared. 'I ain't scared of these people.' He would hold out for his version to be restored.

'I don't want to be quoted with the word "ludicrous",' Frank Price retorted, 'but the picture is already playing nationally.' He conceded that the studio had deleted one scene after Bogdanovich had handed the picture over, 'an artistic difference which we felt improved the film and eliminated four minutes.' As for the music, the Springsteen record label had made outrageous demands, including a cut of the video rights, that the studio had not been prepared to grant. And Bogdanovich, he claimed, had been aware of the problem.

The full-page open letter in *Variety* Bogdanovich organised, with almost two dozen directors backing his stand, was the first of two such embarrassments that Universal would suffer that year.

During the uproar Frank Marshall, situated on the Amblin lot at Universal, was delighted to welcome his old boss Bogdanovich as a lunch guest. Regret was expressed that so much time had passed since their last get-together. They joked, as best they could, about the *Mask* impasse. That Bogdanovich seemed almost penitent was best summed up in his opening remark, accompanied by a sheepish smile, 'I guess I've done it this time!'

With *Mask* a considerable hit, Bogdanovich was persuaded to drop his action. 'Frank Price was the culprit,' he still claimed. 'He was the one who screwed it all up. I think it had something to do with *Out of Africa* being a more expensive picture and very much his baby. Really *Mask* was Sid Sheinberg's, and there was tremendous conflict between these two guys. In the end it boiled down to ego between me and Frank and Sid, and also ego between CBS Records and Universal. And *Mask* got caught in the middle and was the loser.'

Midway through 1985, apart from keeping Spielberg and Price from each other's throats, and allowing the *Mask* controversy to float gently over his head, Sid Sheinberg was having problems of his own – with another maverick sonofabitch filmmaker named Terry Gilliam. All Sheinberg wanted to do was fit Gilliam's *Brazil* into Universal's cookie-cutter and have it come out standing to attention at under two hours, and with a happy ending. What was wrong with that? Plenty, according to Gilliam, declaring he would fight to the death for his movie. When Sheinberg kept delaying *Brazil*'s opening – Twentieth Century-Fox, owner of the foreign rights, having already released it in Europe – Gilliam decided it was time to maximise the embarrassment factor. But how? He decided on the Bogdanovich Solution. The October 2, 1985 edition of *Variety* carried a full-page ad that simply asked the question:

> 'Dear Sid Sheinberg,
>     When are you going to release my movie, *Brazil*?
> Terry Gilliam'

The answer from Sheinberg and Universal was deafening silence as far as the outside world was concerned. Internally, differences began to emerge. Anxious not to let the fuss deflect attention, honours too, from *Out of Africa*, Price told Sheinberg he should go ahead and release *Brazil* and get it over with. That way, he argued, the movie and the controversy would be out of the way and forgotten by the end of the year. Holding it back, on the other hand, might hand *Brazil* the sympathy vote at Oscar time. 'It could really fuck us up,' Price warned.

If anything, Price's sermon only made Sheinberg dig in even harder. And maybe Sheinberg had an agenda of his own as Spielberg's greatest champion. *Out of Africa* was one consideration. But what about his friend's *Color Purple*?

A visit from Gilliam's producer, Arnon Milchan, pleading his director's artistic rights, stiffened his resolve. 'Terry Gilliam is not yet Picasso,' Sheinberg exploded. 'He's not Steven Spielberg. Or George Lucas. Or Sidney Pollack. He hasn't won any Academy Awards.' Pausing to get his breath back, Sheinberg renewed his attack: 'In Texas, we have a saying, Arnon, "Put your money where your mouth is, or shut up." I'm sure there is a Hebrew equivalent.'

Stung, Milchan retorted that coming from 'an assimilated Beverly Hills Jew', that was rich. As to Sheinberg's suggestion that he buy the movie back from Universal? That was *too* rich.

Knowing the pull Spielberg had with his long-time mentor, Gilliam called him up, asked him to look at *Brazil*, then help talk Sheinberg into seeing sense. Spielberg agreed to screen *Brazil* at Amblin and get back to Gilliam. When he did, he reported that he 'loved the movie', but had to agree with Sheinberg, the ending was too dark for him too.

'Spielberg tried to help, at least he watched the movie,' Gilliam told me, 'but his talking to Sheinberg had no effect. I'd hit too many nerves with Sid. As people grow up in the studio system, great chunks of their brains get cut away. It became a gauntlet with Universal. I had to run through it to get to the public.'

The method Gilliam now chose was to sneak his full-length version of *Brazil* out of Universal's vaults, only days before the crucial year-end, and show it to the Los Angeles film critics. The result: in a stinging slap in the face to Sheinberg, Price, Spielberg, *Out of Africa* and *Color Purple*, they voted it 'Best Film of 1985'.

'I think Terry Gilliam is a genius,' Spielberg is on record as saying. Maybe he does, but wouldn't it have been great if he'd really put his weight behind *Brazil*? Or would that have been too much like adding another competitor, on top of *Out of Africa*, to vie with *The Color Purple* in the awards race? As it turned out, he needn't have worried. The 'too dark' *Brazil* was left out of the Oscar stakes.

If *The Color Purple*'s $90 million at the US box-office came as a pleasant surprise to all concerned, the New York *Times* considered more glad tidings at the Academy Awards were foregone conclusions. 'The only thing left for Spielberg to do,' they predicted, 'is to decide which tux to wear as he picks up his Oscar.' Staggeringly, the eleven nominations for *The Color Purple*, including Best Picture, pointedly *excluded* Best Director.

How was it possible? One explanation the pundits put forward: in campaigning so hard for Akira Kurosawa's inclusion in the list of five nominees for *Ran*, his fellow director Sidney Lumet may have edged Spielberg out of the list. The New York *Post* headlined 'Omission Impossible!' Peter Bogdanovich cut to the chase: 'Anyone who says that envy didn't affect Spielberg's chances are crazy.' Clint Eastwood weighed in with, 'He's too successful. He's too young. His genius is too great. They'll never give him the gold.' Whoopi Goldberg, one of three cast members nominated for their performances, threw caution, and probably her Oscar chances, to the wind, blaming 'a small bunch of people with small minds who chose to ignore the obvious'.

John Huston, nominated for *Prizzi's Honor*, dismissed the storm of protest. 'Spielberg has had so much success,' he scoffed, 'he can afford to miss a beat.'

Unlike Goldberg, Margaret Avery had no intentions of losing out. She still did, largely thanks to a brainwave – or was that a brainstorm? – she had. There's nothing wrong with taking out an advert in the trades, although it's better if your studio does it for you. Better too when your message isn't designed to freeze the blood, the function Avery's performed:

'Dear God,
My name is Margaret Avery. I knows dat I been blessed by Alice Walker, Steven Spielberg and Quincy Jones, who gave me the part of 'Shug' Avery in *The Color Purple*. Now I is up for one of the nominations fo' Best Supporting Actress

216

alongst with some fine, talented ladies that I is proud to be in the company of. Well, God, I guess the time has come fo' the Academy's voters to decide whether I is one of the Best Supporting Actresses this year or not. Either way, thank you, Lord, for the opportunity.

 'Your little daughter,
  'Margaret Avery'

She got her nomination, so I guess the good Lord done answered that child's prayers. Unfortunately, he wasn't so obliging with the award itself.

When Oscar producer Stanley Donen invited Spielberg to present the 'Best Actor' award at the ceremony, he declined in a justifiable huff. It was just as well, for it would have been difficult, even for the best actor in the world, to have sat through eleven nominations – *without a single win*. It was a shocker, and a dubious honour shared only with 1977's *The Turning Point*.

Equally galling, the winner for Best Picture and Best Director was the dreaded Price's *Out of Africa*. While Spielberg's earlier Directors' Guild Award had been appreciated – 'If some of you are making a statement,' he'd said in his acceptance speech, 'thank God, I love you for it' – it still served to rub salt, along with balm, into the wound. His penultimate words on the subject, though flippant, concealed a deep hurt: 'When I'm sixty Hollywood will forgive me. I don't know what for, but they'll forgive me.'

Once again the old question had been raised: How could the director of a nominated 'Best Picture' be excluded from nomination? More and more it looked like a Hollywood establishment shut-out personally directed against Spielberg. His players too, for many had considered at least one award a given for nominated actresses Whoopi Goldberg, Margaret Avery and Oprah Winfrey. 'There are times to speak,' Spielberg tersely declared, 'and times to move on to your next musical number. I'm moving on to my next number!'

Warner Bros was not so reticent, issuing a public statement that the company was 'shocked and dismayed that the movie's primary creative force, Steven Spielberg, was not recognised'.

Frank Price's cup, on the other hand, was full and running over. And not only because of his Oscar triumph. Universal's income had rebounded in his first full year of releases, albeit in large measure due to the performance of Amblin's *Back to the Future*, Spielberg's unintended welcome-home gift to Price (produced and marketed, at Spielberg's insistence, outside Price's control).

Price's euphoria was to last only a mere matter of months. Cue further lashings of irony, for his *coup-de-grâce* was delivered courtesy of Spielberg's friend George Lucas.

The movie that failed to fly in August, that crashed to earth with a dull thud, was Universal's *Howard the Duck*, a $35 million disaster Price had allegedly championed. Producer of this misguided fantasy? George Lucas.

'Duck Cooks Price's Goose' was the *Variety* headline that accompanied his ignominious exit, preceded – it was whispered – by an ungentlemanly fist-fight between him and Sheinberg over just who had given the turkey (the duck, that is) the green light in the first place. Now, according to 'a source at Universal', *Variety* reported that 'Price's appointment had never been intended as a long-term relationship'. Price left after serving under three years of his five-year, $3 million-a-year contract, the balance settled by Universal.

The basic problem had been communication, Sheinberg claimed: 'It got to the point where we couldn't work with him. He is the W.C. Fields character who looks at his cards like this' – snuggles a hand close to his vest and peeks – 'and you walk over to him and he puts his cards down.'

Sheinberg denied that Lucas's misfire had indeed cooked Price's goose. 'I don't fault Price for the deal to make *Howard the Duck*,' he said, talking from his office on the fifteenth floor of Universal's Black Tower. 'That is a bullet that could have hit anyone at the studio. He'd always been interested in *Howard the Duck*. He'd optioned the project back when he was running TV. He was very interested in making it. (Then) Lucas had a desire to be connected to it.' Surprisingly, Sheinberg asserted that he had never personally read the script, which many considered unusual for such an expensive project.

Sheinberg also poured cold water over *Variety*'s headline. 'Those people who claim that *Howard the Duck* was a catalyst in (Price's) departure, that's ridiculous,' he said, offering to 'take a lie detector test' anybody wanted to give him. He granted that if the movie had made $200 million, things might have been different, but that basically Frank Price and MCA had failed to click: 'The problem is it should have been dealt with a year earlier, two years earlier, and I take the responsibility for that.'

So how big had 'the Spielberg factor' registered in Price's ousting? 'Steven wanted to relate to me, I wanted to relate to Steven,' said Sheinberg. 'To be jealous of that relationship, somebody has to be sick, or very insecure. It was a sign of how small he was.'

The outspoken Sheinberg's acerbic pronouncements on Price were exceeded only by the bile he unleashed on others. Like Michael Eisner, late of Paramount, busily turning Disney around with Jeff Katzenberg to the point where a takeover bid for MCA was becoming more and more of a realistic threat: Eisner was 'an egomaniac'. As for Sheinberg's ex-colleague Ned Tanen, they no longer spoke because Tanen was 'angry at me because I neglected to phone when one of his wives killed herself'. Not for nothing was Spielberg's supporter rapidly becoming known as 'Jaws' Sheinberg.

If a distancing between Universal and George Lucas might have been considered in order following the *Duck* débâcle, forget it! The old saw, 'It's not what you know, but who you know' is the golden rule in Hollywood. Price's successor at Universal, after a blink-and-you've-missed-it holding of the fort by another hopeful, Bob Rehme, was Tom Pollock – Lucas's ex-attorney. Yep, the same one who'd been handed the terms of *Raiders of the Lost Ark* deal to flog around Hollywood. The same one who had originally negotiated twenty per cent of *American Graffiti*'s gross for Lucas and watched as Universal's brains trust had agreed, laughing at such foolishness behind their collective backs, for how much could that amount to? (The answer: five per cent of Lucas's $13.4 million *Graffiti* windfall had gone straight into Pollock, Rigrod and Bloom's company coffers. A further $2 million followed, their cut of the $40 million Lucas made out of *Star Wars*.)

Now Sheinberg went on to claim that Pollock's appointment was inspired precisely because Lucas's attorney proved such a stickler about squeezing money out of Universal for *Howard the Duck* despite the studio's sea of red ink on the project. The two men had met at Sheinberg's Beverly Hills home, where Pollock had been prevailed upon to forego pre-arranged cash payments due from *Duck* regardless of whether or not the movie bombed. Pollock was adamant: an agreement had been made, and he insisted on behalf of his client that the agreement be kept. Hurting as he was, Sheinberg – by his account – took another look at the tenacious attorney: 'It occurred to me that he was a really terrific guy to run the motion picture group at Universal . . .!'

For Pollock the appointment meant a quick visit to Rodeo Drive and the nearest tailor. His normal working attire of casual shirt, jeans and sock-less moccasins would never do at the Black Tower, where Lew Wasserman's dress code of dark business suit and tie still held sway.

Despite the mixed reviews accorded *The Color Purple*, Spielberg seemed to take heart from the public response. Even with the issues he'd chosen to duck, he regarded it as his 'coming-of-age' movie. Having reached that watershed, he was reluctant to regress once more. There was always Amblin to churn out the commercial-formula movies. After a year of 'Steven Spielberg Presents' that included *The Goonies*, *Young Sherlock Holmes*, *The Money Pit* and *An American Tail*, a fellow director decided to break ranks and go public with his discontent.

'The only thing Steven Spielberg and I have in common is our birthday, December 18,' said Alan Rudolph. 'This past year, certifiably the worst year in recent movie history, is a case of the studios getting exactly what they want, and Spielberg has to take his share of responsibility for that. Amblin produced and reproduced several films last year that have all the high concept nonsense involved, and yet really no point of view. And the audience says, "Well, I've seen this before."'

Contrarily, as Rudolph himself admitted, the total gross of all *his* movies combined didn't equal the first weekend figure Spielberg achieved with one of his blockbusters.

It's ironic that Spielberg's *Sugarland Express* is a better movie, in my opinion, than the best of Rudolph's. Ironic too that if *Sugarland* had been a hit, it might have been adopted as the benchmark of excellence by Spielberg, rather than the mush into which his career descended, no matter how successfully in monetary terms, with *Close Encounters* and *E.T.*

# 24

# 'Ting!'

*'Empire of the Sun was an interesting thing, because all
the critics who liked my films before, hated it, but all the
highbrow critics who never liked anything I did, loved it.'*

*'Empire of the Sun was dismissed. There's nothing worse
than being dismissed.'*

STEVEN SPIELBERG

*'It's a baby boy!' Spielberg heard the nurse say, although it was hardly
necessary. He was there, he had watched the child emerge, he had heard
its first, squawking cry, he had watched as his child was cleaned up,
swathed in blue robes, cradled in Amy's arms. Like many a father before
him, he felt as if his was the only child ever born in the history of the
world.*

*'Can I hold him?' he asked, half crying with the strangest mixture of
excitement, pride and relief.*

*'Of course you can,* daddy,' *Amy replied with a smile, extending her
arms, proffering the little bundle. 'Just for a moment now, Mr Spielberg,'
he heard the midwife counsel.*

*Gazing down into his son's face, his heart skipped a beat as the little
eyes flicked open. 'Hi, Dad,' he heard the infant say. 'How ya doin'? Any
chance of dinner? I'm* starving.'

*Spielberg looked at his son in blank amazement. 'You can t-t-talk?' he
stammered.*

*'You betcha.'*

*'But I don't understand. New-born babies aren't supposed to—'*

*Astonishingly, the baby was tugging his right arm from its restrictive
wrapping and wagging his index finger admonishingly. 'There are more
things in heaven and earth, dear Horatio,' he intoned, 'than have ever
been dreamed of in your philosophy. Now take me to the nearest Burger
King. Then mebbe we could do a movie. Hasn't Brian got a screening of*

221

Body Double *coming up? So I hear the buzz ain't so good? So what else is new?'*

Spielberg *gazed at his wife in astonishment. She seemed happy enough, not too concerned, smiling placidly. Was he the only one to appreciate the momentous nature of what was happening? Now he turned to the matron, struggling to find the words. 'Isn't th-this – a l-little unusual? I mean – to arrive, so* gifted*?!'*

*'Not really,' she replied, very matter-of-fact. 'When you've attended as many deliveries as I have, you've seen and heard it all. Why, the other week we had a baby girl who began reciting Rabbie Burns' "Tae A Moose" as soon as her little head popped out. What could we do? Her parents weren't even Scottish! Oh, look, he's closed his little eyes and gone to sleep. I wouldn't bother about it if I were you. It'll sort itself out.'*

*'It'll sort itself out, darling.' He heard Amy repeat the words, only this time they seemed to come from a distance, and carried with them a weird echo.*

*He woke up with a start.* God, *how realistic it had been. And hey – what a great idea for a movie! Naw, something called* Look Who's Talking *was already in development. Well, what if the baby turned out to be an alien? Shit, been there too, with* E.T.'*s baby-gurgling. So it needed a little work already. Maybe Matthew and Bob would be interested in the concept for* Amazing Stories. *Hey, waste not, want not.*

The arrival of his son changed Spielberg in ways he could never have imagined. Although everyone had told him what it would be like being present at the delivery, watching the miracle of birth overwhelmed Spielberg. The dream that had seemed so real, the birth of an all-talking, streetwise baby, was soon all but forgotten. This was reality, this was *his* son, *his* child. Now he had a second career, that of family man and father. And Brian De Palma had a new role as well. That of a real-life Godfather.

All young Samuel Max had to do in the mornings was to smile at his dad, and appointments were instantly forgotten. A four-day week replaced the punishing regime Spielberg normally set himself, and it was a 9.30 start in the mornings instead of 7.45. Before Max he had seldom left Amblin's offices before 10 pm, now he never missed his son's bedtime. And there was another unexpected by-product of fatherhood: now that he had a child of his own, the imperative he'd felt to make movies featuring children, and be a surrogate father, was gone.

Spielberg felt there was a strong possibility, as his son grew older, that he might be able to relive his own childhood yet again, recalling more clearly the funny and scary times, the miserable times too, he had as a boy. Meantime, it wasn't just the son who had a lot of growing up to do, but the father as well. From now on his personal projects would reflect that growth, as would an unusual acquisition.

A long-distance telephone bid to Sotheby's in New York City brought Rosebud, *Citizen Kane*'s beloved boyhood sled, into Spielberg's possession. The expected price tag had been $20,000, which Spielberg termed 'an insult'. Instead, he upped the ante to $60,500, the highest price ever paid for a piece of movie memorabilia.

'It will go over my typewriter to remind me that quality in movies comes first,' he declared.

Sorry about the irreverent thought, but wasn't Rosebud consumed in a fire at the end of the classic movie? Or was that a sledge double? Or just another example of movie magic? And didn't Spielberg already owe Welles a debt, having borrowed from *Kane*'s finale in *Raiders*, with the Ark of the Covenant hidden away in some dusty archive?

In Spielberg's position any piece of work capable of being bought was his for the asking. Many resented the fact that Thomas Keneally's *Schindler's List* was on his shelf and had been for years. Who did this lightweight think he was, even contemplating the depiction of the Holocaust on screen, his dithering denying other, more worthy filmmakers the chance to offer the subject the justice it cried out for?

There was further gnashing of teeth in the film community with the announcement that Spielberg had snapped up rights to J.G. Ballard's semi-autobiographical memoir of a childhood spent in a Japanese concentration camp, *Empire of the Sun*. Spielberg had his answer ready. He hadn't bought it for himself at all, but for the venerable David Lean. It seemed that Lean had been aware of Spielberg's career from the beginning, ever since the release in Britain of *Duel*. 'I knew immediately that here was a very bright director,' he declared. 'Steve takes real pleasure in the sensuality of forming action scenes, wonderful flowing movement. He is the way movies *used* to be. He is entertaining his teenage self – and what is wrong with that? I see Steven as a young brother. I suppose I see myself in him. I have rarely felt so at ease with anyone. Curious thing, that.'

It was indeed curious, in so far as Lean, whatever the undoubted merits of his film work, has always been known as a distinctly chilly, even downright unpleasant individual. In Kevin Brownlow's *David Lean: A Biography*, Lean emerges as someone who betrayed all six of his wives with a string of mistresses, and cheated on those second-stringers as well with innumerable one-nighters – this, all the way

223

through to the grand old age of seventy-eight. A sacred monster indeed! There was more:

Item: When seventy-five-year-old Dame Peggy Ashcroft was laid up in her hotel, having suffered a fall while making *A Passage to India*, it seemed that Lean refused even to walk a few doors down the corridor to see how she was. Sympathy for a laid-up old lady? Forget it.

Item: When a second-unit filmed a storm scene not only wisely but far too well, Lean, in a jealousy-inspired hissy fit, refused even to talk to the individuals responsible. And he regularly dropped technicians, once they'd outlived their usefulness and become, in his words, 'surplus to his requirements'.

Item: If the only way he could persuade Charles Laughton to appear in *Hobson's Choice* was to threaten to expose his homosexuality, so be it.

With his passion for making movies, to the exclusion of winning friends and influencing people with the warmth of his personality, Lean possessed a cold gene that rendered him indifferent to the struggles and concerns of those he regarded as constituting the lower orders. His fellow-feeling for Spielberg, the way he regarded him as a kindred spirit, is instructive. Although it manifests itself in different ways, it could be argued that Spielberg displays the same cold gene in many of his dealings.

The partnership between the two on *Empire of the Sun* was fine while it lasted, which wasn't for very long. Although willing to forego the director's seat in favour of Lean, it seemed that Spielberg had secretly coveted the subject all along. When Lean chose to pass and move on to developing Joseph Conrad's *Nostromo* instead – under Spielberg's aegis once more – the path was cleared.

The main character in *Empire* was eleven-year-old Jim Graham, who had grown up middle-class and spoiled. There the resemblance to everything Spielberg had ever known ended. The book was stark, uncompromising, unsentimental, brutal. Stand by, many declared, for another whitewash job, tears and laughter among the barbed wire and bayonets. Well, maybe . . .

Spielberg declared himself 'inspired' by Jim's character, seeing him as a survivor in a world that didn't allow survival. And maybe, now he had turned forty, it was time for a different kind of film-making. What if he set out to shoot the movie Lean himself might have made? Spielberg suddenly realised that he had the opportunity to please a side of himself he had never seriously entertained before, a side that wouldn't necessarily think of the audience with every thought and breath. Eyebrows were raised when heavyweight playwright Tom Stoppard was brought in for screenplay duty.

After checking out locations in Buenos Aires, Vienna, Lisbon and Hong Kong, Spielberg sought permission from the People's Republic of China to film part of the movie in its authentic Shanghai location. Frank Marshall and Kathleen Kennedy flew across the Pacific to Beijing as his personal ambassadors in the quest. The deal took a year to set up; *Empire of the Sun* would be the first major Hollywood movie filmed in China since the 1949 revolution.

A nine-month talent search was conducted before thirteen-year-old Christian Bale was chosen from among 4,000 applicants for the role of Jim. Oddly enough, he and Spielberg already had a smidgeon of shared history – for Bale had been featured, as the Czar's hemophiliac son, with Amy Irving in the TV mini-series *Anastasia*. So had Irving put in a word for young Bale? No, she hadn't. Founder member of Chicago's Steppenwolf Theater Group John Malkovitch, having made a considerable impact in his first movie, *Places in the Heart*, was cast as Basie, Jim's unsentimental, uncompromising 'guardian'.

With its polyglot mix of Chinese and European culture, Shanghai had changed little since Japan had taken over the city on December 8, 1941. This suited Spielberg and his unit, although there were certain glaring exceptions. First, the stylish Tudor homes where Jim and his parents had lived were now only suitable for exterior shots, since each of them had been sub-divided and was occupied by up to fifteen Chinese families; interiors would be built in Britain at Elstree Studios. Second, rickshaws were no longer around to provide the necessary period colour; fifty were built from scratch. Third, all of the posters stuck on hoardings had modern Chinese characters; 1,000 had to be specially designed, printed and posted using classical Chinese.

Apart from that, and the first assistant director shouting 'Ting!' instead of 'Cut!' for the benefit of the 5,000 Chinese extras on day-leave from their regular jobs, filming went smoothly at Shanghai Film Studios and on location throughout the city. Ahead lay the move to Elstree, then it was on to Jerez, in the heart of Spain's sherry-producing country, to film the Japanese prison camp scenes. There the advance unit unexpectedly encountered five solid weeks of rain as they dug in for their scheduled three months. Toiling by the banks of the Gualalquivir river, they erected the prison camp pagoda, bunkers, a railway line and turntable, together with a fully operational 1,000-feet runway for the World War II planes the unit would employ – three US P51 Mustang fighter planes (collector's pieces valued at half a million dollars each), together with actual Japanese Zeros built by Mitsubishi (with a dozen assorted one-third scale versions for long shots).

Kathleen Kennedy caused a furore when she went public about what she saw as Spanish-style rip-offs, with exorbitant sums being demanded for the most basic materials. An enraged Spanish government countered that the unit had flown their entire crew of technicians from Elstree, denying work to local craftsmen – a situation that, in reverse, would never have been tolerated in Britain. Look at the daily expenses, *per diems*, the unit must be paying! Why, Amblin was even continuing to employ a British catering company!

Kennedy fired back, pointing out that thousands of locals were being given employment as extras, that had a Spanish crew been flown from Madrid, they would have been collecting *per diems* just the same; the only excess in flying the British out lay in the extra air fares. And the British caterers had been on the job from the start, even out in Shanghai, and were totally familiar with the dietary requirements of the cast and crew.

If the Spanish government had no answer, Spanish mosquitoes were happy to oblige. Following the five weeks of downpour, a plague of the insects descended upon the unit and for close on two weeks made life hell for all concerned.

The constantly recurring motif with which Spielberg chose to festoon the movie was wings: wings of real, full-scale planes; wings of pretend, three-quarter scale planes; wings of Jim's vast collection of toy planes; wings decorating limousines; shining wings turning to rusted wings; even Jim's boys-own comic is entitled 'Wings'. Fair enough, since it was the boy's obsession, and since it was the loss of one of his favourite models that led to the separation from his parents.

Although superimposed on Jim, the 'wings thing' can be traced directly back to Spielberg. 'It's a fetish,' he cheerfully admits. 'I consciously like flying and I have flying in all my films. But yes, I'm afraid to fly in real life. So there's a conflict there, I guess.'

Spielberg was bemused by the critical notices for *Empire of the Sun*. His usual supporters deserted him en masse, while those highbrows who normally slammed him – while by no means issuing rave notices – managed to find some words of praise.

His army of fans among the public were equally bemused. In place of the cute and cuddly boy hero they might have expected, they were faced with Jim, an initially dislikeable, occasionally pathetic, distinctly brattish kid who goes on to suffer a prolonged nervous breakdown in the course of the movie. As for the grown-up lead, the 'protector' played by John Malkovitch, he was a cynical user, perfectly prepared at a moment's notice to drop Jim and move on, attaching himself like a leech to whoever came along next. With no one among the principals to root for, audiences were turned off.

That *Empire of the Sun* came over as the least likely Spielberg movie ever can be traced to Tom Stoppard, the author of the screenplay. With his literate, drily humorous script Spielberg had moved into erudite, intellectual territory. And paid the box-office price. That he had also remained completely faithful to Stoppard's bleak vision, and refused to compromise Ballard's original intention, was a cause for celebration. In turning his back on cuteness and sentimentality, Spielberg revealed a new, hitherto unsuspected depth of vision. Without using spectacle for its own sake, he showed himself as a world-class filmmaker fully up there with Lean, achieving in *Empire of the Sun* exactly the correct balance between masterfully handled crowd scenes – the breathtaking evacuation of Shanghai, the desolation and brutality of the prisoner-of-war camps – and the interaction between the foreground characters. The movie is a stunning achievement, and one can understand Spielberg's disappointment at the cool, even baffled reception it received.

In the old days music hall performers were booked to perform 'as known'; the intention being that no impresario would be stuck with Dame Nellie Melba performing handstands instead of hitting high notes. With *Empire of the Sun* Spielberg had refused to perform 'as known'. And paid the price. The message was not lost on the world's most pragmatic filmmaker.

Meanwhile, Spielberg had another sure-fire revenue-earner on the horizon. His canny refusal to consign *E.T.* to video had created an unprecedented demand that the 1985 theatrical re-release only served to whet further. Whether or not it was to balance the books in what for him was a relatively thin revenue year, Spielberg would finally give in to Universal's entreaties in October 1988.

As expected, the theatrical record-setter went on to shatter existing sell-through records. With memories of the video-game nightmare still imprinted on his brain, Steve Ross must have thought, 'If only . . . !'

One answer Steve Ross proposed to the $1 billion losses WCI suffered in 1984–5 was to remove the company from the market place and make it a privately owned corporation. How? In a then-fashionable leveraged buy-out financed by junk bonds and organised by Michael Milken. Spielberg would be cut in on the deal, Quincy Jones would get a piece, Streisand and Eastwood too, maybe Dustin Hoffman if he played his cards right and joined the inner circle. Several factors prevented attempts at the buyout proceeding, not least the Ivan Boesky scandal and the collapse of Milken's paper world.

Ross's second answer was to pull off one of the biggest coups of his career – the buyback of WCI's half of the Warner/Amex joint cable venture from American Express on extraordinarily advantageous terms. Thanks to this and a string of successful movies and records, WCI began a dramatic recovery from the dark days of Atari's collapse.

If Spielberg was the 'Magician of the Movies', Ross, shrugging off would-be raiders along the way like Rupert Murdoch and Chris-Craft's Herb Siegel, was surely the 'Wizard of Warner', the escape artist supreme. After all, he had the ultimate threat up his sleeve: 'If I go, kiss goodbye to Spielberg and the rest, they're only here because of me.' Which was undoubtedly true.

As Spielberg would declare at WCI's 1987 board meeting, just in case a particle of doubt remained in any maverick shareholder's mind, 'I am too secure in my line of work and too fat as a result of it, to be seduced by deals and perks and promises. I have settled down to live and work in only two houses – MCA and WCI . . . Steve is as obsessed with the creative development of this company as I am in the making of my movies, and I just wanted to come here and say that as long as Mr Ross remains the skipper of this battle wagon, I will never leave my station and will continue to make films here that hopefully will please you and your families.'

After reading out a like-minded epistle from Clint Eastwood, he continued, 'There are hundreds of creative people in my home town who second everything that Clint and I have just said. We really do love Steve Ross. We believe Steve Ross *is* WCI.'

As, of course, did Steve Ross.

A few months after the meeting, in December 1987, Ross proposed that WCI grant Spielberg 200,000 share options, Eastwood and Barbra Streisand 100,000 apiece. If a cynic might have regarded the options as representing payment for encomiums rendered, their apportionment permitted an intriguing look at the relative value Ross placed on the stars of his little galaxy. Where Eastwood might have grunted and taken the valuation in his stride, the walking ego known as Streisand might have reacted rather differently.

David Geffen? He was the little boy that Santa Steve forgot – in terms of his total exclusion from the options. In also refusing Geffen a $5 million a year advance against his record royalties, and opting instead to hand over full ownership of Geffen Records in 1990, Ross had made one of the worst decisions of his business life.

*

228

While the mosquitoes had been biting on *Empire of the Sun*, another Amblin production, the cutely titled *\*batteries not included*, had been up to its ill-conceived neck in trouble back in the US, on the poverty-stricken Lower East Side of New York City. The plot of the movie was the apotheosis of Hollywood High Concept – a tenement-load of elderly and disadvantaged tenants being forced out by an unscrupulous landlord are saved by the intervention of tiny alien 'fixers' . . . !

Spielberg's company had rented a flattened slum as location site for the movie – free of charge, thanks to a grateful New York City – which just happened to be directly across from a series of ancient, run-down occupied tenements. For months those tenants were forced to watch a fortune being spent on construction destined to be torn down when filming was complete. 'It's obscene for Spielberg to make a film in which aliens are the only resort for the poor and elderly,' one tenant organiser declared. 'It's appalling that he spends millions to construct the façade of housing in an area where real housing is so desperately needed, only to blow it up while returning nothing to the community.'

Well, he didn't blow it up. He burned it down instead. And left behind exactly what he'd found in the first place. In the process, Spielberg produced one of the worst-ever Amblin films. Again, there were charming moments. How could there not be with Jessica Tandy and Hume Cronyn in the cast? But even they were defeated by the cretinous concept, which even called up not one but two of the 'little guy' aliens to pretend-die in the well-worn Disney tradition Spielberg had borrowed. The movie was not only an insult to the intelligence of movie audiences everywhere, but – more seriously – to the unfortunate denizens of the Lower East Side and all impoverished people.

*\*batteries not included* – wouldn't you know it, another grotesque outgrowth of the calamitous *Amazing Stories* – became the latest in a series of Amblin failures, following *Young Sherlock Holmes* (redubbed *Young Sherlock Holmes and the Pyramid of Fear* in some foreign territories by a panic-stricken Paramount), the Richard Benjamin-directed Tom Hanks vehicle, *The Money Pit* (dubbed 'gruesomely unfunny' by *Variety*), and the surprising box-office dive of *Innerspace*. Spielberg wanted it both ways. Cash gushers from junk and acclaim for adult ventures like *Empire of the Sun*. For the time being he had to settle for neither.

The birth of their son was the glue that kept Spielberg and Amy Irving's marriage together. For about three and a half years. From the start Irving felt her persona vaporising, caught in the long shadow her husband cast. 'When I first got married,' she recalls, 'men crossed the street to avoid eye contact with me. I think it had to do with Steven being such a powerful force in the business. What I lost was that cocky security that I could enter a room and men would be attracted to me.'

Soon after tieing the knot the couple established a routine of spending each weekend at their beach retreat with young Max. Monday was a different matter: he would be handed over to a babysitter, allowing them to spend the day alone together on an extended date of shopping, lunch, movies, dinner. The four-day week remaining, Irving insisted, was enough for her husband now that he had a full staff taking care of business at Amblin. Spielberg didn't argue. At least, not publicly. At least, not at first. Close friends saw the other side of the supposedly idyllic marriage. 'It was no fun to go over there,' says Matthew Robbins, 'because there was an electric tension in the air. It was competitive as to whose dining table this is, whose career we're gonna talk about, or whether he even approved of what she was interested in – her friends and her acting life. He really was uncomfortable. The child in Spielberg believed so thoroughly in the possibility of a perfect marriage, the institution of marriage, the Norman Rockwell turkey on the table, everyone's head bowed in prayer, all that stuff. And Amy was sort of a glittering prize, smart as hell, gifted and beautiful, but definitely edgy and provocative and competitive. She would not provide him with any ease. There was nothing to go home to that was cosy.'

Irving was happiest when she was working, and welcomed the break filming *Anastasia* in Austria. Spielberg arrived in Vienna on the day she was preparing for her 'mad scene', bearing a birthday gift of an exquisite 1914 Fabergé egg locket with a musical 'A' for Anastasia attached.

The first half of 1988, with Joan Micklin Silver's *Crossing Delancey* awaiting release, found the couple ricocheting between their Los Angeles home, the New York apartment in Trump Tower, and the renovated Pennsylvania Dutch barn in East Hampton that Steve Ross had secured. The couple's third marriage anniversary was celebrated in a private dinner at the American Hotel in Sag Harbor. They arrived wearing each other's gifts, Spielberg outfitted from top to toe in Ralph Lauren mock-rugged pseudo-Western sheepskin jacket, brown cords and lace-up shoes, green-flecked brown socks and sweaters, tie and cowboy hat, Irving floating in a brown Issey Miyake pantsuit, cream pleated Matsuda blouse and matching satin vest, brown suede Maud Frizon shoes completing the elegant picture.

Irving's choice of outfit for her husband was an expansion of the influence she had brought to bear in the choice of Amblin's Tex-Mex architecture. Left to himself, she often despaired, God alone knew how Spielberg would dress himself. The comic nadir had been reached with the arrival of a present from his mother of a yellow striped sweatshirt. Teamed with a pair of blue or black jeans, the eyesore might have been tolerable. Instead, Spielberg had acquired a pair of matching yellow pants that he considered made a complete outfit. 'It's a reflection on me,' Irving had pouted when she saw him posing. 'Don't go out looking like that.'

When Spielberg decided to take a stand against his wife's fashion cop, Irving coaxed the pants off him and promptly cut the legs off. Defiant, Spielberg donned the cut-offs and headed for work, leaving Irving not knowing whether to laugh or to cry. There was no such problem when her husband reappeared that evening. The yellow cut-offs had frayed to the stage where his underpants were showing.

The façade the couple kept up was seen through by many friends. Beyond dubbing the singing voice of Jessica Rabbit in *Who Framed Roger Rabbit?* there was no question of Irving participating in one of her husband's movies. That would have represented too much of a climb-down, an unacceptable admission that her own career was running out of steam. Irving's choices, despite her early success, had become more and more limited.

She openly scoffed at the suggestion that marriage to Spielberg should have opened all doors for her. 'It's really only been a hindrance,' she maintained. 'I can name two separate occasions in which I've *lost* jobs because people haven't wanted a representative of Steven's camp in their team. It's an ego thing. Any director who hires me gets Steven on the set at least once or twice, and if you're not secure enough in your own work, you don't want him seeing what you're doing, or hearing about it from his wife over breakfast. You can't count on anything in this business. No matter who you're married to.'

Appearances on stage in *The Road to Mecca*, and in an ill-advised movie version of *Rumpelstiltskin* filmed in Israel by the Cannon cousins Menahem Golan and Yoram Globus – a real family affair for Irving, with the movie scripted and directed by her brother David, and featuring Priscilla, their mother – had to serve to keep her name before the public until *Crossing Delancey*. Once again, as she had with *Yentl*, Irving felt she had the platform from which she could soar. Even as Spielberg was flying to New York for the movie's premiere, rumours were flying that Kate Capshaw had re-entered his life. Irving knew it was time to make a final move.

After living separate lives for several months, the final split came in April 1989. 'Our mutual decision, however difficult, has been made in the spirit of caring,' their announcement ran. 'And our friendship remains, both professional and personal.'

Spielberg lifted that cosy cover just two months later. Asked to comment on the break-up, he replied, 'I've never talked to the press about my private life. *She* talks about it.'

Over the years Denis Hoffman continued to meet with Spielberg. Some of their discussions seemed to hold out the prospect of work, one movie specifically discussed being *E.T.* Kathleen Kennedy duly called up. 'This is just a little picture,' he recalls being told, 'and we've very little money. Very small budget.'

'Look, I'll do anything you want,' he replied.

'OK, I'll send a copy of the titles over. We're just going to have them over a black background, or maybe over a scene. Something real simple.'

Hoffman quickly prepared a budget of just a few thousand dollars, and called back. Kennedy was out to lunch/taking a meeting/had just slipped out. The runaround. Eventually she got back to him: 'We're not quite ready yet. I'll be out of town for the next week or two, but I'll get back to you after that.'

Two weeks later Hoffman called, to be assured by Kennedy's secretary, 'Oh, she knows about you. You'll be hearing.' He did. With a turn-down. Kennedy was 'very, very sorry', but they'd decided after all to go with fairly complex special effects below the titles that called for nothing less than George Lucas's Industrial Light and Magic. Her last words: 'Talk to you next time.'

Cut to a few months later when Hoffman, like millions of others, lined up to see *E.T.* There the title was, in purple letters, on an *absolutely plain* black background, no special effects, nothing. And at the end of the movie the credit, 'Titles by Pacific Title'. *Not* George Lucas's ILM, but one of Hoffman's competitors.

A few years later Hoffman was put through a re-run. At another meeting Spielberg acted as if he'd just had a brainwave. 'You should do *all* my titles,' he recalls him saying. 'You're in the optical business, aren't you? This is crazy!'

'I'd love to do your titles, Steven.'

'Of course! I'll call my people right away! You're gonna do it!'

Once again, as he had so often before, Hoffman left Spielberg's office walking on air. This was it! The big break! A few weeks passed before he got a call from Neil Canton on the Amblin lot. Strangely, he sounded brusque, rude even. 'Gee, I'm supposed to call you,' he recalls their conversation beginning. 'I've got a note on my desk,

232

"Call Denis Hoffman". Except, I'm not sure what I'm supposed to call you about.'

'Who's the note from?'

'Well, I guess it's from Steven. Yeah, it's in his writing. What is it you do?'

'I have a company that does titles and opticals for movies.'

'Ohhhh! That must be what this is all about! You know, I use this guy at MGM to do my titles and I've been using him for years. But you know, I guess if Steven wants you to do something, I could give you a shot. Maybe we could get together and talk about it.'

'I'd very much like to talk about it. At your convenience.'

'OK, let's see, I'll be out of town for a while, and anyway, the next one's still a long way off, we're not ready yet to think titles. Why don't you call me in six weeks?'

Cue the same old runaround: Taking a meeting/Still out of town/Just slipped out. Leading to precisely zip.

If Hoffman's forbearance seems to pass all understanding, bear in mind his impression that Spielberg had no direct obligation. If he was content to play the good cop to Kennedy and Canton's bad cop, what was he supposed to do about it? A commission from Spielberg remained something not to be kissed off in a fit of pique.

What remained hurtful to him on a personal basis, in view of their shared history, was never receiving as much as a preview ticket to one of Spielberg's movies. One other slight had particularly stung. Hoffman spent $350 on an elaborate, one-foot tall music box carousel he bought as a gift for Spielberg's first-born. He had it specially engraved, 'Samuel Max's Carousel', and proudly called Spielberg's Amblin offices. 'I have a gift for Steven's son,' he explained.

'Oh, that's wonderful. Bring it on over,' a secretary told him.

When he did, he was asked to leave it in a room with what looked like a couple of dozen other gifts. To this day Spielberg has yet to acknowledge Hoffman's gesture.

Later in the mid-eighties Hoffman went to Spielberg with what he considered a solid business proposition. Having observed for years the second-rate snacks served up on movie locations, Hoffman had the idea, while remaining in the titles and opticals business, of setting up what became Designer Donuts, a company that would supply caterers with an upscale doughnut, croissant and muffin. Would Spielberg consider either a loan, or joining the other backers he had lined up? Spielberg replied while he didn't loan money, he would consider an investment 'under certain circumstances', and his business people would spell out just what those conditions would be.

Grateful as he was for Spielberg's eventual help, which did include a loan, an equity investment, and an equipment lease, there were extremely stringent conditions attached. Like Hoffman having to second-mortgage his house to guarantee Spielberg's security. Like having to agree to take no more in salary from the company than any other employee. Like being forbidden to employ any family members. (Hoffman had to obtain special dispensation before his son could be hired.) And as the largest investor, with $25,000, Spielberg insisted on getting his stock cheaper than anyone else. In all, $70,000 was put up through one of his investment companies.

Hoffman looks back reflectively on the six months of negotiations necessary to obtain the loan, the agreements he had to sign, the second mortgage he was forced to take out. 'It's rather different from the original contract I drew up with Steven,' he points out, adding, 'But I guess that's why he is where he is today and I am where I am!'

# 25

## To Stand Naked

*'I'm making the third* Indiana Jones *movie to apologise for the second. It was too horrific. There's not an ounce of my own personal feeling in Temple of Doom.'*

*'We had snakes in* Raiders of the Lost Ark *and bugs in* Temple of Doom. *But supposedly man's greatest fear is public speaking. That'll be in our next picture.'*

STEVEN SPIELBERG

*Although there was no truth in the rumour that Warren Beatty wanted him to play Mumbles in* Dick Tracy, *Spielberg was all too well aware that public speaking was not his forte. Other perceived inadequacies could be hidden, but the more successful he had become, the more the spotlight fell on his inability to articulate with confidence before an audience. Could they see the flop sweat breaking out on his brow, trickling down his cheeks, dribbling off the hair on the back of his neck and saturating his collar? Could they sense the tension that gripped him like a vice?*

*Were they secretly laughing at his discomfort? On Spielberg's list of 'All-Time Greatest Fears' creepy-crawly bugs had been relegated to second place, way behind holding forth at public gatherings.*

*There was no way, therefore, that he would willingly submit to this form of torture. Except – maybe, he told himself, practice would make perfect. Why should he accept any limitation? The fear had to be faced down, overcome . . . but how? The answer: why, out of the spotlight, of course, at low-key affairs where the pressure would be that much less. The ideal opportunity soon arose. Would he address a group of law students? Yes, he darned well would!*

*Came the day he felt good, he felt confident, this would be a breeze, a piece of cake, a walk-over. Just look at all those eager young faces, bursting to hear what he had to tell them about the big wide world and the opportunities it afforded. He marched confidently up to the podium fol-*

*lowing his introduction and began to speak. It was great, he was flying, improvising on the few notes he had made, soaring even.*

*Suddenly he froze. Dried up. Seized up. Died.*

*N-o-t-h-i-n-g!! How long would it take before the audience realised that this was more than merely pausing for effect? It wasn't so much that he had lost his train of thought, more that his command of language had suddenly deserted him; the 'Delete' button had been pushed on his knowledge of English. His mind raced. What were the alternatives?* Amo, amas, amat, amamus, amatis, amant? *Forget it!! He could try a few lines in French, but would his schoolboy proficiency pass muster with these Bright Young Things? Was* 'Un Film de Steven Spielberg', *last spotted on the Champs Elysee, about to turn into* 'Un Débâcle de Steven Spielberg'?

*In those few seconds Spielberg experienced a terror that gripped his heart. Now he knew how Indiana Jones had felt when confronted with those 7,500 snakes, how Jimmy Stewart's character had felt staring down those limitless canyons in* Vertigo *that reached all the way from ladder top to floor. This was a moment old Hitch would have relished; he would have found a way to portray the agonising internal panic, to . . .*

*As suddenly as he had froze, Spielberg heard in his head the clanking of gears that told him he was about to recommence his speech. Sure enough, there it was, as crisp and clear as it would ever be given his tendency to swallow his vowels and smother his consonants, taking up exactly where he had left off, finishing the argument he'd posited, answering all questions, clearing all doubts, the consummate filmmaker at ease with the world, shining the beacon for all these enquiring young minds; enlightening, inspiring. Although hardly another day, another dollar, those Young Turks had provided a further stepping stone, mercifully out of the limelight, in Spielberg's self-therapy course in public oratory. Maybe, who knows, fear of all things buggy will be back at Number One at some point in the future.*

Having disavowed the sadism and violence he had served up on a platter in *Temple of Doom*, Spielberg might well have chosen to pass on a third Indiana outing had he not originally committed to the idea of a trilogy. On the other hand, there was the argument that this time, with *Indiana Jones and the Last Crusade*, he could make 'a movie he could stand naked on top of'.

Spielberg was knocked out by the notion of having Sean Connery play Indiana Jones' father. Apart from the Bond series, Spielberg had admired the star's acting skills in movies as far back as Sidney Lumet's *The Hill*, although his all-time favourite 'Connery' to date was without question John Huston's memorable *The Man Who Would Be King*. Now, courtesy of Brian De Palma's

236

rough cut, he had caught a preview of Connery's latest performance, the one that would land him his first Oscar, playing the tough, weathered Irish cop in *The Untouchables*. God, he thought, the guy was *so* powerful, if anything even more so than in his younger days. Who better to give Harrison Ford, no slouch himself at filling the big screen, a real run for his money. But could he get him?

Intrigued as he was at the call from Creative Artists that both Spielberg and Lucas were interested in him for the role of Professor Jones, Connery was concerned over the team's refusal to hand over a script. Could it be that one of them was less than wholly enthusiastic? Connery was correct. 'George wasn't thinking in terms of such a powerful presence,' Spielberg later admitted. 'His idea was for a doting, scholarly presence, played by an older British actor.'

Connery turned down the script he finally managed to extract. After months of teasing secrecy, an approach not best appreciated by the Scot, ploughing through the material provided a real sense of anti-climax. This was pale, uptight stuff, not at all Connery-worthy, with Indiana's dad portrayed as more wimp than warrior. Lucas was shaken to learn how Connery saw the role, how he based it on the personality of the explorer Sir Richard Burton, someone who would have been totally indifferent to his son's upbringing, who would have disappeared into the jungle for months on end without so much as a backward glance, devil take the hindmost, utterly guilt-free.

The sheer un-Americanism of Connery's approach, its politically incorrect finger raised at the very core of apple-pie values, blew a circuit in Lucas's brain. Even the relatively emancipated Spielberg initially vetoed the idea of Indiana's father enjoying carnal knowledge of the movie's heroine along with his son. 'Why?' Connery wanted to know. 'It's been done before, you know. Some of the old Greeks were ahead of you.'

Only when the prudish pair came round to his way of thinking, with Lucas screaming and protesting to the last, did the redoubtable Connery sign on. It turned out that Harrison Ford had also been less than thrilled with Jeffrey Boam's first script drafts, considering them far too thin in characterisation and adding nothing to Indy's personality. Although better pleased with the final version, one worry remained. Wasn't Connery just a bit young to play his father? He was, after all, only twelve years older than him—!

When Connery and Ford first arrived on the set of *Last Crusade*, the entire crew fell respectfully silent. It was like royalty had arrived. 'The two *are* like royalty,' Spielberg agrees. 'Not the royalty you fear because they can tax you, but the royalty you love because they make your lives better.' The wily Scot made sure he was involved in every rewrite that took place during production. He also cannily succeeded in having his role expanded, moving his first scene from page seventy in the script to page fifty.

Although Connery bows to no one in his admiration for Spielberg's visual sense, he lightly qualifies his praise when discussing his comprehension of actors' motivations: 'He understands what he wants to try and get – but he's not absolutely certain about how to get it in terms of performance.' A mischievous ear-to-ear grin. 'But then he's young, eh?'

If Connery senior and the 'twenty ideas a day' he threw at Spielberg were a lot to cope with, the arrival of junior, in the shape of real-life son Jason, served only to up the ante. There was a distinct touch of surrealism as Jason watched his father interact with his 'movie son' both on-set and off. The feeling reached mind-boggling proportions with River Phoenix playing Indy as a youngster.

After three weeks of shooting in Spain, the unit departed at the beginning of June 1988 for what Spielberg and his crew called their 'good luck studio', their overseas Holywood home, Britain's Elstree at Borehamwood, Hertfordshire. A major shock awaited him. While filming *Raiders of the Lost Ark* there, an out-of-control fire had almost levelled the site. Now another cliffhanger was being played out. Already sold by EMI to the Cannon Group, the venerable studio had been re-sold for $36 million by the bankrupt Cannon to an investment consortium led by City of London financier Peter Earl. His intention: to put the site on the market for sale to the highest bidder. Frank Marshall felt personally betrayed. 'Two years ago,' he tersely spelled out, 'when we made the deal to shoot the movie, Cannon promised not to do that.' There was a palpable, disheartening sense of insecurity among all of the studio's 'permanent' personnel.

The resultant 'Elstree SOS' was publicly supported by Spielberg. The campaign that followed persuaded Hertsmere Borough Council, Elstree's ruling authority, to impose a six-month preservation order on the site, to give the Department of the Environment a chance to consider designating the Elstree studio a historic site. Spielberg was one of a delegation who visited the House of Commons personally to hand in a petition to save the studio. 'Straight from the set in the morning to the House of Commons in the afternoon,' Marshall marvelled, shaking his head. 'An unusual day, to put it mildly!'

The collapse of Cannon's house of cards apart, the long-term problem was that Elstree as a studio was worth an estimated $20 million; as a real estate development site for supermarkets or apartments, maybe double that figure. Although Spielberg talked passionately about raising $20 million, it was never going to be enough in the face of financial realities. Unless a compromise could be found.

It was. Half of Elstree's thirty-one acres were eventually sold off to the Tesco supermarket chain. The balance was acquired by Hertsmere Council, enabling 'Gate Studios' to emerge from the ashes of the old Elstree.

For the *Last Crusade* crew it was off to Italy after their bittersweet Elstree stay, followed by the ancient city of Petra in Jordan. 'We're all tired,' Marshall admitted as shooting wrapped. 'Ten years ago we signed on for all three, and now we're ready to move on to other things. It's been a fun and fulfilling series, but there are other movies out there waiting to be made.'

Spielberg felt the same way, but gratefully acknowledged the learning curve the series had provided. 'I've learned more about movie craft from making these movies than I did from *Jaws* or *E.T.*,' he declared. 'And now I feel as if I've graduated from the Lucas Cliffhanger University. I ought to have paid tuition!'

The three Indiana Jones features tell plenty about the escalating budgets of movies. At the beginning of the eighties *Raiders of the Lost Ark* had been brought in for $20 million and grossed $242 million. Three years later, with the same shooting schedule, the same cast and crew had been hard put to hold *Temple of Doom* down to $30 million. Gross: $180 million. Three years further on and *Last Crusade* was looking at $44 million, with above-the-line costs for the main participants Spielberg, Lucas, Ford and Connery accounting for less than twenty per cent of the total. Gross: $197 million.

One thing that hasn't changed over the years is the mutual regard between this unique producer/director partnership. To an unexpected extent. 'Steven is a good friend and we think so much alike,' says Lucas, 'that there were even rumours that we were the same person. At a sci-fi convention somebody remarked that we were never seen in the same place in the same time, we were one alien being who could change form.'

As if to perpetuate the legend, Spielberg admits to occasionally signing Lucas's name when asked to give an autograph.

Back in Martha's Vineyard during the protracted shooting of *Jaws*, Spielberg had discovered that he shared a favourite movie with Richard Dreyfuss. Victor Fleming's *A Guy Named Joe*, starring Spencer Tracy, Irene Dunne and Van Johnson, had wrung tears from both of them as young scuds. After obtaining the rights from

MGM in 1979, Spielberg – temporarily ignoring Dreyfuss's warning: 'If you cast anybody else in Tracy's role, I'll kill you!' – sounded out Paul Newman and Robert Redford to star in *Always*, his proposed reworking of the original. Only after they declined – they both wanted to play Tracy's Pete – did Spielberg call in Dreyfuss, his original fellow-enthusiast.

Instead of the World War II airman Tracy had portrayed, Dreyfuss would play a fire-fighting pilot who dies before coming back as a guardian angel to inspire a young pilot and enable his grieving lover to find happiness anew. Spielberg never paused to think that maybe such mawkishness had had its day. Pressing on, he caught an episode of *Roseanne* and signed John Goodman to update Ward Bond's Al. Holly Hunter's performance in *Broadcast News* convinced him he had the ideal replacement for Irene Dunne's Dorinda. With the addition of newcomer Brad Johnson as Ted, the young pilot Van Johnson had earlier played, there remained only the cameo role of the guardian angel to fill. This, he felt, called for a bold casting coup that would rocket the movie into the stratosphere.

Sean Connery was his eventual choice, and for a while it looked set – until Connery begged off, pleading other commitments. It was time for a drastic rethink. What if the guardian angel was a woman? What if he could get Audrey Hepburn?! He did – for a fee of $1 million, payable direct to UNICEF, the organisation on whose behalf Hepburn worked tirelessly. There was an odd thread running through her casting: Dalton Trumbo had written the script for *A Guy Named Joe*; years later, blacklisted, he had worked in secret on *Roman Holiday*, the movie that catapulted Hepburn to stardom.

Like the kid in the candy store who can have anything he wants, Spielberg assumed he could commandeer Irving Berlin's classic 'Always' for his movie's main theme. He had reckoned without the estate of the late Berlin. Permission was withheld. This was a new experience for Spielberg. He could buy the remake rights to a whole movie, he could buy movie rights to whatever book or play he wanted, yet he was denied *one lousy song*?

Well, if he couldn't have 'Always' – and dozens of follow-up phone calls and messages only confirmed the position – he would use another tried and trusted sentimental favourite, Jerome Kern's haunting 'Smoke Gets In Your Eyes'. Wait a minute, though, he could hardly call the movie *Smoke Gets In Your Eyes*, especially since his pilot hero goes down in flames. Could be misunderstood. Better to stick to *Always*, even without a matching movie theme. It never seemed to have occurred to Spielberg to stay with the song used in *A Guy Named Joe*, 'I'll Get By (As Long As I Have You)', despite its undoubted lyrical fit. Maybe he felt it didn't punch the appropriate emotional buttons.

With a budget set at $29.5 million, which even many of Spielberg's supporters felt was on the high side for such slender material, the unit moved to Montana for location work. Amidst predictions of stardom for Brad Johnson, pleasure at being reunited with Dreyfuss, and the professional ease Holly Hunter and John Goodman brought to the enterprise, the stand-out for Spielberg was directing Hepburn. As he shouted 'Cut!' after her final, poignant scene, he had no way of knowing that he had just directed the actress in the last role she would ever play. Her remaining months were spent once more travelling the world in the service of UNICEF.

After viewing the rough cut of the movie, Spielberg felt that there were a couple of scenes between Dreyfuss, Hunter and Goodman that could be played more effectively. Ignoring the cost, he asked them to reassemble. The redone scenes safely in the can, he presented each of the three with a brand-new $25,000 Mazda Miata bearing personalised number plates reflecting the characters they'd played.

The generous gesture, unimaginable even five years earlier, was widely put down to Steve Ross's influence. Ross regularly showered the likes of Streisand and Spielberg with expensive presents, a practice not approved by everyone at Warners. Over the years Robert Daly for one had personally considered it over the top – until the enormous success of the *Lethal Weapon* series. Flush from the box-office bonanza, he'd finally capitulated and dished out seven Land Rovers to the movie's main participants.

*Always* would not prove a Spielberg highlight. 'Was there no one among Spielberg's associates with the intellectual stature to convince him that his having cried at *A Guy Named Joe* when he was twelve was not a good enough reason for him to remake it?' David Denby asked in *New York* magazine. Pauline Kael in *New Yorker* was next to take aim. 'Now that Spielberg is no longer twelve,' she wrote, 'hasn't he realised that there's a queasiness in the idea of playing Cupid to the girl you loved and lost, and fixing her up with the next guy?' Sheila Benson was no kinder in the columns of the Los Angeles *Times*. 'A better title for *Always* might be *Forever*,' she suggested, 'which is roughly its running time. *A Guy Named Joe* was dreadful the *first* time round.'

For once audiences marched in time with the critics. *Always* was all but unwatchable, the early 'cutesies' between Dreyfuss and Hunter unbearable. Spielberg's notion that in Brad Johnson he had discovered the next screen heartthrob was another misjudgement –

the school jock he had cast as a teenager could hardly have been more wooden.

For Spielberg it was never going to be enough that he had several of the biggest box-office successes of all time to his credit in the live-action field. What, he asked himself, endured decade after decade, never went out of fashion, always came up brand-new, never dated? Answer: Walt Disney animated features. If they relied on their initial business alone, many would have failed to recover their production costs, but look at the legs displayed by *Snow White and the Seven Dwarfs*, *Fantasia*, *Pinnochio*, *Dumbo* et al., in their many revivals, not to mention the new fortunes they had found on video.

Persuaded by Spielberg, Universal funded an animation factory in London, where 350 of Europe's finest animators were recruited and 'Amblimation' was formed. With artwork presided over by animator Don Bluth, a Disney refugee who'd already struck out with an independent effort, *The Secret of Nimh*, the first outing under Spielberg produced a hit in *An American Tail*.

Spielberg's interest in animated subjects happily melded with the adaptation of *Who Censored Roger Rabbit?* that had been on the stocks for years at Disney. Robert Zemeckis was first approached by Michael Eisner and Jeff Katzenberg after the success of *Back to the Future*, and declined. Then a call came from Spielberg. What if Amblin joined forces with Disney to co-produce the movie? This time Zemeckis was persuaded.

Even the combination of the Disney magic, Richard Williams' artwork, Spielberg's input and Zemeckis's direction, still spelled a risk at the movie's planned budget of $35 million. Two tortuous years were spent marrying artwork with live action before *Who Framed Roger Rabbit?* finally emerged, its budget dangerously swollen to $50 million. With a further $32 million spent on its launch, the movie proved the biggest hit of 1988, grossing $154 million in the US, another $174 million round the world.

Any gnashing of teeth in Hollywood emanated mainly from two sources. One was from the mouth of Sid Sheinberg. 'That ravenous rat', his favourite term for the Disney outfit and Eisner in particular, had done it again, *and* in partnership with his favourite son. If time spent away from Universal meant the loss of a Spielberg project for one studio, the same applied at Warners, his second home. Cue at least a degree of gnashing from Steve Ross. At least a degree of compensation was on the way for Ross as Spielberg pressed ahead with his animation unit, initiating a *Tiny Toons* TV-series for a grateful Warners.

Problems arose with Don Bluth's second feature, *The Land*

*Before Time*, when Spielberg described the cut that was proudly unveiled as 'too scary and too violent for little children'. Not so, Bluth declared, pointing to the classic Disney cartoons that Spielberg, of all people, knew from first-hand experience were capable on a good day of scaring the living bejeesus out of any child. Spielberg dug in: Not in *my* cartoons – oh, and by the way, Don, maybe that's why your *Secret of Nimh* failed at the box-office . . .!

Given little choice, Bluth made the changes Spielberg ordered. It spelled the end of their relationship. Now busy over at Twentieth Century-Fox after a spell with his own animation department in Ireland, Don Bluth describes Spielberg as 'basically an ideas man'.

As for his much-vaunted storyboards: 'Well, Steven's drawings aren't too good.' Fully on a par, in fact, with Bluth's storytelling skills.

# 26

# Seismic Shifts

*'I think it would be a real boring community if all of us sat around and made wonderful little films like* Driving Miss Daisy, The Commitments *and* Boyz 'N' The Hood. *Now these are terrific, but if every studio made films like these, there would be a tremendous craving for* Terminator II *or* Batman IV.'

*'The power of the cinema is a lot stronger than the power of literature, because more people have access to it for one thing, and one picture is worth a thousand words.'*

STEVEN SPIELBERG

The roots of the Sony Corporation of Japan's search for a Hollywood studio lay buried beneath a still-livid corporate scar. Never again, they vowed, would a repetition of the VHS vs Beta débâcle be allowed to favour their competitors. Sony's Beta, widely considered the technically superior system, had lost the mass-market race due to the company's reluctance to sub-licence. The breach had been eagerly filled by their arch-rival Matsushita.

Just as their earlier purchase of CBS Records had been the conduit to software that complemented Sony's range of hardware stereo, compact disc systems and digital audio tape technology, so a major movie company would yield a library of movies, as well as a constant stream of new features, enabling them to achieve pre-eminence with their version of any new technology. In theory, at least.

Sony chiefs Akio Morita and Norio Ohga stressed to CAA's Mike Ovitz, their appointed broker, the importance of avoiding the adverse publicity that had accompanied their takeover of CBS Records, characterised in tabloids as 'a prime slice of America's soul sold to Nippon'. All in the past, they were assured. Ovitz first pointed them in the direction of MCA's Universal. Great company, he told them. Solid management. Spielberg and Amblin making magic on the backlot. Unbeatable library. Too rich for our blood, they replied. Months of negotiation with Kirk Kerkorian at MGM followed. With the library, including the precious *Gone With the Wind* negative, already carried off in Ted Turner's gunnysack, all that remained looked suspiciously like an empty box. It was time to get down to serious business. Namely Columbia Pictures.

The new object of Sony's affections scarcely represented virgin territory. Columbia had first been seduced by Coca-Cola in 1982, then all but abandoned six years later following the remarkable discovery that the performance of movies did not unfailingly follow the sales-graph of watered-down syrup. The current captain of the ship, Victor Kaufman, made clear his intentions to move on if and when a takeover was agreed.

As negotiations slowly proceeded, the question of Kaufman's potential successor was raised. To Sony's astonishment Mike Ovitz indicated that he was prepared to talk. The only snag: he wanted the Kingdom of Heaven plus. The Japanese equivalent of 'Forget it, Mike' was swiftly conveyed, together with much embarrassed bowing.

Besides, the head of CBS Records, Walter Yetnikoff, had a better idea. How about Peter Guber and Jon Peters? Look at their record! *The Color Purple! The Witches of Eastwick! Rain Man!* (Forget *Vision Quest, Who's That Girl?, Innerspace, Gorillas in the Mist.* And forget the clinkers Warners had rejected – *Youngblood, Clan of the Cave Bear, The Legend of Billie Jean, Clue, Head Office, High Spirits.* The Polygram loss? Ancient history!)

All the other warning signs about the team were ignored. The way Jon Peters had treated director Frank Pierson on the set of *A Star is Born* had long since passed into Hollywood legend. The list of credits Guber claimed from his years at Columbia had included every hit they'd made, and ignored the major flop he'd championed, producer Ross Hunter's *Lost Horizon* musical remake. Although Spielberg had possessed the clout to have it written into his contract that neither man be allowed to set foot on his *Color Purple* set, *Witches of Eastwick* director George Miller had not been as fortunate.

The volatile Peters was 'genuinely thought-disordered' according to Miller, his creative process 'without any predictable intelligence. It depended on the last movie he'd seen. If *Aliens* was out, he'd say, 'We've got to make it more like *Aliens*.' The next week it'd be a Whoopi Goldberg movie.' Per *Witches*' production designer Polly Platt: 'As a filmmaker it broke my heart to see what I saw, and I don't blame Peters alone. Where was Guber? Towards the end it was just grotesque.' With filming complete, Miller had fled to Australia to edit *Witches'* footage, refusing to return unless Peters was removed from the post-production process.

And the original *Witches'* producers, Rob Cohen and Don Devlin, had found themselves pushed off the movie. 'We had to renegotiate our deal so that we were no longer the producers, Guber and Peters were,' said Cohen. 'Warners president Mark Canton used his own brother Neil as the third producer. We were treated abominably. Subhumanly.'

A 1988 merger of their company with Burt Sugarman's Barris Industries had produced the 'Guber-Peters Entertainment Company'. With Sugarman's backing, a $100 million offer was mounted for a twenty-five per cent interest in MGM. After two weeks and a look inside the studio's 'empty box', the bid was withdrawn. Within a year, following a $19 million loss on revenues of $24 million, Sugarman had sold his stake and departed, leaving Guber and Peters holding their ailing baby. The 'karmic twins' were in trouble.

One year later everything had changed. *Rain Man* – put into turnaround by Warners and produced once more without the benefit of the team's presence – was a smash. Then came *Batman*, the largest grosser in Warners' history. Variously reviled in the industry as 'used car salesmen', 'nitwits', and 'dishonourable', Guber and Peters had beaten the odds.

For years, it seemed, Yetnikoff had 'schmoozed, schmingled and bingled' with the team, and Guber had told him a year earlier that they would be interested in running whichever studio Sony settled on. But surely they were under contract to Steve Ross at Warners? No problem, Guber had declared, an 'oral agreement' had since been reached. The gypsy's warning from Ovitz that it might not be as simple as that was dismissed as sour grapes.

Even as Sony's bean-counters were at work on Columbia, Steve Ross was concluding the deal of his life, the deal that would assure him a place in history. Just like politicians, old buildings and whores, Ross had hung in long enough, and returned from the corporate boneyard with sufficient regularity, to be judged respectable. If only he'd been allowed to proceed with the WCI share swap originally proposed for Time Inc. his triumph would have been all the sweeter, for the debt left at the end of the agreed merger would have been $2.6 billion, manageable for a company with a stock market valuation of $15 billion and an annual revenue flow of $10 billion. Paramount punctured that pretty balloon with a cash offer for Time Inc. of $10.7 billion, leaving the media giant with no alternative – if they wanted to stick with their preferred bedmate – but to mount a leveraged takeover for WCI. It cost them $14 billion. The result: a hefty long-term debt load for the combined Time-Warner of $16 billion. Still and all, Ross had prevailed.

From running funeral parlours to joint-CEO of the movies, music and publishing colossus that Time-Warner represented – the world's largest-by-far media empire – it had been one hell of a ride.

Sony's successful $4.7 billion bid for Columbia was followed by their recruitment of Guber and Peters at annual salaries of $2.75 million each, together with a $50 million bonus pool available to share among themselves and three top executives on the fifth anniversary of their contract. In addition, Sony paid out $200 million to purchase the 'Guber/Peters Entertainment Company' after Guber let it be known that 'in all fairness' to the company's shareholders it should be valued with its rights intact. Even though their slate of projects, including *Batman* sequels, remained at Warners. Even though one quarter of the purchase price was going straight into the pockets of Guber and Peters. Even though the total figure would climb to $260 million once financial charges were thrown in. Reaching for their calculators, analysts estimated that Sony had paid at least fifty per cent over Guber/Peters Entertainment's market value.

Steve Ross reacted to news of their appointments with an outburst of rage. After all his generosity to the team, supporting them through good times and bad, this was his reward? Just one month earlier, following the $19 million loss suffered by their company, Guber had asked Ross to consider an investment. Although he'd declined, Ross had taken the time to offer Guber advice on other ways to stoke up the company's finances. And all the while the sonofabitch had been schlepping back and forth to Tokyo behind his back!

Following Columbia's formal approval of Sony's offer at the end of September 1989, Warners filed suit against Sony seeking $1 billion in damages, alleging that Guber and Peters had been hired 'unethically and illegally' in defiance of a cast-iron, freshly negotiated contract with WCI. 'Oral agreement'?! *Forget* it!

It was the end of Sony's dream of a problem-free, low-profile takeover. Latent US xenophobia was unleashed in banner headlines across the country, with a poll conducted by *Newsweek* indicating that readers placed fear of Japan's economic might over the power of the Russian military. Rather than face certain defeat in court, Sony buckled. Steve Ross had won. Big time. Yes, he would release Guber and Peters, but on his own terms:

247

Sony would give up Columbia's thirty-five per cent share in the Burbank Studio they shared with Warners. They would be cast out to Culver City to the old MGM lot Warners had acquired in an earlier takeover of Lorimar Pictures. (Columbia's interest at Burbank would receive a subsequent independent evaluation of $25 million more than Culver City in its entirety.)

Warners would be given a fifty per cent stake in CBS's Columbia House Video and Record Mail Order Club – for free. (Estimated advantage to Warners: between $225 and $400 million.)

Warners would acquire the basic cable rights to the Columbia/TriStar library, for which they would deduct a distribution fee. (Estimated advantage to Warners: between $200 and $400 million.)

If the magnitude of Steve Ross's pound of flesh soured relations between Sony and their 'dream team', a brave face was put on it. Not so brave in Ovitz's case. Faced with his bill for $10 million for services rendered, Norio Ohga pronounced himself 'appalled' and demanded to see his time sheets.

'In Hollywood it's all about the size of your dick,' an exuberant Guber declared – even as he prepared, in a symbolic act, to remove the ponytail that had caused the Sony bosses the odd twinge of anxiety.

'Is that so?' came the reply from a columnist on the Los Angeles *Daily News*. 'Well, as my old mother would have said, "Where does he get the balls to say that?" And if what he says is true, him and Peters must be hung like horses. Or should that be by the neck?'

In all, Sony had shelled out over $1 billion for the services of Guber and Peters. 'That does it!' one stunned studio executive declared. 'The floodgates are open! This town, and every one in it, are up for grabs!'

Even if Steve Ross subscribed to that view, never in his wildest dreams would he have imagined that the first tongue lapping up Sony's sushi would belong to Spielberg. How wrong can you be?

With *Back to the Future III* providing the only bright spot on Amblin's horizon as the eighties became the nineties, it began to look as if Spielberg had painted himself into a corner of diminishing returns. Whether going the absurdly sentimental route of the dreary *Dad*, indulging John Patrick Shanley's fantasies in *Joe Vs. the*

*Volcano*, cooking up a new batch of little monsters in *Gremlins II*, planning a futile return to the adventures of Fievel and the Mousekawitzes in *An American Tail II*, attempting to transfer *Noises Off* from stage to screen, or turning Frank Marshall loose among the spiders in *Arachnophobia*, nothing really clicked.

Spielberg's call to Shanley, hot from *Moonstruck*'s script, had followed a submission of *Joe Vs. the Volcano* to Amblin. 'I've just read your script,' he told the writer. 'I think it's great and I'd like to make it.'

'That's great.' (To his wife, standing nearby: 'It's Spielberg!')

'I heard that you want to direct it.'

Shanley had mentioned this little item to one or two friends. 'Uh, yeah,' he replied.

'Well, I think that's a great idea. Let's do it.'

'Okay.'

As Spielberg rang off, Shanley replaced the receiver and looked across at his wife. 'I think we're in big trouble,' he said. Whether joking or not, his remark proved prescient. Despite the casting of Tom Hanks and Meg Ryan, the movie bombed. Another Warners strike-out.

Based on a William Wharton novel that *Family Ties*' Gary David Goldberg had purchased for his directorial feature debut back in 1983, the supposedly uplifting message of *Dad*, as interpreted by Goldberg, was that nothing could match the magic of cancer to bring an estranged father and son together. 'The syrupy quality that's become endemic to Spielberg's Amblin productions stifles several memorable performances,' wrote *Variety*'s critic, detecting 'cloying sweetness, annoying excesses'. Bombs away at Universal.

While *Gremlins II* did better abroad than on its home turf, any talk of further sequels for Warners was squelched. Another franchise had bit the dust, and this time with a movie many – Spielberg strangely excluded – considered even more anarchic fun than the first. Spielberg had seen the finished product as too dark and, perhaps anticipating the type of reaction accorded *Temple of Doom*, had asked Warners to remove his name from the finished movie. Steve Ross had talked him out of it, pointing out what a negative message would be relayed. Much as he admired the guy who had given him his big break, Joe Dante admits he would not have been too distressed had Spielberg had his way. 'The problem is that when people see Spielberg's name up there,' he says, 'they assume he directed the movie.'

After enjoying Michael Frayn's London and Broadway success *Noises Off*, Spielberg outbid all competition for movie rights to the farce. The problem was: how to film the fairly complex play within a play? The man who had given Frank Marshall his start back in the late sixties on *Targets* had the answer. Or so he claimed. Marshall had never lost touch with his benefactor and friend, and when Peter Bogdanovich called one day out of the blue, Marshall listened.

Despite Bogdanovich's spotty record after *Mask*, Spielberg's conviction was that someone who had made great movies in the past could make great movies again. The go-ahead was given for *Noises Off*, with Marshall producing, and Spielberg, Bogdanovich and Frank Marshall executive-producing for Amblin/Touchstone, with a cast including Michael Caine, Carol Burnett, John Ritter, Julie Hagerty, Christopher Reeve, Nicolette Sheridan and Denholm Elliott. It would have been nice to have been able to report that Marshall's twenty-fifth anniversary reunion with Bogdanovich turned out a great success. Regrettably, even with all this talent and expertise aboard, the movie sank like a stone upon its brief release in 1992. Once again, stage farce had failed to transfer successfully to celluloid.

The problem with *Arachnophobia* was the hype surrounding its release, with predictions of a minimum $100 million blockbuster. Although the sphinx-logoed Hollywood Pictures finally had the epithet 'If it's the sphinx, it stinks' laid to rest – Marshall's movie was no stinker, just too rambling and not nearly scary enough – the movie struggled to achieve its $50 million gross. Very respectable, but still judged a disappointment.

*An American Tail II – Fievel Goes West*? Another franchise petered out. With the *Back to the Future* series also having run its course, there was an urgent need to restock the pipeline.

Looking around for a winner, several projects were picked up, then dropped. Spielberg considered directing his sister Anne's screenplay for *Big* until scheduling conflicts made it impossible. Similarly, he spent five months working on the script of *Rain Man* before giving up in favour of *Indiana Jones and the Last Crusade*. 'I was very upset not to have been able to direct *Rain Man*,' he declared, 'because I've wanted to work with Dustin Hoffman ever since *The Graduate*. But I couldn't go to my best friend and say, "I know I'm a whore, but I found something I like better – hire George Miller."' (Despite the success of *Rain Man*, don't count Spielberg as one of its admirers. He is on record as having found it 'emotionally very distancing' and claims he 'would have pulled tears out of a rather dry movie'.)

Spielberg and Amblin came up with a real hybrid in *Cape Fear*. In the wake of their get-together on *Amazing Stories*, there had been talk of Spielberg and Scorsese forming a New York production company based at Robert De Niro's Tribeca HQ. This had never materialised; neither had Scorsese's all-but-announced participation in *Schindler's List*. The nail in that particular coffin was undoubtedly the movie a worried Universal had released in 1988, *The Last Temptation of Christ*.

Cancelled by Michael Eisner at Paramount back in 1983 only weeks away from the start of principal photography, Scorsese had been forced to shelve his cherished project for years until his return to commercial viability – courtesy of the same Eisner, now esconsed at Disney – with *The Color of Money*. Eisner's magnanimity did not extend to reconsidering *The Last Temptation*, even with the budget pared-down from the original $15 million to a meagre $6.5 million. For that money Universal stepped in, after a personal plea from Michael Ovitz, anxious to impress Scorsese and snare him as a client.

Knowing from the very beginning they were courting controversy, Universal had insisted on a 'Religious Adviser' being appointed to oversee the production. The idea backfired when the individual walked out after a few weeks. The walk-out was widely reported and led to the beginning of a misinformation campaign. *Temptation* was sacriligeous! Jesus was being portrayed as a homosexual! Mary Magdalene was nothing more than a whore! The stage was set for a stormy opening, and that's exactly what the Religious Right achieved. Twenty-five thousand demonstrators paraded outside Lew Wasserman's home protesting the movie's 'attack on the very basis of Christianity and Roman Catholicism' that had been financed by 'Jewish money'. Although passions cooled as the movie went into limited release, Wasserman as an individual and Universal as a studio were shaken to their foundations at the unprecedented vehemence of the initial attacks and the sporadic picketing of theatres. Director Franco Zeffirelli's vicious attack was another blow, and although he denied using the words 'Jewish cultural scum' he refused to allow his new movie to be shown at the same festival as *The Last Temptation of Christ*. An alternative title that one wag suggested, *The Last Straw for Lew Wasserman*, surely nixed any chance of Scorsese being trusted with the directorial reins on *Schindler*.

For some time, against the background of the controversy, De Niro and Spielberg had been deep in discussions on a remake of the black-and-white original *Cape Fear*, the J. Lee Thompson thriller that had starred Gregory Peck and Robert Mitchum. The way De Niro recalls it, 'Steven and I were looking for other directors. We discussed several we both knew.' For one reason or another, there were no takers, and in between talking to them De Niro kept mentioning the movie to Scorsese.

Perhaps worried it would be seen as a come-down, a sell-out – as

251

had *The Color of Money* – or worse, a scrap tossed from Spielberg's table, Scorsese initially demurred. Finally, a meeting was set up at Amblin where they discussed tailoring Wesley Strick's script to Scorsese's sensibilities. Yes, the Bowden family could be made a lot more conflicted than they were in the original. Sure, Max Cady could be made more terrifying, violent and sadistic than even Mitchum had made him. A scene with the Bowdens' daughter that would be loaded with menace and latent sexuality? No problem. Spielberg did hold out for one stipulation. Here's what it amounted to: Scorsese could do basically what the hell he liked with the Bowdens – just so long as they were all alive at the end of the movie. This was all well and good and certainly added considerable depth to Scorsese's version. Until, that is, he abandoned any pretence at realism and opted in the second half of the movie for shlock horror on a level with Freddy Krueger and the *Nightmare on Elm Street* series. Scorsese's descent was all the more startling coming from someone widely considered America's finest director. The first *Cape Fear* had never been considered a masterpiece, just a decidedly nasty, but very effective and believable thriller. Scorsese's version had the unusual effect of making it look better than it was. Spielberg was right on the money, though, in having the Bowdens survive the carnage. It was the one item left intact from the original.

While 'helping out' one contemporary buddy with *Cape Fear*, Spielberg inadvertently helped set in motion his closest friend's greatest disaster. One of the things that had kept him close to Brian De Palma over the years, through his own unprecedented rise and rise, and De Palma's thick and mainly thin, had been the ruling out of any question of direct collaboration. So it would remain.

For his part Spielberg relished the unbiased critiques, completely devoid of envy or bullshit, he regularly received from his friend. In his position he had fewer and fewer people he could turn to who would give him their fully honest opinion, without stopping to bear in mind what it was he wanted to hear, let alone how an overdose of frankness might cool the relationship. Even as Spielberg railed about how Hollywood's power centres had been eroded with the death of the high rollers, *he* had become the new centre of power, the high roller revived, with the emergence of Amblin as virtually a new stand-alone studio. If a project was given the bum's rush at Warners or Universal, it could still be *released* by Warners or Universal, if Amblin picked up the pieces.

As far as De Palma was concerned, Spielberg was still the same semi-serious, semi-nutty kid he had met almost twenty years earlier, someone so different from him that he might have come from another planet. He was secretly flattered that Spielberg spent so much time on his concerns, and it pleased him when he read something Spielberg had said about his 'intellectualism, his European aspect'.

Spielberg provided a constant safe harbour when things went badly, as well as playing the wonderful cheerleader when things went well. He had advised him to hold on through some of the ugliest notices on *Scarface*, and had been proved right when the movie was recognised for what it was. When *The Untouchables* had gone through the roof, anyone would have thought Spielberg himself had a stake in the movie. His support through the making of *Casualties of War* had been overwhelming, and his description of *Casualties* as 'a great movie, possibly the most powerful statement yet on Vietnam' had provided much-needed balm to soothe the largely critical notices. 'Brian's career has taken the most dramatic turn,' Spielberg had claimed, 'because he has started to tap into the great playwrights, to blend his own brilliant visual lifestyle into terrific literature.'

It was a call to Spielberg from another close friend, Warners' Terry Semel, that changed De Palma from a 'Probably' to a 'Definite' candidate to helm the movie version of Tom Wolfe's bestseller, *Bonfire of the Vanities*. The basic question Semel asked after meeting with the safari-suited De Palma: 'What do you think of him for *Bonfire*?' Spielberg's basic answer: 'You won't be sorry.'

When the Guber/Peters team exited Warners to head Columbia while the movie was in pre-production, Semel looked around for a replacement producer. Either not knowing or not caring about the golden rule in the relationship between Spielberg and De Palma, never to mix business with pleasure, he called Spielberg. When he turned it down, De Palma agreed to take on the double role.

The complete failure of the movie, both in critical and box-office terms, devastated De Palma. Spielberg had been perhaps more diplomatic than completely honest at a fiftieth birthday party for his friend thrown the day he first saw *Bonfire*, and just twenty-four hours before its crucial test screening in San Diego. 'I want to make a toast to this great movie I saw today!' he announced.

Trying to contact De Palma after the first weekend's figures were in, with less than $3 million in the kitty, was futile. As it was for weeks afterwards. Dawn Steel, De Palma's backer at Columbia on *Casualties of War* during her brief tenure, invited both De Palma and Spielberg to attend the unveiling of *Lawrence of Arabia*, the restoration of which both men had championed. Spielberg made the date; De Palma was a no-show.

Spielberg leapt to his friend's defence as one Warners' suit after another distanced themselves from *Bonfire*. It was a difficult juggling act, for although Steve Ross was far above the storm, the same could hardly be said for Bob Daly and Terry Semel. 'Look, every executive at Warners was in on every decision Brian made,' Spielberg argued. 'If they objected, they *could* have objected. They saw the dailies. Half that movie was filmed on the lot. It wasn't shot in Armenia or Pakistan. They were *there*. They *liked* the film when they saw it.'

At the same time Spielberg's thoughts were with his friend. 'Brian's a survivor,' he declared. 'It'll only hurt him until his next big hit. The worst thing that could happen out of all this would be if he directs *Home Alone II* or a safe little Disney comedy. If that happens to Brian, I'd know his spirit would be broken.'

Despite Spielberg's spirited defence, De Palma chose manfully to shoulder the blame for the way *Bonfire* had turned out. 'This is a mea culpa,' he declared. 'Yes, Warners gave me feedback, but *I* made the decisions. No matter how many memos I got, it was my fault. I was wrong.' If for nothing else, those uncompromising sentiments alone explain why De Palma, if he lives to be a hundred, will never be totally absorbed in the ways of Hollywood.

Instead of Disney, it was Universal, Spielberg's home turf, where a home was found for his next project, *Raising Cain*. By his own standards this was seriously minor, not to say highly derivative De Palma, and the movie quietly died. Reaching for what had, after a rocky start, gone on to glory, he next re-teamed with his *Scarface* producer Martin Bregman and star Al Pacino. There was a persuasive symmetry in the move. Back in 1982, De Palma had worked for 18 months on *Prince of the City* before being dropped in favour of Sidney Lumet. With *Carlito's Way* the traffic was reversed – it had been offered first to Lumet before De Palma took over. It would be nice to report that De Palma was back on top with *Carlito's Way*. Unfortunately, many saw it as a case of *Scarface* revisited, and after a decent opening, and many fine reviews, the movie faltered.

Next time out, on the atypical *Mission: Impossible*, would prove a different kettle of fish entirely for this most stylish, idiosyncratic director. Having enjoyed much of his work in the past, particularly *Obsession, Carrie, Dressed to Kill, Blow Out* and *Body Double*, it's a pleasure to welcome De Palma back into the winner's circle.

# 27

# Corporate Kabuki

*'I think MTV has been one of the most destructive
influences on the current crop of movies that are being
made. And the news has had a negative effect, since we're
getting stories of epic disasters in sound bites no longer
than a couple of minutes.'*

*'I had always played to the adult audience who were able
to remember their childhood and enjoy the movies along
with their children. But when I began playing to the kids
directly, I found that I stumbled on my shoelaces. Then I
realised, when you're making movies, you can't do things
consciously.'*

STEVEN SPIELBERG

Naturally Spielberg had been kept fully informed. Even so, it still
came as a considerable shock. Lew Wasserman and Sid Sheinberg
were selling out to Japanese electronics giant Matsushita? It was
unbelievable. Selling out not just a piece, but lock, stock and barrel?
Even Spielberg's little adobe hacienda?! Going the Columbia route
with Sony, and through the same broker, CAA's Mike Ovitz? It was
the end of an era. Wasserman, the colossus of Hollywood, was cash-
ing in his chips and going to work as an employee? How had it
come to this? And *why*?

The answers to both questions: in stages.

First: Rupert Murdoch and his News Corporation's takeover of
Twentieth Century-Fox in 1985 had provided a wake-up call. It was
a great big world out there, and some gentlemen callers were more
gentlemanly than others.

Second: an investment that had gone sour. In May 1986, MCA
purchased a large stake in the 1,680-screen Cineplex-Odeon chain
for $159 million. Soon afterwards Cineplex-Odeon's apparent

success story fizzled; by October 1990 one analyst was claiming that the chain was losing MCA $16 million a quarter.

Third: a monumental pain in the backside. That's what it took, back in 1987, to convince Lew Wasserman that a friendly suitor was preferable to a raider's attack. Languishing in hospital following surgery to remove a polyp from his colon, he had been forced to watch, helpless for once, as the value of his company's stock increased by ten per cent on the off-chance he might die and a marauder might launch a raid on MCA. Within a week Universal had mounted a rights issue designed to fortify existing shareholders' positions – it boosted Wasserman's stake to seven per cent and the stock he indirectly controlled to twenty-two per cent – and to make the company, through the additional assumption of debt, less of an attractive sitting duck. The result: another frustrating 13 per cent stock hike.

If the raiders had known just how close the hospitalisation had brought Wasserman to his maker – he hovered between life and death for almost twelve hours, not because of his operation, but after groggily biting through a thermometer – the stock would have gone through the roof. The episode underlined to Wasserman that MCA would be torn apart within months of his demise. The thought was intolerable, but how, midway through his seventies, could he keep MCA, his indisputable fiefdom as it was presently constituted, intact? What, Wasserman agonised, would Jules Stein have done?

Far from easing his anxiety, two more events in 1989 had sent his blood pressure soaring – Time Inc.'s takeover of Warner Communications, and the swallowing of Columbia Pictures by Sony. Said Sid Sheinberg of the new Time-Warner, 'It was the final recognition that what may have passed for an ability to compete in a certain kind of world had to be re-evaluated.'

For a while there was talk of MCA amalgamating with Paramount. Unsympathetically portrayed in the media as two scared domestic giants proposing to huddle together, the better to defeat any foreign invasion, those talks came to nothing. 'We're a 200-pound gorilla in a game with a 1,000-pound gorilla,' Wasserman fretted. 'We've got to become a 1,000-pound gorilla or get out of the game.'

It was against this background that Matsushita, true to their tradition of 'followership', made their first approach. Whatever else might be there in Universal's mixture – access to Spielberg and Amblin notwithstanding – it was the strength of the studio's library, the vital software, that was a key attraction.

With $126 billion in cash and $136 billion in securities,

Matsushita were the twelfth-largest industrial company in the world, with revenues in 1989 of over $44 billion. That they could afford MCA was beyond question. How well they might fit with the Wasserman and Sheinberg regime, together with their star tenant Spielberg, was another matter entirely.

During an initial exploratory meeting in Honolulu in November 1989, Mike Ovitz was impressed that Matsushita had dispensed with the usual planeload of low-level executives to get talks started. Instead, their modest delegation was led by company president Akio Tanii's second-in-command, Masahiko Hirata. By early the following summer Ovitz was given the green light from Osaka and intimated Matsushita's interest to the MCA board. Let's take this as far as it will go, was the word from Wasserman. With reams of sensitive financial data obtained from MCA under strictest confidentiality, Ovitz assembled 125 hand-picked personnel at CAA's offices to sift through the mountain of information.

By early September Matsushita were informed that they should consider the parameters of $75 and $90 a share for MCA. Aware that they had the field pretty much to themselves, Hirata applied the brakes, requesting further stacks of financial data. There was the falling value of Los Angeles real estate to consider, he argued, and what about the fiasco of Universal Studio Florida's much-hyped June opening? Fully three months after the first eager line of kids had torn through its gate, three of its biggest attractions were still riddled with bugs. And talking of bugs, Federal investigators had recorded conversations that seemed to indicate mob infiltration in MCA's record division. Then there was Cineplex-Odeon . . .

The 'pearl beyond price' was not without its flaws, Hirata declared. Worse was to come. The cover of the entire operation was about to be blown sky-high.

Back in 1986 Steve Ross's abrupt refusal either to hand out an advance, or to purchase his record company outright for $50 million, had left David Geffen stunned. A year later he had made the offer again, asking $75 million this time, the increased figure based on Geffen Records' ever-escalating number of chart placings. Again Ross had turned him down flat. Never mind that Geffen would instead own the whole show by 1990! So much for being one of Ross's two golden boys! Would Ross have turned down Spielberg's Amblin so cavalierly? There would come another day, Geffen vowed, and another buyer. 'I guess he kept hoping I'd have a bad year and he'd get the company for less,' he later rationalised.

By the late eighties Geffen's movie output had been through several ups and downs: Ups with *Risky Business* and *Beetlejuice*, downs with *Lost in America*, Scorsese's *After Hours*, the non-Spielberg *Little Shop of Horrors*, the strange, offbeat *Defending Your Life*. Geffen Records was a different story altogether. Already strong with Peter Gabriel and Cher, Geffen had struck a seam of pure gold clad in denim and leather with heavy metal bands Whitesnake and Guns N' Roses. His revenues for 1989 were a record-busting $175 million, doubled in just two years.

In the Spring of 1990, as Matsushita were preparing their final assault on Universal's 'Black Tower', Geffen sold his company to MCA for 10 million shares of stock. The value: $540 million. 'I *love* Steve Ross,' he gloated. 'Had he been a different guy, he would have bought my company for $50 million. And I'd have been killing myself today!'

Stressing the sensitive nature of the discussions and the crucial importance of maintaining secrecy, Sid Sheinberg formally notified the MCA board in mid-September 1990, that talks with Matsushita were underway. After breaking the news to Spielberg separately, he sought out David Geffen, the company's largest shareholder of six months' standing.

Within days of their discussion the *Wall Street Journal* published an in-depth article blowing the lid off the talks. The day before the leak MCA's stock had been languishing at $34.50. The day after it soared to $54.20. For anyone holding 10 million shares, as Geffen did, another $197 million had descended from heaven.

An infuriated Matsushita, convinced that the betrayal emanated from MCA's board, were forced to disclose their interest. Little did they know how much the leak had briefly united Wasserman, Sheinberg and Ovitz in a blizzard of embarrassment. 'There have been various talks of this nature regarding mergers and acquisition, but nothing has materialised as of today,' was their terse announcement, followed by a reluctant admission that movies, television, property, books, records and other forms of entertainment software represented 'a field that will be increasingly important in the future'.

One week later they had sufficiently recovered their sangfroid to issue a further press release: 'Matsushita Electronics will continue to have contact with MCA regarding a possible business combination between the two.' They added that there could, of course, be no assurance that the contacts would lead to any kind of conclusion.

A mid-October morning saw Ovitz anxiously escorting Hirata and another Matsushita executive, Keiya Toyonoga, to Wasserman's elegant Beverly Hills home. The objective: fence-mending. Handshaking and bowing was followed by an hour of exchanges on everything from politics to star performers. Helped along by discreet quantities of domestic wine, the process was still rendered wearisome through the necessary presence of interpreters. Any lingering suspicions that MCA had deliberately leaked news of their talks were never aired. Wasserman gently but firmly nipped Hirata's notion of a partial bid for the company's film and record divisions in the bud. The meeting was friendly, conducted with courtesy, an exercise between honourable gentlemen. The ambience created appealed to Wasserman.

Ten days later he had good reason to reconsider. This time the bombshell burst with a Nikkei news report that Matsushita wanted a 'cool-off period', with negotiations to be resumed in mid-November. Their plan: to allow MCA's stock, which had peaked at $63.50, to 'run out of steam'. A livid Wasserman watched as MCA's stock plummeted so badly that market trading had to be suspended twice. Prospects looked bleak for a deal, let alone by the Thanksgiving deadline Wasserman had hoped for.

In an attempt to clear the air and move forward, Ovitz invited the main participants – Wasserman, Sheinberg, Hirata, Toyonoga – to a dinner in the neutral territory of New York's Hotel Plaza Athenee. Talks resumed in Sheinberg's Trump Tower apartment next morning. Assuming a price could be agreed, how would the company be run after the takeover? Hirata stressed Matsushita's desire that the current management, together with their precious contacts, remain; as long as MCA stayed within a budget limit laid down from head office in Osaka, they could remain autonomous. Wasserman's position as chairman was guaranteed for the rest of his life, or until he chose to retire. A $21 million 'golden parachute' set up for Sheinberg back in the days of hostile takeover threats would remain in place; the chairmanship was his for the asking if Wasserman chose to leave.

Early in the afternoon, Hirata ominously began a circuitous dissertation on how much the world had changed in recent months. He revealed that Matsushita now preferred to use their cash pile to buy up US properties at their newly distressed price levels, simultaneously taking advantage of the yen's strength. Where did that leave MCA? Well, rising interest rates and a sagging Tokyo stock market had made its purchase extremely difficult. The bottom line: because of the recession, the threat of war in the Middle East and the uncertainty of oil supplies and prices, the best Matsushita could contemplate was $60 a share. Tops.

The pleasantries that preceded Hirata's announcement were over. 'You're so far off it's not worth talking,' he was informed.

One day later Hirata's 'top' was raised to a 'limit' of $64.

Wasserman was realist enough to know that in the sick economy prevailing in the US, the $100 a share he might have hoped for a year earlier was no longer achievable. The $75 mentioned at an early stage, however, he had regarded as $70 bottom, $80 top. Troubled economy or not, he regarded $60, even $64, as not only a personal insult, but an outrage. Wasserman said he would put the offer to his board. However, he would be recommending against acceptance.

Hirata stood firm. They were prepared to go to $64 and no further. Ovitz was told that there was no point in remaining in New York, he might as well catch the next plane back to Los Angeles.

Over dinner that evening with his advisers, Wasserman had calmed down. He accepted that what had become known as 'the Geffen leak' had had the debilitating effect of not only locking Matsushita into a deal, but MCA as well.

Stonewalled by Hirata and mindful of the share plunge that would certainly follow the announcement of the breakdown of talks, Wasserman indicated that 'for a few dollars more' the deal could yet be salvaged. A dawn call to Ovitz, back in LA, urged him to contact Hirata one more time.

As the noon deadline for MCA's conference call approached, the call came through. The bid had been raised to $66. With Wasserman's blessing, and after twelve hours of discussion, the MCA board accepted. Matsushita had their prize.

The selection of goodies their 'due diligence' had thrown up looked dazzling indeed. Movies apart, Matsushita had gained illimitable dominion over a ready-made, up-and-running, superstreamlined entity programmed for success. The amazing array included:

MCA Music Entertainment, encompassing MCA Records, Music Publishing, the Universal Amphitheater, MCA Concerts, Facility Merchandising and Winterlands Concessions (with merchandising licences for stars such as Bruce Springsteen, Madonna, George Michael, Billy Joel, Janet Jackson and The Who, as well as exclusive licences to produce imported sportswear for the Hard Rock Cafe, Levi Strauss, Esprit, Major League Baseball and the National Football League).

Spencer Gifts, headquartered in Atlantic City, New Jersey, with 437 retail stores, named 'Retailer of the Year' in 1989.

MCA Book Publishing, with record revenues for the third

consecutive year from G.P. Putnam's, Berkeley Publishing Group, and Putnam and Grosset.

WWOR-TV, serving the TriState New Jersey, New York and Connecticut areas (under Federal regulations this would have to be divested with a majority foreign ownership in MCA).

The USA Network, a TV cable service among the nation's top-rated stations.

MCA Recreation Services:
Universal Studio Tours, with five million visitors in 1989, a twenty-five per cent hike on the previous year;
Yosemite Park and Curry Co: awarded George Bush's 'Take Pride in America' award in 1989;
Universal Studios Florida, scheduled to open in the second quarter of 1990, with Britain's Rank Organisation as an equal partner.

MCA Developments:
The Sheraton-Universal Hotel.
A fifty per cent ownership in ten Universal City Plaza office buildings.
A 'substantial investment' in the Cineplex Odeon cinemas chain.

MCA Merchandising: revenues flowing from merchandise sales ranging from the *Back to the Future* series to Universal-TV's *Miami Vice* and the Woody Woodpecker cartoons.

MCA Home Video: 4 million copies of Spielberg's animated *The Land before Time* had been sold, backed by the first video campaign to involve two promotional partners, the US Postal Service and Pizza Hut.

Universal-TV: A leading supplier of primetime TV programming, with four series returning for the 1989/90 season, *Murder She Wrote*, the ABC *Mystery Movie*, *Quantum Leap* and *Coach*. MCA-TV Entertainment was supervising the preparation of twenty *Movies of the Week* ordered by its sister company, USA-TV, together with six ordered by Showtime and HBO.

MCA-TV International had again achieved record results in

1989, springing from a new private channel in Germany and TV series licensing in the UK.

Universal Studios: The largest in Hollywood, covering 450 acres, with thirty-six soundstages, two Technicolor film labs, the 'Black Tower' admin building, the 'Alfred Hitchcock' Preview Theater, and 10,000 employees. Plus the Spielberg connection through Amblin Entertainment's presence on the backlot.

All this, plus the second-highest movie revenues in Universal's history, with prospects for their seventy-fifth Anniversary year in 1990 regarded as bright. Overall revenues stood at a record $3.38 billion, with net profits a record $192 million.

Excellent as these figures were, the real pearls for Matsushita – Spielberg and Amblin apart – remained the fabled contents of MCA's vaults, the fruits of almost seventy-five years of theatrical production, together with over thirty years of television. Over three-thousand feature-length productions lay carefully stored, together with 13,500 TV episodes. From any standpoint it was quite an eye-ful, and a tribute to the incredible organisational and delegational skills of Lew Wasserman, the band-booker's assistant. What a band-booker! What an assistant! And with just a little help from their friends . . .

Although their cash-out was spectacular, Wasserman's translating to $327 million, Sheinberg's to $120 million, the duo were now employees of Matsushita. And Spielberg, in turn, was several branches further removed from the top of the tree. With nowhere, it seemed, to climb.

# 28

# By Hook or By Crook

*'It's so boring falling in love with the director. There's no
way I thought that would ever happen to me.'*

KATE CAPSHAW, 1982

*'Some actresses marry directors with the understanding
that they'll work together. I think it's a tacit understanding
and that's what keeps them going. In our case, it's our
family that keeps it going.'*

KATE CAPSHAW, 1995

For years in the early eighties there was talk of a Spielberg version of
*Peter Pan.* Surely the story of the little boy who wanted to stay a child
was the archetypal Spielberg project, the summation of his own life
and career? How could he *not* make it? And there was another superstar for whom the tale of arrested development had a special
significance. Michael Jackson had vacationed in the Hamptons with
Spielberg, they had made home movies together, Jackson had
watched *Jaws* '100 times', *E.T.* 'at least forty times'. 'He will always
be young,' he said of his host. 'I love Steven so much, it almost
makes me cry. He inspires me more than anybody on Earth today.'

Spielberg moved quickly to scotch any notion of a collaboration,
declaring in 1984, 'Michael Jackson is a very close friend of mine,
but he never was, and never will be, Peter Pan.' Cue wrenching
sobs from the vicinity of Jackson's Neverland hideaway.

In 1986, after working for several months on the music for a
*Peter Pan* adaptation, John Williams was disappointed when
Spielberg announced he was dropping the whole thing. Now he had
a child of his own, the story ran, he no longer felt the same com-
pulsion to bring Barrie's story to the screen. It took several years, an
update, a complete change of concept – and a human sacrifice
named Nick Castle – before Spielberg would take another run at the
tale.

Columbia honchos Peter Guber and Jon Peters were determined to begin their tenure for new owners Sony with a bang, eager to announce to the world that the studios, semi-moribund for years, were back in the mega-budget business. Adapted from several of Barrie's works, *Hook* was a screenplay by Jim Hart that had been sold to Columbia's TriStar in 1989 by producers Craig Baumgarten and Gary Adelson, with director Nick Castle attached from the project's inception. It was considered a definite 'go', and it remained that way when Guber and Peters appointed a new boss at TriStar. Except that Mike Medavoy, fresh from the wreckage of Orion, just happened to have been Spielberg's very first agent way back when. Except that he saw what an enormous scoop it would be, both for the Guber/Peters team, and for himself, if he could rekindle his old client's well-known interest in Master P. Pan. So another director was attached? Nothing that couldn't be sorted out. Behind it all, cheering from the sidelines, was Spielberg's brand-new agent, master puppeteer Mike Ovitz.

According to Spielberg, the project was brought to him without mention of another director. Frank Marshall (no disappearing act on this occasion) supports his ex-boss's story: '*Hook* came to Steven without his knowing that there was another director attached. When he found out, he was horrified.'

If Spielberg hadn't known from the first moment, he knew before too long. 'I didn't think that this particular director could pull it off and get the best cast, but Steven didn't want to take another director off,' says Medavoy. 'I told him it was my responsibility.' And that, it seems, was enough. As long as someone else was prepared to play the heavy, it was fine by Spielberg. Castle was history, save for a payoff check and story credit. But how to minimise the damage? Medavoy's answer was to promise the director another TriStar movie at some unspecified time in the future, and to describe the charge that Spielberg had thrown his weight around as 'completely undeserved'. Moreover: 'He's been meticulous about *not* doing it. This guy suffers from a rap that is unfortunate.' We'll give the suddenly vocal Marshall the last word on the subject: 'Here's the problem. If someone sends you a script to read and you like it, you assume you can do it. Especially if you're Steven.'

Even in a Hollywood that seldom dares to speak out against its royalty, this was too much. Suddenly, although to a man it was done anonymously, Spielberg and Amblin came under fire. 'It's a damn disgrace,' one entertainment lawyer volunteered. 'Steven Spielberg isn't interested in any game where he doesn't own *all* the marbles. Amblin's like a black hole. So much goes into development, so little comes out.'

Per another of the same species: 'If you want to submit something to Amblin, you're forced to sign their egregious submission agreement that means you'll never get paid if they use your material.' According to an agent: 'This man is not the same as the soft and cuddly characters he creates. He's always been a very strong, very tough businessman. It's the Rule of Kings: "I am the King, I make the rules."' Step forward a studio chief: 'The amazing thing about Spielberg is that he would truly be happiest if he owned every property in town.'

Spielberg did find one valiant defender, none other than Dustin Hoffman's lawyer Bert Fields. 'Steven is very active going after properties,' he conceded, 'but I haven't seen any behaviour that I would call deceitful or unscrupulous.' How about that 'egregious submission agreement'? Fields admitted he hadn't actually *seen* the document, but he had his rationale ready: 'When you are in Steven's position, you get literally thousands of submissions, and some of them may be somewhat similar to ideas you're already developing. You have to be able to protect yourself against someone who comes forward and says, "I came up with the idea for *Jaws*" just because he submitted a story about trout fishing.'

Nick Castle, as it happened, was not the only individual deposed by Spielberg on his arrival. And this time, regardless of the protests, there was no question whose handwriting was all over the deed. One of the original producers of *Hook*, Craig Baumgarten, suddenly discovered that 'complications' had arisen. As in he was *out*. As in Spielberg was *insisting*, as part of his CAA package, that *his* production team of Kathleen Kennedy, Frank Marshall and Gerald Molen be awarded *sole* production credit. *Forget* that Baumgarten had been with the project from its inception. Per Baumgarten, 'All the power was on *their* side of the table.'

Help came from an unlikely source. From under the mighty Ovitz's nose, from within CAA, *notwithstanding* the fact that Baumgarten was signed with another agency. How come? Step forward Ron Meyer, an acquaintance of Baumgarten's, a partner of Ovitz's, and someone with a more acutely developed sense of fairness than is generally rampant in Hollywood. Spielberg had put himself in the wrong, Meyer concluded. Calls were made, heated arguments were forwarded, reason finally prevailed: Baumgarten found himself reinstated with a co-producer credit. 'He did it solely because it was the right thing to do,' a grateful Baumgarten said of Meyer's support. 'I had nothing to give him.'

Back in the mid-eighties, long before Amblin had grown so powerful, Kathleen Kennedy had been more voluble than either of her partners on the bad rap Hollywood producers in general, and

Amblin in particular, were handed. 'I think here is a Hollywood mystique that isn't necessarily what Hollywood is,' she had claimed. 'When we at Amblin find material we like, we sit down and meet the people. If we like the people we go ahead, and if we don't like the people, that may be one of the reasons we don't go ahead. At Amblin we want to stay small. We feel that the only way we can function the way we do, which is not through fear or by swinging our weight around, is to stay small and keep a hands-on quality to all our movies.' Many considered that 'manifesto', if it had ever existed, no longer typified Amblin's operation.

Writer Michael Kaplan may have been referring to Kennedy herself, as well as a typical Spielberg staffer, when he wrote, 'Spielberg has insulated himself from the real world. His fanatically loyal staff continues to shield him from the impact of hostile public opinion.'

The torrent of complaints meant precisely zilch to an exuberant Guber, Peters and Medavoy. Maybe, who knows, Spielberg as well. 'I've always been Peter Pan,' he declared. 'That's why I wanted to do this movie. In a way, it's typecasting for me to do this, because I've always felt an affinity for the character.'

No expense would be spared to bring *Hook* to the screen! Look at the stars! Robin Williams for Peter Pan! Dustin Hoffman for Captain Hook! Julia Roberts for Tinkerbell! Behold the stellar supporting players! Maggie Smith as Wendy! Bob Hoskins as Smee! Feel the budget! $65 million!

The deal Ovitz worked out for his clients was spectacular. Forty per cent of the movie's gross rentals of the first $50 million would be divided between Spielberg, Hoffman, Williams and Roberts. After that TriStar retained all gross revenues between $50 million and $120 million. If and when they exceeded $120 million ($240 million box-office) the director and stars would once again share forty per cent of the excess.

The way the deal was structured, it was a win-win situation for the above-the-line participants. For TriStar, collecting only $30 million from the first $50 million in gross rentals, the situation was different. On a budget of $70 million, plus $30 million to lay out on prints and ads, the company had to claw back $100 million in gross rentals, a box-office tally of $240 million, just to break even. This had been well within the reach of Spielberg several times in the past; hopes were high in both Los Angeles and Tokyo that 'the magician of the movies' could bring it off again. 'Am I crazy?' was the question on Medavoy's mind as he re-examined the terms.

Some observers wryly noted the irony in Spielberg rushing into Sony's embrace. Would he do the same for Matsushita? And how did Steve Ross regard Spielberg's flying the coop for the delinquent Guber and Peters, whether it was a one-off deal or not?

In Jim Hart's script Peter Pan was now an unhappy grown man, who has to return to Never-Never Land to rediscover his childhood ideals and sense of innocence. That was fine as far as the leading role was concerned, but it wasn't nearly enough for Cap'n James Hook's Hoffman. At his insistence *Once Again*'s screenwriter Malio Scotch Marmo was called in to beef up his dialogue and character. Apart from their numerous contacts through Steve Ross, as a favour Spielberg had already directed Hoffman narrating *Strokes of Genius*, a TV documentary Ross's wife Courtenay had produced on the life and work of abstract impressionist Willem de Kooning. They had often talked of making a *movie*-movie together, with Ross entertaining extravagant hopes of a slam dunk for Warners – in vain, alas.

Shooting on *Hook* commenced in February 1991, with no less than six stages constructed on what had just been rechristened 'Sony Pictures Entertainment Studio' at Culver City (previous occupants: Metro-Goldwyn-Mayer and Lorimar). A life-size pirate ship constructed on the giant stage seven, all of five storeys high, became a must-see for the regular stream of celebrities eager to catch a glimpse of the goings-on, not the least of which was the constant stream of badinage between Hoffman and Williams, good-naturedly described by Spielberg as 'the clash of the Titans'. Amy Irving came along for the tour and was greeted warmly by her ex-husband. Bruce Willis showed up and was greeted less warmly by the assembled technicians. It was only days after the star's reported trashing of film crews, attributing the high cost of movies to their outrageous demands. Willis found himself lightly showered from the rafters; when he got back to his car someone had spat all over the windscreen.

Even cloudier was the atmosphere surrounding the blue-screen work an extremely high-strung, supposedly 7-inch Tinkerbell was shooting. The break-up of her relationship with Kiefer Sutherland had left Julia Roberts feeling raw, betrayed and highly emotional. A complicated lighting set-up found her visibly upset at the delay. 'I'm *ready*,' Spielberg was informed, and there was no mistaking the mixture of anger, frustration and impatience behind the words.

'And *I'm* ready,' Spielberg shot back, giving as good as he got. He pointed to the lighting technicians, frantically trying to finish. 'And *they're* ready when *they're* ready.'

It worked. Roberts went quiet as a lamb, if still decidedly fretful. Spielberg conceded that it was a difficult time for his star and described her treatment by the press as 'an unfair experience'. Despite it all he would later claim that 'she did the movie proud'.

One visitor to the set was privy to a rare glimpse of Spielberg's habitual playing of 'good cop' to a female deputy's 'bad cop'. It began during a scene in which Robin Williams was being immersed for take after take in a water tank, surrounded by topless, body-painted mermaids. As close as the visitor can remember the conversation, it went like this:

Spielberg (as Williams bobbed up for the umpteenth time): 'Robin, you were wonderful. Now just one more time?'

As Williams obligingly disappeared into the tank, Spielberg's deputy tugged at his arm: 'Steven, don't forget Robin's leaving town for a week the day after tomorrow. And we've got a whole bunch of other retakes to do.'

Spielberg: 'Really? He's leaving town after tomorrow?'

Deputy: 'Yes, and I don't think we'll be able to finish by then. It'll mean calling him back. Expense.'

Spielberg: 'OK, you take care of it when he bobs up.'

As soon as Williams had scrambled out of the tank, the deputy collared him, with Spielberg still by her side: 'Robin, we'll need you to stay next week for retakes.'

Spielberg (immediately, highly indignant): 'Retakes? *What* retakes?! Robin can't do that stuff next week. He's out of town. He's very busy. What are you talking about?'

Deputy: 'But Steven, we've gotta get those shots.'

Spielberg: 'Oh, my God, this is crazy. Robin can't possibly—'

Williams (smiling sheepishly): 'Hey, Steven, I'll do it. Maybe I can postpone the trip.'

Mission accomplished.

Backscratching became the order of the day as the shoot lumbered along. 'You won't meet anybody who knows his craft more,' Dustin Hoffman declared within earshot of his director. 'He operates, he knows lenses, and he doesn't have to consult.' Turning to Spielberg, he addressed him directly: 'You know more than anybody I've ever worked with.'

Spielberg was all modesty. 'No, Kubrick,' he demurred. 'He knows more than I do. And Coppola knows a lot. The three of us call each other up all the time.' Then there was Scorsese: 'The best American film director working today.' With those, it seemed, any summit meeting would have been complete.

Hoffman's admiring 'I haven't seen a movie like this before' continued the encomium as Spielberg ambled off. 'It's his own beast,' he added. 'It's traditional, yet it's new. I guess you have to call it the Spielberg genre.' Hoffman remained surprised at how Spielberg seemed to combine both incredible security with unexpected insecurity. 'I couldn't have known it,' he declared, 'but he says he comes to work every day wanting to vomit.'

'I just get nervous,' Spielberg amplified. 'And the queasiness comes basically in all my movies when I get on to a set.' He had additional reasons to be nervous when *Hook* ran over schedule. By the time it finally wrapped, after a hectic 160 days, budget scare stores abounded. Had $65 million become $100 million? Rumblings in the press later began about problems with the finished article, deemed an over-stuffed turkey well in advance of its first public screening.

The sneak preview in Texas proved agony for Spielberg, for he could tell that the movie simply wasn't working for the audience. After forty minutes he got up, walked out to his waiting limo and fell asleep. Strangely enough, the score cards filled out produced a ninety-six per cent approval rating, at least according to the press release TriStar execs concocted. Could triumph yet be yanked from disaster's maw?

The answer: sort of. After a slow start that caused fits from Culver City to Tokyo, the movie went on to squeeze past the $100 million mark at the US box-office; this despite reviews that were almost overwhelmingly negative. In any list of critical notices there's always one or two that stand out. This time there was a beaut. Henry Sheehan, who'd earlier gone overboard in one direction with *Raiders of the Lost Ark*, describing it as 'one of the most inhuman, un-human and anti-human movies of all time', now alleged in the pages of *Film Comment* that 'With *Hook* Spielberg establishes himself not just as a mere commercial force, but as a major artistic personality and a legitimate aspirant to greatness.' To which all I can say is – BULLSHIT!! – and go along with James Verniere in the Boston *Herald*, who described *Hook* as 'a turgid, bombastic mess'. After an interesting start with the grown-up, uptight Peter trying to cope with his children and career, the movie flew – literally – straight to hell.

Before *Hook* had even finished shooting, Jon Peters was out as co-CEO of Columbia Pictures. Oh, what it had seemed to be! Having already rid themselves of one wild man in their firing of Walter Yetnikoff, Sony had quickly discovered they had another in Peters. He denied it, but a workman at his country home claimed Peters had pulled a gun on him. He denied it, but it was claimed he'd dispatched a corporate jet to London bearing fresh-cut flowers for his girlfriend. *This* was one-half of the partnership they'd paid hundreds of millions for?

And not even Sony's deep pockets, it seemed, could keep up with his and Guber's free-spending ways at Culver City, where $100 million was being expended to bring the studio's facilities up to scratch. Someone had to take the fall, and Peters was it. Suitably compensated, of course, and with a rich production deal at the studio. Was there no end to the madness?

Kate Capshaw's career had failed to soar after *Temple of Doom*, largely due to an unfortunate series of career decisions. Co-starring with Dudley Moore and Eddie Murphy in *Best Defence* had seemed like a good idea at the time: 'I'd just seen Dudley in *Arthur* and loved it. Everyone said Eddie couldn't be hotter. But nobody had looked at the script!' Four movies in one year, all flops, followed. Then there were the missed opportunities. Her new agent Mike Ovitz asked her to consider a comedy about stealing babies. This was *not* Capshaw's idea of fun and her role in *Raising Arizona* was filled by a grateful Holly Hunter. A unique television opportunity was next to be passed up: 'I was asked to see the producers on this new series. I wasn't that keen on television, but, more importantly, I read the pilot and said, "Why would a woman with an Ivy League education stop at a bar and work there and never leave?" I thought that was the most ridiculous thing I'd ever heard.' Guess what that turned out to be? *Cheers*! Oddly enough, it was a role strikingly similar to that of Willie Scott in *Temple of Doom* – a broad working abroad as a nightclub entertainer, with Shanghai replaced by Osaka – that marked her return to major movies in Ridley Scott's *Black Rain*. Hardly the stuff Oscar nominations are made of, but you can't win them all . . .

If his get-together with Kate Capshaw during *Temple of Doom* had been just a fling at the time for Spielberg, Capshaw would claim it had always meant much more for her: 'I think it was just the way he smelled. He smelled like my family. It was a smell of familiarity.' Capshaw wasn't just talking metaphorically, but olfactorily as well: 'They say that once a woman takes a whiff of her infant you can blindfold her and march twenty babies in front of her and she'll pick hers, and that's how it felt to me. I felt like I was blindfolded and took a smell and said, "This is the guy!"'

According to Capshaw, her attraction to Spielberg even predated their initial get-together on *Indiana Jones and the Temple of Doom*. She attributed it to an article she read in which Spielberg talked about *E.T.*: 'I just felt that I had a love connection. I just could feel that he was sweet.' Capshaw's conversion from Methodism to Judaism was seen by many as her final game plan in a long campaign to land Spielberg. It certainly did no harm, although she claims she was always drawn to the Jewish faith because of its emphasis on the importance of the family: 'When I converted, Steven was delighted. But then all the people in his family who were supposed to fall to their knees in exultation didn't say a word. They wanted me to know it didn't matter to them.' Since the couple had been living together out of wedlock for two years, their reaction may have been quiet relief at the increased prospect of a marital union. One more point: Bernie Adler's Lubavitcher beliefs would have rendered him unable to attend their eventual wedding had Kate not converted.

Even before the divorce from Amy Irving was final, Spielberg and Capshaw had had their marriage plans worked out. Each would be bringing a child from a previous union – Samuel Max, on a shared basis, from Spielberg's first go-round; Jessica, from Kate's first marriage. And together the couple had already added a daughter, new-born baby Sasha. There was just one other little matter to settle.

Spielberg had determined that never again would he be taken to the cleaners, at least not to the extent Irving had achieved. His answer was to propose a $2 million pre-nuptual agreement to Capshaw, the cash to be paid in one lump sum. In Hollywood terms, this was considered miserly.

Capshaw's reaction was to consult her lawyers and come up with an alternative pre-nup, one that more accurately reflected Spielberg's ability to shell out. 'I love you and I want to marry you more than anything else,' her intended was informed, according to one source, 'but I have to protect myself too. I want a guarantee of $2 million for each year we are married if it lasts longer than five years. If we divorce before five years, I want a guarantee of $20 million. And a $10 million trust fund for each child we have.'

The explanation of the bigger payday if the marriage doesn't make it to their fifth anniversary? According to a friend: 'She feels that clause will protect her from Steven running off with a bimbo and chucking the marriage shortly after they wed. Kate feels that if the marriage lasts five years, it'll last forever.'

Cue the hearts and flowers as the wedding date of October 1991 was set, the ceremony to take place at Spielberg's Long Island estate, on the banks of Georgica Pond in the Hamptons, with Steve and Courtenay Ross, Harrison Ford and Dustin Hoffman among the 100 guests. Spielberg informed a friend, 'My heart stopped for a minute there when Kate told me what she wanted, but then she pointed out that it was I who had asked for a pre-nuptual agreement in the first place. She was looking after her interests, just as I was. I thought it over, but the fact is I love her and I want her. She's no gold digger. I proudly told her, "Dear, you're worth every cent!'"

Ain't love grand! Expensive, too. Spielberg's marriage to Irving lasted three and a half years, with $100 million reportedly the post-bop settlement. The bill per day: around $78,000, making Irving one of the highest-paid boppers in the history of the universe.

Compared to her, gorgeous Kate was strictly cut-rate.

# 29

## Stuck In Amber

*'I reached a point in my life where I wanted to put
something back into my films, not just take out.'*

STEVEN SPIELBERG, 1993

*'The story is so sickly it's a wonder Steven Spielberg
hasn't shot a remake with Richard Dreyfuss playing the
old Jewish tailor.'*

KEN RUSSELL, reviewing Carol Reed's *A Kid for Two
Farthings*

Sid Sheinberg, who purchased the movie rights to the novel
*Schindler's List* (*Schindler's Ark* in Britain and the Commonwealth)
for a $500,000 guarantee, had first brought the book to Spielberg's
attention late in 1982. He claims never to have thought of Spielberg
as a 'popcorn movie' director, despite the tag attached by others,
and was convinced that his best work lay outside the strictly commercial field: had everyone forgotten *Duel* and *The Sugarland
Express*?

Spielberg's reaction was quickly to scan a couple of reviews of
the book. 'It'll make a helluva story,' he told Sheinberg. 'Is it true?'
(Referring, presumably, to the individual actions and characters
portrayed, not to the authenticity of its setting.) Sheinberg urged his
friend to read the book. When Spielberg did, it brought him face to
face with 'the great murder' his parents and grandparents had
talked about in his childhood, the one aspect of his boyhood memories he'd chosen not to pursue, the Holocaust perpetrated during
World War II by Hitler on six million Jews. Maybe now it was time.

While all concerned realised that any movie version would have
to stand as the ultimate remembrance of this ultimate evil, Spielberg
was fascinated with the 'Rosebud' aspect of the book – what had
motivated the hitherto profit-orientated Oskar Schindler? Why had
a philandering, hedonistic bon vivant – an expert at playing both

ends against the middle for his own selfish purposes, cosily allied with the Nazis, with a wife back in Germany, a German mistress tucked away in his Krakow pied-à-terre, and a Polish secretary on the receiving end of his advances – decided, against all the odds, to do the decent, humane, courageous, altruistic 'right thing', saving the lives of his Jewish employees, together with those he rescued from the death camp at Auschwitz? What turned a German industrialist who set out to exploit Jewish slave labour into the saviour of over eleven hundred Jews?

Spielberg was convinced that it wasn't a case of heroics for its own sake, for a degree of modesty had been part of the man's charm. That was too facile. There had to be some other explanation, one the book had failed to provide. Perhaps it would emerge during the production process if he decided to go ahead . . .

Another huge question nagged Spielberg night and day. Was he really the man to bring Schindler's story to the screen? One thing was for sure, as he thought and re-thought the events unfolded in the book. Whoever undertook the formidable project, whether himself as director, or someone else under Amblin's production umbrella, the treatment must preclude a re-run of the storm of protest over the perceived dilution of Alice Walker's *The Color Purple*. This was no issue to be softened, but one to be portrayed uncompromisingly, without fear or flinching. A small voice continued to nag.

As Kathleen Kennedy recalls it, 'Whenever we would finish a movie, we would start talking about *Schindler's List* again. But there was always a problem with the screenplay or who to cast. The thing is, when Steven wants to make a movie, *he makes it*. The screenplay gets fixed, the actors found. At the heart of it, he was suffering anxieties as to whether he was intellectually and emotionally mature enough for it. To deal with the complexities of the movie, he felt he had to be a complete adult.'

There were several other directors interested, the still-spry Billy Wilder notable among them. Much as Spielberg admired Wilder, the thought of handing over the reins of what could be a watershed project tested his resolve; the same small voice held him back. At other times the resolve weakened, and twice he tried to offload it on other directors, first Sidney Pollack, then Martin Scorsese. Both protested: 'This is *your* material. Why are you giving it to us?' After Scorsese agreed for a while to take it on, Spielberg felt himself missing it. In the end he was unable to let go.

Fred Schepisi, who adapted an earlier book of Keneally's, *The Chant of Jimmie Blacksmith*, pleaded with Spielberg to turn *Schindler's List* over to him, saying that it would be ruined as a glossy big-studio project. 'Give it to me,' he begged. 'I don't think you have the courage to not use the crane and dolly.'

One Universal executive suggested that Spielberg drop the whole idea of making what was an intrinsically uncommercial project, and allow the studio to make a donation to the Holocaust Museum instead. As Spielberg recalls it: 'That really put a fire under my *tokus*.'

Still he kept delaying. 'I had to grow into it,' he explains. 'I had a lot of projects on my shelf that had "social deed" written all over them, even "politically correct". And I didn't make those films, because I was censoring that part of me by saying to myself, '"That's not what the public will accept from you. What they will accept is thrills, chills, spills, awe and wonder, that sort of thing." I was afraid people would say, as some of them did about *Color* and *Empire*, "Oh, it's the wrong shoe size. And it's the wrong style. What's he doing? Who does he wanna be like? Who's he trying to become – Woody? Or is it David Lean? Or Marty Scorsese? *Who does he think he is?*" And I listened to that criticism, it gets to you. I almost slept in that bed they made, that I was a kid for life . . .' A pause, a hesitation, finally a confession: 'No, I made that bed for myself.'

Twin beds he had lain in, he now realised, were those of indifference and denial. He berated himself mercilessly for looking without seeing for most of his adult life. On the set of *Raiders of the Lost Ark*, the uniforms of the extras, emblazoned with red and white swastikas and other Nazi emblems, had given him no pause whatsoever beyond a quiet satisfaction in their authenticity. He had sat with them, drank his Dr Pepper, ate his sandwich – and never once thought what their neatly starched apparel truly represented. Absorbing himself in the graphic horrors of *Schindler's List* provided 'a real strong wake-up call'.

One surprise emerged during the research process. Where a reluctance to open up their records might have been anticipated from the Polish authorities, the opposite proved to be the case. And when the documents were examined, it was clear no rigging had occurred, that the historical truth had been carefully preserved. An even bigger surprise was an emissary from the Polish government showing up at Amblin's offices in 1985. 'Please shoot this movie in our country,' the Minister of Culture pleaded to Spielberg. 'We need closure,' seemed to be the subtext.

Keneally's 220-page script, on which Spielberg placed his initial hopes, proved a disappointment. In this version Schindler developed enough relationships to sink a whole mini-series. A script from *Out of Africa*'s Kurt Luedtke took over three years to deliver. Luedtke's problem, it turned out, lay in his failure as a hard-nosed journalist to swallow Schindler's heroics wholesale as detailed by Keneally. (He touched a nerve there: Keneally had written the book as a novel, and it had been submitted as such, and won Britain's prestigious Booker prize.)

Spielberg realised that the movie had to be a document, not a melodrama, that he had to be a reporter as much as a director, yet unlike Luedtke, he had no problems accepting what Keneally had written. On the other hand, after *Awakening*'s Steven Zaillian had been called in by Scorsese, Spielberg felt that his first 115-page script failed to flesh out the characters of Schindler's Jewish workers, as Keneally had managed in his book. He conceded that while it was strong, it was too contained. 'That's not the way I see it at all,' Zaillian protested. 'I see this as an overview, not an internal view.'

Spielberg listened. Certainly the last thing he wanted was 'a movie about those five Jews whose story we were telling'. If audiences came away from the movie saying, 'Oh, yeah, the Holocaust. That thing that happened to those five people,' it would be a disastrous disservice to the memory of the millions who had perished. And he had in mind the criticism levelled at an otherwise honourable attempt to portray the events while adding melodrama, some would say banality, in NBC's 1978 TV mini-series, *Holocaust*.

It took until 1992, and one field trip to Poland, before Zaillian completed his script to Spielberg's satisfaction. At last he felt ready to commit: 'Finally, a few roads met.' One of those 'roads' was Spielberg's unexpected discovery of his own Jewish heritage through his children. Although he had endured a painful childhood growing up as a Jew, he made a conscious choice that he wanted his children to be brought up in the faith. Reading materials were brought into the house to teach his kids what the various holidays meant. In the process Spielberg himself became re-interested in the religion he had, for all intents and purposes, turned his back on for years. This particular 'road' intersected at just the right time with the forward momentum of Oskar Schindler's story. Apart from anything else, Spielberg felt the real world intruding: Saddam Hussein's attempt to eradicate the Kurdish race; the horrors of the 'ethnic cleansing' in Bosnia. Had 'the murdering sons of bitches' ever gone away, or had that part of mankind's makeup simply been lurking, latent, waiting to re-emerge?

Tom Pollock wanted Spielberg to shoot the movie in colour. It could be shown in black-and-white in cinemas, he argued, then restored to colour for video release. Spielberg resisted. 'It would have looked pink-and-white,' he protested. There were disputes with many at the studio who wanted what Spielberg calls his usual 'big cathartic moment', like having Schindler dropping to his knees like a traveller on the road to Damascus. Not in this movie, they were informed. In an atypical Spielbergian act, he waived the gross participation terms that normally allowed Amblin to make money from the first box-office dollar, informing Sheinberg, 'I don't want to make any money until you guys get all your costs back.' On that basis Spielberg won a budget of $22 million. There was just one pre-condition. Spielberg had to make *Jurassic Park* first as the price of *Schindler's List*'s green light.

Even Spielberg, never let us forget, was still working for the man, still a working stiff no matter how successful, highly paid and exalted. It was a state of affairs, amidst all the pan-Pacific corporate shuffling, far from lost on him.

In a surprise move Frank Marshall and Kathleen Kennedy departed Amblin Entertainment in January 1993, setting up their own Kennedy/Marshall shingle on the Paramount lot, where a multi-picture three-year deal had been negotiated. Their first three projects to receive the nod were the Melanie Griffith comedy, *Milk Money*, the classic children's fable, *The Indian in the Cupboard*, and a Michael Crichton novel, *Congo*, over which Spielberg and Brian De Palma had haggled a decade earlier.

Apart from his second-unit stints with Spielberg, Marshall had already wet his feet as a fully fledged helmer on Amblin's *Arachnophobia*. On leave from Amblin, he was the first director set for Disney's ill-fated *Swing Kids* before wisely opting only to exec-utive-produce the project and switching instead to direct *Alive*, a co-production of Disney and Paramount, produced by Kennedy and based on Piers Paul Read's real-life shocker about plane crash survivors resorting to cannibalism in the Andes.

In case there were any doubts that their split from Spielberg had been entirely amicable, Marshall was ready to lay them to rest. 'Steven has been very supportive and we talk all the time,' he declared at the end of the team's first year at Paramount. 'He sent me a snowmobile for Christmas.'

Although Marshall and Kennedy took *Congo* with them to Paramount, it was a relative crumb from the master's table, one of author Michael Crichton's leftovers revived to cash in on his latest blockbuster, *Jurassic Park*. Those rights were securely held by Spielberg himself. Crichton's original 'wish-list' to direct the movie, apart from Spielberg, had included James (*Terminator*) Cameron and Richard (*Lethal Weapon*) Donner; Cameron had been 'too busy', Donner had claimed he 'lacked the stamina' for the under-taking. In the end, Michael Ovitz had helped broker the deal between Crichton and Spielberg.

Kathleen Kennedy was set to produce *Jurassic*, scheduled to begin shooting on August 24, 1992, just a few months before her departure for Melrose Avenue and the welcoming Paramount gates. Co-producing was Gerald Molen, Amblin's newly appointed head of production, who had joined the company full-time after working on *Hook*. The script was by David Koepp, from what was described as 'an adaptation of the book' by Michael Crichton and Malia Scotch Marmo.

Crichton's role in the adaptation had been far from straightforward. To start with, he had little desire to become involved in the script at all, even with the extra $500,000 on offer. Having sweated the book out, he wanted to get away from the characters he'd created, and move on. Then he began to reconsider. 'I really felt that I knew the direction of the story,' he says. 'It was like a boat. Pull one part out and the water starts rushing in. Oops, don't do that! Do something else and the boat starts sailing too fast or in the wrong direction. I had already made a lot of these mistakes in my earlier drafts and I felt I knew the pitfalls.'

A preliminary meeting with Spielberg provided a few parameters from both parties. 'I'll do a draft for you and cut it down to budget size,' Crichton agreed, 'but then you're going to want somebody else to polish the characters.' Crichton felt he had surprised the director, since the typical writer's reaction was seldom 'Get someone else.' For his part, as he accepted, Spielberg explained what he liked best and least about the book.

Seven months later, Crichton produced a first draft that nobody much cared for. 'Steven was really good about identifying what was wrong,' Crichton recalls. 'He said, "The movie starts too fast."' It was back to the drawing board to work out a more detailed prologue to the action. Spielberg also proposed that Crichton tackle the redraft in 40-page chunks, rather than spend more months possibly heading down the wrong track. It took a month to come up with the first 40 pages, and from then on it was relatively plain sailing. Per Crichton: 'Steven was amazing to work with, intelligent and sane, not at all like the Hollywood crowd.'

While Spielberg had assembled an impressive cast for *Jurassic* in Sam Neill, Laura Dern, Jeff Goldblum, and Sir Richard Attenborough, playing his first role in front of a camera for fifteen years, it was clear from the outset who the stars of the movie had to be. In preparation for filming Crichton's tale of genetically engineered prehistoric monsters running amok in a contemporary jungle theme park, special effects teams had already been working for eighteen months, developing a variety of extinct species, from the mighty Tyrannosaurus rex to airborne pterodactyls, to poison-spitting dilophosaurs and pack-hunting, vicious velociraptors. Initially the thought had been solely to construct life-size robotic creatures using the latest scientific information, with Stan Winston at the drawing board. Then Industrial Light and Magic's Dennis Muren entered the scene with computer graphic imaging. Working in tandem with Winston's amazing creations, they planned to integrate the 'animals' (Spielberg's definition; as opposed to 'monsters') with actors and background in a way never before achieved on the screen. T. rex ended up forty-foot long and weighing 9,000 pounds, the other creatures' scale varying between twelve and twenty per cent, with the six-foot tall velociraptors at the upper end.

Early scenes on the Hawaiian island of Kauai got shooting off to an unexpectedly rocky start. Hurricane Iniki, the worst storm to strike Hawaii this century, killed three people, injured 100 more, rendered 8,000 homeless. Even Spielberg, the master of spectacle, was overwhelmed as he watched uprooted palm trees flying overhead. A petrified Laura Dern was among the actors and crew amused and delighted by his idea of protectiveness as they sheltered from the storm and awaited their evacuation. With all the lights blacked out, he first held a torch over Dern's head, then under her chin, rapidly repeating the process as he alternately called out, 'Love story! Horror movie! Love story! Horror movie!' Back on the relatively safer ground of California, filming continued on the stages and backlots of Universal and neighbouring Warner Bros.

With Spielberg's departure to make his long-planned *Schindler's List*, there was a degree of concern expressed at the studio at the rough assembly of *Jurassic Park* left behind. No special effects or model work had been added, and without music, the whole thing looked like mere shadow play. There was only one thing for it. As the special effects and computer imaging were added, they would have to be beamed by satellite to Poland. Spielberg would have to work overtime after filming *Schindler's List* by day.

# 30

# Epiphany

*'I know I'm sentimental, I just really like people a lot. I'm always siding with the positive in human nature, so that tends to drive most of my movies into a category which some people can rightly claim is sweet and soft. To keep that from happening in* Schindler's List *I held most of the performances back.'*

*'I don't look at sad, ugly things very often . . . I'm a real strong avoider. Most of my movies aren't real life. There were moments in* Purple *and* Empire *that had real life in them, but they're not start-to-finish real life. And this time, on* Schindler's List, *I knew I had to look. Then, when I started looking, I couldn't stop.'*

STEVEN SPIELBERG, 1994

If Steve Ross's ascension to joint-head of the Time-Warner behemoth was the peak of his career, and the price he extracted from Sony's poaching trip yet another triumph, his pursuit of a financial tie-up with Toshiba and Itochu of Japan must be counted as his last hurrah. Whatever else he was – scoundrel, charmer, benefactor and nemesis; no matter how brilliant, twisted, greedy and generous; regardless of his wit, selfishness, warmth and venality – he remained, like all of us, merely mortal.

He had been cut to the core of his being when David Geffen turned on him after the windfall sale of Geffen Records to MCA. 'Steve's biggest get-off,' the ingrate had declared, rubbing salt into the wound, 'is when he can sit there after a deal is made and say how he took someone to the cleaners.' Coming from someone he'd promoted and backed for over twenty years, it was a bitter pill to swallow. Why the bitchery?

True, he'd been obliged to fire the little bastard back in the mid-seventies when his involvement in movies hadn't worked out, and it had boiled down to losing either Geffen or several others at Warners. But who knew the guy was about to be zapped with a cancer scare? Besides, hadn't he accepted him back into the fold later? Okay, okay, there had been that unfortunate fracas over *Personal Best*. But Geffen had piled on the drama in his claim that the movie could have brought him down. And yes, he had turned down Geffen's offer to sell his company, turned down also his request for advances. That had been his mistake, Geffen's good fortune. True also, he had excluded Geffen from the Spielberg/Streisand/Eastwood share option deal back in 1987, and again with a similar, but relatively minor share-out just before Time Inc.'s takeover. Maybe his greatest sin, though, had been in not taking Geffen to one side and telling him about the Time-Warner deal in advance. Yes, he could imagine how that must have crazed the little sucker.

Stung as he was by Geffen's public outburst, coupled by widespread press criticism of the reported $78 million payout he'd awarded himself following the takeover, together with a subsequent, ill-conceived rights offering that had been laughed off the board, the beleagered Ross took some comfort from Spielberg. He was the one true friend who stood by him, one guy who truly seemed to understand, one solid tower of strength amidst toppling straw men like Geffen.

Spielberg saw how unhappy the bad PR was making Ross, and claimed that his understanding of what the mogul was going through had been gained from first-hand, ongoing, bruising experience. 'People don't see my movies,' Spielberg complained, 'they see my success, they think of how much money I make. Steve used to say that people don't understand. They want to knock the statue off the pedestal. They want to *kill* Steve Ross. They want to *be* Steve Ross.'

In the autumn of 1991, with the Toshiba and Itochu financial partnerships secured, prostate cancer that had been first diagnosed in the mid-eighties was found to have spread despite surgery Ross had undergone years earlier. Spielberg was the only one outside of the immediate family circle to spend time with the ailing tycoon, nursing him through terrible depressions, talking him through his lowest points as he endured a year of radiation and chemotherapy treatment. They fooled each other with straight-faced talk of buying a yacht together when his health was restored. Finally, a solitary ray of real hope was held out in the form of fresh surgery. Ross did initially rally after the operation was carried out, but died two months later in the early hours of December 20, 1992.

For the first time in his life Spielberg had had someone he could

281

completely open up to, talk over personal problems with, truly confide in and relax with. Now he had lost that someone, the man he'd considered not only a great friend and mentor, but the father he would have chosen had the option been his. Ross, Spielberg was convinced, had been someone who cared about him, as opposed to what he could do for them. Who'd counselled him through the years not to follow his example, rampaging through life as if the devil was on his heels, as if making it in business was the one, the only goal.

Spielberg wasn't the first to absorb the lesson that – hey, you're a long time dead, bud, do you really want to go through the pearly gates, your proudest boast that you made it to the top of your profession, to the detriment of caring for your family, cultivating real friends, being loved? Lord knows Spielberg was hearing the lesson from someone who hadn't always practised what he preached. Ross had never been the quintessential family man, he'd let friends take the rap for his misdeeds, if he'd been loved, he'd been hated in equal measure. But why quibble about the source when you're absorbing one of life's greatest lessons?

Spielberg eloquently spelled out the desolation he felt at the funeral service. 'For the past couple of days,' he said, 'I feel cold, I can't keep warm, I feel that there's a draught through my heart. And I know that Steve is up there, trying to figure out a way to plug up the holes.'

Geffen, it later turned out, had indeed been mortally offended at being excluded from the share options granted to 'these friends of his', Spielberg, Streisand and Eastwood. 'Here I was, an associate for twenty tears,' he raged, 'and I didn't get a single share option.' It was Ahmet Ertegun at Atlantic Records, Geffen now maintained, who'd been more of a father for him: 'Steve never took a fatherly interest. I was an asset of his.' His valedictory comment: 'He didn't have an easy life, Steve. He didn't make it easy for other people, but he sure didn't have an easy life.'

Watching a documentary on Oskar Schindler's life, Spielberg had been struck by what he saw as similarities with Steve Ross. 'If you were an actor,' he'd told him, 'I'd cast you in this part.' Instead, he tested a whole series of hopefuls, including Liam Neeson, an actor who'd been through the process several times with Spielberg for other roles that had gone elsewhere. Was this another? the actor thought. Maybe not, for hadn't Spielberg always said in the past he was saving him for 'something special'?

After a first test in September 1992, Neeson heard nothing, apart from the odd press report that Kevin Costner and Mel

Gibson had both expressed interest and been turned down. It took until the following December, and a performance he'd just given on Broadway in *Anna Christie*, before he heard further.

Spielberg, his wife and mother-in-law had been in the audience. Mrs Capshaw was still in tears, overcome by the power of the play and the performances, when they met the actor backstage. Kate Capshaw watched as Neeson, a gentle giant of a man, put a comforting arm around her mother. 'That's what Schindler would have done,' she told her husband later.

Watching him in the play, Spielberg was suddenly aware of the tremendous power the normally understated actor was capable of unleashing. Less than two months later Neeson was in Poland on the set of *Schindler's List*, shivering along with the rest of the cast and crew in minus 15-degree temperatures. Anxious for Neeson to see that he didn't have to emphasise the character's charm, or himself as an actor, Spielberg had showed him some of Steve Ross's home movies. There was something in there, he was convinced, whether body language, expressions or mannerisms, that would help Neeson capture the elusive flavour of Oskar Schindler. Other than that, the man's deeds should, if Neeson's interpretation was successful, speak for themselves.

Spielberg had met with Ben Kingsley, his first choice for the role of Itzhak Stern, Schindler's accountant as well as the voice of his conscience, the man who helps convince his master that there's more than one bottom line in life. Before accepting, Kingsley had expressed his concern about the possible collapse of the boundaries between an actor and his role due to the emotionalism involved in the subject. He arrived for a second round of discussions hoping to hear the word that would sum up and justify both his and his director's approach. 'Witness' would have been his first choice; instead Spielberg came up with 'conscience'. This Kingsley happily accepted.

Spielberg had searched long and hard for someone to play the sadistic Amon Goethe. Struck with Ralph Fiennes' portrayal of T.E.B. Lawrence in TV's *A Dangerous Man*, as well as his unusual interpretation of Heathcliff in the unreleased *Wuthering Heights*, he called the actor in for a test. 'Ralph did three takes,' Spielberg recalls, 'and I still, to this day, haven't seen takes two and three. He was absolutely brilliant. I saw *sexual evil*. It is all about subtlety. There were moments of kindness that would move across his eyes. Then they'd instantly turn cold.' It was exactly the mixture he wanted, for the delineation of great evil could never, Spielberg felt, be one-dimensional, there had to be shadings that served to make the man's cold-bloodedness truly monstrous.

283

'Steven didn't get involved in motivation or my interpretation of Goethe,' says Fiennes. 'He wasn't dictatorial or autocratic. He *trusted*, and that trust built. But he did tell me not to make Goethe a clichéd Nazi.' When he also asked the actor to put on some weight for the role, Fiennes obliged, turning up on location 25 pounds heavier.

Janusz Kaminski, the Polish-born cinematographer chosen for the project, had heard some 'pretty scary things' about Spielberg and his attitude to crew members, especially with regard to the director's highly specific ideas on lighting. 'Sometimes the photography Steven was familiar with and suggested would have been too glamourous,' he recalls. It was with considerable relief that Kaminski found Spielberg open to suggestions of a change to his usual style, not to make the film look 'too beautiful, just real'.

Spielberg spent almost five months shooting the movie 'sick in my life and sick in my stomach'. The unit was greeted with billboards daubed with anti-Semitic symbols, a hardly needed reminder that as a Jew in Poland he would have been dead fifty years earlier. Worse, there had been no physical change in the country in the half-century since the horrors; unlike the camp at Warsaw, Krakow had not been razed to the ground. The actual house Schindler lived in was used in filming, also the factory where he'd turned out his munitions; they now made radio parts. Because there was a monument on the site of the actual Plaszow forced labour camp, it was re-created 800 yards away on the site of an open mine.

A last-minute decision was made to amplify and extend the harrowing sequence of the liquidation of the Jews from the Krakow ghettos. Allocated just two pages in Zaillian's 192-page script, Spielberg spent three weeks filming it. 'He thought I'd lost my mind,' Spielberg recalls, 'but really I felt strongly that the sequence had to be almost unwatchable.'

As he had anticipated, Ben Kingsley had days when he found it difficult to function, when, like Spielberg, he was overcome with the enormity of the evil that had been perpetrated on millions, with the awful, rending closeness to the events their script and location brought them. In a bar one night Kingsley watched as a middle-aged German businessman approached one of the Israeli actors and asked, 'Are you a Jew?' When the answer was a nod, the individual drew a finger across his throat, then jerked an imaginary noose tight. 'Hitler should have finished the job!' he muttered. Kingsley had to be physically restrained, and the incident ended with the German being forcibly escorted from the bar, still screaming racial epithets.

'How are you?' Spielberg greeted him the following morning as a shot was being set up.

'I'm fine,' Kingsley replied. Tight-lipped, he added, 'I'm in a state of rage.'

'I'm in a state of rage too,' Spielberg replied, stone-faced; the incident had been reported to him too. 'Let's get to work.'

What helped Spielberg retain a sense of equilibrium during the shoot – 'my salvation', he calls it – was the presence of his wife and children back in their hotel each night, as well as their occasional visits to the set. Without that link to normality, he doubts if he could have got through *Schindler*.

To Liam Neeson he confided, 'I mustn't use my Spielbergian bag of tricks here. I must simply eavesdrop with the camera, just tell the story, keep peeling that onion away, get very, very bare and stark.' The question was: *Would* he be able to resist the same 'bag of tricks' that had served him so well in the past? *Could* he avoid lapsing into melodrama?

Neeson, having recently worked on *Husbands and Wives*, found unexpected similarities between the techniques that movie's director had employed, and those Spielberg was calling into play. 'Spielberg's direction was a bit like Woody Allen's,' he claimed. 'We didn't know how he was going to shoot a scene. You just had to be prepared in *not* being prepared.' The method added a decided edge.

Spielberg recalled something Francois Truffaut had told him on the set of *Close Encounters of the Third Kind*. 'You can't create a story that you haven't yourself lived in some way.' He felt that while this was normally true, *Schindler's List* would prove the exception to the rule. Yes, most films were about imagination, but this was different. For the first time in his career Spielberg felt unrestricted, released from his own fantasies, able to enter a terrible world far removed from anything he had personally experienced. His own Jewish faith aside, and that had seldom been either a guiding or a limiting factor, he felt as if his own humanity was on trial in the production of *Schindler's List*. This was the ultimate test, not just as a filmmaker, but as a man.

Halfway through filming Spielberg called up his friend Robin Williams. 'I haven't laughed in seven weeks,' he told him. 'Help me.' Williams obliged with twenty minutes of long-distance schtick, providing a rare break.

After Spielberg had conceived the way he wanted the movie to end, the laying of the stones by a group of survivors on Schindler's grave, 128 Schindlerjüden were flown to Jerusalem. Four hours were spent filming the colour sequence.

Back at Universal the first assemblage of the movie came in at over four hours; almost an hour had to go. Neeson was sorry that what he considered one of the best sequences was sacrificed, with Schindler playing a game of '21' with Goethe for Helen, his Jewish maid. Spielberg's reasoning was simple. Anything that smacked of old celluloid was out: the scene was 'too Hollywood, too *Cincinnati Kid*. Everything that reminded me of another movie I cut out of *Schindler's List* because I'd made a career of reverberating my past in my films, if not flagrantly, then subtly.'

Not content with that, Spielberg went on to confess how much, despite his previous denials, he had borrowed, Peter Bogdanovich-style, from past masters of the art of cinema. 'I know how to put Cecil B. De Mille on screen,' he declared. 'I can do a Michael Curtiz. If my mojo's working I can put one-tenth of a David Lean image on the screen. But I've never really been able to put *my* image on the screen, with the exception of *E.T.* perhaps. And certainly not until *Schindler's List* was I really able *not* to reference other filmmakers. I'm *always* referencing everybody. I didn't do any of that on this movie.'

The admission, made in the confessional atmosphere surrounding the production and aftermath of *Schindler's List*, was a significant one. Bogdanovich had paid the price for his honesty back in the seventies, and had been lambasted ever since. Now that Spielberg felt unassailable, it was own-up time. And why not? Call it the 'Oskar Schindler syndrome'.

With two dreadful years behind them since Matsushita's takeover of MCA, everyone at Universal was nervous, from Lew Wasserman to Sid Sheinberg to Tom Pollock. The Tom Selleck vehicle *Mr Baseball* had got things off to a bad start under their new owners, then the Sylvester Stallone comedy misfire, *Stop! Or My Mom Will Shoot* had followed with Ron Howard's big-budget *Far and Away* adding to the misery along with *Leaving Normal, Dr Giggles* and *Out On a Limb*. Since then the record had gone from bad to disastrous, with one flop following another – *Mad Dog and Glory, Heart and Souls, Army of Darkness, Matinee, The Public Eye* and *Lorenzo's Oil*. Universal's last $100 million grosser had been Amblin's *Back to the Future II*. Way back in '89.

Since then Tom Pollock had largely opted for the timid approach, with a string of what looked, and performed, like B-movies. They badly needed a certified smash. With *Jurassic Park*'s $65 million-and-climbing bill, the eyes of Universal's new masters were certain to be trained on the company as never before. All their eggs appeared to be in one basket, or as one top agent put it, 'They don't seem to have an agenda, *except* for *Jurassic Park*.'

286

All doubts were instantly swept away as the US opening weekend figures were fed into computers: *Jurassic Park* was certain to generate a minimum of $125 million, maybe as much as $185–200 million at the box-office. Instead, it took $100 million in just nine days, passed $200 million in twenty-three days, finally achieving $350 million by the end of its run. Spielberg's worldwide record take of $645 million with *E.T.* was about to be exceeded by almost fifty per cent, with over $900 million in box-office receipts gathered round the globe.

Spielberg had opted to take no money at all upfront for *Jurassic*, choosing instead to go for ten–fifteen per cent of the movie's adjusted gross. The result was one of the biggest paydays in the history of motion pictures, variously estimated at between $30–50 million (equalled or exceeded only by Jack Nicholson's reported $50 million cash-out from *Batman*). On top, Spielberg had what Jack had failed to negotiate – a hefty cut of the merchandising, with 1,000 products, from board games to models and picture books, licensed to over 100 manufacturers.

The sigh of relief that followed the box-office returns was heard all the way across the Pacific. 'The success of *Jurassic Park* is the sole factor that nudged up Matsushita's consolidated profits,' a Merrill Lynch analyst confirmed.

Once again critics had been left in the dust. '*Jurassic Park* isn't as sorry a mess as Spielberg's last movie, the unspeakable *Hook*,' Andrew Sarris had reported in the New York *Observer*. 'It's the same kind of mess, though . . . Remarkably tedious and toothless.' *Variety* had been closer to the people, overcoming their reservation about the 'often dim and even clunky' story and characters to offer their money verdict: 'The movie delivers where it counts – in excitement, suspense and the stupendous re-creation of giant reptiles. A monster hit.'

Perhaps under the weight of all those millions it's foolish to talk of the artistic low that *Jurassic Park*, hot on the heels of *Hook*, undoubtedly represented in Spielberg's canon. Or perhaps not. It all depends on one's point of view – if there are no low points, how can the high points stand out?

Liam Neeson sees his involvement in *Schindler's List* as 'a defining experience'. Although he was always aware it was going to be a very special movie, he had no idea of the event it proved to be. Apart from 'the great joy of working with a master like Steven Spielberg', he felt he had experienced Hollywood expertise at its best, as part of a team working at their peak. At the same time he had never viewed the project as a Hollywood career enhancer. The main reason: 'I'm not playing an American hero.'

When Sid Sheinberg first viewed the movie, he had a reaction he was unable to cope with: 'After a few minutes I broke down.' The tough-as-nails executive was nonplussed. 'We're supposed to be *professionals* here,' he argued. 'This is supposed to be a *film*. We're supposed to be *marketing* it. It's *business*.' He tried to compose himself, but was totally destroyed. Then he looked over at Michael Kahn, the editor who'd spent every day of the shoot on the set with Spielberg, followed by six weeks in a rented studio near his director's East Hampton home. Kahn was crying like a baby.

Universal rolled out exactly the right campaign for the three hour, thirteen-minute movie, dignified yet strong, totally in keeping with its subject matter, with none of the hype and hoopla reserved for potential blockbusters.

At the opposite end of the spectrum from the studio's reserve came totally over-the-top statements from the likes of Spielberg's friend Jeffrey Katzenberg. 'I think *Schindler's List* will wind up being so much more important than a movie,' he raved. 'It will affect how people on this planet think and act. At a moment in time, it is going to remind us about the dark side, and do it in a way in which, whenever that little green monster is lurking somewhere, this movie is going to press it down again. I don't want to burden the movie too much, but I think it will bring peace on Earth, goodwill to men. Enough of the right people will see it that it will actually set the course of world affairs. Steven is a national treasure. I'm breakin' my neck lookin' up at this guy.'

Peace on Earth, goodwill to men? Come on, Jeffrey, only a few months later you'd be locked in a battle to the death with Michael Eisner, your long-time senior partner at Disney! Spielberg had a much more modest, and realistic goal in mind: 'I wouldn't have done *Schindler's List* if I didn't think a story like this would remind people, in a way that they don't really like to remember, that these events occurred only fifty years ago. And it could happen in all its monstrosity again.'

Liam Neeson provided further welcome, down-to-earth counterbalance to Katzenberg's high-flown rhetoric. 'In today's world the individual is gradually being squashed,' he noted. 'Switch on CNN any night of the week and you get that feeling from the former Yugoslavia and Rwanda. You think, "My God! Human beings are worth nothing." Then a film like *Schindler's List* comes out and reminds us that individuals can do something. I don't think movies can change society – never have, never will. But they can give people pause for thought.'

The initial reviews of *Schindler's List* were almost uniformly favourable – we're talking over ninety per cent – the common theme being astonishment at Spielberg's 'transformation' from lightweight to heavyweight contender in one fell swoop. Per the New York *Times*, 'The film ensures that neither Spielberg nor the Holocaust will ever be thought of in the same way again.' In *New Yorker*: 'The movie will take its place in cultural history and remain there.' David Ansen in *Newsweek* declared, 'This movie will shatter you, but it earns its tears honestly.'

As surely as night follows day, there was a backlash. It started in America, with J. Hoberman in *Village Voice* declaring, 'Leave it to Steven Spielberg to make a feel-good movie entertainment about the ultimate feel-bad experience . . . And don't worry about dinner afterwards – it's a tasteful movie.'

*Forward*, the Jewish newspaper, criticised the hailing of a Nazi hero while portraying all Jews as ineffectual victims. Another commentator had his own take on Schindler's conversion from black marketeer. Although he had without question helped many Jews survive the earlier years, his 'buying' of 1,100 lives in the summer of 1944, with the end of the war and the German defeat all but a foregone conclusion, could be interpreted, he maintained, as smacking of pragmatism, the desire to come out the far end of the tunnel smelling of Ashes of Roses rather than ashes of dead Jews. And hadn't some Schindler survivors described paying bribes to his Jewish office staff to have their names added to the list, in effect purchasing their 'buy-out'? All this, he argued, had been swept under the rug in Keneally's book, let alone Spielberg's movie.

Leon Wieseltier weighed in via the pages of *New Republic*. 'I do not doubt that the glibness of Spielberg's film is glibness in a good cause,' he conceded. 'But Americans are quickly moved. There is something a little exhibitionistic about all these tears. I'd prefer a bit more stunning into silence.'

Armond White in *Film Comment* was another who questioned the movie's approach: 'Spielberg's skills see him through, but *Schindler's List* is weakest as history, strongest at depicting the emotionality of the events. Of all the techniques he employs – fast cutting, chromatic shifts, emotive lighting – the most specious is the pretence toward documentary realism. It's a desperate, unoriginal tactic.'

Two other *Village Voice* writers questioned 'a film so enamoured of a benevolent German entrepreneur that it barely portrayed the Jews he saved as characters in their own right'.

Ethnic musicologist Henry Sapoznik, informally employed as a music consultant on the movie, bemoaned the sacrifice of 'fidelity to historical detail on the altar of blockbuster immediacy.' He had advocated the use of the Yiddish and Jewish songs of the period as resistance music that would have shown the Jews as more than just victims. Instead, what had been used was 'Juzak', with its preference for melodrama over historical rigour.

Across the Atlantic other naysayers lay in wait. 'Of course the film isn't a masterpiece,' author Howard Jacobson informed readers of *The Independent*. 'It wouldn't be reasonable to expect a man who is so fond of childish things to put them away overnight. A well-behaved Spielberg film gives us nothing to cheer about.' In the same newspaper their regular critic Adam Mars-Jones described *Schindler's List* as 'three partial films in one – a harrowing pseudo-documentary, an effective melodrama, and an embarrassing piece of kitsch moviemaking. Authentic intensity, emotionalism and botch.'

Geoff Brown in *The Times* was little more impressed. 'The manipulative Spielberg style may be held back,' he noted, 'but it peeps out nonetheless. Artfulness surfaces in the treatment of children, the smart cross-cutting, and the dreamlike appearance of Auschwitz, almost pretty in the falling snow. Compared to the horrifying footage gathered in Resnais' *Night and Fog*, and other documentaries, *Schindler's List* takes place in Disneyland.'

Even after its sweep at the Academy Awards – giving Spielberg not only his long-awaited 'Best Director' award, but also the 'Best Picture' accolade – the doubters continued to express their reservations. 'Despite its seven Oscars,' Jason Epstein wrote in the *New York Review of Books*, 'I doubt that *Schindler's List* will survive its season as a memorable film, or as a comment on the concentration camps, for the evil that Spielberg tries to portray lies beyond his imagination.'

The main fault I found with *Schindler's List* is that it's neither fish, flesh, nor fowl, rather the uneasy mixture of the three that Mars-Jones summarised. Although I didn't accept everything in Keneally's book as gospel representation, I found it almost unbearably moving. Spielberg's movie, on the other hand, scarcely moved me at all. Perhaps to someone coming across this most terrible of all modern examples of man's inhumanity to man for the first time, it was enough, for they would have no documentary reality against which to judge the movie's ersatz texture. Perhaps my childhood memories of newsreel footage of the Allied relief of Belsen and other concentration camps remains too vivid to be superceded by any dramatic reconstruction. And while few would dispute that the movie is superb in purely technical terms, calculation was there in spades. Despite his protestations, Spielberg had indeed resorted to the 'bag of tricks' he claimed to have locked away. If the *Cincinnati Kid* sequence was gone, there remained the scarcely credible misfiring guns episode. Yes, it was in the book, but wasn't that a *novel*? And yes, miracles can happen, but was this the movie in which to include one?

Even Thomas Keneally felt compelled to speak out about Schindler's speech and breakdown at the movie's climax, complete with weeping violin, where he cries out that if only he'd sold his car and a few more diamonds, more lives could have been bought. Which Oskar Schindler was this? Surely not the same one who'd quietly disappeared, *in untidy real life*, into the night with his wife and a carload of diamonds? Spielberg defended the scene as 'absolutely necessary'; Schindler wasn't speaking for himself, but 'for all of us, what we might do someday'. The scene remained terribly phoney, and it could well be the reason that Neeson was denied an Oscar for his otherwise exemplary performance; no actor alive could have made the scene ring true.

Astonishment was also expressed at the dedication, 'For Steve Ross', which Spielberg chose to include on the final credits. Meaningless to millions perhaps, inappropriate to many who knew. So too, in view of the gravity of the subject, was the final, inappropriate credit line. It read 'An Amblin Entertainment'.

A disturbing insight into how one segment of America's youth received the movie was provided by a teacher from a predominantly black high school in Oakland, California. Several among her group of students laughed out loud at a scene showing a Nazi shooting a Jewish woman. Spielberg was concerned enough to visit the school and talk to the people involved. 'How can they be expected to respond when they have no idea of their own history, when they live in a society that cares so little for them?' he was asked.

Since Pauline Kael was one of the first to single out Spielberg's talent, we'll give her the second-last word, for the moment, on *Schindler's List*. It would be a tragedy, she wrote, if Spielberg were fooled into thinking he had made a 'great film'. If that was his conclusion, the effect on the remainder of his career might be sad indeed.

The thoroughly shocking *last* word would be uttered two years later, and from someone much closer to the real Oskar Schindler than either Kael, Keneally or Spielberg had ever been.

Uncomfortably close.

# 31

## Monkeys and Typewriters

*'It all begins with the writer. It's a fundamental dictum, but somehow it keeps getting forgotten along the way. No filmmaker, irrespective of his eclectic bag of tricks, can ever afford to forget his commitment to the written word.'*

*'I dream for a living. Once a month the sky falls on my head, I come to, and I see another movie I want to make. Sometimes I think I've got ballbearings for brains; these ideas are slipping and sliding across each other all the time. My problem is that my imagination won't turn off. I wake up so excited I won't eat breakfast.'*

STEVEN SPIELBERG

The business that carried on before, during and after *Schindler's List*, looked like business as usual with Amblin's one-two announcement of *Casper* and *The Flintstones*. The hectically pre-occupied Spielberg maintained his hands-off policy on both projects, while maintaining his right to provide a touch on the tiller whenever it was deemed necessary. What he concerned himself with most was the original choice of the most appropriate writers and directors, together with a fairly rigid adherence to the original concept. First and foremost, he continued to seek out new talent as ready and bursting for that first big break as he had been when Sid Sheinberg was persuaded to take that fateful look at *Amblin'*.

There are enough parallels in the careers of Spielberg and the young director of *Casper* to qualify for the description 'eerie'. Thirty-year-old Brad Silberling's first inkling that he'd like to be a director had dawned after seeing *Jaws*. Like Spielberg, he'd 'acquired' his dad's camera, in his case a Super 8, and shot movies while in elementary and junior high school. A short graduate film, *Repairs*, had landed him in a programme at UCLA. This had led in turn to a directing contract at Spielberg's old alma mater, Universal-TV.

Spielberg was alerted initially by some of Silberling's TV work, including episodes of *Doogie Howser, M.D.*, *LA Law* and *NYPD Blue*. Most of all, he was impressed by his adroit handling of a comedy and drama mix. Spielberg called him up, offering a comedy-drama he was prepping for Warners. 'I could see you were trying to make a movie,' he told him, referring to an episode of *Brooklyn Bridge*, 'and I know what that's like on those schedules. Maybe it's time you got a crack at really doing it.'

When the studio nixed the project, perhaps feeling that Spielberg's constantly repeated theme of a family divorce was wearing just a teensy-bit thin, Silberling's big break was on hold. He was still jubilant, and confident that his time would come. 'It was so great to meet Steven and talk to him,' he says, 'because the experience I had he literally had himself. I spent my first year at Universal feeling, as he calls it, like a company mascot. You're this young guy and everyone hits you on the buns and says, "Isn't he cute? Look, he's a director!" But meanwhile nobody wants to hire you, because the risk is so great, especially in TV.'

It was while working in Hawaii on a pilot for Steve Bochco that he got his second call from Spielberg, immediately after Alex Proyas, his first choice, had exited *Casper* in favour of *The Crow*, citing catch-all 'creative differences'. The good news for Silberling: 'This one is really going.' The bad news, thanks to Proyas's abrupt exit: 'It's going soon.'

When Spielberg went on to explain the nature of the ectoplasmic delights in store, all of them to be computer generated, Silberling expressed grave doubts. 'Let's be honest,' he suggested. 'You know that other than some blue-screen work in TV, I have basically zero background in special effects, and I've never dealt in character animation, whether or not it's going to be computer graphics.'

'I know, I know,' said Spielberg, waiting patiently for the other shoe to drop. It did soon enough.

'Listen, if you're prepared to go there,' Silberling declared, 'I'll go there too.'

What followed was more than a year of intense labour, painstakingly attempting to coordinate human action with animation and special effects. At the end of it all Silberling felt he deserved a doctorate in the arts. Had he gone to any reference work to study the processes, he realised that would have been a limiting mistake; instead he had been lucky enough to have worked with experts in a field so revolutionary that new rules were being constantly written. Even since the 'latest' computer technology showcased to perfection in *Jurassic Park*, the science had taken giant strides.

Silberling describes his benefactor as contributing 'the perfect amount of involvement' in *Casper*. After his chores on *Jurassic Park* and *Schindler's List*, Spielberg would drop by the set, his 'big toy' on the backlot, take a look at the intricate work in which Silberling was involved, and say, 'Wow, looks great! Glad you're doing it and not me!'

*Casper* wasn't a movie for critics, nor for naysayers like Michael Medved in the New York *Post*. '*Casper* doesn't stand the ghost of a chance of living up to its hype,' he predicted. 'It's a pale imitation of what entertainment ought to be.' Although I agreed with the latter half of his comment, there's no doubt that Silberling delivered at the box-office, aided and abetted by the $100 million in marketing support the movie received from the combination of Pizza Hut, Pepsi-Cola, Choice Hotels, the Thermos Company and Tiger Electronics. After an opening weekend of $22 million, *Casper* went on to top $100 million in the US, more than doubling that sum abroad.

As if to give the lie to Spielberg's much-vaunted support for 'authors' moral rights' and the sanctity of the written word – maybe that should be *rewritten* word – a staggering total of either thirty-two or thirty-five writers (it depends who's counting) laboured mightily to produce the enormous mouse that emerged as *The Flintstones*. 'What Universal did was create a mess and dump it in our laps,' declared a frustrated Writers' Guild spokesman, as he attempted to unravel who had written what and when.

*The Flintstones* went on to put all movie critics on their mettle, reaching for variations of Fred Flintstone's trademark expression. Hence 'Yabba-dabba-*dumb*' from Jay Carr in the Boston *Globe*, 'Yabba-dabba-*don't*' from Tom Crow in LA's *Village View* and 'Yabba-dabba-*doo-doo*' from Carrie Rickey in the Philadelphia *Enquirer*. The Los Angeles *Times* topped them all with its 'Yabba – *oh, let's just forget it!*'

'What makes *The Flintstones* grotesque,' wrote Frank Rich in the New York *Times* under the headline, THE PALEO-HUCKSTERS, 'is not that it's a lousy movie, but that it isn't a movie at all. It is instead a greedy marketing scheme, so naked in its contempt for the audience that the moviegoers at my Saturday night show experienced a deep funk.'

None of the criticism prevented the movie from taking $37 million at the box-office over the US Memorial Day weekend, then comfortably exceeding $100 million before conquering foreign shores.

With all those millions sloshing around, one would have thought that the powers-that-be would have been in a generous mood when it came to any question of settlements for infringements of rights. Not so. Sued for unauthorised use of the late Mel Blanc's voice, MCA apologised for their 'mistake'.

And offered $500 to his estate as compensation.

There was a welcome element of diversification evident in a couple of other Amblin projects. *How to make an American Quilt*, the Whitney Otto novel that had eight women weaving tales of their past, came first. Producers Midge Sanford and Sarah Pillsbury, keen to secure the rights, discovered that they had already been optioned by Amblin. They were handed the project to develop, and asked Spielberg to pay for a script when it became clear a major-studio pitch wasn't flying with the book alone. Unusually – for the normal process is only to commission a screenplay when a project has a home – Spielberg agreed. He also approved their choice of Jane Anderson for the job, as well as Jocelyn Moorhouse to direct, on the strength of *Proof*, the blind photographer drama she'd helmed back in her native Australia. Although it was no block-buster, *Quilt* turned out a sensitively made, well-received, affecting drama.

Amblin's second 'diversification', on the other hand, was an unmitigated disaster. *To Wong Foo, Thanks for Everything, Julie Nemar*, while employing the undoubted talents of director Beeban Kidron, best known for *Oranges Are Not the Only Fruit* on TV and *Used People* on the big screen, was a desperately unfunny drag queen epic that seemed to borrow freely from the Aussies' *Priscilla, Queen of the Desert*. They really shouldn't have bothered.

Mid-'94 saw the opening of Dive! the submarine-sandwich restaurant Spielberg and Disney's Jeff Katzenberg had dreamed up and developed in association with Levy Restaurants of Chicago. Well placed inside the Century City Shopping Center, close by the busy AMC multiplex, the 300-seater was a hit from the very first day. It could hardly be missed, not with a huge yellow sub docked outside, an equally giant olive and toothpick skewering its funnel.

In between guzzling the french fries and sandwiches (eighteen varieties, from cold cuts to Italian meatballs, brick oven-roasted steak, fajitas, Chinese chicken salad) kids thrilled as the portholed room darkened at regular intervals, sirens blared, red lights flashed, ('Prepare to dive!'), a 210-foot screen echoed the sentiment – D.I.V.E! – amidst a flurry of bubbles, a bell rang and a voice announced, 'We have reached periscope depth.' A boy's voice, filled with patented wonderment: 'What do you see, cap'n?' Answer (sung by Johnnie Nash): 'I Can See Clearly Now.'

On the way out, a selection of nautical-emblazoned Dive! merchandise lay in wait, everything for the aspiring sailor and his mate from T-shirts to caps and boxer shorts, including plugs for Spielberg's fast-sinking *seaQuest DSV* TV-series. Jules Verne, Captain Nemo, and *20,000 Leagues Under the Sea* certainly had a lot to answer for. More than they knew, for Dive! – soon expanded into Las Vegas and Barcelona in Spain, with New York's Times Square being eyed for the future – would prove only the first of Spielberg's and Katzenberg's business ventures together.

The second would be a real whopper.

During rehearsals in April 1994 for Arthur Miller's play, *Broken Glass*, Amy Irving – now happily domiciled with Brazilian movie director Bruno Barreto, their four-year-old child Gabriel, and Max, her son by Spielberg, on a shared custody basis – was ready to face the fact that she, rather than her ex-husband, had placed most, if not all of those career pressures on herself. She was also ready to talk about the life experiences that had enabled her to interpret the troubled character she was playing, a woman obsessed with the Holocaust. (Still competitive? You bet. No prizes for naming the project, mulled for over a decade, which Spielberg was preparing to shoot.) Her character's twin obsession with a tyrannical husband? It's possible to read too much into her acceptance of the role. Still and all – 'I have a lot to draw on,' she admitted, 'and not *just* the marriage fuck-ups. It's a lot of growing up and experiencing loss, whether it's through death, career disappointments, or marriage failures.'

She had spent considerable time exploring strong issues with her father before his death in 1979, with Spielberg, with her new partner Barreto – each relationship having involved, one way or another, 'a loss of identity': 'You start out being Jules Irving's daughter. And you finally break away from that to become Amy Irving. And then you become Steven Spielberg's girlfriend. During my marriage to Steven, I felt like a politician's wife. There were certain things expected of me that definitely weren't me. One of my problems is that I'm very honest and direct. You pay a price for that . . .'

Irving resorted to therapy after the breakup to resolve her feelings. 'I could have remained angry,' she says, 'but I know it takes two to break up a marriage.' She and Spielberg have today achieved the kind of edgy friendship reserved for couples who have been through the marriage mill and come out the other end bloody but unbowed, able to weigh up honestly the good with the bad, to accept that there were faults on both sides, willing to off-load the baggage of the past. And move on.

In October 1994, five years to the day that he and Jon Peters had taken over at Columbia, Peter Guber's resignation was announced. After a string of flops including *Radio Flyer, Wolf, Last Action Hero, Lost in Yonkers, Geronimo* and *I'll Do Anything*, it seemed long overdue. Although ousted three years earlier, Peters had remained on the lot until February 1994 before heading back whence he came – to Warners.

Guber too would initially remain, with a $20 million contract settlement, the biggest offices on the lot, and one of the most lucrative deals in Hollywood history for his brand-new Mandalay Entertainment, including a $275 million revolving fund to finance his cherry-picking of projects already in development at Columbia. What had he done to deserve this? Why, apart from the string of moneylosers, he'd splashed out a cool $100 million refurbishing Culver City, added to the fleet of corporate jets, and landed Sony with a massive $2.7 billion write-off on its investment, announced just one month after he ducked out, head held high.

All this madness has to be seen against a background of the utter turmoil that had prevailed at Columbia ever since the fateful Japanese takeover. Walter Yetnikoff, whose schmoozing, schmingling and bingling had been responsible for Guber and Peters' transfer from Warners, had been first to go in September 1990, his dreams of a move into pictures with his hand-picked team but a fond memory. Frank Price – *yes, Frank Price*, Spielberg's worst nightmare, ex-Universal-TV, ex-Columbia Pictures, ex-Universal Motion Pictures, soon to be ex-Savoy Entertainment – was appointed Motion Picture head at Columbia under Guber and Peters. The arrangement lasted exactly two years, when he was replaced with Mark Canton, one of Guber and Peters' pals from Warners. (Oddly enough, no great protest from Warners on this occasion. Wonder why?) Mike Medavoy, Spielberg's first agent, rescued from the ailing Orion, was in charge at TriStar for a few summers, then ousted.

Sony chief Akio Morita's stroke in December 1993 seems to have been the cue for his US deputy Mickey Schulhof to go wild in the country, installing sushi bars at Sony's New York HQ in Madison Avenue with tinkling streams running through them, and one of the city's top chefs handcarving equally pretty fishballs for his delectation and delight.

Through it all, joining Guber as Columbia president and CEO just two months after he began his reign, was Alan J. Levine, his ex-attorney at Guber/Peters Entertainment. Yet another tongue in the trough! All it needed to complete the picture was a hearty chorus of 'The Gang's All Here', and a high-kicking chorus line led by Heidi Fleiss to engulf the studio in a tidal wave of scandal. That too came soon enough.

With Guber and Peters gone, who did Schulhof have left to blame? Why, Levine and Canton of course. Enter Nobuyuki Idei as Sony's new president in April 1995. One look at those tinkling streams, the jet fleet, the deal Schulhof had awarded Guber, the millions upon millions irretrievably down the drain, and Schulhof was shown the door. Leaving Levine and Canton still running the circus, their ex-boss Guber hand-waving distance away on the road to Mandalay. Only in Hollywood!

Among all the head-shaking that took place, there were actually kind words for Spielberg. 'Say what you like about Steven,' one producer told me, 'but hey, the guy makes money not just for himself, but for other people too. And when you see the outrages perpetrated around here, can you blame him for wanting to grab every cent? Wouldn't you, rather than see it disappear down some corporate drain, or paid out to some asshole who's contributed zip to the bottom line? And he's creative, that nobody can deny. I mean, it's not like a bunch of old pals signing cheques to each other, you sign mine, I'll sign yours, that passes for corporate conduct in this town.'

After *Schindler's List* there lay ahead an unprecedented lay-off from directing for Spielberg. An adaptation he had considered of Robert Waller's best-seller, *The Bridges of Madison County* with Clint Eastwood and Meryl Streep, was left to Eastwood and Amblin.

For once Spielberg had something on his mind other than movies, the establishment of 'The Survivors of the Shoah Visual History Foundation', a non-profit organisation he intended to seed-finance, then look for major corporation funding. It would operate with the bare minimum full-time staff, with volunteers devoted to recording the testimony of Holocaust witnesses and their families. 'I cry every time I get involved in watching someone's story,' he confessed. 'But I don't turn away. If I do, what can I expect others to do?'

Through the foundation, his true 'sequel' to *Schindler's List*, 'more important than any movie', he wanted his friends, his children, and the whole world, to be aware of the terrible events that had taken place in Europe in the middle of the century. 'We must do a better job of teaching tolerance,' he declared. 'We need to know about the Holocaust. We need to know about segregation. It's not just history. Tolerance is an understanding of people and their experiences, a visceral understanding of their pain and a realisation that their pain is our pain.'

Two incidents during the filming of *Schindler's List* in Poland had bookended his interest in the need to collate and preserve Holocaust experiences and attitudes before the estimated 200,000–300,000 survivors, now in their seventies and eighties, passed on. The first sparked a realisation of the spiritual release such a record would provide.

'I just read Keneally's book,' one of the Polish extras had declared. 'Now it's *safe* to tell all of you I was one of Schindler's Jews.'

Then there was the dark side of the equation, the need to recognise and attempt to grapple with the hatred that still existed. A young German actor playing a small part in the movie, overwhelmed at the revelations of systematic extermination from which he'd been shielded, had asked his father if he'd played a part in the process. 'Yes, I did,' his father told him. 'I was a guard at three different concentration camps. I was responsible for the deaths of thousands of Jews.'

Utterly taken aback at the shocking suggestion of – what? Surely not *pride*? – in his father's voice, the son had asked, 'But – how do you feel about that now?'

Nothing could have prepared him for the chilling answer: '*I didn't kill enough of them.*'

Spielberg acknowledged that a rounded picture of the atrocities perpetrated by man against man would have eventually to include, among others, the treatment of Blacks from Africa and the virtual extermination of the North American Indians. He might have added the many millions slaughtered by Stalin, he could have brought the picture up to date with recent horrors perpetrated in Rwanda and the former Yugoslavia. Or would that be too all-encompassing and render the entire project futile? Instead of supporting what rapidly became known as 'Steven Spielberg's Shoah Foundation' – rightly so, if the New York *Daily News* columnist Liz Smith was correct in claiming that *all* Spielberg's profits from *Schindler's List* were being sunk in the project – wouldn't it be just as effective to arrange network airings on an annual basis of the harrowing *Chronicle* documentary on the opening-up by the allies of the German concentration camps? Beyond these unimaginable sights, what further testimony is needed?

Personally, I'd feel happier if the $60 million Spielberg has reportedly raised, to provide thousands upon thousands of hours of videotaped testimony, was putting food into the mouth of even one starving baby, or supplying medicine to even one deprived out-post. After all, his inter-denominational 'constituents' around the world have raised him to his present level. Aren't these same con-stituents entitled to equal consideration and benefit from the wealth and clout they've bestowed?

# 32

# The End of the Beginning

*'After all these years Jeffrey and I discovered we're better friends outside the business – because we're too competitive.'*

STEVEN SPIELBERG, pre-DreamWorks

*'Stay a dreamer and never go public.'*

STEVE ROSS: Advice to Steven Spielberg

### $$$ 'PLAYA VISTA, HERE WE COME!' $$$

The three of them had come a long way since that first statement of intent fourteen months earlier. Now, in December 1995, as they stood in a hazy drizzle over overlooking the muddy site where Hollywood's first new studio in fifty-five years would rise, a welter of emotions bubbled beneath the surface jocularity.

Left to Jeffrey Katzenberg and David Geffen, Spielberg's partners in 'DreamWorks SKG', the company would have operated indefinitely out of rented space at Universal. It was at Spielberg's insistence that the construction of a new studio, to exist separately from an animation facility already established in Glendale, had even been considered. Now here they were, allied with Maguire Thomas Partners and the Howard Hughes Corporation, the anchor tenant in the biggest land development in Los Angeles history, the largest commercial construction in the US in a decade, a 1,100-acre spread that would accommodate their centrepiece 100-acre studio in the new Playa Vista community of 13,000 apartments, schools, restaurants, libraries, commercial space and marina.

After a year of complex negotiations the $6 billion civic project had been granted $70 million in tax breaks from the City of Los

Angeles and State of California, their members determined that Spielberg and his partners would build from the ground up and forget about rival bids from Burbank and other interested out-of-State parties, especially the threat of a move to the East Coast. Other tenants already established included Silicon Graphics and IBM, both of whom had signed joint venture agreements with DreamWorks to help develop their 'digital' studio, ensuring the company the latest in cutting-edge technology.

As the three of them surveyed the site, hundreds of guests, including the Governor of California and the Los Angeles Mayor, awaited them at a reception being held in a giant wooden aircraft hangar below. There was a sense not only of history being made, but of it being *remade*, for this was where Howard Hughes had built his enormous Spruce Goose over half a century earlier. The hangar would house six of DreamWorks' soundstages, with an additional nine being built outside, together with backlot bungalows for producers, directors and actors, with offices encircling an eight-acre man-made lake.

It was Geffen who broke the silence, a teasing smile playing across his impish features. 'Who spent this money?' he asked.

'*We* did,' Katzenberg replied, shrugging. 'This is theatre, David. Remember, it's all theatre.'

Spielberg turned to face his colleagues. 'No,' he corrected. 'This is a romantic dream.'

'You made this happen, kid,' Geffen pointed out. 'This is your fault.'

'I won't apologise yet,' Spielberg replied. After looking around for another few moments, 'Yeah,' he added, the smile broadening, 'I like it!'

Many others in the Hollywood community, many highly placed others, *didn't* like it. Ever since the announcement of their alliance, the powerful individuals with whom the lives of Spielberg, Katzenberg and Geffen had interconnected over the years had been thrown into disarray. The result was a *danse macabre* in which the predominant refrain was a lusty version of 'Change Partners'. As at any tripping of the light fantastic, there had to be a wallflower. Barry Diller, ex-ABC, ex-Paramount, ex-Twentieth Century-Fox, now stuck in TV Home Shopping hell, amply filled the role on this occasion. The dancers, joining Spielberg, Katzenberg and Geffen, included Universal's Lew Wasserman and Sid Sheinberg, Disney's Michael Eisner and CAA's Michael Ovitz. And the unexpected arrival of a surprising new face on the floor, just as the 'Excuse Me' was beginning, would have a galvanising effect.

To start with, they hadn't even thought up a name for their new company. That was for later. First came the announcement in October 1994. Spielberg, Geffen and Katzenberg were joining forces to form a brand-new motion picture, animation, television and multi-media entertainment company. 'I want to start something great,' Spielberg declared at that first press conference. Over the years, he added, he'd had an almost religious fervour in *not* investing his money in showbusiness. That was then, this was now: 'Not in my wildest dreams would I have guessed that this trio would have come together. Now I can't think of a better place than this to invest in our own future.'

The idea had been first sparked – if you ignore the wake-up calls provided first by Sony's takeover of Columbia, then by Matsushita's absorption of MCA – during a phone call of commiseration from Spielberg soon after the news reached him, at Robert Zemeckis's holiday home in Jamaica, that Katzenberg had been bounced from Disney. A mere matter of hours earlier Michael Eisner had closed the door on any question of Katzenberg's assuming the No 2 position at the company vacant since the death of Frank Wells. Katzenberg was a shattered man. As Spielberg talked to his friend, Zemeckis caught the gist of the conversation. 'Why don't you guys do something together?' he shouted from the sidelines, loud enough so they both could hear.

'Jeff, let me quote you a line from *Back to the Future*,' said Spielberg. 'It's Christopher Lloyd's last line in the movie, "Where you're going you don't need roads."'

'What do you mean, "you"?' Katzenberg replied, his mind buzzing with the echo of Zemeckis's semi-serious, semi-joking suggestion. 'I'm talking "we".'

Katzenberg later acknowledged he had been teasing. Yet the idea lingered. And kept on lingering. Until it finally took shape. One week later Katzenberg met with Spielberg at his Pacific Palisades home. 'I'd love to be in partnership with my friend and partner from Dive!' he told him. 'What do you think about starting a brand-new studio from scratch?'

Spielberg took a deep breath. The nudge from Zemeckis, it seemed, had lingered with him too. Suddenly his situation had been crystallised. If one minute you were working for Lew Wasserman and Sid Sheinberg, the next for some Japanese company that made refrigerators, the world was up for grabs. 'The idea of working with you is thrilling,' he replied. 'But you left Disney because you were invited to leave. I have no reason to leave MCA. That would be very hard.'

Katzenberg's next step was to pull David Geffen into the charmed circle, the move designed to increase Spielberg's comfort level not only with the diversity of creative talent, but also the hard-nosed financial acumen he would bring to the party. 'Why do you need me?' was Geffen's first, perhaps disingenuous reaction. 'You guys cover all the bases.'

Even as Spielberg gave his answer – he didn't mind owning up to his awe of Geffen's wheeling and dealing ability, and who better to maestro-mind any record division the new company might consider? – Geffen's mind was racing back to his and Spielberg's days as Steve Ross's 'boys'. How they had vied with each other in the quest for Ross's approval! There had even been discussions back then of what they might do together on a single-project basis, and Geffen, in a fit of bonhomie, had introduced Spielberg to John Napier, his production designer from *Cats*. The result: one Hollywood minute later Napier had been hired to work on the *Indiana Jones* series. And Geffen, of course, had introduced his *Little Shop of Horrors* songwriters, Alan Menken and Howard Ashman, to Katzenberg. The result: award-winning Disney scores for *The Little Mermaid* and *Beauty and the Beast*. Now, he had to admit, it felt good lying back and having his ego stroked. Tell me more, Steven! Do it again, Jeff!

In their company, Spielberg grew increasingly confident. The wee small hours were the problem, for the more he thought about their plans, the more he had *time* to think about them, the more trepidation he felt. Life at Amblin was cosy. Life with Kate was cosy. The last thing he wanted or needed was something to disrupt his charmed life. Yet the idea of being part of the first new Hollywood studio in over half a century was overwhelming. Maybe, with the correct discipline, with the help of his partners, it was possible to reach for that golden goal without sacrificing what he had. Of all the people in the world who might influence his final decision, he knew that only two would have the ultimate power of veto. One was his wife. The other was Sid Sheinberg.

Kate Capshaw is many things – a beautiful woman, a capable actress, a great homemaker. Her expertise does not necessarily extend, however, to evaluating multi-million dollar business proposals. Nor was that the advice Spielberg either sought or received. 'I love Jeffrey,' she made clear. 'But I never want you to *become* Jeffrey. I don't want you to become involved in that lather of workaholism.' Just as long as Katzenberg could have her husband's services only from 8.30 am to 5.30 pm Monday through Friday, and he belonged to her and their five children the rest of the time – Max, Jessica and Sasha having been joined by Sawyer, a son born in '92, and Theo, their adopted black child – she gave her blessing.

Presented with those ground rules, Katzenberg declared that he understood and accepted them. For the moment, though, outside of the weekday slog, he accepts that 'Everything else is Kate's.' Kate's dictum had to be run past Geffen also. He showed less concern, shrugging it off with the equivalent of 'Whatever, Steven.'

Breaking the proposition to Sid Sheinberg was a nerve-wracking experience, even for the mighty Spielberg. This was the man, after all, who had nurtured him through those difficult early years when he could easily have foundered. He had strayed before, but had always found his way back to find a welcome mat waiting. Now it was time to sever the umbilical cord. 'Why do you *need* this?' Sheinberg asked. 'How does this *benefit* you?'

'It benefits me,' Spielberg replied, 'because the idea of building something from the ground up, where I could actually be a co-owner, where I don't rent, I don't lease, I don't option but actually own, *that* appeals to me.'

Inevitably Sheinberg's own position at MCA found its way into the conversation. He and Lew Wasserman, just back from a trip to Osaka, were deeply unhappy with the attitude of their lords and masters at Matsushita, and for the first time in decades Sheinberg was facing an uncertain future. Deal after deal had been stymied since Matsushita had tightened its grip on the corporate purse-strings. Like the acquisition of Virgin Records that would have transformed MCA into the world's largest recording organisation. Like the chunk of NBC that would have opened syndication and network doors.

Although Wasserman and Sheinberg strove to give the outside world the impression that throughout the new regime they had remained super-successful, in every way living up to Matsushita's expectations, their track record told a different story. Their idea of filming *Mr Baseball* with Tom Selleck in Japan contained eerie echoes of another major miscalculation in cosying up to new masters; Wasserman's fellow-octogenarian Ray Stark had chosen Atlanta, under the very noses of Coca-Cola, to film *The Slugger's Wife* almost a decade earlier. The result in both cases: deserted theatres. And a multitude of misfires had followed in amongst the few hits.

So many things, in fact, had changed since the takeover in 1990 – and not only faces, but attitudes. President Akio Tanii and his team had been swept away following a multimillion dollar recall of faulty Matsushita fridges. His successor, Yoichi Morishita, had nothing to prove, no allegiances, and had made his feelings clear from the day and hour of his appointment in the autumn of 1993.

The Osaka visit had been an attempt to persuade Morishita to allow MCA to join with ITT in a $5 billion bid to swallow the CBS network. Whether it was intentional or not, they had been kept waiting for hours in an outer office while the new man attempted to absorb their presentation. Back home, still seething, Sheinberg had fired off a letter of protest to Morishita's boss, Masaharu Matsushita. Even if they had no respect for him, how dare they humiliate the venerable Wasserman! So much for fabled Japanese politeness! A follow-up meeting was demanded with the very head of Matsushita's house. Spielberg's waxing lyrical about the joys of ownership provided Sheinberg an unfortunate reminder of his and Wasserman's predicament.

'Look, Sid,' said Spielberg, 'if you don't want me to do this, I won't. You don't even have to explain yourself. You can just say, "No." I'll call Jeffrey and David.'

Sheinberg may have experienced a whole gamut of feelings. About the partners with whom Spielberg had chosen to ally himself. About 'Jeffrey', until recently part of his nemesis, the dreaded Disney. About 'David,' whose leak had infuriated everyone concerned with the Matsushita negotiation. And hey, at no stage of their discussion had Spielberg even *hinted* that there might be a place at the table for Sheinberg. At fifty-nine, was he being regarded as a burnt-out case? Or, more realistically, did Spielberg simply have enough on his plate to bother with such trifles as his and Lew's hatching masterplan to reclaim MCA?

'I'm in no position to stop you from this amazing venture,' he told Spielberg, 'when I'm unsure what I want to do with my own life.'

The more he thought over his discussion with Spielberg, the more Sheinberg became convinced he'd been handed a trump card to play in the next round with Matsushita.


## $$$ THE SEARCH FOR MONEY $$$

Katzenberg in particular was cockahoop over his partnership with Spielberg and Geffen. Sure, he'd had offers from NBC and CBS immediately upon leaving Disney, but he wanted more than just another stint as an employee. Eisner, the man he'd faithfully served for over a decade, had stabbed him in the back *and* the front, and if it took him a lifetime, he would get even.

The next step for 'the Dream Team' was to figure out the financial angle. They would invest $100 million between them from their own resources, awarding themselves a *two*-thirds share in the venture. A further $900 million would be sought in equity financing, the participants to share the remaining *one*-third. With the granting of a $1 billion bank facility, their happiness would be complete.

There were those in the financial community who had the temerity to ask: Hold on just a second! What's wrong with this picture? *Two*-thirds for $100 mil, *one*-third for $900 mil?! The team's answer: Here's what you're getting, folks:

Spielberg: producer/director of six of the ten biggest movie hits of all time, including *Jaws* ($420 million worldwide), *E.T.* ($700 million) and *Jurassic Park*, at $900 million+ the current record-holder.

Katzenberg: the guy who helped steer Disney from a $1 billion total-revenue also-ran to a number-one studio winner with revenues of $8 billion from worldwide interests. The spark that ignited the revival of Disney's animated features from *The Little Mermaid* to *Aladdin* to *The Lion King* and *Pocahontas*.

Geffen: Eagles, Nirvana, Guns N' Roses, Cher on CD and vinyl; *Cats* on the boards; *Risky Business* to *Beetlejuice* and *Interview with the Vampire* on celluloid.

Dazzling, huh? Except, have we got this right? For Spielberg/Katzenberg/Geffen's ten per cent they get sixty-seven per cent of the profits? And 100 per cent of the voting control? And how are the three going to struggle along in the meantime? Well, each of them get a seven-year contract, plus expenses, plus perks, plus $1 million annual salary, plus a $2 million pool for personal loans, plus no flying together, plus security guards, all of it neatly wrapped up in a bright, shiny LCC package. LCC? 'Limited Liability Company', taxed like a partnership, with profit passing directly to the owners, on the owners' level – *but*, as with a corporation, an LCC protects its holders from personal liability in the event of litigation—!

So how much of Spielberg's attention, for example, could DreamWorks' lucky shareholders expect? According to his contract, he 'will endeavour to direct no fewer than three films for the company over the seven-year term. However, if he fails to so direct three films, he will have no contractual liability.' So maybe something, maybe nothing. Great deal! So were investors lining up with fistfuls of cash? 'It's like stacking hour over Kennedy airport,' Spielberg claimed.

Laying hands on his one-third of $100 million was no problem for Geffen. Positively awash with greenbacks from the sale in 1990 of Geffen Records to MCA, he was now acting 'Mr Cool' about his wealth with consummate professional ease. 'Steven and I have enormous amounts of money,' he conceded. 'You can't spend or even use most of it. It's just on some financial statement, and other people are playing with it. So I'm not in this because I need or want to make another billion. That would have no value. It's all in the doing, all in the journey.'

Whether or not he was bullshitting about 'the journey' – the statement has to be weighed against one assessment of Geffen as 'money-obsessed' – he was dead right about Spielberg and his money. Finding $33.3 million was no big deal for him, not with a net estimated worth of $600 million that would easily swell to over $1 billion if Amblin was ever cashed-out.

For Katzenberg, who had laboured in the shadow of Eisner's salary and record-setting bonuses, and whose payday had been relatively modest, it was one helluva stretch. One that involved mortgaging the ranch – or in his case two ranches, a brand-new beachhouse in Malibu and a home in Utah's Deer Valley.


## $$$ APPLYING PRESSURE $$$

Spielberg swore it on a stack of bibles. The timing of the troika's announcement of their intention to climb into bed together had nothing, *positively* nothing, nothing *whatsoever*, to do with the second trip Wasserman-san and Sheinberg-san were about to make to meet with their Japanese elders and betters. 'I'm really interested in natural childbirth and not an adoption,' Spielberg ambiguously declared from the sanctity of his Amblin base. 'I want to start my own company with David and Jeffrey and I want MCA involvement. But *how* they'll be involved I don't know.'

So the timing, a week before Lew and Sid once more took their show on the road, was just serendipitous? 'The news was going to get out anyway,' Spielberg claimed. Indeed, he had gone to Sid and Lew to apologise for any innuendo that might arise. Spielberg chose his next words with particular care: 'The timing of the announcement was not a power chip or any kind of lever to suggest that we have an interest in taking over MCA.'

Which didn't seem totally to exclude his complicity in any threat Sid and Lew might care to drop.

A chorus of 'Oh, What A Lousy Name' could be heard all the way from LA's Mulholland Drive to New York's Madison Avenue when the name of the new enterprise was finally announced. 'DreamWorks' followed by the trio's initials 'SKG' – was this really the best they could come up with? The extremity of the reaction could be seen as a foretaste of how their first venture might be received, if it turned out to be even fractionally less than stupendous. Spielberg's friend Tom Hanks understood the politics of envy that would colour the unveiling. 'Everybody is rooting for their failure,' he declared. 'I guarantee that when their first film opens, everyone will say, "This is it? This is what these three geniuses have come up with?"'

By the end of November 1994, the team had reached agreement to produce TV programming for Capital Cities' ABC network. The announcement set executives from rival NBC foaming at the mouth. It wasn't so much the loss of a potentially valuable supplier that crazed them, more resentment that Spielberg had bypassed them despite their imagined 'relationship'. Quite apart from their unprecedented support for *Amazing Stories* in the dim and distant, the network had recently paid $50 million for two airings each of *Jurassic Park* and *Schindler's List*. And they had stuck with Spielberg's waterlogged *seaQuest DSV* – the series inspired, like Dive!, by his boyhood daydreams of being Captain Nemo – despite the subtitle that was soon affixed, 'Voyage to the Bottom of the Ratings'. This was their reward? Analysts were as puzzled as NBC were angry. Why had the new company limited themselves by signing up with one network? Wouldn't it have been better to shop around for the best deal when the product flowed on stream?

One answer arrived in short order, with Capital Cities/ABC's announcement of an investment of $27 million in DreamWorks SKG, the same amount three other investors were ponying up – Chemical Bank, Microsoft and the Ziff brothers. On top of that, Microsoft founder Paul Allen was bringing $492 million to the table, receiving a twenty per cent equity stake in exchange for seeing no return on his money for six years.

Allen's deal was celebrated by Spielberg and Katzenberg taking their wives Kate and Marilyn to see *Bye, Bye, Love*, the movie set in a McDonalds restaurant, directed by their brand-new TV division signing, Gary David Goldberg, the man who gave the world *Family Ties* and the Jack Lemmon bummer, *Dad*. (Batty comment from Goldberg: 'Ultimately I believe the DreamWorks group, who have been friends, will love me in success and they'll love me in failure.'

Yeah, *right!*) Then it was on – no, not to McDonalds, silly – to Dive! Their meal may have gone down better than the movie, and presumably they didn't have to wait in line for a table.

The second answer lay in the real genesis of the Capital Cities' deal. When Katzenberg first cut loose from Disney, Capital Cities' president Robert Iger had been one of the first to headhunt. When Katzenberg allied himself with Spielberg and Geffen, Iger renewed the sport. Conveniently, he had just settled an old quarrel with Spielberg. The setting: a White House dinner for Boris Yeltsin at which they were seated together. The beef: Iger had withdrawn his support for a Civil War project Amblin's TV division had been cooking up. The problem: Ted Turner had beaten Spielberg to the small screen with the same theme. Iger's suggestion: 'That's in the past, Steven. Let's patch it up and move on. There's lots of other stuff we'll be doing together.'

Despite his earlier comparison with Kennedy's stacking hour, lining up other investors involved a tedious round of entertaining that left Spielberg bored and occasionally fractious. He doesn't even remember meeting with suits from Calpers, a pension-fund institution, although Katzenberg says he met them twice. (Having been stiffed by an earlier investment in Weintraub Entertainment, and after eyeing DreamWorks' less-than-overwhelming prospects for outside investors, Calpers backed out anyway.)

In February 1995, hoping to close a deal with Samsung's Lee Kun Hee over dinner at Pacific Palisades, Spielberg was obliged to ask his wife to drive to the nearest mall for extra table linen to accommodate the party of twelve that turned up. Luckily there was enough Chilean sea bass and white wine to go round, with the sober-sided Katzenberg, as usual, sticking to Diet Coke. 'The word "semiconductor" must have been used about twenty times during that two-and-a-half-hour encounter,' Spielberg recalled. 'I thought to myself, "How are these people going to know anything about the movie business when they're so obsessed with semiconductors?"'

Whether or not his annoyance communicated itself to Lee Kun Hee, the potential investment, variously put between $500–800 million, was never made. A consolation prize: Lee's thirty-six-year-old niece Miky invested instead, along with brother Jay, through their newly formed One World Media Corporation (an offshoot of Cheie Foods and Chemicals Inc., makers of Spam; the company itself spun off from Samsung) to the tune of $300 million. In exchange for a ten-year deal to distribute DreamWorks movies and videos in Asia (excluding Japan, Australia and New Zealand) she was handed 10.8 per cent of the equity. A senior Far Eastern analyst with Warburg Securities, Jonathan Dutton, estimating a $90 million interest charge on the $300 million by the year 2002, described the investment as 'bizarre', for although Cheie had $1.6 billion in assets, they were largely tied up in share-price disputes with disgruntled Samsung shareholders. A personal visit in November 1995 by Spielberg and Katzenberg to attend a pour organised by Lee (their second-largest investor after Paul Allen) in Seoul's Grand Hyatt ballroom, may have helped calm investor's nerves. Or not, as the case may be, for wasn't Miky Lee bidding fair to be the latest in a long line of Easterners eager to chase the chimera of Hollywood riches? Another sucker, following Sony, Matsushita, and the other, lesser lights like JVC, already taken, bedazzled then filleted, to the cleaners? Only time will tell. Meanwhile, Miky, keep selling that Spam!

An extra $750 million required for the team's contribution to Playa Vista's construction costs – unanticipated at the outset – was taken care of by advances from Home Box Office, and the sale of the remaining worldwide video and free-TV rights to DreamWorks' future movie slate. Terms for the HBO deal, which also took in Time-Warner's sister company Cinemax, were instructive. Although the payout *could* amount to as much as $1 billion over ten years, and revenues for any animated or Spielberg-directed movies would command a premium higher than the rest, the cash paid, in the *final* analysis, would be related to the box-office performances of the movies. At last, some common sense.

311

# 33

# The End of the Beginning – II

*'Did you ever see* Dumbo*? If you remember, Timothy
Mouse gives Dumbo a magic feather, and he can only fly if
he has the feather. In the end, he loses the feather and has
to fly without it. He flies just fine. Well, Jeffrey
(Katzenberg) was the feather.'*

Roy Disney

*'I've always said that Michael built Hollywood Records
and Euro Disney and that Jeffrey's responsible for
everything else.'*

David Geffen

## $$$ THE SOUP THICKENS $$$

The bottom line amidst all the hoopla remained in DreamWorks'
ambitious plans. This was to be no slow roll-out. On the movie side
they planned three features in 1996, a further five in '97, going up
to seven in '98, a total of nine in '99 and beyond, with a revolving
$800 million set aside for their production. The 'Amblin' logo
would remain, but only until all commitments under the banner
were honoured – like sequels for Universal to *Jurassic Park*, *Casper*
and *The Flintstones*, together with other items to be cleared off the
shelf like *Zorro*, with the Roberto Rodriguez/Antonio Banderas
team, and *Men In Black*, starring Tommy Lee Jones and Will Smith,
to be directed by Barry (*Get Shorty*) Sonnenfield. At the same time
as taking care of those hot little items, the new Amblin husband-
and-wife team of Walter Parkes and Laurie MacDonald would
oversee the live-action DreamWorks slate under Spielberg.

Katzenberg was to take charge of animated features, the first of
which, *The Prince of Egypt*, was due by Christmas '98, with one a
year scheduled thereafter on a revolving $200 million fund. He
would also be in charge of TV development and programming.

What looked like his exclusion from DreamWorks' live-action domain was a surprise. How would Katzenberg, known for his almost pathological inability to keep his fingers out of every known pie, hold back from two dozen live-action features, probably the very items that would decide the success or failure of the entire venture? Answer: Before you could say 'hyperkinetic', Katzenberg was immersing himself not only in DreamWorks' movies, but Amblin's as well.

With only months to go before he was free of his contractual obligations to MCA's Geffen Records, Geffen would start up DreamWorks' record label. His first scoop: snagging a bunch of disgruntled ex-Warner executive stalwarts in Mo Ostin, Lenny Waronker and Michael Ostin. His second: securing US rights to George Michael's next two albums, in exchange for a hefty reported $90 million pay-off to Sony, and $55 million advance guarantee to Michael, both items co-funded by Virgin Records in exchange for non-US rights. The only question begged: After a five-year lay-off – a lifetime in pop music terms, resulting from his ultimately failed lawsuit against Sony – how hot was Michael? And Sony was still entitled to issue a 'Greatest Hits' collection, as well as sharing in revenues from the two Geffen/Virgin albums. It depends, I guess, on how you define 'scoop'. Some would call it buying sales, and at one helluva cost – with more money sunk into this one deal than the partners coughed up for the entire DreamWorks shebang.

Geffen's third scoop was longer in coming, but no less potentially significant: beating out stiff competition, he landed album rights, reportedly for close on $1 million, to Broadway's newest smash, *Rent*.

The fact that Geffen would continue his own programme of movies for DreamWorks provoked decidedly mixed reaction from the financial community. Sure, he's had winners, all the way from *Risky Business* to *Interview with the Vampire*, just like the hand-out claimed. He'd also had expensive bummers, from *Personal Best* and *Lost in America* to *Defending Your Life*, the dismal *Last Boy Scout*, and the disastrous *M. Butterfly*.

Lest anyone think that Spielberg had recovered from his initial stage fright and was proceeding with these grand schemes like some super-confident colossus, think again. 'After our first planning session at DreamWorks,' he revealed, 'I thought about how much easier it would be to start with a single film, make it, see how it does, and if it does well, make a second picture. That's the contradictory, play-it-safe side that haunts me before I fall asleep at night.'

313

Many were astonished at the apparently callous way in which Disney supremo Michael Eisner had treated his deputy, Katzenberg. Those with long memories recalled that Frank Wells had first been offered the top post by Roy Disney back in 1984. David Geffen's advice had been particularly cogent on that occasion: 'Michael will never work for you, Frank. It'll never happen. You're gonna have to be the number two guy.' Wells had accepted the advice and unswervingly served under Eisner for a decade.

Following Wells's untimely death in a helicopter crash in April 1994, a head count of the denizens of Buena Vista Boulevard would have produced a landslide for Katzenberg's chances of moving on up to fill the vacancy. And a greater landslide still after Eisner's emergency quadruple heart-bypass surgery three months later.

The lanky, open-faced Eisner – unkindly dubbed 'Mr Potato Head' by many Disneyites – darkly maintained that he had excellent reasons for not promoting Katzenberg, alluding both to 'logical' and 'intuitional' arguments. And he knew he could rely on support from the section of the company where it counted most, for Roy Disney had been disgruntled for years over the credit Katzenberg had grabbed for the success of the studio's animated programme. 'It was a hard decision,' Eisner stoutly maintained, 'and I didn't make it in one day and I didn't make it lying in the hospital. Jeffrey wanted to be completely in the spotlight, and he was no longer in the team unless he was the captain. I believe we had enough information over and over again that he should not have the job.' The death of Wells had left 'an impossible void', and the more Katzenberg had touted himself as his natural replacement, the less Eisner had liked it.

Just to add insult to injury, he had already composed a press release announcing Katzenberg's departure – 'with heartfelt thanks and obvious regret' – *before* telling the man himself. And just ahead of their meeting, he'd called Joe 'I love sports movies' Roth, ex-Twentieth Century-Fox, and offered him Katzenberg's job.

Ever the amateur psychiatrist, known for urging Katzenberg at one point during a Disney mid-life crisis to seek help, Geffen had this to say about his colleague's ex-boss: 'Michael Eisner is a liar. And anybody who had dealt with him, really dealt with him, *genuinely* dealt with him, knows he is a liar. There's something very, very damaged in his background.' So no love lost there.

Geffen claimed that he was the guy who had at first advised his friend to stick it out and stay at Disney. He was the guy who'd been astonished when Katzenberg, fearful it would restrict his promotion chances, had refused to join the Disney board and sign a contract that would have yielded him an extra $100 million. (It would also have forced him to declare his earnings, the very thought of which was anathema to Katzenberg. It wouldn't have looked good to all the talent he'd screwed down to the last dollar. As Alec Baldwin said of him after his experience on *The Marrying Man*: 'He's the eighth dwarf – Greedy.') He was the guy who'd assured his friend that Eisner would never dare let him go. Now Geffen was enraged at rumours that one reason straightarrow Katzenberg had been fired was because of his friendliness with the gay community both inside and – for Geffen, most pointedly – outside the studio. (After years of proclaiming his bisexuality, Geffen had finally come out of the closet completely at a 1992 AIDS benefit. 'When they want to say the worst about you,' he fumed, 'they call you a fag.')

Geffen and Eisner had not always been at loggerheads. Far from it. They had first got to know each other in the mid-seventies, when Eisner was at ABC and Geffen, pre-firing and pre-cancer scare, as VP at Warner Bros, had offered him the job of heading Warners' TV division. When Eisner's ex-boss Barry Diller heard about the offer, he'd grabbed him for Paramount instead. Rebuff One. If Geffen was miffed, he soon had other, more pressing medical matters on his mind.

Fast forward to 1984. When Diller departed to Rupert Murdoch and Fox, and Paramount chairman Martin Davis denied Eisner Diller's chairmanship, Geffen had come forward once more: let's the two of us set up a company and go 50–50. Instead, Eisner had gone to Disney, where Geffen's advice to Frank Wells, already recruited by Roy Disney, landed him the top job. Rebuff Two.

Fast forward again to 1989. Aware that Eisner had earlier backed off from acquiring CBS Records – a move he'd had cause to regret, with its purchase price of $2 billion now worth an estimated $10 billion – Geffen offered Disney his record label for $400 million. After protracted negotiations, Eisner chose to start up in-house Hollywood Records instead. Three rebuffs, you're out? Well, getting there, at least. 'Michael would say X one day and the next day he didn't say X,' is how Geffen characterised their talks. 'I could have lived with him saying he'd changed his mind. But I cannot live with him saying, "I never said that."' Geffen's conclusion: 'Eisner couldn't stand the idea of having me in the company.'

His subsequent MCA windfall apart, there was considerable satisfaction, not to say undisguised glee, to be gained from the disastrous missteps Eisner made in setting up Hollywood Records, starting with the pay-out of $12 million to pop group Queen, while lead singer Freddie Mercury lay dying of AIDS. Although Eisner would dismiss the entire record-label misfire as costing only $10 million, a multiple of eight times that was considered more appropriate.

That Katzenberg had advised against the venture tightened his ties with Geffen, already someone he regarded as 'his older brother'. Their relationship had begun when Geffen, returning with Barry Diller in the late seventies from a cruise on Sam Spiegel's yacht, had first observed Diller's gofer animatedly and expertly hustling and bustling their goods through customs, dancing rings round the bemused officials. 'Who the hell is that guy?' he had asked.

Over the years they'd had their fall-outs, most notably when Katzenberg tried to coax Geffen's *Risky Business* scripter Paul Brickman into a move to Disney. 'Jeffrey, you'd better decide whether winning at all costs is worth my friendship,' Geffen had told him, 'because you cannot be my friend and try to fuck me.'

'You're absolutely right,' Katzenberg had replied, shamefaced. 'I will never do it again.' He hadn't, and the friendship grew. Geffen provided a shoulder to cry on when it was needed, in between Katzenberg's almost non-stop workaholism. When his wife Marilyn had twins, the joke amongst Katzenberg's colleagues was that it was a smart move to save time.

Saving, in fact, had swiftly become a religion at Disney, a fact that had rebounded on the company when economy and good housekeeping had crossed over to downright mean-mindedness. And not just in squeezing cutthroat deals upfront. Item: the veteran singer Peggy Lee, having written a half-dozen songs and voiced four characters in Disney's animated *Lady and the Tramp*, was obliged to sue the company, turning up every day at the courthouse in a wheelchair, to gain an award of $2.3 million, her share of the $32 million net profit windfall the company earned from the movie's release on video. Item: after providing Disney with the voice of *Aladdin* for peanuts, Robin Williams felt he was entitled to a share of the loot from the bonanza the movie went on to make. Told no dice, he vowed never to work at the studio again. Item: early in 1994 Geffen had called Frank Wells, upset about what he saw as Eisner's latest affront to humanity. An AIDS benefit had been organised honouring Katzenberg, and with their corporate enemies Wasserman and Sheinberg giving $100,000 to the cause, Eisner had proposed just $25,000 spread over a four-year period. Wells described himself as 'ashamed' and promised to do his best to sway Eisner. The direct result: an outright $100,000. The indirect result: another fraying in the relationship between the growing Katzenberg/Geffen alliance and Eisner.

Geffen was not the only one to single out Eisner as

DreamWorks' potential *bête noire*. Even before the company had taken shape, Spielberg had darkly predicted, 'Jeffrey's exit will be Eisner's Machiavellian loss.' Cool to frosty.

Spielberg and Geffen were surrounded by others who felt the same way. The way Sid Sheinberg told it, Eisner suffered from a 'failure of character'. And Mickey Mouse was 'a ravenous rat' after Disney had threatened to open a theme park in Florida, prompting the allegation that the company had stolen the idea from a plan MCA put to potential partner Paramount, back when Eisner was in situ.

Barry Diller had been at war for years with his former protégé, daggers having been drawn after a below-the-belt petition from Disney, under Eisner, questioning the 'fitness' of the Fox network, under Diller, to provide children's afternoon programming. Describing the studio as 'the Evil Empire', Diller – repeating Spielberg's high-horse with Frank Price – refused even to enter the same room as Eisner. Only the prospect of enlisting Disney's muscle to help in a concerted bid for CBS had produced a convenient thaw by mid-1995. Well, sort of. Diller, Take One: 'Michael looks like Goofy, and he often acts like Goofy, and he's definitely in the body of Goofy, but he's one of the most smartly spirited minds that I've ever come across.' Diller, Take Two: 'Michael is competent, but he's also paranoid. Eighty-five per cent of his toughness is for good reasons; fifteen per cent is over the line. There is an excessiveness that has always bothered me. Disney makes deals that are too tough, and when a deal is too tough it never works out in the end.'

Eisner himself had been no slouch at the well-aimed slights. Aware of the relationship that had existed over the years between Spielberg and Katzenberg, consolidated in business terms with the emergence of Dive!, he referred to the venture, with thinly disguised contempt, as 'Jeffrey's deli'.

Eisner declined to chair a fund-raiser for the Simon Wiesenthal Center and Museum of Tolerance when he learned that Katzenberg and Spielberg would be gracing it with their presence. 'I just thought I would stay away from that group,' he declared. Then, as an afterthought: 'I'm sure I gave money.'

If he did, it was more than he was inclined to grant Katzenberg, who threatened to sue after his dismissal, claiming he was owed millions from profit points in Disney's animated features. 'Prove it,' came the invitation from the Magic Kingdom. Hints were dropped by Katzenberg of a smoking gun in the form of a deal memo from the late Wells. Geffen, meanwhile, stoked the flames from the sidelines. 'To not pay him is shameful,' he declared on one occasion. On another: 'I'm not afraid of Eisner. That's why he's so angry with me.

I am the only one in this town willing to say the truth.'

Disney was riding high on several fronts, on Broadway with the sell-out *Beauty and the Beast*, in the movies with the biggest film of the year, *The Lion King*, and on TV with the number-one show, *Home Improvement*. Those who disputed Katzenberg's contribution to the revival of the studio's animated features were pointed in the direction of Roy Disney' s last solo outing, *The Black Cauldron*, an animated bomb. Fortunes can change, of course, and for every hit there is a miss. If Katzenberg had been the driving force behind Disney's acquisition of the cutting-edge independent Miramax, he was also responsible for signing Merchant/Ivory's first-look deal and greenlighting their worst movie in years, *Jefferson In Paris*. And among the legacy he left behind, *Quiz Show* and *Ed Wood*, despite ecstatic reviews, would lose fortunes. Maybe, after all, it was a good time for the 'Golden Retriever' to move to another kennel.


## $$$ OMIT OVITZ! $$$

The team had been aware from the beginning that Mike Ovitz would be miffed, to put it mildly, at being kept 'out of the loop' on such an important deal as the formation of DreamWorks. All three had their reasons for the exclusion.

Never a great friend of the CAA chief, all the way back to the brouhaha in the early eighties over *Personal Best*, through to Ovitz's accusation that he had prematurely leaked the news of Matsushita's MCA takeover for his own rotten gain, Geffen took a positively mischievous delight in including Ovitz out.

As for Katzenberg, at Disney he had been the antithesis of the free-spending Hollywood studio boss with whom Ovitz had enjoyed making his rich deals. 'This time you've stepped over the line,' he'd raged, following Ovitz's attempt to renegotiate Dustin Hoffman's *Billy Bathgate* salary at the eleventh hour. Ovitz had been infuriated over Katzenberg's reference to his client Bill Murray in another outburst: 'Actors used to make a living,' he'd declared, 'they got a paycheque each week. Now they strike a fortune.' They had fallen out again over the bonuses withheld from Robin Williams for voice-overs rendered on *Aladdin*. Ovitz was known to be acting for Jim Henson's heirs when their attorney accused Disney of attempting 'the outright theft of Henson's legacy' .

Spielberg? From the first, when he had finally given in to years of Ovitz's blandishments and joined CAA in 1990, the arrangement had been a compromise that reflected both men's view of their power and partially answered the question – why did Spielberg, at this stage of the game, with access to whatever and whoever he wished, need an agent at all? Spielberg's answer: sure, if Ovitz came up with a real juicy, irresistible project that caught his imagination, CAA would get its usual ten per cent. Otherwise, on projects Spielberg initiated himself, the fee would be negotiable.

Kate Capshaw neatly characterised her husband's exclusion of the CAA supremo from his DreamWorks plan: 'It was like going to the sandbox with your buddy, and suddenly a new person comes in to play with them. In business or politics or general affairs you can usually reduce things to simple human relationships: envy, jealousy, feeling excluded. It's like Mike was saying, "Why are you playing with so-and-so instead of me? I thought you were my best friend!"'

## $$$ THE LEW AND SID FOLLIES $$$

The duo's second meeting with Matsushita, moved at the last minute from Hawaii to San Francisco when word reached the press gallery, proved a total bust. Wasserman and Sheinberg presented two propositions.

First, their ideal: sell us our goddam company back. (Although Spielberg had held back from any question of commitment, the two men still hoped that once the DreamWorks team saw what was on the table, they would ante up some of the necessary cash to facilitate a buyout of MCA.)

Second, and not so ideal, but we could live with it: play along and loosen the pursestrings, give us back control.

The alternative: say 'no' to both and we'll walk in December 1995 when our contracts expire. And take Spielberg with us, and with him the chance of participation in any aspect of DreamWorks. No, better than 'chance'. The near-certainty. No, better than 'near'. The *certainty*.

The Japanese team stonewalled the pair. Worse, they went on the offensive. Why should they increase MCA's cash flow? Why wasn't the company self-supporting, as they had been promised? Even with the mighty grosses from *Jurassic Park*, their investment in MCA still represented a major disappointment. And what about the currently-in-production *Waterworld*? At $125 million and climbing, it would need to approach *Jurassic*-style business just to make its money back.

As for selling the company back to Wasserman and Sheinberg, ominous looks were exchanged before the stern Japanese equivalent of 'Strictly no comment' was trotted out. If his predecessor had been held back from inner-sanctum expressions of dismay, even disdain, at the cocky, thumb-snooking Sheinberg, Morishita was labouring under no such restrictions. All a perplexed Sheinberg would say after the encounter was, 'I'm not sure if it was a good or bad meeting. Do I know that anything will be accomplished? No.' A further meeting was scheduled for January 1995. Per one Japanese columnist, 'The Hollywood pair didn't seem to realise that their proposals were regarded as nothing short of treachery.'

Matsushita's disillusionment with the movie business in general, and MCA in particular, was complete. It was true the company had been spared the brutal $2.7 billion write-off Sony had suffered at Columbia. But for how long? Several of their board felt that the *Waterworld* débâcle had been deliberately hatched; if not, it certainly suited Wasserman and Sheinberg in many ways. Whether *Waterworld* was *truly* out of control, or whether it was Wasserman and Sheinberg who were out of *their* control, the situation was intolerable. Offloading MCA was a top priority. And there was no question this side of sainted cherry blossom of settling it on those individuals who had brought about this sorry loss-of-face.

The third meeting, back in Osaka this time, went even worse. This time Wasserman and Sheinberg had gone on the record in advance: if nothing was settled, they would definitely ankle MCA. 'I am out of the business of talking with those guys,' Sheinberg had raged. 'I am dropping a black cloth on the subject. Do you know what the word *ausgespielt* means? I am tired!'

This time their threat of a walk-out was met by a bout of polite coughing, followed by Matsushita's chairman's cool-as-a-cucumber announcement that Michael Ovitz, their original broker, was due in Japan within a matter of days and would help the company quantify the pair's worth. This was too much for Wasserman, who rose to his feet in high dudgeon, the lenses on his horn-rimmed glasses thoroughly steamed. 'I've been in this business for sixty years,' he spat out, 'and I'm not going to have my performance evaluated by Michael Ovitz.'

Although it was a great exit line, he and Sheinberg may have felt as they trundled out that this time they had really burned their bridges behind them. What had happened was outrageous! Why, they had been taken at their *word*! Didn't these guys know from *anything*?

# 34

## New Fields to Conquer

*'These people have married each other and I wish them the best. I share the view of the world that they'll have great children. I also know that the reality is that 50 per cent of all marriages in America end in divorce. So we'll have to wait and see.'*

SID SHEINBERG on DreamWorks' formation

*'Steven Spielberg is selfish, self-centred, egomaniacal, and most of all – greedy.'*

DAVID GEFFEN, quoted by Julia Phillips

### $$$ OVITZ OVULATES $$$

Beginning with his ill-fated brokering of Sony and Matsushita's entry into the Hollywood studio system, the tag 'most powerful man in Hollywood' had draped itself around Ovitz's neck like an albatross. 'Power is really a misleading word,' he now demurred. 'It creates a resentment that shouldn't be there. It totally gets in the way. I don't think I'm any more or less powerful than a dozen people in this town.' Such new-found modesty was very becoming, but note the less-than-humble 'or less'!

Yep, Ovitz may have collected $40 million for arranging Matsushita's takeover of MCA for $7.5 billion, but had it been worth the opprobrium? And although it wasn't true, many saw him as the architect of Sony's disastrous hiring of the Peter Guber/Jon Peters team that had led to Warners claiming Columbia's half of the Burbank Studio and banishing Sony new-found pride and joy to the outer reaches of Culver City. Being hired by Credit Lyonnais to shepherd the long-troubled MGM back to some semblance of its former glory – the better to sell it off to the highest bidder – had brought forth a storm of protest about conflicts of interest, and not only from rival agency ICM's Jeff

Berg. Then there was CAA's hi-jacking of the Coca-Cola advertising account, not to mention the deal to help Bell Atlantic, Nynex and the Pacific Telesis Group develop video programmes to be broadcast over phone lines. Hey, wasn't this guy getting just far too big for his boots? If MCA had once been called the 'Star-Spangled Octopus', wasn't Ovitz bidding fair for the title of 'Beverly Hills Hydra'? Enough was enough already.

At a conference in New York partly organised by the showbiz rag *Variety* to discuss the shifting economics of the movie industry and the leverage agents had acquired, Ovitz gallingly found himself singled out by Katzenberg as the major contributor to the high cost of moviemaking. The shouting match that followed was dubbed 'The Clash of the Titans' by amused Hollywood observers. And this was only the overture, as other industry heavyweights weighed in – notably veteran producer Ray Stark, closely followed by Geffen. The two of them had opened up their hearts, it seemed, to LA *Times* reporter Alan Citron, confounding those who would have sworn that neither possessed such an organ, and providing the harmony to Katzenberg's main refrain.

Clearly nursing deep-seated resentment at being no longer considered a major player, octogenarian Stark – having, in truth, helped create the monster Ovitz had become – now barked, 'It's no longer agents. It's *secret* agents!' Per Geffen, 'Making movies has gone from being a business where everyone could make money to a business where it's likely that the only profit is in agents' commissions.'

The riposte that Ovitz made was widely seen as a blast at pointsman Katzenberg, rather than the relatively behind-the-scenes Eisner. 'Disney wants everyone to adapt to their religion,' came the blast from CAA's increasingly embattled tower.

Coming from Ovitz, the ultimate 'My way or no way' man, this was rich. It was also new, for Ovitz had himself made a religion of never responding to the slings and arrows. A shift was going on. For Ovitz it was never going to be business as usual. He had to make a move. The problem was *where*?

'If there's anything that Michael Ovitz wants to do, he can do it. *Anything*.' Thus spake Ovitz fanatic Jeffrey Logsdon, an entertainment industry analyst with the Seidel Companies. No limitations? 'If he wants to produce a movie, if he wants to *act* in a movie, *anything*,' Logsdon elaborated. Of course! Can't you just see them lining up for Mikey Ovitz in *Brother, Can you Spare a Percentage?*, the heartrending tale of a millionaire in mid-life crisis. At everyone's blasted beck and call! All these 2 am calls, collect already, from Sean Connery! His minimalist-gorgeous Wilshire Boulevard digs ridiculed as the CAA gun-fucking-turret! Limited to a percentage

322

of his goddam clients' earnings! Based on a true story! 'Our fingers are all thumbs!' chorus Siskel and Eberts. 'A heartwarming family picture!' smarms Michael Medved. Now playing in a mall near you! I don't *think* so.

Not that he would ever *really* contemplate a move to running a studio, according to Logsdon. The way he had it figured: 'Right now, he's getting a piece of *everybody's* action. The profit margin on theatrical films is 4.5 per cent on a high capital-investment base. For Michael, it's zero capital-investment base and he gets ten per cent or fifteen per cent!' Ergo: 'It's smarter to be in his business than the movie business!'

Logsdon's argument was a persuasive one – unless one knew how Ovitz's mind works. No matter how successful he had made CAA, he would always be regarded, among the high-falutin deals with the Coca-Colas and Nynexes of the world, as just another flesh-peddlin' agent. And yes, goddamit, Sean Connery *did* wake him up at 2 am with collect calls from the Brazilian jungle, he *was* bored out of his skull with the once-fashionable austerity of his HQ, and his percentage of performer's earnings was becoming increasingly negotiable. As in downwards. Look at the Spielberg fire sale! More and more the role of superagent was becoming down-right *undignified*!

When Matsushita had last spoken to financier Herbert Allen, he had passed on a personal message from Spielberg to Matsushita: if Wasserman and Sheinberg were retained, they would be in the running for a piece of the DreamWorks action. Not only that, but Spielberg and his partners were prepared to fly out to Osaka to offer confirmation in person. Matsushita's response to Allen had been crisp: outline all our disposal options, and don't tell Wasserman and Sheinberg what we're up to. Come to that, don't tell Ovitz either, because he represents Spielberg and he might spill the beans. Allen had assured them that Ovitz wouldn't breathe a word. The code of the Bushido, or some such nonsense. And Ovitz was the man to talk to round their boardroom table.

One thing Ovitz knew for sure at the end of that first round of discussions with Matsushita. There was no way he could remain allies with everyone – not the Spielberg/Katzenberg/Geffen triplets, not the Wasserman and Sheinberg twins, perhaps not even Matsushita, much as he prided himself on having mastered their games of corporate kabuki. The question was which relationships to retain and which to discard, always bearing in mind the other participants, past, present and potential in the game of Hollywood catch-as-catch-can. One new player in particular would be touted during the presentation he intended to make in

323

Osaka that would make eyes pop when the time came.

Meantime, he had Wasserman and Sheinberg, Spielberg too, to face down at Sheinberg's sixtieth birthday bash. He had all his answers ready. Would they have expected him to turn Matsushita's invitation down? Of course not. What had he told them? Why, that they'd be crazy not to appease the best team in the business. And if Sid and Lew were indeed leaving, why should Matsushita be denied his sky-high, glowing evaluation of their worth? Had there been talk of a sale to a third party? Not to him.

And while offering Spielberg his heartiest congratulations on the formation of DreamWorks, he suggested that they all behave like grown-ups instead of children – no matter how impossible a demand that would make on petulant little David in particular – and let bygones be bygones. Life was too short. All that jazz.

Ovitz completely wrongfooted Spielberg, Katzenberg and Geffen, as well as a Hollywood community used to absorbing seismic shifts above and below ground. In particular, he wrongfooted Spielberg, who clearly underestimated the depth of Ovitz's disenchantment with the whims of superstar clients.

'There were strained feelings between Ovitz and the three of us that have recently been resolved,' Spielberg claimed soon after the party. 'It was important I resolve it, because I needed to determine if Michael was going to continue to represent me as a director. I resolved my feelings towards Michael, and I think he resolved his feelings about not being part of the DreamWorks inception.' Even while Spielberg was signalling that Ovitz and the DreamWorks team had kissed and made up, that their little spat was a dead issue, that all was sweetness and light, that sheep may safely graze once more, the CAA chief was moving right along with his own agenda. Spielberg and his Merrie Men had purposely excluded him from their little party. Spielberg still regarded him as a mere agent – OK, make that superagent. He'd show *them*!

## $$$ NEW KID ON THE BLOCK $$$

When producer Ron Kass offered to despatch Alan Parker's first script, *Melody*, to a potential investor in Seagram's Edgar Bronfman, neither Parker nor his colleague David Puttnam held out any great hopes. It was the end of the Swinging Sixties after all, and Hollywood's disenchantment with the decidedly non-swinging English scene was all but complete. Had the decision been left to Bronfman, their pessimism would have been fully justified. Although it was true that the drinks magnate, having just divested himself of a large chunk of MGM he'd held for two years, was looking to make a modest investment in movies on a per-project basis, *Melody* was not his idea of a good time. If the script hadn't fallen into the hands of his fifteen-year-old son, Parker and Puttnam would have been obliged to move on the next piggy-bank. As it was, Bronfman listened to his offspring and agreed to put up two-thirds of the movie's $1 million budget.

After flopping all over the world, the movie was released in Japan and scored a major hit. Then it turned out that the negotiator of the Japanese contract had awarded Bronfman, Parker, Puttnam, et al., a percentage of the *gross*, rather than the *net* they had expected. *Melody* was in the black, home free. If he hadn't been before, Edgar Bronfman Jr was the apple of his dad's eye. The experience began a lifelong fascination with the movie business that included acting as a gofer on a couple of Puttnam projects. Then he moved to Los Angeles, hellbent on carving out a career in movies, and determined, whatever happened, to defy his dad and stay out of the liquor business.

For the next ten years the tall, handsome Bronfman succeeded royally – in defying his dad, that is. And little else, unless you count the useful contacts he made for the future that speak more of Hollywood's propensity for sniffing out potentially rich pickings than any great faith in the young man's capabilities. Among those cosying up were Mike Ovitz and Barry Diller, two men who wouldn't have given a disenfranchised Bronfman the time of day; Diller in particular was regarded as a mentor. Bronfman's estrangement from his father deepened when he insisted on marrying Sherry Brewer, an African-American actress, in 1979. What brought father and son together again, oddly enough, was a flop movie the young man produced in 1982, Tony Richardson's *The Border*, starring Jack Nicholson and Harvey Keitel; Bronfman's biggest problem had been coaxing superstar Jack Nicholson out of bed and down to the studio on time.

Suddenly it was reconciliation time back at the Seagram ranch, with the heir-apparent agreeing to work himself up in the company just like anyone else. How about if he started as assistant to the office of the president? Hey, you can't get much lower than that! A few months later he was off to Europe to take care of the international end of the business. Back in the US by 1984, bingo, the lad assumed the presidency of the House of Seagram. In 1991, with one son and two daughters, the marriage to Brewer was dissolved; three years later he married Clarissa Alcock, the daughter of a Venezuelan oil executive.

By 1993 Seagram's was prospering. Not only under Bronfman's

firm hand, but mainly to do with a twenty-five per cent stake his father had taken in the DuPont Corporation back when *The Border* was emptying cinemas across the country. Now his son felt he was ready to make a similar diversification. What better field, given his lifelong passion, than movies? In February he put his toe in the water, acquiring 4.9 per cent of Time-Warner stock – one more fraction of a percentage point and he would have been obliged publicly to declare Seagram's stake, upping the price for subsequent purchases. Uncomfortably aware that Bronfman's 'toe-testing' had made Seagram's their largest shareholder, Time-Warner's board, fearing a hostile takeover, adopted a 'poison pill' defence that kicked in when outside ownership reached fifteen per cent. Bronfman's response was to build up Seagram's holding by a further ten points to 14.9 per cent.

News travels fast, especially when the messenger is an old acquaintance. On Mike Ovitz's return from talking to Matsushita in Japan, Bronfman found himself being briefed on a truly unique opportunity: It seemed that the company was thoroughly sick of Wasserman and Sheinberg's threats, which had escalated beyond DreamWorks in their latest dispatches to 100 Universal execs prepared to abandon ship with them. Matsushita was looking for someone with deep pockets to take MCA off their hands; Ovitz had put forward Seagram's as a possibility.

It was time for a change of strategy. Bronfman's softly-softly approach to Time-Warner had been met with a cloud of poison gas and wounding accusations of being callow, inexperienced and starstruck. Now there was another, even tastier fish to fry, and nary an insult in prospect. MCA-Universal was simply too good to pass up. *If* the price was right. *Provided* he didn't land in the same mess as Matsushita, tied hand and foot to joined-at-the-hip Wasserman and Sheinberg. *Especially* if he could, in the process, retain Spielberg's goodwill and capture distribution rights for DreamWorks movies and records. But how to do that while getting rid of the old guard and replacing them with his own supremo? 'T'was a puzzlement. One that had to be solved. But he was getting ahead of himself. With Time-Warner on hold, it was a question of first things first. To hell with delegations. Devil take the hindmost, this rising son would take himself off *personally*, *alone* to the Land of the Rising Sun.

## $$$ LANDING THE PRIZE $$$

After Seagram's Gulfstream jet had reached its destination and unloaded its solitary passenger on to Japanese soil, the journeys from Kansai International to the Miyako Hotel, and on to a guest-house in the old town of Kyoto, were but short limo rides. Awaiting Bronfman was Yoichi Morishita, Matsushita's chunkily built, bull-headed president.

Nothing so crude as figures was discussed at that first meeting. Instead, through an interpreter, Bronfman impressed the Japanese with his air of well-bred gravitas as he spelled out his love of movies, music and entertainment in general. Next morning, in Matsushita's opulent headquarters in Osaka, the two men got together again. This time the language was less ethereal. Bronfman explained he had no wish to find himself involved in an auction. Morishita should present valuations of MCA's various divisions, then give Bronfman time, on an exclusive basis, to frame any proposal. Morishita granted him eighteen days, on one condition: Wasserman and Sheinberg must be kept in the dark. If that cover were blown, the whole deal would follow. Bronfman agreed.

When Matsushita ordered bookkeepers in to MCA, the heads of the house refused to believe what was being contemplated. Maybe they just wanted a valuation so they could float off a piece. If they were looking at anything as dramatic as an outright sale, Ovitz would have told them, right? Wrong. 'I did feel obliged to tell Sid,' Ovitz would later declare, 'but I had a confidentiality agreement with Matsushita. And I had given Edgar my word that everything would remain confidential. There was no deal yet. Everything was in the talking stage. What could I do? Ultimately, I'm a businessman bound by a code of ethics. It was a tortuous experience.'

By March 24 Bronfman made his second trip to Osaka, this time with an offer in his pocket for eighty per cent of MCA/Universal for $5.7 billion. Although less than totally thrilled – they had hoped for $10 billion for the whole shooting match – Matsushita indicated that the offer would be favourably consid-ered. That was enough for Bronfman.

With Seagram's sale-back of its Dupont holdings for $8.8 billion a couple of weeks after his return to the US, Bronfman's war chest overflowed. Gathered together on April 9, 1995 in Los Angeles, flanked by proud godparents Herb Allen and Mike Ovitz, and with Morishita sat across the table from them, both senior and junior Edgars prepared for the official signing that would mark the deal's consummation.

First they had to make a couple of courtesy calls – late, perhaps, but better late than never. Bronfman Sr's was to Lew Wasserman. Bronfman Jr's was to Sheinberg. That formality completed, Bronfman Jr applied his signature. The majority controlling interest in MCA/Universal had just changed hands.

The telephone calls from Bronfman indicated to Wasserman and Sheinberg that a meeting scheduled for later in April with Matsushita had been nothing more than a decoy to put them off the scent. Their fury at the deception found a voice in MPAA president Jack Valenti. 'I've never seen business behaviour as sordid and squalid as the Japanese treatment of Lew Wasserman and Sid Sheinberg,' he spluttered.

## $$$ MONUMENTAL STUPIDITY? $$$

News of Seagram's Dupont share sale, and their takeover of MCA/Universal, stunned the stock market. Some analysts, harking back to Sony's $2.7 billion write-off at Columbia only weeks earlier, described it as 'a joke', and a cruel one at that; shareholders who'd thought their money was safe in chemicals and liquor suddenly found themselves hostage to fortune in the entertainment industry, and at the very studio that had the year's biggest potential disaster on its books in *Waterworld*. Many had regarded Seagram's Dupont holding as the company's greatest asset, accounting as it did for almost half its annual profits. And look at MCA's operating income of $400 million – actually *less* than when Matsushita had taken over five years earlier! When the news leaked out that Wasserman and Sheinberg had not even been available for due diligence discussions because of the secrecy of the takeover discussions, they were even more incredulous. 'Monumental stupidity on the part of Edgar Bronfman,' Scott Black of Delphi Management railed. 'Stupid to get out of Dupont. And the real dumb thing is to go and pay seventeen times cash flow for MCA.' *The Wall Street Journal* scoffed at the deal, alluding to Bronfman's 'lifelong infatuation' with Hollywood and suggesting that a suitable title for his first movie would be *Dumb and Dumber II*.

While Seagram's shares plunged eighteen per cent, wiping $800 million off the Bronfmans' thirty-six per cent holding, Matsushita also faced stormy criticism on their home ground, notably from the *Nihon Keizei Shimbun*, Japan's leading financial newspaper. The $1.9 billion hit they'd taken in exchange losses, they wrote, was enough to plunge Matsushita into the red. 'Money can buy a company,' they pointed out, 'but it cannot develop the company's human resources. This is especially true in the software and network business, a factor Matsushita probably overlooked. During the bubble era, many Japanese companies recklessly used their surplus funds to acquire businesses. This hasty foray into a new business line has backfired. Matsushita has paid for it in the end.' If

Morishita had imagined that the twenty per cent holding still retained in MCA was enough to save face, he'd been mistaken. If Matsushita had been unable to control events in Hollywood with a 100 per cent stake, what chance did they have with twenty per cent? At least Sony's new president Nobuyuki Idei had bitten the bullet and clung to full control of Columbia – for the time being at least.

Bronfman had his answer ready to those who raised the thorny subject of *Waterworld*. 'We bought MCA with no debt,' he revealed. 'Matsushita has eaten the costs of *Waterworld*. Let's say that between post-production and marketing the movie will cost us $57 million. That's one per cent of what we paid for MCA. If it is the biggest hit in creation, it won't make any difference. And if it's the biggest flop in creation, it won't make any difference either, from a financial point of view. But if you're going to print that, print this: You stand behind your creators in good times and bad. Kevin Costner is a great star and filmmaker. I want to stick with him, and I've told him that.'

## $ $ $ WINNERS AND LOSERS $ $ $

It was easier than Bronfman had thought. At eighty-two Wasserman was in a mood to be put out to pasture, so long as it was on the Universal lot in suitably dignified digs. And he wanted to retain his seat on MCA's board, and the title of Chairman Emeritus, *and* a seat on Seagram's board. Granted. As for Sheinberg: 'I don't want Lew's old job,' he declared at the outset, 'I want to do something else.' Specifically, what he had in mind was a housekeeping deal at Universal for the 'Bubble Factory' production company he intended to form with his sons Jonathon and Bill. Granted.

Spielberg, of course, Bronfman had already talked to – on April 11, before the ink was even dry on the deal to take over MCA. Flanked by his DreamWorks partners during the meeting held on Spielberg's homeground at Amblin, Bronfman had been much encouraged. Universal, he discovered, already had Amblin tied to sequels to *Jurassic Park*, *The Flintstones* and *Casper*, among several other projects. Whether or not Matsushita had been fully aware that this continuity was in place, or whether they were denied the information, is another matter. And yes, DreamWorks was prepared to talk about non-US distribution rights, on suitable terms. Bronfman was elated. The centre of power was with him.

At an early meeting with studio execs headed by Tom Pollock, Bronfman skilfully laid to rest fears of the kind of bloodbath

Hollywood normally expects with a change of proprietor. (Pollock may have experienced twinges that told a different story.) He related how, during his last stint at the studio, producing *The Border*, he had asked for his bungalow to be painted a colour other than 'Universal white'. He had asked all the way up to studio head Ned Tanen before realising that 'Universal white' it was going to be; that was pretty much the way things had been. It was a clever story, for although it summed up the way Universal had always been run under Lew and Sid, it was only gently, and amusingly critical.

All that Bronfman now lacked was a new studio head. All along he'd had two names in mind. Although Barry Diller, busily preparing a bid for the network of his dreams, CBS, disavowed interest, many doubted that he had even crossed Bronfman's mind for the job. Mike Ovitz was the front runner from the beginning – and yes, there was a possibility. But how would the DreamWorks trio feel about Ovitz in his new role? They'd all had their differences in the past, and there was no question that Ovitz had played both ends against the middle in his recent dealings, both with them as individuals and with their friends at MCA.

Geffen, of all people, had already put Bronfman's mind at ease on that score during the meeting at Amblin. 'We're perfectly willing to work with Ovitz,' he'd clarified. Geffen also had a few encouraging words to the press about Bronfman, as well as a put-down for the Doubting Thomases. 'MCA is a great company that has been run by conservative businessmen,' he declared. 'It's an underexploited asset, the equivalent of where Disney was when it was taken over eleven years ago by Michael Eisner. Frankly, Edgar's gotten a good deal.' Geffen's statement caused many a double take. Were they mistaken, or had Geffen just paid Eisner the Antichrist a rare compliment? Could there be a reconciliation in the air?

The problem with Ovitz, it quickly transpired, lay in the endless litany of his demands. If they had stopped short of salary, bonuses and stock options, Bronfman might have been able to live with them. They didn't, and he couldn't. 'He's asking too much,' close colleagues were informed. Ovitz wanted to take with him a whole chunk of CAA, the valuable advertising side that included the Coca-Cola account – naturally, with Bronfman paying the bill and absorbing it within the structure of MCA. Bronfman's view was that it had nothing to do with his new company's core business. And he recalled the mess Sony had got themselves into turning ridiculously expensive somersaults to get their chosen team of Guber and Peters. That way lay disaster. Every man has his worth. Ovitz had overpriced himself. And come to that, was he really the best candidate for the job? Oh sure, the media would ooh-and-aah for a month or two, and MCA's stock might jump temporarily on news that Bronfman had captured such a prize. After that, though, Ovitz would have to perform. And although he was unquestionably a legendary dealmaker, did that automatically make him a great project-picker? All the deal-making skills in the world hadn't translated into hit movies for the hapless Victor Kaufman, the man who'd run TriStar and had packaged Columbia for sale to Sony before departing to set up Savoy Pictures, a busted flush after three short years and hundreds of millions of dollars down the drain. How would Ovitz perform when he was on the other end of the deal, negotiating for an actor's services instead of awaiting his cut at the end of the day? The more he thought it over, the more Ovitz had edged himself out as far as Bronfman was concerned.

Wasserman, still smarting at what he saw as Ovitz's double-dealing, seized the opportunity of a gathering of Universal execs to underscore the general reaction. Addressing Bronfman, he said, 'I think I speak for all of us at this luncheon in telling you how pleased we are that the deal didn't work out.'

Bronfman was fully up to the occasion. 'Thank you for your candour', he said in reply, 'and I just want you to know that I reserve the right to hire someone equally offensive.'

All the arguments against Ovitz also applied to Ron Meyer, one of Ovitz's two original partners. Or did they? First off, Meyer was one of the best-liked agents in Hollywood. His style was more laid-back than the buttoned-up, tightlipped Ovitz. He didn't come with all the baggage of the 'most powerful man' jazzbo in which Ovitz had originally luxuriated. And boy, how his clients loved him.

The announcement of Meyer's appointment caught everyone by surprise. After consideration, it seemed to reflect nothing but credit on Bronfman. Here was a man prepared to start the way he meant to finish, someone prepared to solve a problem with lateral thinking. Some of the naysayers who'd criticised his betting the House of Seagram on MCA/Universal, who'd seen him casting the company adrift on the stormy seas of movies rather than remaining docked in the safe harbour of Dupont, began to shift their positions. So far, there had been none of the missteps that had characterised Sony's takeover of Columbia, neither was there under Bronfman the remotest prospect of the hands-off stance that both Sony and Matsushita had adopted with their supposed plums. There was a sense of – Hey, this could work!

The feeling was reinforced with Bronfman's announcement of a ten-year deal to distribute DreamWorks' movies in foreign territories, together with worldwide rights to DreamWorks' homevideos and record labels. With Wasserman and Stein taken care of, Spielberg had come through. His support continued in a ringing endorsement of MCA's new chief: 'As talented a businessman as Edgar Bronfman is, he is equally a gentleman of honour. Honour, loyalty and fairness are the values under which I strived at Universal Studios for twenty-six years under Sid Sheinberg and Lew Wasserman.'

With Ron Meyer's drafting in of deputies Casey Silver and Sandy Climan, something had to give, regardless of 'honour, loyalty and fairness'. In March 1996, Tom Pollock resigned following a boot upstairs. Completing the picture, a buffer was installed between Meyer and Bronfman in the shape of Frank Biondi, the executive ousted by Viacom's Sumner Redstone. That played remarkably well with Meyer, freeing him up as it did to concentrate on matters creative while Biondi made with the paperwork. Bronfman was emerging as a canny tactician. All he needed now was a string of hit movies.

## $$$ THE BEST PART OF BREAKING UP $$$

The media world was prepared for a shakeup with the battle between Barry Diller and Westinghouse over CBS. This was one battle, pundits believed, that Diller could ill afford to lose after his besting a year earlier by Sumner Redstone's Viacom in his bid for Paramount Pictures. The news of Westinghouse's $5.4 billion triumph, announced towards the end of July 1995, left the unhappy Diller sidelined once again, The Man Without a Network. (But who knows what will emerge from his raggle-taggle Silver King Communications?)

News of the takeover barely had time to sink in when it was superceded by a real bolt from the blue. Michael Eisner's end-run around the DreamWorks team, and round deputy dawg Katzenberg in particular, came with his announcement that the Walt Disney Company was acquiring Capital Cities/ABC for $19.6 billion.

Even as pundits weighed up the implications – Katzenberg, courtesy of DreamWorks deal with ABC, was back working for Eisner?! Would the Dream Team void the $200 million joint venture?! – the Disney chairman struck again. His new studio head? None other than Michael Ovitz, Bronfman's elusive butterfly, acquired on the rebound from his rejection at MCA.

Incredibly, after all the mud that had been slung, the ensuing weeks brought the glimmer of a reconciliation between Katzenberg and Eisner. Egged on by Spielberg and Geffen, Katzenberg seemed suddenly anxious to avoid a situation smacking of 'This town ain't big enough for both of us'.

'Michael, we've had nineteen fabulous years and ten terrible months. Let's not make it eleven,' he wrote Eisner.

Ain't understanding mellow! Not on this occasion. In early April 1996, following the breakdown of settlement talks, Katzenberg's lawyer Bert Fields served notice on Eisner and his new president Ovitz, that he intended to file a lawsuit against Disney on behalf of his client. One week later Fields made good on his threat. *Real* good. The amount he was seeking? 'At least' $250 million.

The suit followed months of fruitless behind-the-scenes negotiations in which, strangely enough, that highly skilled negotiator Ovitz had failed to effect a resolution to Katzenberg's claims. In Fields' submission, a key element of Katzenberg's compensation was an incentive bonus provision providing for payment to him by Disney of two per cent of Disney's profits from product put into production or acquired for distribution during Katzenberg's employment. (Think *Aladdin*! Think *The Lion King*!! Think the stage version of *Beauty and the Beast*!!!) The later of his two contracts spelled out that the bonus would continue subsequent to the end of the term of the contract. According to the lawsuit, 'The profits expected to be received by Disney . . . have a net present value believed to be in excess of $12.5 billion.' Hence the $250 million claim!

Before the suit was filed, Michael Eisner, true to form, was defiance itself, describing the prospect of a legal tussle as 'a speck on the horizon', adding that 'it is irrelevant to the course of our company whether his contract is settled, or whether in fact he has a contract at all'.

Some 'speck'. There again, some horizon. But hang on, what exactly did Eisner mean by 'whether in fact he has a contract at all'? It sure sounded ominous, and indeed it was.

It took Disney until May 17 to file their answer to Katzenberg's claims in Los Angeles Superior Court. Bombshell! The company claimed that a new pact Katzenberg signed in 1988 had waived his right to future bonuses, in exchange for having his contract terminated in 1994, rather than 1996, as Disney would have preferred. So, having already settled up 'the full amount of bonus compensation due to him' and having 'accelerated and paid him deferred bonuses', Katzenberg, per Disney, was 'not entitled' to anything further. Not even 250 bucks, let alone 250 million . . .

Bert Fields immediately blasted back. 'It's absolutely an absurd interpretation of the agreement,' he claimed. 'Katzenberg would have to have been incompetent and insane to make the contract they claim he made.' Was it just my imagination, or did he hesitate for a moment before adding, 'And Katzenberg is neither!'

Not expected to open at a courtroom near you before 1997, the case may well be settled quietly before then. Otherwise, with the prising open of the Disney books, the world at large will get a protracted peek at a range of Hollywood salaries, bonuses and perks, not to mention bookkeeping finesse, of the type normally kept well away from prying eyes. After O.J., another windfall for Court-TV!

# 35

## What a Difference a Year Makes

*'Actually, I was nineteen and down at Cal State at Long
Beach when it all started to happen. I made a short film
called* Amblin', *financed by a very young producer named
Denis Hoffman. He had money and I didn't; we joined
forces.'*

STEVEN SPIELBERG, quoted in the New York *Post*,
June, 1975

*'To Denis, You Were The First. Love, Steven.'*

Inscription on *E.T.* poster sent to Denis Hoffman by
STEVEN SPIELBERG

The journalist who called Denis Hoffman for an appointment in
August 1994 was keen to explore his association with Spielberg in
connection with a biographical piece. The whole thing seemed
innocent enough, as indeed it was in intent, until there came an
awkward pause after Hoffman finished explaining why the original
contract between them had been declared void. 'Spielberg's a year
older than he says he is,' his guest informed an incredulous
Hoffman. And the journalist had the proof from several sources.

A friend vividly recalls the normally placid, laid-back Hoffman
calling him once the interview was over. 'HE LIED TO ME!' he shouted
down the line. 'HE LIED TO ME!'

'Denis, what on earth are you talking about?' the startled friend
asked.

'SPIELBERG LIED TO ME!' Hoffman replied.

Soon after, final proof lay in Hoffman's hands, direct from the
Hamilton County of Ohio's Records Office – a faxed copy of
Spielberg's birth certificate registering his arrival on Planet Earth as
having indisputably taken place on December 18, 1946. *Not* 1947,
as Spielberg and his lawyer had claimed. The date also directly con-
tradicted the mountain of biographical material written about

335

Spielberg over the years, including listings in *Who's Who* and *Film Encyclopedia*. Not only that, but further investigation revealed that December 1947 was the year listed *by Spielberg himself* on his driving licence, on his voter's registration, even on his children's birth certificates. As far as Hoffman was concerned, he had been suckered into signing away his right to a Spielberg-directed movie.

Friends put Hoffman in touch with Robert C. Rosen of Rosen & Associates, who agreed to take on his case, together with Pierce O'Donnell of Kaye, Scholer, Fierman, Hays and Handler (O'Donnell having successfully represented columnist Art Buchwald in his landmark case against Paramount Pictures regarding the movie, *Coming to America*). Before proceeding to file their complaint, Rosen and O'Donnell contacted Spielberg's attorney Bruce Ramer. 'Please tell Hoffman not to file a suit under any circumstances,' the duo was informed. 'Steven wants to settle this matter and does not want it to go public.'

As negotiations with Ramer proceeded through May 1995, retired Judge Tanner was called in to mediate what was considered a fair settlement of the matter. At an October meeting between attorneys, Spielberg's Marshall Grossman declared, 'We are going to come back to you with a substantial offer by next Wednesday. So please hold off filing your complaint until then, because we need to talk to Steven.'

On the Tuesday, twenty-four hours before the promised settlement proposal, Grossman, in a pre-emptive strike, filed suit instead on Spielberg's behalf, claiming 'financial harassment', alleging that Hoffman was trying to extort millions of dollars from Spielberg. While acknowledging the existence of the 1968 agreement between them, Spielberg was denying outright that Hoffman had brought him any scripts to consider, and maintaining that in 1976 Hoffman had in fact asked him to buy out the contract between them. Spielberg declared that he had complied with this request, also that he had given Hoffman's Cinefx work on 'at least one' of his films, as well as partly financing Hoffman's company, Designer Donuts. Then Hoffman had come along in May 1995, claiming tens of millions of dollars based on his claim that the 1977 buyout had been obtained fraudulently. Spielberg was seeking a declaration that the buyout was valid, and that no further money was owed Hoffman, together with unspecified damages, costs of the suit, and general relief. 'Over the past several months,' Grossman elaborated, 'Hoffman's demands for money became more intense and Hoffman seeks to publicly embarrass Spielberg by portraying him as ungrateful for the financial assistance originally provided by Hoffman nearly thirty years ago. Mr Spielberg is simply saying, "Enough is enough."'

Bob Rosen responded immediately on behalf of Hoffman, describing the suit as 'a bad-faith first-strike attempt on the part of Spielberg to stop the facts from coming forward. They're trying to destroy my client . . . This is a typical David and Goliath lawsuit.'

It took just two days before a counterclaim was filed, with Hoffman suing Spielberg for $33 million, the calculated average return to the producers of the three theatrical movies produced within the span of their agreement, *The Sugarland Express*, *Jaws* and *Close Encounters of the Third Kind*. With interest, Rosen reckoned, a judgement could amount to $170 million, excluding potential punitive damages. Supporting his claim that their contract had been settled solely based on Spielberg's fraudulent statements regarding his age, Hoffman submitted birth and bar mitzvah newspaper reports, together with an actual copy of Spielberg's birth certificate and other documentation.

'Steven lied to Denis and said, "My contract with you is not enforceable because I was a minor when we entered into our agreement in 1968 . . ." Hoffman's attorney back in 1977 would never have recommended settlement unless he believed they didn't have a leg to stand on,' Rosen pointed out. Pierce O'Donnell chipped in: 'Why else would Denis Hoffman give up one of the most valuable pieces of paper in Hollywood for thirty grand?'

While acknowledging that Spielberg was indeed born in 1946 – and therefore indisputably a twenty-one-year-old adult while signing on the dotted – Grossman and spokesman Marvin Levy steadfastly refused to clarify why their client had neglected over the years to correct the scores of misstated references to his birth year, even on the many occasions when his age was quoted as part of a question personally addressed.

Instead, Grossman chose to pour cold water over Hoffman's claim that he was misled back in 1977. 'If age was such a big deal back then,' he argued, 'wouldn't a careful and prudent lawyer have insisted upon a written representation or done the minimum amount of investigation necessary to satisfy himself on that issue?'

Hoffman's reps had a ready answer: countless journalists and biographers from magazines like *Time*, *Newsweek*, *Rolling Stone*, *Interview*, *Penthouse*, *Variety* and *People*, and newspapers like the Los Angeles *Times* and New York *Times* (in January 1988 their piece was entitled 'Spielberg at 40: The Man and the Child'), had also 'got it wrong'. Even the official record in *Current Biography* was incorrect, not to mention Spielberg's falsified licence filed at the Department of Motor Vehicle records in Sacramento, and Spielberg's voter registration.

'I'm sure there's an answer,' was Grossman's attempt to brush this off. 'Maybe he didn't care what people said about his age. He cares about one thing. Making films.'

Not films for Denis Hoffman, though. The Los Angeles *Times*, not best known for the snap and crackle of its humour, came up with an unusually succinct summary: 'Steven Spielberg once directed a problem-plagued movie called *1941*. Now he has a new problem: 1946.'

A court date, likely to be sometime in 1997, is awaited. Meantime, here is Hoffman's case, as spelled out by Rosen and O'Donnell in their suit:

*Introductory Statement*:

1) Denis C. Hoffman was the person who started the stellar career of defendant Steven A. Spielberg, the only person who would support defendant Spielberg when no-one else, even defendant Spielberg's own family, would back his film aspirations. Spielberg has repaid Hoffman's faith and trust by cheating him through a fraud. Hoffman is the innocent victim of a deliberate and outrageous lie perpetrated by Spielberg in a calculated and malicious scheme to avoid his legal obligations to Hoffman and to deprive Hoffman of the considerable benefits of the binding written contract he made with Hoffman on September 28, 1968. Instead of honoring his written agreement with Hoffman to direct any script Hoffman wanted in the decade after Hoffman produced and financed *Amblin'*, Spielberg unilaterally breached that contract by means of a flat-out fraud. Pretending he was underage when he signed the agreement, Spielberg deceived Hoffman into believing the agreement was unenforceable, and induced Hoffman to surrender his valuable contract rights for a tiny fraction of their real value.

2) Spielberg has (with Hoffman's assistance) become the most successful director in the history of motion pictures. Spielberg's films such as *Jaws*, *Close Encounters of the Third Kind*, *E.T.*, the *Indiana Jones* trilogy, *Schindler's List* and *Jurassic Park* have met with overwhelming critical acclaim and enormous commercial success. Spielberg's company 'Amblin Entertainment' is named after the project Hoffman created with Spielberg, and which was the catalyst for Spielberg's success. None of this would have occurred, however (or, it would not have occurred at the time, and in the

338

same manner and by the same means as it did in fact occur) but for the contributions and endeavors of Hoffman.

3) Spielberg's acts and conduct are reprehensible and deserving of the strongest possible censure. Hoffman seeks damages on account of Spielberg's fraud and breach of contract. Hoffman further seeks punitive damages to deter Spielberg from engaging in the same conduct in the future, and to set an example to the entertainment industry that a deal is a deal and that this basic principle applies equally to powerful directors.

### Facts Common to all Causes of Action:

1) In early 1968 Hoffman was approached by a friend who worked in the editorial department of Universal Pictures. Hoffman's friend desired to introduce Hoffman to a young college student who was loitering around the editing rooms at Universal. While he had no industry background or experience, and no apparent mastery over the many nuances of directing a motion picture, he had abundant desire. This person was defendant Spielberg.

2) Hoffman met with defendant Spielberg over lunch at the Old World Restaurant in Hollywood. During the course of the meeting, defendant Spielberg said he would do anything Hoffman wanted, if Hoffman would only finance a film for and on his behalf. Defendant Spielberg recited his history of unsuccessful attempts to develop a film with major motion picture studios such as Universal. Defendant Spielberg stated no-one was willing – not even his family – to assist him in any way to finance a first film he could use to showcase his talents to a studio.

3) Hoffman was impressed by defendant Spielberg, and expressed interest in collaborating with him. Before the lunch was over, Hoffman and defendant Spielberg made a verbal agreement to develop and produce a short-subject film together. Hoffman would finance and produce the film, and defendant Spielberg would direct it. In consideration therefore, defendant Spielberg offered Hoffman a percentage of his income for the next three years. Concerned this might be too onerous for defendant Spielberg, and despite defendant

Spielberg's willingness and enthusiasm to make such an offer, Hoffman did not accept this proposal. Instead, in return for financing and producing the film, Hoffman proposed a contract in which defendant Spielberg would commit to direct a film from any script of Hoffman's choice within ten years. Defendant Spielberg's director's fee for this film would be $25,000 plus five per cent of any profits after expenses. Both parties orally agreed to these terms.

4) Defendant Spielberg then submitted several story outlines to Hoffman. All of them reflected a naive and unrealistic approach, and none of them were suitable. Hoffman then established certain parameters for defendant Spielberg to guide him, with a view towards maximising the likelihood that defendant Spielberg (as an inexperienced, unknown, first-time director) would be able to deliver a film that was technically and commercially satisfactory. Hoffman's primary guidelines were: not to use dialogue; to use music for continuity; and to make extensive use of optical effects. The absence of dialogue would eliminate the necessity to record sound on location and to synchronise the dialogue with the visual images of the film. The use of music for continuity would serve as a substitute for dialogue. Optical effects would enhance and stylise the film. In furtherance of these objectives and his partnership obligations to defendant Spielberg, Hoffman contributed both the compositions and performances of October Country, a band of musicians Hoffman then represented, and also the services of Cinefx, an optical company owned by Hoffman. The story outline eventually delivered by defendant Spielberg – which later was named *Amblin'* – made use of all of Hoffman's suggestions. The title itself (*Amblin'*) was a collaborative decision between Hoffman and defendant Spielberg.

5) As partners in *Amblin'*, Hoffman and defendant Spielberg agreed to press forward and make the project a reality. Jointly, they established a budget and shooting schedule. At the time, defendant Spielberg had no job and little money. Principal photography took place in August of 1968 on various locations, including Hoffman's studio facilities that he donated to the production. Even though defendant Spielberg vastly exceeded the budgeted production costs, due to defendant Spielberg's lack of experience, Hoffman paid all such costs without complaint. As producer, Hoffman supervised the

340

production and creation of all elements used in connection with the film.

6) During this period of time, Hoffman saw a great deal of defendant Spielberg. Defendant Spielberg made many visits to Hoffman's home, and the two became good friends. The relationship between Hoffman and defendant Spielberg, however, developed beyond mere friendship. As the filming of *Amblin'* progressed, the partnership relationship between Hoffman and defendant Spielberg matured. It became a personal relationship based on mutual trust and confidence that reflected their close business links as partners, each contributing to the production of *Amblin'*. For example, when defendant Spielberg needed transportation, Hoffman often loaned him his car, sometimes for days at a time. And when defendant Spielberg was short of money, Hoffman gave him cash to keep him going.

7) On September 28, 1968, Hoffman and defendant Spielberg signed a 1-page written agreement, memorialising their earlier oral agreement. This express written contract set forth defendant Spielberg's promise to direct, at any time of Hoffman's choosing before September 28, 1978, and for a fee of $25,000 plus five per cent of net profits, any script selected by Hoffman. (A true and correct copy of this contract, 'The Agreement', is shown at Appendix 'A'.)

8) When he signed the Agreement, defendant Spielberg did not represent to Hoffman that he was under any restrictions that might inhibit his ability to perform under or pursuant to the Agreement, or that otherwise might frustrate Hoffman's legitimate contractual expectations of defendant Spielberg's diligent and conscientious performance of all of the Agreement's material terms and conditions.

9) *Amblin'* was finished and released in December 1968. Although *Amblin'* was a first film without dialogue by an unknown director, Hoffman was successful in obtaining contracts for both domestic theatrical exhibition and foreign distribution. Due to screenings caused by this exhibition, and submissions by Hoffman to film festivals, the movie received great public and industry acclaim. *Amblin'* won the 'Silver Phoenix' award at the 1969 Atlanta Film Festival. The award reads 'Silver Phoenix – The Atlanta International Film

Festival – World's Best Short Subject *Amblin'* Denis C. Hoffman'. (Copy of the plaque: See Appendix 'B'.) The Council on International Non-theatrical Events congratulated Hoffman for *Amblin'*, which was 'selected for its excellence to represent the United States of America in international motion picture events abroad'. (Copy of the 'Golden Eagle' Certificate: Appendix 'C'.) *Amblin'* was also accepted as the official US entry into the Venice Film Festival – another prestigious industry event. Because of *Amblin'*, Universal signed defendant Spielberg to an exclusive seven-year contract.

10) Over the next several years following the release of *Amblin'*, Hoffman repeatedly asked defendant Spielberg to fulfil his contractual and fiduciary obligations to direct a movie pursuant to his obligations, Hoffman proposed several scripts, but defendant Spielberg continually informed Hoffman he presently was unavailable because of ongoing commitments.

11) Early in 1975, right after defendant Spielberg's huge box-office success with *Jaws*, Hoffman and defendant Spielberg met for lunch at the Universal commissary. During the meeting, Hoffman told defendant Spielberg he was neglecting the obligations the Agreement imposed on him. Defendant Spielberg confirmed his intention to meet all the Agreement's terms. Defendant Spielberg said his contractual commitments to Universal made it hard to perform just then. Defendant Spielberg added, however, that he was about to commence pre-production on what would be another hugely successful film, *Close Encounters of the Third Kind* for another studio – Columbia Pictures. Defendant Spielberg assured Hoffman he had not forgotten about the Agreement, and that he would make a film for Hoffman as he had promised as soon as his presently existing contractual commitments had been met.

12) Hoffman and defendant Spielberg met several more times in 1975. Hoffman attempted in good faith to identify a suitable property for the film defendant Spielberg was obligated to direct. Throughout the time, Hoffman relied to his detriment on defendant Spielberg's statement; Hoffman's partnership relationship with defendant Spielberg; the apparent sincerity of defendant Spielberg's various representations and promises to Hoffman; defendant Spielberg's repeated reaffirmations of the Agreement; Hoffman's complete confidence in defendant

Spielberg's personal honour and integrity; Hoffman's considerable contribution to defendant Spielberg's career; and their express contract that defendant Spielberg would in fact honour and perform in good faith his contractual promises and commitments, as set forth in the Agreement.

13) Hoffman is informed, believes and thereon alleges that, at no time, did defendant Spielberg disclose to Universal the existence of his previously existing contractual commitment to Hoffman under and pursuant to the Agreement.

14) In July 1975, Hoffman telephoned defendant Spielberg and left many messages for him regarding the status of the project. Eventually, defendant Spielberg returned these calls. To Hoffman's shock, during their telephone conversation, defendant Spielberg asserted that, in his opinion, the Agreement was unenforceable. Hoffman's astonishment at defendant Spielberg's assertion was exacerbated and enhanced by Hoffman's consistent attempts until then, in trying to identify a suitable property to develop and produce, and defendant Spielberg's apparent sincerity to comply. Defendant Spielberg invited Hoffman to contact his attorney, Bruce Ramer, of the law firm known as Gang, Tyre, Ramer and Brown.

15) Negotiations between Ramer and Hoffman's counsel lasted more than a year. Ramer maintained the Agreement was illegal and unenforceable. According to defendant Spielberg and his attorney, on September 28, 1968 when defendant Spielberg entered into the Agreement, defendant Spielberg was only twenty years old. As a minor, defendant Spielberg therefore lacked the capacity to contract, and disavowed the Agreement. Ramer and defendant Spielberg told Hoffman that, because the contract was void, defendant Spielberg had no legal obligation to Hoffman. Ramer advised that, under the circumstances, Hoffman should settle for anything he could get.

16) Hoffman called defendant Spielberg. Hoffman specifically asked defendant Spielberg how old he was in September 1968 when he executed the Agreement. Consistent with numerous press articles and reviews and studio materials discussing his career, defendant Spielberg unequivocally represented to Hoffman that he was born on December 18,

343

1947, and that at the time they entered into the Agreement, he was twenty years old. In fact, defendant Spielberg was born on December 18, 1946, and was over twenty-one years old when he executed the Agreement. Defendant Spielberg's express representation to Hoffman was an outright lie. Hoffman relied on this false representation in accepting the assertion that the Agreement was void.

17) Eventually the parties settled for the sum of $30,000. Because of the representations of defendant Spielberg, Hoffman believed his Agreement was unenforceable and worthless and had no chance of success in any litigation to attempt to enforce the Agreement, and that he had no option but to accept defendant Spielberg's modest offer. On or about January 3, 1977, the parties entered into a settlement agreement and mutual general release.

18) As a condition of the Release, Hoffman surrendered to defendant Spielberg all of Hoffman's rights to use the name *Amblin'* in connection with any business venture. Significantly, defendant Spielberg later named his production company and billion-dollar business empire 'Amblin Entertainment'.

19) Hoffman made considerable contributions to *Amblin'*. These included: guiding the development of the story from inception; financing the film; serving as producer; providing optical effects, music and film facilities; publicising and placing the film in distribution and at film festivals; and investing considerable time, attention, energy and effort in its production and subsequent exhibition. The film, and Hoffman's efforts and contribution, in turn made an incalculable contribution to defendant Spielberg's subsequent commercial success. Hoffman, however, received negligible return on his investment.

20) Rarely did defendant Spielberg give Hoffman any credit for Hoffman's contributions in connection with the making of *Amblin'*, or for Hoffman's discovery of defendant Spielberg and his introduction to the film community. For example, the American Film Institute presented defendant Spielberg with a Lifetime Achievement Award at a presentation that was nationally televised on NBC on May 28, 1995. In his acceptance speech, instead of acknowledging

344

Hoffman's contributions to his success, defendant Spielberg attributed his discovery and first directing opportunity to Sidney Sheinberg, an executive with Universal. Great acclaim and accolades attend all of defendant Spielberg's projects, which in turn inures to the substantial economic benefit of all those associated with any of his projects. People associated with defendant Spielberg are able to use that association to develop and produce properties for film or television, to enhance and augment their professional careers, and to derive favourable contractual relationships and prospective economic advantages. As the person who discovered Spielberg, and produced, financed and guided him in the making of his first film, Hoffman would have been the beneficiary of this effect, had defendant Spielberg not spurned him and cast him aside.

21) In August 1994, a freelance writer contacted Hoffman for an interview about Hoffman's early associations with defendant Spielberg. The writer visited Hoffman at Hoffman's personal residence, and spoke with Hoffman for approximately three hours.

22) At the end of the interview, the writer commented he recently had discovered Spielberg actually is one year older than his stated age. Hoffman was so astonished that he asked the writer to repeat his remark several times, to be sure he had heard the writer's statement correctly.

23) Encouraged to investigate the writer's claim himself, Hoffman now has independently confirmed his statement. Although defendant Spielberg has repeatedly and publicly asserted his birth date is December 18, 1947, in truth and fact he was born on December 18, 1946. (A copy of Spielberg's birth certificate is shown at Appendix 'D'.)

24) Any suggestion that Spielberg does not know his real age, for some reason, is dispelled by Appendix 'E'. This is the announcement from a Phoenix Jewish community newspaper of defendant Spielberg's Bar Mitzvah. The Bar Mitzvah occurred shortly after defendant Spielberg's thirteenth birthday. Since the time of Moses, almost every Jewish boy goes through his Bar Mitzvah at age thirteen. If defendant Spielberg was ever confused about his date of birth, the timing of his Bar Mitzvah assuredly resolved any such doubts.

The fact is that defendant Spielberg has long lied about his age – and intentionally – to the detriment of Hoffman.

25) Hoffman has been viciously and cruelly defrauded by defendant Spielberg. The one and only reason why Hoffman forfeited and relinquished his rights under the Agreement was because of defendant Spielberg's unequivocal representation that he was a minor when he entered into the Agreement, and therefore lacked legal capacity to contract. Defendant Spielberg, however, lied about his age. In truth and fact, he was not a minor, but was legally competent to enter into a legally binding contract. Instead of honouring his contractual obligations, however, defendant Spielberg lied to and deceived Hoffman, attempting to insure he would not have to fulfil his contractual obligations, because at that point he was on to bigger and better things. Had Hoffman known the true facts, Hoffman would have insisted upon defendant Spielberg's timely performance of the Agreement.

26) Defendant Spielberg has orchestrated and perpetrated an extensive media campaign, during the course of which defendant Spielberg has lied about his age to this day. Defendant Spielberg's false statements regarding his age have appeared in numerous books, biographies and articles that have been written about him by various authors and journalists; in press releases and publicity announcements, disseminated (directly and indirectly) by defendant Spielberg and his publicists; and in various other print and video media. For example, at the American Film Institute dinner previously described, Tom Hanks, who was the Master of Ceremonies, stated defendant Spielberg was twenty years old when he directed Joan Crawford in an episode of the television series, *Night Gallery* entitled 'Eyes'. In fact, defendant Spielberg was twenty-two years old at that time. Tom Hanks' remarks not only were made directly to defendant Spielberg, and acknowledged by him, but also were televised to a large viewing audience. One terrible consequence of this publicity campaign has been to perpetuate the fraud initially committed by defendant Spielberg upon Hoffman, deceiving and deluding Hoffman as to the fact of defendant Spielberg's true age, and deterring Hoffman from taking action against defendant Spielberg.

Suing for Punitive and Exemplary Damages for Fraud and Deceit, Hoffman and his attorneys maintained that defendant Spielberg had 'acted with ill-will, oppression and malice' towards Hoffman, and with 'reckless disregard' for Hoffman's rights, having 'intentionally concealed or suppressed the fact of defendant Spielberg's true age with the intent to defraud Hoffman'.

Spielberg and his legal eagles immediately began exercising spin control and misinformation.

Item: They claim Hoffman spent eighteen months trying to find a lawyer willing to take on his case. (Fact: Rosen and Associates was his first and only port of call.)

Item: The trial has been shifted from downtown LA, where the jury would have run the spectrum of minorities, to Burbank, where an all-white, middle- to upper-class jury is much more likely – and Spielberg-friendly. (The move, engineered by Spielberg's attorneys, was based on a technicality: Hoffman gave a premise address in Burbank when applying for a licence for Designer Donuts.)

Item: Hoffman's alleged 'financial harassment' of Spielberg. (Fact: Hoffman hasn't spoken to Spielberg personally for several years. All contact, ever since the journalist spilled the beans back in August 1994, has been through his legal team. The closest Hoffman came to contact was through third parties at Amblin, when he was asked to provide materials to accompany a showing of *Amblin'* at the Venice Film Festival. This he did. As Hoffman puts it, '*This* is financial harassment?')

Item: Spielberg's associates claimed their client has never seen any dividends from his investment in Designer Donuts. (Per Bob Rosen: 'What has that got to do with the validity of Hoffman's claim that he was lied to regarding Spielberg's age? *That's* the issue here.' And Hoffman has, in fact, repaid the majority of Spielberg's loans to the company.)

Item: Spielberg's attorney Marshall Grossman has described Hoffman as a 'litigious' individual. Fact: Hoffman has never sued anyone in his life.

Let's sit back and think about this for a minute. Does all this flak come from the unimpeachable Spielberg, the model of personal integrity, a filmmaker raised to sanctified heights with the critical accolades garlanding *Schindler's List*. Surely it can't be true? Say it isn't so! Spielberg's Amblin Entertainment is based on a cheat? A fraud? A swindle? A scam? Even if he *had* been under twenty-one at the time of signing the agreement, didn't he have more of a moral obligation to Denis Hoffman, the man responsible for sparking his career, than a $30,000 pay-off, title work on 'at least one' of his films(!) and loan guarantees more than adequately supported by a second mortgage on Hoffman's home?

Where I come from in Scotland a man's *word* is his bond, let alone a piece of paper. And a moral obligation is more important than a few printed words. Especially when the get-out clause is based on a fudged birthdate.

Maybe Spielberg has been Goliath for so long that he's completely forgotten what it's like to fill David's role. Part of his strategy towards *Amblin'*, it seems clear in retrospect, has been to seize every opportunity over the years to downplay the turning point it provided in his career. He has variously referred to the little movie as 'the slick byproduct of a kid immersed up to his nose in film', 'an attack of crass commercialism' and 'a Pepsi commercial'. This is what impressed Sid Sheinberg enough to hand Spielberg his Universal contract? That went on to win the Atlanta Film Festival award, then a prize at Venice? That, following its blanket release supporting *Love Story*, represents Spielberg's very first theatrical exposure?

It's a puzzlement? No longer. At least, not nearly as much as it used to be.

Other, albeit relatively minor aspects of Spielberg that fail to jibe with the image of the all-round, politically correct good guy he projects, came to light in the wake of the Hoffman suit.

Take the whisky commercial he made for the Japanese market, secure in the knowledge its transmission would be confined solely to that Pacific Isle. Not that Spielberg is alone in hawking goods in Japan he might hesitate to be associated with in his own backyard. Like that well-seasoned Scot Sean Connery promoting – no, not Scotch, silly – but the local Suntory Whisky. Or Arnold Scharzenegger touting Nissan cup noodles. But Spielberg promoting *whisky*?! For what possible reason? Surely not just the filthy lucre? No, it must surely have something – no matter how remote – to do with 'artistic philanthropy'. How so? Well, it's become something of an Amblin, now a DreamWorks, catchphrase to explain everything. Consider:

In 1994 Spielberg established an alliance with actor/director Don Scardino, founding the Off-Broadway 'Playwrights Horizons' to finance work by young playwrights. The first fruit of the endeavour, Nicky Silver's *Fit To Be Tied*, was scheduled for an autumn 1996 Off-Broadway preem. 'Playwrights Horizons/Amblin/DreamWorks are delivering on what we set out to do: create real opportunities for playwrights,' Spielberg claimed in a *Variety* report, before going on to describe the venture as an example of 'artistic philanthropy'.

First off, the idea of any Hollywood money filtering through to help struggling playwrights has got to be good news. Now let's take a closer look. In return for the peanuts involved, what do early backers like Spielberg get in return for their strictly limited largesse? Why, first crack at movie rights, and, more often than not, an option on the playwright's follow-up project. Plus, a cheapo jump on their competitors in their search for happening new talent. Except that Spielberg now has lots of company, with New Line Cinema and Twentieth Century-Fox, among several others, jostling for a piece of the action. Would you believe Peter Guber's Mandalay Entertainment as one of Spielberg's fellow-'philanthropists'? Whatever it is, call it what you will, it's still good for all those young playwrights out there, and all credit to Spielberg for starting the ball rolling. But why try wrapping it as bullshit 'artistic philanthropy' when it's nothing of the kind? Questioned in the same *Variety* report regarding Spielberg's claim, New Line's senior VP of production Lynn Harris did a creditable double-take before replying, 'I think philanthropy is a wonderful thing. And if a philanthropic effort comes out of our programme, great. But we're looking for it to be productive.'

Ask John Clark, actress Lynn Redgrave's husband, manager, and producer of her hit play, *Shakespeare Round My Father*, about Spielberg's 'artistic philanthropy' and he may well choke up. Despite offering to read for Spielberg, Ms Redgrave will not be appearing in Amblin's maiden outing, the appropriately titled *Fit To Be Tied*. The reason: A pay dispute; Amblin won't make with the requisite bucks. Per Clark: 'The theatre, instead of being about class, is becoming something of a freebie.' Or, as Redgrave puts it, 'God knows we need the writers and the movie deals might help a theatre company get its air-conditioning, but the actors are getting more and more shortchanged. The theatre actors' work is being devalued, devalued, devalued.'

Even the modest aim of an air-conditioning unit, alas, might be beyond the reach of all the heady philanthropy flowing. Where playwrights might typically expect around the $40,000 mark for their commissions, a typical Tinseltown handout tends to be limited to the $5,000-10,000 range.

And if Spielberg really wants to help theatrical causes, why doesn't he start on his own doorstep and take an interest in East Hampton's Bay Street Theater in Sag Harbor? Now in its fifth season, this non-profit (maybe that's a clue) enterprise operates year-round serving the community, with new plays preemed during the busy summer months. Two instructors visit four local schools during the off-season and teach a ten-week acting and writing workshop, ending in March with the production of the best student one-act plays. On the professional side, Bay Street

349

has had eight of its thirteen productions in the last four seasons transferred to commercial stages in New York City. (In June 1996 The Jewish Repertory Theater presented Cynthia Ozick's first play *The Shawl*, directed by Sidney Lumet and starring Dianne Wiest, and first staged at Bay Street in 1994 under the title *Blue Light*.)

'We've sent an invitation to Steven Spielberg to each of our productions,' says one of the founder members, ex-Mrs Richard Burton Sybil Christopher. 'He hasn't come yet. But he will.' Ah, hope springs eternal.

As it did, at least for one afternoon in May 1996, for 7,000 rain-soaked students and 8,000 other eager spectators gathered in New York's Washington Square Park to hear Spielberg's commencement speech, the traditional accompaniment to accepting an honorary degree from New York University. When it finally came, Spielberg's eagerly awaited address consisted of the words 'Take the future by storm.' Then he immediately resumed his seat. Well, it *was* raining and blowing a gale, after all. 'This is what we waited three hours for in pissing rain?' one student asked, shaking his head. 'A bullshit crumb from the master's table?!'

Admittedly Spielberg did no worse than his immediate predecessor on the platform, the equally clipped Robert De Niro with his 'Break a leg!' But was that the example to follow? To leave NY Grads, as the New York *Post* put it, 'Speechless'? 'I think it's incredibly selfish. It's a slap in the face,' said one drama student. 'Where are our words of inspiration?' asked a second. A third: 'What did they do for a friggin' degree anyway?'

Over the years Spielberg has amassed a superb collection of guns ancient and modern, probably one of the finest in California. The reason he seems to keep this a deep, dark secret? Probably because it's something else that might not be considered in the Spielberg tradition. He has never talked about his passion for guns to the press, nor has he ever been seen in public handling a gun, let alone shooting one – not since his boy-scout sharpshooter days, then the skeet-shooting forays with John Milius. The only time he's allowed his knowledge of firearms to slip, oddly enough, was in a comparison he made with British movies: 'I keep wondering, "Why is it that the British film is so marvellous for me?" I think it's because they're so careful. A British film is as carefully made as a fine shotgun from Purdey. Every part is hand-tooled.'

What blew his cover was an application filled out for a personal hand-gun. That requires the completion of a government form, making it a felony if incorrect information is given. You guessed it.

Birthdate: December 18, 1947. Instead of a felony charge, the Justice Department announced that Spielberg would probably be let off with no more than a slap on the wrist.

In these days of celebrity justice, Denis Hoffman could not be blamed for having some trepidation over the eventual outcome of his lawsuit, regardless of what he sees as the absolute justice of his case. Money and power arguably enabled Spielberg's lieutenant Frank Marshall to escape being subpoenaed, many saw celebrity status as having allowed John Landis to escape a prison sentence, and – to bring the story up to date – a large percentage of the world's population is convinced that O.J. Simpson got away with a brutal double murder. Will the Burbank jury look at Spielberg during his day in court and simply see cuddly, adorable E.T.? We'll have to wait a while for the answer to that.

Although many things can be censored, truth has a habit of slipping out, whether it's the Denis Hoffman saga, or something reaching much farther back. Since *Schindler's List* represents the pinnacle of Spielberg's career to date as well as his personal ascension into sainthood – producing drivel similar to that spouted by Oprah Winfrey ('I sometimes feel you aren't a real person, Steven, but that God has loaned you to us') – his defensiveness about the central figure is understandable. There comes a time, however, when the sad truth has to be acknowledged, even when the character of the venerated main player is up for grabs.

In March 1996 the voice of Oskar Schindler's eighty-eight-year-old widow Emilie was heard publicising her memoirs – and blasting her husband as nothing more than a greedy profiteer whose rescue of Polish Jews was primarily profit-orientated. As for Spielberg's movie, it was dismissed as 'packed with lies'. 'What does he know about my life?' she railed. 'Absolutely nothing.' His movie, she went on, 'portrays Oskar as a hero of this century. That is not true.' Instead, he was 'a greedy man, whose main interest in compiling "Schindler's List" was to have cheap labour to keep his china factory going'.

An irreverent thought occurs. Maybe with hindsight, the resemblance to Oskar Schindler Spielberg saw in Steve Ross wasn't so far off the mark. And maybe, in view of the hard-to-sell but bitter apparent reality, Spielberg might consider a 'Special Edition' of *Schindler's List* with 'Emilie's Lies' edited out. Hey, it would make for a much shorter movie. Shorter still if he dropped that patently phoney speech at the end, and simply have Schindler drive off into the night with his carload of diamonds. Come to think of it, he could even change the title to *Schindler's Loot*. Or how about simply cutting to the chase and calling it *Spielberg's List*?

351

Memo to CNN: If you have any plans to interview Spielberg any time soon and wish to avoid his hand-waving antics and walk-out when questioned about *Twilight Zone – The Movie*, avoid any reference to Emilie Schindler and her book. Or, for that matter, to the Denis Hoffman case.

# 36

## Father of the Man

'*To Denis, You Started My Engines With* Amblin'
*Love, Steven*'

Inscription on a publicity photograph Steven
Spielberg sent to Denis Hoffman in the early eighties

'*All my movies are wishful thinking. In many of my films I
find I have created the family warmth I wish I had
experienced.*'

STEVEN SPIELBERG

While watching *Temple of Doom* on TV one night, Kate Capshaw
turned to her husband. 'What happened to my career after that
movie?' she asked, smiling quizzically.

'You weren't supposed to have a career,' he replied. 'You were
supposed to be with me.'

Capshaw seems to accept that. 'Oh, I absolutely feel that way,'
she has said. 'I think you have to have a great deal of ambition, these
careers of our A-list ladies don't happen by accident. And if they do
they don't sustain. My focus is on Steven and a large family. In
many ways I *prefer* not working. It looks like I can do many things at
once, but I'm not comfortable doing that. If a couple of things go
right, like taking care of Steven and the children and being home
and having friends, I'm really happy. Some actresses marry directors with the understanding they'll work together. I think it's a tacit
understanding and that's what keeps things going. In our case, it's
our family that keeps it going. Because Steven is surrounded by
such a rich creative world, day in and day out there are people who
always come to see him, I "play" with him a lot. He'd prefer my not
working.'

Capshaw has still managed in the recent past to squeeze in a co-
starring role with Sean Connery in *Just Cause* and a supporting role
in Warren Beatty's *Love Story*, together with a small part in Amblin's

*How to Make An American Quilt*, all presumably to keep from getting too rusty. For the ensemble *American Quilt* she ideally wanted to play *all* the parts, 'the white gals, the black gals, the young ones, the old ones. But there weren't many I could go in and read for except Sally, Winona Ryder's mother.'

Capshaw claims her test for the movie had to be viewed and approved by its executive producer before she was hired. Since her husband filled this position, there was never all that much doubt over the outcome.

It seems the 'large family' is now complete, with six kids sharing both the Hampton barn – with the breathtaking Charles Gwathmey-designed guest house added, its sweeping windows overlooking the waters of the Georgica Pond – and the light and airy $12 million Pacific Palisades home. Six kids? Yes, the 'sixth and final addition', per a cheerfully adamant Capshaw, is Mikaela George, born February 28, '96.

To meet his newly adopted daughter Spielberg flew from Los Angeles to East Hampton immediately after the Oscar ceremony, where he presented a Lifetime Achievement Award to Kirk Douglas. 'I'd make them into a sitcom,' he once joked, 'except I don't do so very well on TV. I don't want to screw around with my family and fail.' (The comment was made before the arrival of Mikaela George, and also predates his Amblin-produced *E.R.* smash.)

There's more than ample room for all of them, whether at the spacious Hamptons, or among the five and a half acres of palms, ferns and sculptured gardens at Pacific Palisades, where the screening room, guesthouse and office quarters are set aside from the main house, and the circular drive has its own set of traffic signals. David O. Selznick composed endless memos from the same Mediterranean-style digs while producing *Gone With the Wind*, Douglas Fairbanks Jr was the occupant before his permanent move to England. The ghosts of Cary Grant and Barbara Hutton nightly replay their marriage. Inside, a small, exquisite Modigliani graces the living room wall, a Monet is nearby, Norman Rockwell is everywhere. Three scripts lay under a glass-topped table – the originals of *Citizen Kane*, *Casablanca*, and Welles' Martian invasion radio broadcast.

The couple's summer in the Hamptons in 1995 often found Capshaw left with the kids by day while Spielberg trundled into New York for an endless series of DreamWorks meetings. A typical evening would find him coming home and saying, 'I met with twelve different people over twelve interesting projects. Honey, what did you do all day?' To which Capshaw's reply would be something like, 'Look at the way I arranged our drawer of Saran Wrap. I got it all lined up.'

Despite this, she seems to believe in the message that seeps through *American Quilt*, that relationships can fail for lack of nurturing. With Capshaw, you can't help feeling that there's little chance of that happening. And yet . . .

With everything the couple have going for them, the buzz among friends has them asking questions like, 'Is that all there is?' and studying Judaism in an effort to find the answers they seek to the Great Meaning of Life. Meantime, it is said that only selected personnel at Amblin/DreamWorks, specially trained in the art, are allowed to bring Spielberg anything even remotely deemed 'bad news'. Lest his equilibrium be disturbed, apparently. Another rumour has him hell-bent on buying up every one of his old family homes, from Ohio to New Jersey, Arizona and Northern California. Why? Maybe to turn them into the DreamWorks equivalent of Shakespeare's birthplace or Burns' Cottage. *Spielberg's Shrines?*

If anyone out there was wondering just what it would take to bring Kate and her predecessor together, the answer turned out to be pretty simple – Samuel Max, the son whose custody they shared. With Amy planning a return to living in New York, she got together with Kate to make a tour of every suitably snooty prep school in the area, covering Horace Mann, Riverdale, Dalton and Trinity before settling on the somewhat surprising choice of West Side's Ethical Cultural School. 'I wanted something more progressive,' Amy explained. 'My kids, especially Max, need freedom.'

From Kate and her husband, absolutely no comment.

Tom Hanks' friendship with Spielberg easily survived their two Amblin flops, *The Money Pit* and *Joe Vs. the Volcano*. The two men have a lot in common. Both are highly successful. Both are wary of close personal relationships with outsiders, leaving them able to count really close friends on the fingers of one hand. And they also happen to be neighbours. 'The nice thing about being with Tom,' says Spielberg, 'is that when he feels comfortable around you, he doesn't feel a responsibility to spearhead the conversation. You know that Tom is your friend, and you his, when you can sit in a room, independently reading or doing other things, and not speak to each other for an hour.' Nor is there any of the nervousness left between them that Spielberg often feels in his relationships with other men. As he puts it, 'I think when you can get rid of the nervousness in a friendship between two guys, then it becomes an older kind of relationship. Now we just take our kids to school and talk about the quality of the American teaching system . . . !'

The two share another trait, Spielberg maintains, that they were both loners who met 'terrific women', who also happen to be best friends. Where Spielberg and Hanks would happily act like couch-potatoes, Kate and Hanks' wife Rita insist on dragging their respective spouses out to restaurants and other social occasions, often together. 'I've never seen Tom as a lonely person,' says Spielberg. 'I think that Tom is just really in touch with himself, and you can't be in touch with yourself if you are always serving others. I think he has to spend time alone getting familiar with that part of him that he needs as an actor, as an artist.'

Spielberg defends the actor's oft-criticised, emotional, rather jumbled speech, after winning the Oscar for his performance in *Philadelphia*, on the basis that his heart was in the right place in pleading tolerance for AIDS victims everywhere. Considering the vast audience his heartfelt message reached – far greater than the total number who would ever actually see *Philadelphia*, as Spielberg points out – he is undoubtedly right.

To Hanks Spielberg remains the same high-school geek, the one forever carting movie projectors and a couple of reels of film around, the only one able to thread them up. 'I was the same way,' he admits. 'So when we go out and do "guy" things, it's not like we're out, you know, parasailing. We're not spearfishing, or anything like that. We're out just talking about a bunch of stuff and waiting to pick up our kids.'

Hanks, never let us forget, comes from the world of stand-up comedy, and at the drop of a hat he'll produce a tellingly hilarious riff on how he sees a typical DreamWorks meeting. Katzenberg would be 'Mr Bottom Line, Mr Brass Tacks', who operates every meeting with a strict agenda, not least that the duration is twenty-two minutes, no more, no less. Geffen would be the diffident smoothie who'd declare, 'We think you're great, and if you want to work with us, fabulous; if not, we still think you're great' – in contrast to Katzenberg's hard-push 'You're great, and here are seventeen reasons why you need to be with us.' Spielberg? He'd say, 'I love that thing you did in that movie five years ago where you had the platypus dancing on the edge of the table, and if you could do that, you could do anything.'

Naturally, the meeting would be over in twenty-two minutes flat.

While in Italy to receive a Golden Lion Award, Spielberg heard that Federico Fellini was in Ferrara, hospitalised following a stroke. Whatever had been actually said, either spontaneously or otherwise, whether both their remarks in the wake of *Jaws* had been warmed over, brushed up or just plain invented by the press, it was time to rebuild any damaged bridges. Spielberg's note to Fellini ran:

'As you read this, I hope you are feeling better. I have been a fan of yours ever since I could see. It is an additional thrill to know I've been awarded the same honour you received for the body of your work recognised and saluted a few years back. Your films have been a great source of inspiration to me. They have contributed more than most other men's in defining film as an art. I'm sorry I didn't get the chance to meet you in Venice, but I'm sure our paths will cross in the future. All my best, as I continue to look at your films and gain more and more inspiration.'

It was the last letter, so the story goes, that Fellini read before his death.

Despite the grey thatch and grizzled beard he now sports, Spielberg still presents the image of an overgrown boy in a baseball cap, sipping his soda, playing video games on modem with Robin Williams, even permitting himself the occasional luxury of laughing at himself. If you're quick and walk through the elegant doors of his Trump Tower apartment – designed, like the Hamptons extension, by David Geffen's architect of choice, Charles Gwathmey – what do you find? Why, a large blow-up of a childhood snap depicting Spielberg as a scrawny eight-year-old with enormous ears, holding a half-eaten apple, bones sticking out of his bare chest, the unsure grin creasing his face worthy of a 'Mad' magazine cover.

Why 'quick'? Only because 'his Trump Tower apartment' never really was his, so it is said, but owned by Universal and let to their favourite son. And now that he's struck out on his own with his DreamWorks pals, he's moving to the San Remo apartment building, where extensive – and noisy – alterations went on for over a year, much to the annoyance of his high-toned neighbours.

Don't be fooled, in any case, by Spielberg's occasional, atypical, lapse into humour. You can be sure that, away from the cameras, he's still negotiating the tightest of deals on a daily basis. And lashing out furiously when he feels he's being mocked or thwarted.

The strict limits of his jocularity were defined, oddly enough, in an offshoot based on 'Mad' magazine, the Fox network's *Mad TV*. In the summer of 1995 the programme makers dared to compile a skit entitled *Schindler's Lost*, the 'true story of a man with a sense of justice, but no sense of direction'. Shot in black and white, this had

357

Schindler and his wife careering all over town in their little car looking for the railway station where Nazis are about to leave with a group of Jews. Schindler gets his directions wrong and ignores his wife's traffic instructions, so that when they finally arrive at the station all that remains is a pile of luggage. 'No-o-o!' Schindler screams. 'I failed. I did not save one of them.'

'I hate to say it, but I told you so,' his wife retorts.

All in the worst possible taste, of course, but isn't the very essence of satire to hold nothing sacred? Spielberg reportedly went ballistic upon hearing of the sketch and complained bitterly to Sid Sheinberg. Just to add insult to injury, it turned out that the executive producer of the show was none other than Spielberg's old friend Quincy Jones! From there it was all the way to the top of the News Corporation tree, with Rupert Murdoch next to have his ear singed. The all-too-predictable result? As one dispirited Fox executive put it, 'Basically, the sketch has been censored.'

In March 1996, champing at the bit between movies, Spielberg became deeply involved in the production of the DreamWorks TV series, *High Incident*, to the extent of serving as camera operator. Already upset by the mid-season cancellation of the company's first sitcom, *Champs*, he persuaded ABC to 'double-pump' an episode of *High Incident* when the first airing belly-flopped. ABC bowed to his request and repeated the episode the following week, bumping the top-rated *NYPD Blue* from its prime-time slot in the process. Then they did it again a week later, infuriating viewers who tuned in expecting to see a brand-new *NYPD* – as listed in 'TV Guide' – and were faced with a repeat of the second episode of *High Incident* instead.

Spielberg, it seems, now has the power of determining not only what we *will* see, but what we *won't*. The 'little bully' lives, with far more power than he ever had over his sisters.

Spielberg's relationship with his father is better than it has been for years. One of the reasons, apart from the healing passage of time, is a greater understanding of the processes that have driven them as individuals. Spielberg recalls being bored to tears when Arnold invited colleagues over to his house in the old days, for all the talk would be computers this, computers that, computers the next thing. B-o-r-i-r-g, especially to someone who, even in his adult life, would list on his 'technical proficiency' resumé an ability to reach for the Yellow Pages when something breaks down.

*Jurassic Park* was one catalyst that made the difference. 'I practically had to take night classes so I could direct the dinosaurs,' Spielberg says. 'I had to learn a whole new vocabulary in computer graphic imaging. I had to learn the same language of my father's vocation . . .' The corollary after all this time? Now semi-retired and in his seventies, Arnold Spielberg also produces movies, be they ever so humble promotional films intended for sales forces. These he sends to his son for comments, advice and guidance.

The second catalyst as Spielberg sneaks past the big 5-0 on December 18, 1996, and enters his sixth decade, was a feeling of oneness with Arnold that dates back to Max's birth. 'My son took away my lost childhood and then he gave it back to me,' he has rationalised. 'When he was born I suddenly became the spitting image of my own father, with all the parental cliches – all the things I swore I would never say to my own children.'

One thing Spielberg the filmmaker had discovered during the shooting of *Schindler's List* was the answer to a question he'd never properly understood: Why certain filmmakers seem *wilfully* drawn to what are clearly offbeat, uncommercial subjects. 'I think I got a little taste of what a lot of directors have existed on all through their careers,' he admitted, 'people like Altman, people like Kazan, even people like Preston Sturges, who made fiercely independent films. I suddenly saw what some of the tug was to the *real* filmmakers, who are always drawn to the subject because it's dangerous.'

Contrarily, since September 1996 he's been shooting an adaptation of Michael Crichton's *The Lost World*, the author's sequel to *Jurassic Park*, which is committed – no, not to DreamWorks (sorry, investors!) – but to Universal. It could be the first movie in history to break through the $1 billion barrier theatrically. As well as a major retrograde step.

Largely thanks to Spielberg, his followers and imitators, the movie world has been polarised. At one extreme: the soulless blockbuster, of which Amblin's *Twister* is the most recent example. It's not *about* anything, it has no emotional centre, it exists only as the crassest example of the Funhouse mentality in moviemaking. *Beyond* Popcorn. *Way* beyond.

Even as *Twister* was smashing its way across US box-offices, the Cannes Film Festival – at the opposite extreme – was unveiling its strongest slate of quality movies in years. Accepting the Golden Palm for Best Movie for his *Secrets and Lies*, director Mike Leigh stated that he found the award 'encouraging for those of us who are trying to make films about people, relationships, real life, love and passion and caring and all the things that matter'. All the things, in fact, that are missing from the bulk of Spielberg's slate.

Since Spielberg – lawsuits apart – now claims to enjoy a life outside movies, let him provide his own happy ending. For most of my career,' he declared shortly before the most recent addition to the Spielberg clan, 'my life was wrapped around film. But, thanks to my wife Kate and my five kids, I now know who I am *without* a script. So the best films are yet to come.'

Maybe the best deals too. And hopefully, more of an inclination to do the right thing by others, as opposed to his own narrow self-interest.

The world waits.

# Afterword

Originally *Flipper*, the first fruit of Sid Sheinberg's independent Bubble Factory production company, was due to be released throughout the US on May 10, 1996. ('Sid's remaking old TV series!' was the comment from his old sparring partner, the ever-naughty Terry Gilliam.) *Twister*, meantime, the latest blockbuster from Spielberg's Amblin Entertainment, was set for a week later, on May 17. When, at the last moment, *Twister*'s release was advanced to May 10, a nervous Universal advanced *Flipper* – hopefully out of harm's way – by one week to May 17. Oops! Thus uncomfortably sandwiched between *Twister*'s $41 million opening weekend and *Mission:Impossible*'s 4-day Memorial Day holiday figure of $56 million, puny little *Flipper* never stood a chance, earning a paltry $4.6 million opening and ending its run with a total box-office gross of $20 million. All's fair in love and war, it seems. Better luck next time, Sid. Meantime, the Bubble's a Bust.

What do patriotism and Hollywood's Humanitarian Awards have in common? Answer: All too often, they're the last refuge of scoundrels. Not always, however. On May 30, 1996 at New York's Waldorf-Astoria, the latest presentation was made to the undoubtedly deserving Edgar Bronfman Jr., still in his honeymoon mode at Seagram's MCA. Flanked by Lew and Edie Wasserman and Ron Meyer, Bronfman accepted the award from Courtenay Ross, Steve Ross's widow. This was, after all, the first annual United Jewish Appeal-Federation of New York's Steven J. Ross Humanitarian Award. The New York *Observer*'s man among the havanas, Frank Digiacomo, reported hearing one cynical, completely out-of-line guest exclaim, 'Steve Ross, *humanitarian*?!'

In the first week of June 1996, *Life* magazine published its list of the '50 Most Influential Baby Boomers'. Spielberg was right in there, heading a list that included Michael Milken, Oprah Winfrey,

Roseanne, John Belushi, Mike Ovitz, Michael Jackson and O.J. Simpson (Yes, really.) 'He's our Homer and our Hans Christian Anderson,' the magazine declared. 'His films, from *E.T.* to *Schindler's List* show us that the human spirit is alive in the most unlikely places – in a creature from outer space or a Nazi concentration camp.' (Like so many others before them, *Life* erroneously listed Spielberg's birth year as 1947.) And when *Life*'s sister publication, *Time*, brought out its own, rather more humble list of the twenty-five most influential people in the US – only a matter of days later – Spielberg, surprisingly, was nowhere to be found.

When Tom Hanks fretted that DreamWorks' first fruits would be looked at askance no matter what, he may not have realized that he might be part of the initial line-up. Yep, chances are he'll be taking the lead in Spielberg's World War II comedy drama, *Saving Private Ryan*. Except, hang on a minute, it looked at first as if DreamWorks' investors could recork that champagne. Spielberg was making it for *Paramount*?! Relax, folks, it could be a DreamWorks/Paramount co-production. If, that is, Spielberg has his way and Paramount buckles under in granting him the 'certain assurances' he's said to be seeking after two solid months of negotiations – namely, that the studio will suspend any other WWII item on its books lest it interfere with *Saving Private Ryan*. Another clear case of influence-a?

With Michael Ovitz's move to Disney, it was a safe bet that his college roommate Frank Marshall would not be long in following. Sure enough, talks that had already been taking place between Kennedy-Marshall and the Mouserie were successfully concluded shortly after Ovitz moved in. Next to switch: Martin Scorsese, on payment of a $6 million refund to Universal towards development costs already incurred. (Ovitz's ex-deputy Ron Meyer did not appear to covet Scorsese's services as much as Ovitz, especially after the less-than-stellar performance of *Casino*.)

With John Travolta's career back in high gear, he was asked about rumours that a Spielberg-directed musical was being discussed that would team him with Barbra Streisand (*My Yiddishe Momma*?!) 'If they wanna do it,' he replied, 'I'll do it.'

No sooner had Kate Capshaw declared her adopted daughter Mikaela George the sixth and positively *final* addition to the Spielberg family than she discovered she was pregnant! The new arrival, predicted to be a baby daughter, is due in December 1996.

362

Political contributions in the US generally come from established organisations. While it's not unknown for a start-up company, one can only wonder what DreamWorks' shareholders made of the company's New York *Times*'-reported donation to the Democrats of $525,000 in the period January through end-June 1996. With not a single movie yet in release, and with the overhead eating up capital, isn't it a bit early to cavalierly hand over half-a-million bucks, whether the total includes cash from individuals or not?

Records are made to be toppled. *Jurassic Park* took nine days to pass the $100 million mark at the box-office. *Batman Forever* took ten days. *Mission:Impossible* did it in eleven, *Twister* in twelve. Then along came Twentieth Century-Fox's *Independence Day*, which grabbed $100 million in seven days. Prompting CNN's Larry King, on July 9th, 1996, to ask Jeff Goldblum (preparing to shoot Spielberg's *Jurassic Park* sequel, *The Lost World*): 'Do you think Steve feels he has to top this?'

Goldblum: 'Yeah, I'll bet he does.'

Chances are he will, too.

# Steven Spielberg Filmography

## MISCELLANEOUS SCREEN CREDITS:

ACE ELI AND RODGERS OF THE SKIES
(Twentieth Century-Fox, 1973) Directed: John Erman
**Spielberg**: Original Story

THE BLUES BROTHERS
(Universal, 1980) Directed: John Landis
**Spielberg**: Actor

GREMLINS
(Warner Bros, 1984) Directed: Joe Dante
**Spielberg**: Actor

LISTEN UP
(Warner Bros, 1990) Directed: Ellen Weissbrod
**Spielberg**: Interviewee

AKIRA KUROSAWA'S DREAMS
(Warner Bros, 1990) Directed: Akira Kurosawa
**'Steven Spielberg Presents'**

## 'DIRECTED BY STEVEN SPIELBERG' ON TELEVISION
### ★Year of Transmission

ROD SERLING'S NIGHT GALLERY
'Eyes' 1969★

MARCUS WELBY, MD
'The Daredevil Gesture' 1970★

ROD SERLING'S NIGHT GALLERY
'Make Me Laugh' 1971★

THE NAME OF THE GAME
'LA 2017' 1971★

THE PSYCHIATRIST
'The Private World of Martin Dalton' 1971★

THE PSYCHIATRIST
'Par for the Course' 1971★

COLOMBO
'Murder by the Book' 1971★

OWEN MARSHALL
'Eulogy for a Wide Receiver' 1971★

NBC WORLD PREMIERE MOVIE
'Duel' 1971★

CBS FRIDAY NIGHT MOVIE
'Something Evil' 1972★

NBC WORLD PREMIERE MOVIE
'Savage' 1972★

AMAZING STORIES
'Ghost Train' 1985★

AMAZING STORIES
'The Mission' 1987★


BALANCE OF 'AMAZING STORIES':
(DIRECTORS)
+ Story Credit: Spielberg

MUMMY, DADDY (William Dear) +
1985

GO TO THE HEAD OF THE CLASS (Robert Zemeckis)
1985

THE AMAZING FALSWORTH (Peter Hyams) +
1985

FINE TUNING (Bob Balaban) +
1985

DOROTHY AND BEN (Thomas Carter) +
1985

THE MAIN ATTRACTION (Matthew Robbins) +
1985

MIRROR, MIRROR (Martin Scorsese) +
1985

MR MAGIC (Donald Petrie)
1985

ONE AMAZING NIGHT (Phil Joanou) +
1985

THE WEDDING RING (Danny De Vito) +
1986

THE GREIBBLE (Joe Dante) +
1986

MISCALCULATION (Tom Holland)
1986

BLUE MAN DOWN (Paul Michael Glaser) +
1986

THE 21 INCH SUN (Nick Castle)
1986

MAGIC SATURDAY (Robert Markowitz)
1986

YOU GOTTA BELIEVE ME (Kevin Reynolds) +
1986

THE DOLL (Phil Joanou)
1986

LIFE ON DEATH ROW (Mick Garris)
1986

THANKSGIVING (Todd Holland)
1986

THE PUMPKIN COMPETITION (Norman Reynolds)
1986

WITHOUT DIANA (Lesli Linka Glatter)
1986

VANESSA IN THE CITY (Clint Eastwood)
1987

MOVING DAY (Robert Stevens)
1987

FAMILY DOG (Brad Bird)
1987

## SPIELBERG FEATURE MOVIES
## EXECUTIVE-PRODUCED:
### *Director

I WANNA HOLD YOUR HAND
(Universal, 1978) *Robert Zemeckis

USED CARS
(Columbia, 1980) *Robert Zemeckis

CONTINENTAL DIVIDE
(Universal, 1981) *Michael Apted

POLTERGEIST
(MGM, 1982) *Tobe Hooper
(Spielberg also Co-Producer, Co-Screenplay, Story)

THE TWILIGHT ZONE - THE MOVIE
(Warner Bros, 1983) *John Landis/Joe Dante/George Miller
(Spielberg also Director of one episode; see Feature
Filmography)

GREMLINS
(Warner Bros/Amblin, 1984) *Joe Dante

FANDANGO
(Warner Bros/Amblin, 1985) *Kevin Reynolds

THE GOONIES
(Warner Bros/Amblin, 1985) *Richard Donner (Spielberg also Story)

BACK TO THE FUTURE
(Universal/Amblin, 1985) *Robert Zemeckis

YOUNG SHERLOCK HOLMES
(Paramount/Amblin, 1985) *Barry Levinson

THE MONEY PIT
(Universal/Amblin, 1986) *Richard Benjamin

AN AMERICAN TAIL
(Universal/Amblin, 1986) *Don Bluth

INNERSPACE
(Warner Bros/Amblin/Guber-Peters, 1987) *Joe Dante

*batteries not included
(Universal/Amblin, 1987 ) *Matthew Robbins

HARRY AND THE HENDERSONS
(Universal/Amblin, 1987) *Richard Dear

WHO FRAMED ROGER RABBIT?
(Touchstone/Amblin, 1988) *Robert Zemeckis

THE LAND BEFORE TIME
(Universal/Amblin, 1988 ) *Don Bluth

BACK TO THE FUTURE II
(Universal/Amblin, 1989) *Robert Zemeckis

DAD
(Universal/Amblin, 1989) *Gary David Goldberg

BACK TO THE FUTURE III
(Universal/Amblin, 1990) *Robert Zemeckis

GREMLINS II – THE NEW BATCH
(Warner Bros/Amblin, 1990) *Joe Dante

JOE VERSUS THE VOLCANO
(Warner Bros/Amblin, 1990) *John Patrick Shanley

ARACHNOPHOBIA
(Hollywood Pictures/Amblin, 1990) *Frank Marshall

AN AMERICAN TAIL II – FIEVEL GOES WEST
(Universal/Amblin, 1991) *Phil Nibbelink/Simon Wells

CAPE FEAR
(Universal/Amblin, 1991) *Martin Scorsese

NOISES OFF
(Touchstone/Amblin, 1992) *Peter Bogdanovich

A FAR-OFF PLACE
(Touchstone/Amblin, 1993) *Mikael Salomon

WE'RE BACK! A DINOSAUR'S STORY
(Universal/Amblin, 1993) *Dick Zondag, Ralph Zondag, Phil
Nibbelink, Simon Wells

THE FLINTSTONES
(Universal/Amblin, 1994) *Brian Levant

CASPER
(Universal/Amblin, 1995) *Brad Silberling

THE LITTLE RASCALS
(Universal/King Features/Amblin, 1995) *Penelope Spheeris

HOW TO MAKE AN AMERICAN QUILT
(Universal/Amblin, 1995) *Jocelyn Moorehouse

TO WONG FOO, THANKS FOR EVERYTHING, JULIE
NEWMAR
(Universal/Amblin, 1995) *Beeban Kidron

THE BRIDGES OF MADISON COUNTY
(Warner Bros/Amblin, 1995) *Clint Eastwood

BALTO
(Universal/Amblin, 1996) *Simon Wells

TWISTER
(Universal/Warner Bros/Amblin, 1996) *Jan De Bont

## FEATURE FILMOGRAPHY AS DIRECTOR:

DUEL (Universal, 1973)
*Screenplay*: Richard Matheson
*Producer*: George Eckstein
*Cinematography*: Jack A. Marta
*Editor*: Frank Moriss
*Music*: Billy Goldenberg
*Production Design*: Robert S. Smith
*Running Time*: 85 minutes (European theatrical version)
*Cast*: Dennis Weaver, Jacqueline Scott, Lou Frizzell, Gene
   Dynarski, Lucille Benson, Tim Herbert, Charles Seel

THE SUGARLAND EXPRESS (Universal, 1974)
*Screenplay*: Hal Barwood, Matthew Robbins (from a story by
   Spielberg, Robbins and Barwood)
*Producers*: Richard D. Zanuck, David Brown
*Cinematography*: Vilmos Zsigmond (Panavision)
*Editors*: Edward M. Abroms, Verna Fields
*Music*: John Williams
*Production Design*: Joseph Alves Jr.
*Running Time*: 108 minutes
*Cast*: Goldie Hawn, William Atherton, Ben Johnson, Michael
   Sacks, Gregory Walcott, Harrison Zanuck, Steve Kanaly,
   Louise Latham, A.L. Camp, Jesse Lee Fulton

JAWS (Universal, 1975)
*Screenplay*: Peter Benchley, Carl Gottlieb (based on the novel by
   Benchley)
*Producers*: Richard D. Zanuck, David Brown
*Cinematography*: Bill Butler (Panavision)
*Editor*: Verna Fields
*Music*: John Williams
*Production Design*: Joseph Alves Jr.
*Running Time*: 124 minutes
*Cast*: Roy Scheider, Richard Dreyfuss, Robert Shaw, Lorraine
   Gary, Murray Hamilton, Carl Gottlieb, Jeffrey C. Kramer,

Susan Backlinie, Jonathan Filley, Chris Rebello, Jay Mello, Ted Grossman, Lee Fierro, Jeffrey Voorhees, Craig Kingsbury, Dr. Robert Nevin, Peter Benchley

## CLOSE ENCOUNTERS OF THE THIRD KIND (Columbia, 1977)
*Screenplay*: Steven Spielberg
*Producers*: Julia and Michael Phillips
*Cinematography*: Vilmos Szigmond (Panavision)
*Additional Photography*: William A. Fraker, Douglas Slocombe, John Alonzo, Laszlo Kovacs
*Editor*: Michael Kahn
*Music*: John Williams
*Production Design*: Joseph Alves Jr.
*Special Effects*: Douglas Trumbull
*Running Time*: 135 minutes
*Cast*: Richard Dreyfuss, Francois Truffaut, Teri Garr, Melinda Dillon, Gary Guffey, Bob Balaban, J. Patrick McNamara, Warren Kemmerling, Roberts Blossom, Philip Dodds, Shawn Bishop, Adrienne Campbell, Justin Dreyfuss, Lance Hendricksen, Hal Barwood, Matthew Robbins
('Special Edition' of the movie released 1980.
    *Running Time*: 132 minutes)

## 1941 (Columbia/Universal/A-Team, 1979)
*Screenplay*: Robert Zemeckis, Bob Gale (from a story by Zemeckis, Gale and John Milius)
*Producer*: Buzz Feitshans
*Cinematography*: William A. Fraker (Panavision)
*Editor*: Michael Kahn
*Music*: John Williams
*Production Design*: Dean Edward Mitzner
*Special Effects*: A.D. Flowers
*Running Time*: 118 minutes
*Cast*: Dan Aykroyd, Ned Beatty, John Belushi, Lorraine Gary, Murray Hamilton, Christopher Lee, Tim Matheson, Toshiro Mifune, Warren Oates, Robert Stack, Treat Williams, Nancy Allen, Eddie Deezen, Bobby DiCicco, Dianne Day, John Candy, Frank McRae, Perry Lang, Slim Pickens, Lionel Stander, Elisha Cook

## RAIDERS OF THE LOST ARK (Paramount/Lucasfilm, 1981)
*Screenplay*: Lawrence Kasdan (from a story by George Lucas and Philip Kaufman)

*Producer*: Frank Marshall
*Cinematography*: Douglas Slocombe (Panavision)
*Editor*: Michael Kahn
*Music*: John Williams
*Production Design*: Norman Reynolds
*Visual Effects Supervisor*: Richard Edlund
*Running Time*: 118 minutes
*Cast*: Harrison Ford, Karen Allen, Paul Freeman, Ronald Lacey,
   John Rhys-Davies, Alfred Molina, Wolf Kahler, Anthony
   Higgins, Denholm Elliott, Vic Tablian, Don Fellows, William
   Hootkins, Bill Reimbold, Fred Sorenson, Patrick Durkin,
   Matthew Scurfield, Malcolm Weaver, Sonny Caldinez

## E.T. – THE EXTRA-TERRESTRIAL (Universal, 1982)

*Screenplay*: Melissa Mathison (from an idea by Steven Spielberg)
*Producers*: Steven Spielberg, Kathleen Kennedy
*Cinematography*: Allen Daviau
*Editor*: Carol Littleton
*Music*: John Williams
*Production Design*: James D. Bissell
*Visual Effects Supervisor*: Dennis Muren
*Running Time*: 115 minutes
*Cast*: Henry Thomas, Dee Wallace, Peter Coyote, Robert
   MacNaughton, Drew Barrymore, H.C. Martel, Sean Frye,
   Tom Howell, Erika Elenian, David O'Dell, Richard Swingler

## THE TWILIGHT ZONE – THE MOVIE (Warner Bros., 1983)

*Producers*: Steven Spielberg, John Landis
*Executive Producer*: Frank Marshall
*Running Time*: 101 minutes
(Steven Spielberg-directed segment, 'Kick the Can')
*Screenplay*: George Clayton Johnson, Richard Matheson, Josh
   Rogan
*Cinematography*: Allen Daviau
*Editor*: Michael Kahn
*Music*: Jerry Goldsmith
*Cast*: Scatman Crothers, Bill Quinn, Martin Garner, Delma
   Diamond, Helen Shaw, Murray Matheson, Peter Brocco,
   Priscilla Pointer

## INDIANA JONES AND THE TEMPLE OF DOOM
(Paramount/Lucasfilm, 1984)
*Screenplay*: Willard Huyck and Gloria Katz (based on a story by
   George Lucas)

*Producer*: Robert Watts
*Cinematography*: Douglas Slocombe (Panavision)
*Editor*: Michael Kahn
*Music*: John Williams
*Production Design*: Elliot Scott
*Visual Effects Supervisor*: Dennis Muren
*Running Time*: 118 minutes
*Cast*: Harrison Ford, Kate Capshaw, Ke Huy Quan, Amrish Puri, Roshan Seth, Philip Stone, Roy Chiao, D.R. Nanayakkaru, Dharmadasa Kuruppi, David Yip, Ric Young, Chua Kah Joo, Rex Ngui, Philip Tann, Dan Aykroyd

THE COLOR PURPLE (Warner Bros./Amblin/Guber-Peters, 1985)
*Screenplay*: Menno Meyjes (based on the novel by Alice Walker)
*Producers*: Steven Spielberg, Kathleen Kennedy, Frank Marshall, Quincy Jones
*Cinematography*: Allen Daviau
*Editor*: Michael Kahn
*Music*: Quincy Jones
*Production Design*: J. Michael Riva
*Special Effects Supervisor*: Michael Sweeney
*Running Time*: 150 minutes
*Cast*: Danny Glover, Whoopi Goldberg, Margaret Avery, Oprah Winfrey, Willard Pugh, Akosua Busia, Desreta Jackson, Adolph Caesar, Rae Dawn Chong, Dana Ivey, Leonard Jackson, Bennett Guillory, John Patton Jr., Carl Anderson, Susan Beaubian, Larry Fishburne

EMPIRE OF THE SUN (Warner Bros./Amblin, 1987)
*Screenplay*: Tom Stoppard (based on the novel by J. G. Ballard)
*Producers*: Steven Spielberg, Kathleen Kennedy, Frank Marshall
*Cinematography*: Allen Daviau
*Editor*: Michael Kahn
*Music*: John Williams
*Production Design*: Norman Reynolds
*Running Time*: 146 minutes
*Cast*: John Malcovich, Miranda Richardson, Nigel Havers, Joe Pantaliano, Leslie Phillips, Robert Stephens, Paul McGann, Christian Bale, Mabato Ibu, Emily Richard, Rupert Frazer, Peter Gale, Takatoki Kataoka, Ben Stiller, Ralph Seymour, Zhau Nai She, Emma Piper

INDIANA JONES AND THE LAST CRUSADE
(Paramount/Lucasfilm, 1989)
*Screenplay*: Jeffrey Boam (from a story by George Lucas and
    Menno Meyjes)
*Producer*: Robert Watts
*Cinematography*: Douglas Slocombe
*Editor*: Michael Kahn
*Music*: John Williams
*Production Designer*: Elliot Scott
*Visual Effects Supervisor*: Michael J. McAllister
*Running Time*: 127 minutes
*Cast*: Harrison Ford, Sean Connery, Denholm Elliott, Alison
    Doody, John Rhys-Davies, Julian Glover, River Phoenix,
    Michael Byrne, Kevork Malikyan, Robert Eddison, Richard
    Young, Alexei Sayle, Alex Hyde-White, Paul Maxwell, Mrs.
    Glover, Vernon Dobtcheff, J.J. Hardy, Bradley Gregg

ALWAYS (Universal/United Artists/Amblin, 1989)
*Screenplay*: Jerry Belson (from Dalton Trumbo's 1943 screenplay
    for A GUY NAMED JOE, from a story by Chandler Sprague
    and David Boehm, adapted by Frederick Hazlitt Brennan)
*Producers*: Steven Spielberg, Frank Marshall, Kathleen Kennedy
*Cinematography*: Mikael Salomon (Panavision)
*Editor*: Michael Kahn
*Music*: John Williams
*Production Designer*: James Bissell
*Running Time*: 117 minutes
*Cast*: Richard Dreyfuss, Holly Hunter, Brad Johnson, John
    Goodman, Audrey Hepburn, Robert Blossoms, Keith David,
    Ed Van Nuys, Marg Helgenberger, Dale Dye, Brian Haley,
    James Lashly, Michael Steve Jones

HOOK (Tristar/Amblin, 1991)
*Screenplay*: Jim V. Hart, Malia Scotch Marmo
*Screen Story*: Jim V. Hart, Nick Castle
*Producers*: Kathleen Kennedy, Frank Marshall, Gerald R. Molen
*Cinematography*: Dean Cundy
*Editor*: Michael Kahn
*Music*: John Williams
*Production Designer*: Norman Garwood
*Running Time*: 135 minutes
*Cast*: Dustin Hoffman, Robin Williams, Julia Roberts, Bob
    Hoskins, Dante Basco, Charlie Korsmo, Amber Scott, Caroline
    Goodall, Glenn Close, Maggie Smith, Phil Collins

JURASSIC PARK (Universal/Amblin, 1993)
*Screenplay*: Michael Crichton and David Koepp (from the novel by Michael Crichton)
*Producers*: Kathleen Kennedy, Gerald R. Molen
*Cinematography*: Dean Cundy
*Editor*: Michael Kahn
*Music*: John Williams
*Production Designer*: Rick Carter
*Running Time*: 90 minutes
*Cast*: Richard Attenborough, Jeff Goldblum, Laura Dern, Sam Neill, Bob Peck, Jerry Molen, Joseph Mazzello, Samuel L. Jackson, Ariana Richards, Miguel Sandoval, Cameron Thor, Martin Ferrero, Wayne Knight, B.D. Wong, Tom Mishler, Richard Kiley

SCHINDLER'S LIST (Universal/Amblin, 1993)
*Screenplay*: Thomas Keneally, Stephen Zaillian (from the novel by Thomas Keneally)
*Producers*: Steven Spielberg, Gerald R. Molen, Branko Lustig
*Cinematography*: Janusz Kaminski
*Editor*: Michael Kahn
*Music*: John Williams
*Production Designer*: Allan Starski
*Running Time*: 185 minutes
*Cast*: Liam Neeson, Ralph Fiennes, Ben Kingsley, Jonathan Sagalle, Caroline Goodall, Emheth Davidtz, Peter Appiano, Joachim Paul Assbock, Hans-Joerg Assmann, Uri Avrahami, Dominika Bednarczyk, Sigurd Bemme, Dirk Bender, Martin Bergmann, Henryk Bista, Tadeusz Bradecki, Stanislaw Brejdygant, Alexander Buczolich

# ADDITIONAL REVIEWS FOR 'SCHINDLER'S LIST':

'This is Steven Spielberg's masterpiece.'
Kevin Lally, *Film Journal*

'Against all odds, Spielberg the box-office champ has made the most demanding and emotionally powerful American movie in years.'
David Denby, *New York*

'Destined to have a permanent place in memory.'
Janet Maslin, New York *Times*

'Spielberg's dismayingly transparent attempt to win the Oscar the Academy has so long and so perversely denied him.'
Dave Kehr, New York *Daily News*

'In his stunning *Schindler's List* Spielberg captures the courage of Holocaust's unlikely angel.'
Jay Carr, Boston *Globe*

'It marks him as one of the world's great filmmakers.'
Peter Keough, Boston *Phoenix*

'After several attempts at making a fully realized, mature film, Steven Spielberg has finally put it all together in *Schindler's List*. A remarkable work by any standard.'
Todd McCarthy, *Variety*

'Lines like Kingsley's "The list is life" ring false. They smack of the dramatic artifice that rears its head in Neeson's final breakdown scene, the subtext of which is "Let's have a big moment here to finish the story."'
Matthew Gilbert, Boston *Globe*

'What is most worrisome about the wild overpraise of *Schindler's List* is the complacency it invites. The hype is already taking on a life of its own.'
Frank Rich, New York *Times*

'No, I don't think *Schindler's List* is a great film, whatever that is, but it was worth doing, and it moved me very deeply at several points. Yet I question much of the hyperbole advanced in its promotion as a cultural phenomenon.'
Andrew Sarris, New York *Observer*

'Spielberg has done something that can't quite be said of any other film about the Holocaust. He has allowed us – for the first time – to see it.'
Owen Gleiberman, *Entertainment Weekly*

'A great movie. It is by far the finest, fullest dramatic film ever made about the Holocaust.'
Terrence Rafferty, *New Yorker*

'A travesty.'
Tony Adler, Chicago *Reader*

'The greatness of *Schindler's List* goes beyond all expectations.'
*Der Spiegel*

'It's a film any director would be proud to see with his or her name above the title.'
Kenneth Turan, Los Angeles *Times*

'This is not the definitive film on the Holocaust. That is yet to be made. This film is certainly worth seeing, but it did not satisfy me emotionally.'
Ed Koch

'Spielberg has done the best directing of his career. Much of his previous work has been clever, but *Schindler's List* is masterly . . . a welcome astonishment from a director who has given us much boyish esprit, much ingenuity, but little seriousness. His stark, intelligent style here, perfectly controlled, suggests that this may be the start of a new period in Spielberg's prodigious career – Part Two: The Man.'
Stanley Kauffman, *New Republic*

AN AGREEMENT


FROM: STEVEN SPIELBERG

TO:   DENIS C. HOFFMAN


To recompense for financing my story to be made into a short film
I agree to direct one feature film for DENIS C. HOFFMAN sometime
during the next ten years.

I will be paid $25,000 plus 5% of the profit after all expenses.

I will direct any script of DENIS HOFFMAN's selection and I will
perform my services for him anytime during the next ten years at
his choosing unless I am involved in a project. In which case I
will make myself available to him immediately following said proje

*Steven A. Spielberg*

*Denis C. Hoffman*

9-28-68

*Cine 1969*

The Council on International Nontheatrical Events
congratulates

Denis C. Hoffman

for the motion picture

**Amblin**

selected for its excellence to represent the
United States of America in international
motion picture events abroad and awards to it

*The Golden Eagle*

# APPENDIX D

I hereby certify this to be a true certified copy of the certificate on file with the Cincinnati Board of Health.     Date Issued: _____     SEP 15 1994

*Richard D. Howard* M.B.A.
Local Registrar, City of Cincinnati
Assistant Commissioner of Health

## OHIO DEPARTMENT OF HEALTH
### COLUMBUS
### CERTIFICATE OF LIVE BIRTH

Reg. Dist. No. 494
Primary Reg. Dist. No. 2D
State File No. 15176
Registrar's No.

**1. PLACE OF BIRTH:**
(a) County  Hamilton
(b) Cincinnati (City, Village, Township)
(c) Name of Hospital or Institution: The Jewish Hospital (If not in hospital or institution, give street or location)
(d) Mother's stay before delivery ___ yrs In this community 26 yrs (Specify whether years, months, or days)

**2. USUAL RESIDENCE OF MOTHER: 66**
(a) State
(b) County
(c) City or village (If outside city or village, write RURAL)
(d) Street No. 817 Lexington Ave. (If rural, give location)

**3. FULL NAME OF CHILD** Steven Allan Spielberg

**4. DATE OF BIRTH** Dec. 18, 1946 (Month) (Day) (Year)

5. Sex: Male
6. Twin ___ Triplet ___ If so—born 1st, 2d or 3d
7. Number months of pregnancy 9
7a. Weight at birth 6-10
7b. Congenital malformation No
8. Is mother married? Yes

**FATHER OF CHILD**
9. Full name Arnold Spielberg
10. Color or race White  11. Age at time of this birth 29 yrs
12. Birthplace Cincinnati, Ohio (City, town, or county) (State or foreign country)
13. Usual occupation Student
14. Industry or business University of Cincinnati

**MOTHER OF CHILD**
15. Full maiden name Leah Posner
16. Color or race White  17. Age at time of this birth 26
18. Birthplace Cincinnati, Ohio (City, town, or county) (State or foreign country)
19. Usual occupation Housewife
20. Industry or business

21. Children born to this mother not including this child 0
(a) How many other children of this mother are now living 0
(b) How many other children were born alive but are now dead 0
(c) How many children were born dead? 0
(The total of a-b-c should equal Item 21)

22. Date serologic test for syphilis 6/1/46
23. (a) If none, give reason
23. Mother's usual mailing address:

24. I hereby certify that I attended the birth of this child who was born alive at the hour of 6:16 P. M on the date above stated and that the information given was furnished Leah Spielberg related to this child as Mother

25. Registrar's signature Grace LePoria, Dep.
26. Date received by local registrar JAN 13 1947

Signature F. A. S. Kautz, M.D. (Specify if physician, licensed midwife or other)
Address 19 W. 7th St.
Date signed 12/16/46

Do not write in this space

381

APPENDIX E

PHOENIX JEWISH NEWS     DECEMBER 25, 1959

8485

Steven Spielberg, son of Mr. and Mrs. Arnold Spielberg, 3443 N. 49th St. will be Bar Mitzvah Jan. 9 at Beth Hebrew Congregation. Rabbi William Greenberg will officiate. A Kiddish will follow the services and an open house will be held Jan. 10. Grandparents are Mrs. Rebecca Spielberg of Cincinnati and Mr. Philip Posner of Phoenix. Out-of-town guests will be Mr. Irwin Spielberg and daughter Jennie of California.

* * *

William Sitzer, son of Mr. and Mrs. Samuel A. Sitzer, 6412 Calle Camelia Rd. will be Bar Mitzvah Jan. 9 at Temple Beth Israel. Rabbi Albert Plotkin will officiate. A Kiddish will follow the service. Grandparents are Mrs. A. Greenspon of Munster, Ind. Miss Estelle Sitzer of New York will be a guest.

* * *

Stuart Leslie Kogan, son of Mr. and Mrs. Sidney M. Kogan, 821 West Amelia, will be Bar Mitzvah Jan. 2 at Temple Beth Israel. Rabbi Albert Plotkin will officiate. An Oneg Shabat will follow services. Out-of-town guests will be his grandparents Mr. and Mrs. Benjamin Kogan of Chicago and Mrs. Helen Swiren of Los Angeles, Mr. and Mrs. D. Ostroger of San Diego, and Pvt. Sheldon Kogan.

**But Ev**

By R

At the biennial conver gregations, held last mo by Mrs. Hiroshi Okamot Union College-Jewish In Reform rabbinical semi standing of Judaism turning to Japan to other Jews.

She pointed out to the gates that American Jud not properly be transpo land like Japan, and Judaism were to take it it would have to be a na nese expression of Jud which would reflect the background and the milieu just as America reflects America.

THE LARGER ISS touched on only in passin our responsibility to the v of unaffiliated people in Upon this the UAHC bi not touch, for there is impetus among congreg: leadership toward activ tism, either among thos nominally Jewish in the of Jewish descent, or a great body of 40,000,00 ated Americans.

The Central Conference

89

382

# Index

387

DreamWorks SKG 301–11; dealmaking 189–90; drops *California Suite* project 33, 34; early contract with Hoffman 16–17, 45–6, 335, 339–41, 375; early difficulty in getting work 22–3; earnings 82, 287; exclusion from Academy Awards 63, 125–6, 138–9, 142, 188, 216, 217; first feature film see *Amblin'*; Hoffman's lawsuit against 335–48, 351; interviews 120, 195; keys to success 134; misstating of age 67, 68, 335–6, 337, 338, 343–4, 345–6; and *Night Gallery* 26; opening of restaurant Dive! 295–6; and press 116; producing 171, 201; reviews 28, 44–5, 82, 99–100, 134, 135, 195, 208–9, 226–7, 241, 269, 287, 289–90, 373–4; screenwriting 74, 120, 124; seven-year deal with Universal 18; television experiences 26, 27, 28, 30–2; turns down *White Lightning* 35; whisky advert for Japanese 348

**Collaborations/Associates:** Bronfman 329, 331–2; feud with Price 211–12; Hoffman *see* Hoffman, Denis; Kahn 75, 114–15, 288; Kennedy 110–11, 123, 203, 274; Landis 141–2, 156; Lucas 23, 96, 97, 104–5, 239; Ross 171–3, 175–6, 179, 190, 281–2, 291; Williams 40, 60–1, 94, 134

**Work Approach:** attitude towards associates 79, 85, 111, 194–5; attributes 40, 191, 206, 268, 278; celibacy during movie making 56; charge of master manipulator 135; commitment to written word 292; control freak 12, 102; directing 25, 80, 89, 118, 197; engrossed with movie making 84; nervousness at work 269; portrayal of violence 116; reference to other filmmakers 286; ruthlessness 74

**General:** on directors 44; establishment of 'Playwrights Horizons' 348–9; establishment of 'The Survivors of the Shoah Visual History Foundation' 298–300; honorary degree from New York University 350

**Personal:** birth of son 222, 229, 359; buying of *Citizen's Kane's* Rosebud 223; characteristics 16, 27, 111, 194–5, 357; clarinet player 61; clothes 230, 231; dark side of nature 141, 198; discovery of Jewish heritage through children 276; family life 354–5; fear of flying 226; gun collection 350–1; houses 173, 354; inability at public speaking 235; likes 96; loneliness 126; and money 124, 190; part of 'bratpack' 96–7; phobias 3; taste in women 86; wealth 308; wearing of sunglasses 114; and women 64, 127

**Relationships:** Barrymore 131, 136–7; Belushi 100–1, 102;

393

seven year deal with 18; *see also* MCA
Ure, Mary 51
*Used Cars* 199

*Variety* 134
Victor, Mark 120
*Village Voice* 82, 289
Voigt, Jon 50

Walker, Alice 203–4, 205
*Wall Street Journal* 209
Wallace, Dee 130, 137
Walsh, Joseph 32–4
Warner Bros 185, 217; files suit against Sony 247–8; recovery under Ross 227–8; takeover of Time Inc. 246–7, 256; and *Twilight Zone* 141, 148, 152, 154, 155; Westchester Theater scandal 174, 182; wooing/recruiting of SS by Ross 171–3, 175–6, 179; *see also* Ross, Steve
*Washington Post* 100
Wasserman, Lew R. 18, 23, 30, 34, 39, 47, 82–3, 129, 175, 331; ascent to Chairmanship of MCA 35; and Bonfman takeover 328, 329, 331; and *The Last Temptation of Christ* 251; and Matsushita 255, 256, 259, 260, 262, 319–20, 305; survival of Stein's wish to dismiss 19, 24, 25
*Waterworld* 319, 320, 329
WCI *see* Warner Bros
Weaver, Dennis 29

Weissman, Eric 67
Wells, Frank 314
Westchester Theater scandal 174, 182
Westinghouse 332
White, Armond 289
*White Lightning* 35
*Who Framed Roger Rabbit* 231, 242
Wieseltier, Leon 289
Wilde, Cornel 66–7
Wilder, Billy 44, 274
Wilder, Thornton 54
Williams, John 40, 94, 134, 193; *Jaws* 60–1
Williams, Robin 268, 285, 316, 318
Williams, Treat 96
Williamson, Bruce 99–100
Willis, Bruce 267
Winfrey, Oprah 205, 206, 208, 351
Winger, Debra 128
Wingo, Dorcey 156, 158
Writers' Guild of America 98
Wyler, William 90–1

Yetnikoff, Walter 245, 246, 297
*Young Sherlock Holmes* 187, 229

Zaillian, Steven 276
Zanuck, Richard 23, 40; *Jaws* 49, 52, 61, 62, 164; *Sugarland Express* 41, 43
Zemecks, Robert 91, 92, 93, 111, 198, 199–200, 242, 303
*Zorro* 312
Zsigmond, Vilmos 83